Beyond the Corporate University

*Culture and Pedagogy
in the New Millennium*

Edited by Henry A. Giroux
and Kostas Myrsiades

ROWMAN & LITTLEFIELD PUBLISHERS, INC.
Lanham • Boulder • New York • Oxford

ROWMAN & LITTLEFIELD PUBLISHERS, INC.

Published in the United States of America
by Rowman & Littlefield Publishers, Inc.
4720 Boston Way, Lanham, Maryland 20706
www.rowmanlittlefield.com

12 Hid's Copse Road
Cumnor Hill, Oxford OX2 9JJ, England

British Library Cataloguing in Publication Information Available

Library of Congress Cataloging-in-Publication Data Available

ISBN 0-7425-1047-6 (cloth : alk. paper)
ISBN 0-7425-1048-4 (paper : alk. paper)

Printed in the United States of America

♾™ The paper used in this publication meets the minimum requirements of American National Standard for Information Sciences—Permanence of Paper for Printed Library Materials, ANSI/NISO Z39.48-1992.

For Susan, Linda, and our children

Beyond the
Corporate University

DATE DUE

WITHDRAWN

Contents

Acknowledgments

We would like to thank all of the contributors, who provided a sense of commitment, intellectual courage, and insight to this project. Special thanks to Stanley Aronowitz, Roger Simon, Ralph Rodriguez, and Amitava Kumar. Henry Giroux would also like to thank Susan Searls-Giroux for reading and editing the introduction. We would also like to thank Dean Birkenkamp and Janice Braunstein for their support and help.

Acknowledgments

We would like to thank all of the contributors, who provided a sense of commitment, intellectual courage, and insight to this project. Special thanks to Stanley Aronowitz, Roger Simon, Ralph Rodriguez, and Amitava Kumar. Henry Giroux would also like to thank Susan Searls-Giroux for reading and editing the introduction. We would also like to thank Dean Birkenkamp and Janice Braunstein for their support and help.

Introduction

Critical Education or Training: Beyond the Commodification of Higher Education

Henry A. Giroux

> Let us even suppose that a democracy, as complete, perfect, etc. as one
> might wish, might fall upon us from the heavens: this sort of democracy
> will not be able to endure for more than a few years if it does not engender
> individuals that correspond to it, ones that, first and foremost, are capable
> of making it function and reproducing it. There can be no democratic soci-
> ety without democratic *paideia*.
>
> —Cornelius Castoriadis (1997, 10)

Beset by the growing forces of neoliberalism and the ravaging politics of the
culture wars, progressive educators and advocates of democratic education
are increasingly pressured to become either servants of corporate power or
detached intellectuals defined by a steadfast allegiance to the dictates of a narrow professionalism. As neoliberalism spreads its ideology, power, and influence over all aspects of society, there is a growing dislike for all things social,
public, and collective. As the obligations of citizenship are narrowly defined
through the imperatives of consumption and the dynamics of the marketplace, commercial space replaces noncommodified public spheres and the
first casualty is a language of social and political responsibility capable of
defending those vital institutions that expand the rights and services central
to a meaningful democracy. This is especially true with respect to the current
debate over the purpose of higher education, the cultural politics of the curricula, the role of academics as public intellectuals, and the centrality of pedagogy as a moral and political practice "that hold[s] open the temporality of
questioning" (Readings 1996, 19). At the same time, while all of these con-

1

cerns point to a crisis in higher education, especially the humanities, they cannot be understood outside of a range of broader social, cultural, economic, and political considerations that constitute a crisis in the very nature of democratic public life.

Beyond the Corporate University represents a partial, but hopefully significant, attempt to both identify and engage the crisis of higher education while simultaneously taking account of those profound transformations in the larger society, especially the forces of neoliberalism, that are waging a full-fledged assault on the welfare state, minorities of class and color, and all those public spheres not governed by the logic of the marketplace. All the chapters in this book share a language of critique and possibility that affirms the legacy of democratic concerns and rights that historically have defined the stated mission of higher education (Slaughter and Leslie 1997). Against the encroaching demands of a market-driven logic, *Beyond the Corporate University* forcefully argues that higher education should be defended as both a public good and an autonomous sphere for the development of a critical and productive democratic citizenry. Rather than instrumentalize reason and commodify knowledge, higher education is defined through its attempts to develop the capacities, skills, and knowledge necessary for students to create the conditions necessary "to govern democratically everyday life, the economy, civil society, and the state" (Panitch and Gindin 1999, 22). Within this discourse, civic education, rather than commercial training, becomes the governing axiom for producing democratic forms of political, social, and cultural agency that are crucial to constructing a society "that is as free and as just as possible" (Castoriadis 1997, 5). Higher education in this context is organized around a sense of critical public citizenship and represents a crucial ethical, pedagogical, and political site for keeping alive not only the tensions between market values and those values representative of civil society that cannot be measured in narrow commercial terms, but also those notions of educated hope that keep alive forms of political agency capable of realizing a life outside of the dictates of the marketplace—and which are crucial to a substantive democracy. *Beyond the Corporate University* recognizes that public and private institutions of higher education must make money in order to survive, but it refuses to reduce higher education to its entrepreneurial function. At the same time, it rejects the often right-wing notion that the purpose of education is about pure contemplation (Tingley 2000). All of the authors represented here believe that while the university cannot dissolve its commercial ties with the larger society its main purpose is civic education, taking seriously what it means to educate students for critical citizenship and political agency. This book takes as one of its central themes that education must not be confused with training, suggesting that educators resist allowing commercial values to shape the purpose and mission of higher education. Theorists as diverse as Stanley Aronowitz (2000), Randy Martin (1998), and

Cary Nelson (1997) have recognized the threat that corporate values pose to education, arguing that the best reason for supporting higher education lies not in its role as a training ground for the corporate workforce or, as Jeffrey J. Williams points out in this book, a "licensed storefront for name brand corporations (e.g., Kentucky Fried Chicken)," but in the crucial values it represents for educating students for the demands and responsibilities of leadership, social citizenship, and democratic public life.

In the first section of this book, the authors directly address how the ascendancy of corporate culture and neoliberalism in all facets of U.S. life have increasingly undermined the distinction between higher education and business that many progressive educators want to preserve. As democratic values give way to commercial values, intellectual effort is often reduced to an instrument of the entrepreneurial self, and social visions are dismissed as hopelessly out of date. Public space is portrayed exclusively as an investment opportunity, and the public good increasingly becomes a metaphor for public disorder. Within this discourse, anyone who does not believe that rapacious capitalism is the only road to freedom and the good life is dismissed as either a crank or worse. Hence, it is not surprising that Joseph Kahn writing in the *New York Times* argues without irony that "These days, it seems, only wild-eyed anarchists and Third World dictators believe capitalism is not the high road to a better life" (quoted in Rothschild 2000, 15).

As the public sphere is consistently removed from social considerations and notions of the public good are replaced by an utterly privatized model of citizenship and the good life, the collapse of public imagination and a vibrant political culture is *celebrated* by neoliberal warriors rather than perceived as a dangerous state of affairs that Americans should be both contemptuous of and ashamed to support (Bauman 1999). Divested of its political possibilities and social underpinnings, freedom finds few opportunities for translating private worries into public concerns or individual discontent into collective struggle. And increasingly, collapsing intellectual ambition and social vision are matched by a growing disdain toward matters of equality, justice, and politics and how such issues might be addressed critically by educators in higher education, especially the humanities.

As corporations become more and more powerful in the United States, educational leadership is stripped of its ethical and political obligations and is redefined primarily as a matter of management, efficiency, and cost effectiveness. In the name of efficiency, educational consultants all over America advise their clients to act like corporations selling products and to seek "market niches" to save themselves. Within this corporatized regime, management models of decision making replace faculty governance. Once constrained by the concept of "shared" governance in the past decade, administrations have taken more power and reduced faculty-controlled governance institutions to an advisory status. Given the narrow nature of corporate concerns, it is not surprising that when matters of accountability become part of the language of school reform, they are divorced from broader considerations of social responsibility.

Similarly, as universities become increasingly strapped for money, corporations are more than willing to provide the needed resources, but the costs are troubling and come with strings attached. Corporations increasingly dictate the very research they sponsor. At the University of California at Berkeley, for example, business representatives are actually appointed to sit on faculty committees that determine how research funds are spent and allocated. Equally disturbing is the emergence of many academics who hold stocks or gain other financial incentives in the very companies sponsoring their research (Cho 1997). As the boundaries between public values and commercial interests become blurred, many academics appear less as disinterested truth seekers than as operatives for multinational interests. This is exemplified by a recent story published in the *New York Times* in which Jonathan R. Cole, Columbia University's provost, argues, without a critical response, that the motivation of the university "is to be entrepreneurial. We've been giving it away for generations. Now we want to get a fair return" (Arenson 2000, A25). Getting a fair return means in this case investing $40 million of the university's $1.5 billion endowment in start-up Internet ventures that translate intellectual capital into financial gain. Academic research is now directly tied to the possibilities of making big profits. How this marriage of commercial logic and academic capital might affect the role of academic research, the purpose of the university, and the rules for supporting particular types of teaching, research, and knowledge production is left unexamined in the *Times* article except for a quote by Dr. Michael Crow, Columbia's executive vice provost, who states: "Columbia has no plans to compel faculty members to cooperate with its own ventures, but hopes to offer them as an alternative to working with outside companies" (A25). Indeed!

However, there is more at stake than academics selling out to the highest corporate bidder. In some cases, academic research is compromised; corporations routinely censor research results at odds with their commercial interests (Cho 1997). As Eyal Press and Jennifer Washburn have reported, "In a 1996 study published in the *Annals of Internal Medicine,* Mildred Cho and Lisa Bero found that 98 percent of papers based on industry-sponsored research reflected favorably on the drugs being examined, as compared with 79 percent of papers based on research not funded by the industry" (2000, 42). Press and Washburn have also provided examples of companies that have censored corporate-sponsored research papers by removing passages that highlighted unfavorable results or negative outcomes. It gets worse. As large amounts of corporate capital flow into universities, those areas of study that do not translate into substantial profits get marginalized, underfunded, or eliminated. Hence, we are witnessing both a downsizing in the humanities as well as the increasing refusal on the part of universities to fund research in public health or science fields that place a high priority on public service. The new corporate university appears to be indifferent to ideas, forms of learning, and modes of research that lack commercial value.

Against the current onslaught to vocationalize higher education, *Beyond the Corporate University* argues that progressives need to defend higher education as a resource vital to the democratic and civic life of the nation. Central to such a task is the challenge to resist what Bill Readings (1996) has called a consumer-oriented corporation more concerned about accounting than accountability. The crisis of higher education needs to be analyzed in terms of wider configurations of economic, political, and social forces that exacerbate tensions between those who value such institutions as public goods and those advocates of neoliberalism who see market culture as a master design for all human affairs. *Beyond the Corporate University* strongly argues that progressive educators must challenge all attempts on the part of neoliberals to either define democracy exclusively as a liability or to enervate its substantive ideals by reducing it to the imperatives of hypercapitalism and the glorification of financial markets. This requires, in part, that educators consider the political and pedagogical importance of struggling over the meaning and definition of democracy, authority, and social responsibility within their courses and situate such a debate within an expansive notion of human rights, social provisions, civil liberties, equity, and economic justice. As oppositional public intellectuals, progressive academics need to create a movement for the defense of public goods and democratic public spheres, one that links the struggles within the university to multiple sites within the larger social order. Such a movement suggests that progressive academics must take seriously the symbolic and pedagogical dimensions of struggle and be able to use these resources in a variety of public spaces to fight for public services and rights, especially the right to decent health care, education, housing, and work. Michael Bérubé (1998) has recently argued that educators need to find ways to ensure that their academic work addresses the imperatives of social policy. For Berube, teaching, research, and writing are indispensable roles for public intellectuals to engage in as critical academics, but they do not fully constitute the possibilities of what it means to do valuable work in the university. Bérubé claims that such intellectuals must connect their work to social policy, especially addressing the role that public policy currently plays in undermining the basic foundations of democratic public life. The leap from teaching to policy is important and complex and *Beyond the Corporate University* attempts to support such a vital connection. At the same time, we want to extend this insight by arguing that the call for academics to link their work to social policy remains too abstract unless it engages the crucial role of pedagogy in developing and enabling forms of political agency among both teachers and students that make such a connection both attractive and viable. Without a viable notion of political agency, such calls

for linking theory and practice become empty and elide the crucial importance of making the pedagogical more political.

What must be challenged at all costs on many fronts is the increasingly dominant view propagated by neoliberal gurus such as Milton Friedman that profit
making is the sole purpose of democracy and accumulating material goods the
essence of the good life. Such a struggle demands new means of communication within the university and among cultural workers from a variety of public spheres within and across national boundaries. But if the notion of the
oppositional public intellectual is to be redefined as part of a broader project
to link learning to social change, such a project will have to create new forms
of communication and solidarity capable of addressing and challenging the
dangerous threats that globalization currently poses to social, economic, political, and cultural democracy. Under such circumstances, the very notion of
what it means to be an oppositional public intellectual will have to change,
especially in challenging the orthodox left notion that the proper, if only, aim
of left politics can be built around the call for economic justice (Willis 1999).
Moreover, rearticulating the relationship between ethics and social transformation will demand a commitment to a pluralized politics that refuses to rely
on one solution or answer. It will also require understanding and contesting
multiple forms of domination, while simultaneously expanding current
notions of justice and rights to include new movements struggling to create
new entitlements and redress diverse forms of oppression. On the contrary,
problems regarding the transformation of society are multiple, interdependent, and complex and involve issues of youth, race, women, bureaucracy, the
environment, population growth, the devolution of the state, the disappearance of noncommodified public spheres, the changing character of labor and
technology, and the problems of urbanism, and more.

In the second and third sections of *Beyond the Corporate University,* a
number of authors redefine the cultural politics of the university and classroom teaching by critically examining the struggle over meaning, knowledge,
and literature as part of an extended attempt to struggle for a radical democratic social order. By focusing on how authority and power shapes knowledge,
how the teaching of broader social values provides safeguards against turning
citizenship skills into training skills for the workplace, and how culture works
to put into place particular forms of agency, these two sections reaffirm the
importance of the curriculum as a site of critique, critical exchange, and social
struggle. Moreover, the struggle over curricula, both hidden and overt, offers
progressive educators the opportunity to challenge those approaches to corporate pedagogy in which knowledge becomes capital—a form of investment
in the economy—that appears to have little value when linked to the power
of self-definition or the capacities of individuals to expand the scope of individual and social freedom. By viewing curriculum as a site of critical inquiry,
contestation, and resistance, pedagogy is defined as a normative and political

practice rather than as a neutral methodology or a fixed a priori discourse. Engaging the disciplines, especially literary studies, in ways that highlight their sociohistorical formations and ideologically laden commonsense assumptions offers teachers and students alike a view of authority that needs to be both the subject of critique and a strategic resource to be used in creating the pedagogical conditions necessary to challenge dominant modes of knowledge. Rather than viewing teaching and learning as a sacred ritual buttressed by forms of authority that appear unproblematic and beyond the range of deliberation, progressive educators would challenge all forms of authority "that would fail to render an account and provide reasons . . . for the validity of its pronouncements" (Castoriadis 1997, 4). At stake here is the attempt to rethink what it means for critical educators to produce knowledge, social relations, and modes of authority capable of challenging those forms of moral and political regulation that perceive higher education as both a training ground for corporate berths and as a guardian of dominant cultural capital designed to benefit a small privileged minority of ruling class students.

Focusing on how higher education puts into place particular forms of temporality, subject positions, and knowledge through which students define themselves and their relationship to the social world (Giroux 1992), a number of authors in *Beyond the Corporate University* argue that the relationship between culture and pedagogy cannot be abstracted from the central dynamics of politics and power. Culture, in this instance, is always tangled up with power and becomes political in a double sense. First, questions of ownership, access, and governance are crucial to understanding how power is deployed in regulating the images, meanings, and ideas that frame the agendas that both structure classroom life and articulate with broader ideological and institutional forces in the wider society. Second, academic culture not only offers up specific knowledge, values, ideologies, and social practices to different groups of students situated within unequal relations of power, it also makes a claim on certain histories, memories, and narratives. As James Young has noted in a different context, such histories tell "both the story of events and its unfolding as narrative" in order to influence how individuals take up, modify, resist, and accommodate themselves to particular forms of citizenship, present material relations of power, and specific notions of the future (1998, 673). In this instance, the representation of politics that shapes the content of the canon, curricula, and literature, in particular, within higher education is inseparable from the institutional conditions, mechanisms of power, and social relations through which questions of meaning, public memory, belonging, and desire are produced, mediated, and distributed.

Within the corporate university, curricula, and classroom social relations, the concept of the social is being refigured and displaced as a constitutive category for making democracy operational and political agency the conditions for social transformation. In this instance, the notion of the social and the public are not being erased as much as they are being reconstructed under circumstances in which public forums for serious debate, including public and higher education, are being eroded. Within the ongoing logic of neoliberalism, teaching and learning are removed from the discourse of democracy and civic culture—defined as a purely private affair. Divorced from the imperatives of a democratic society, pedagogy is reduced to a matter of taste, individual choice, and job training. Pedagogy as a mode of witnessing, a public space in which students learn to be attentive and responsible to the memories and narratives of others, disappears within a corporate-driven notion of learning in which the logic of market devalues the opportunity for students to make connections with others through social relations that foster a mix of compassion, ethics, and hope (Simon 2000). The crisis of the social is further amplified by the withdrawal of the state as a guardian of the public trust and its growing lack of investment in those sectors of social life that promote the public good. Moreover, the crisis of the social is further aggravated, in part, by an unwillingness on the part of many academics to address the importance of higher education as a force for encouraging critical participation in civic life. At the same time, dominant educational discourses give scant attention to how pedagogy functions as a crucial cultural, political, and moral practice for connecting politics, power, and social agency to the broader formative processes of democratic public life. Such concerns are important because they not only raise questions about the meaning and purpose of higher education, but also because they politicize the meaning of pedagogy by connecting it to important considerations of ideology, power, and ethics. Moreover, addressing pedagogy as both an act of intervention and the outcome of historically specific struggles and deliberations offers a challenge to neoliberal cultural warriors who in their attempts to privatize and corporatize all aspects of schooling abstract pedagogy from the realms of power and politics.

Under attack by corporate interests, the political right, and neoliberal doctrines, pedagogical discourses that define themselves in political and moral terms, particularly as they draw attention to the operations of power and its relationship to the production of knowledge and subjectivities, are either derided or ignored. Reduced to the status of training, pedagogy in its conservative and neoliberal versions appears completely at odds with those versions of critical teaching designed to provide students with the skills and information necessary to think critically about the knowledge they gain, and what it might mean for them to challenge antidemocratic forms of power. All too often critical pedagogy, within and outside of the academy, is either dismissed as irrelevant to the educational process or is appropriated simply as a technique for "encouraging" student participation and dialogue. Missing from these discourses is any reference to pedagogy as an ideology and social practice engaged in the production and dissemination of knowledge, values, and identities within concrete institutional formations and relations of power.

Nor is there any sense of the relevance of understanding pedagogy as part of a broader project for democratic transformation as well as for providing the skills and knowledge necessary for students to be critical rather then merely good citizens.

In the final section of *Beyond the Corporate University,* all of the authors address the centrality of pedagogy as a moral and political practice, though they take up what it means to make the pedagogical more political in different ways. In opposition to dominant views of education and cultural politics, these authors argue differently for a transformative pedagogy that relentlessly questions the kinds of labor, practices, affective investments, and forms of production that are enacted in higher education. Similarly, these authors understand that while higher education must be comprehended within an analysis of those wider forces that shape the larger social order, central to such an analysis must be a critical attentiveness to the conditional nature of pedagogy itself. This suggests that pedagogy can never be treated as a fixed set of principles and practices that can be applied indiscriminately across a variety of pedagogical sites and classrooms. Pedagogy must always be contextually defined, allowing it to respond specifically to the conditions, formations, and problems that arise in various sites in which education takes place. Rather than treating pedagogy as commodity, these authors share the assumption, both implicitly and explicitly, that progressive educators need to engage their teaching as a theoretical resource that is both shaped by and responds to the very problems that arise in the in-between spaces/places/contexts that connect classrooms with the experiences of everyday life. Critical pedagogy locates discursive practices within a broader set of interrelations, but it analyzes and gives meaning to such relations by defining them within particular contexts constructed through operations of power articulated among the concrete interactions between texts, teachers, and students.

One consequence of linking pedagogy to the specificity of place is that it extends the possibility of making the pedagogical more political. Not only does it foreground the need for educators to rethink the cultural and political baggage they bring to each educational encounter, but it also highlights the necessity of making educators ethically and politically accountable for the stories they produce, the claims they make upon public memory, and the images of the future they deem legitimate. Pedagogy is never innocent and if it is to be understood and problematized as a form of academic labor, educators must not only critically question and register their own subjective involvement in how and what they teach, they must also resist all calls to depoliticize pedagogy through appeals to either scientific objectivity, ideological dogmatism, or the denunciation of all authority as simply a mask for domination. Far from being disinterested or ideologically frozen, critical pedagogy is concerned about the articulation of knowledge and affective investments to social effects and succeeds to the degree in which educators encourage students to think critically while providing the conditions for them to expand their capacities for individual and social transformation. Moral and civic agency within this pedagogical discourse is encouraged rather than simply molded. Following Readings (1996), the notion of pedagogy that permeates this book is that it is a transaction that can never be concluded. Hence, the "aim of pedagogy should not be to produce autonomous subjects who are supposedly made free by the information they learn. . . . Rather, . . . the scene of teaching can be better understood as a network of obligations . . . [and that] teaching is a question of justice not a search for truth" (19). Crucial to the latter position is the necessity for critical educators to be attentive to the ethical, affective, and subjective dimensions of their own practice and how the latter must become not merely the condition for conducting social analyses, but also for engaging in forms of autocritique.

As diverse as the chapters in *Beyond the Corporate University* might appear, they all share in the assumption that as an act of intervention, education needs to be grounded in a project that not only problematizes its own location, mechanisms of transmission, and effects, but also functions as part of a larger vision enabling students to think more critically about *how* existing social, political, and economic arrangements might be better suited to address the promise of a radical democracy as an anticipatory rather than messianic goal. Educators within this discourse function as oppositional public intellectuals rather than as multinational operatives. Jacques Derrida (2000) has recently suggested in another context that the social function of intellectuals as well as any viable notion of education should be grounded in a vibrant politics, which makes the promise of democracy a matter of concrete urgency. For Derrida, making visible a "democracy" that is to come as opposed to that which presents itself in its name provides a referent for both criticizing everywhere what parades as democracy—"the current state of all so-called democracy" (9)—and critically assessing the conditions and possibilities for democratic transformation. Derrida sees the promise of democracy as the proper articulation of a political ethics and by implication suggests that when higher education is engaged and articulated through the project of democratic social transformation it can function as a vital public sphere for critical learning, ethical deliberation, and civic engagement. Under such circumstances, the meaning and purpose of higher education redefines the relationship between knowledge and power on the one hand, and learning and social change on the other. In doing so, higher education represents the possibility of retaining one important democratic public sphere that offers the conditions for resisting the increasing depoliticization of the citizenry, provides a language to challenge the politics of accommodation that connects education to the logic of privatization, refuses to define students as simply consuming subjects, and actively opposes the view of teaching as market-driven practice and learning as a form of training. In short, *Beyond the Corpo-*

rate University attempts to resuscitate the image of higher education as a public good, the curriculum as a place through which critical teaching and learning can be connected to addressing the most pressing social problems of contemporary society, and pedagogy as a moral and political practice that provides students with the most important knowledge and skills available to enable them to create a pluralized culture, a democratized economy, and a political system that is animated by the most basic and important precepts of democratic public life.

WORKS CITED

Arenson, Karen, W. 2000. "Columbia Leads Academic Pack in Turning Profit from Research." *New York Times,* 2 August, A1, A25.

Aronowitz, Stanley. 2000. *The Knowledge Factory: Dismantling the Corporate University and Creating True Higher Learning.* Boston: Beacon.

Aronowitz, Stanley, and Henry A. Giroux. 1992. *Education Still under Siege.* Westport, Conn.: Bergin and Garvey.

Bauman, Zygmunt. 1999. *In Search of Politics.* Stanford: Stanford University Press.

Bérubé, Michael. 1998. *The Employment of English: Theory, Jobs, and the Future of Literary Studies.* New York: New York University Press.

Castoriadis, Cornelius. 1997. "Democracy As Procedure and Democracy As Regime." *Constellations* 4.1: 1–18.

Cho, Mildred. 1997. "Secrecy and Financial Conflicts in University-Industry Research Must Get Closer Scrutiny." *Chronicle of Higher Education* 43.7: B4–B5.

Cho, Mildred, and Lisa A. Bero. 1996. "The Quality of Drug Studies." *Annals of Internal Medicine* 124:485–489.

Derrida, Jacques. 2000. "Intellectual Courage: An Interview." *Culture Machine* 2:1–15; also see <www.culturemachine.tees.ac.uk/articles/art_derr.htm>. Last accessed: December 2000.

Giroux, Henry. 1992. *Border Crossings.* New York: Routledge.

Martin, Randy. 1998. *Chalk Lines.* Durham, N.C.: Duke University Press.

Nelson, Cary. 1997. *Manifesto of a Tenured Radical.* New York: New York University Press.

Panitch, Leo, and Sam Gindin. 1999. "Transcending Pessimism: Rekindling Socialist Imagination." In *Necessary and Unnecessary Utopias,* ed. Leo Panitch and Sam Gindin. New York: Monthly Review Press.

Press, Eyal, and Jennifer Washburn. 2000. "The Kept University." *Atlantic Monthly,* 20 March, 51–54.

Readings, Bill. 1996. *The University in Ruins.* Cambridge, Mass.: Harvard University Press.

Rothschild, Matthew. 2000. "Quick Hits." *The Progressive* (August): 15.

Simon, Roger. 2000. "The Touch of the Past: The Pedagogical Significance of a Transactional Sphere of Public Memory." In *Revolutionary Pedagogies,* ed. Peter Pericles Trifonas. New York: Routledge Falmer.

Slaughter, Sheila, and Larry L. Leslie. 1997. *Academic Capitalism: Politics, Policies,*

I

HIGHER EDUCATION AND THE POLITICS OF CORPORATE CULTURE

1

Franchising the University

Jeffrey J. Williams

I

To return to an old question, what is the idea of the university? One common-place idea, from Immanuel Kant, is that it is based on the disciplinary divisions of knowledge. A linked idea, from Alexander von Humboldt, is that it is based on the nation-state.[1] In a modification from Matthew Arnold and John Henry Newman, it is based on cultural training—which work to reproduce the national culture, in Arnold's famous rubric staving off anarchy. According to Bill Readings's (1996) oft-cited contemporary update, it is now ungrounded from nations and culture, and based on a dereferentialized notion of "excellence." For me, like that of other public institutions and entitlements, the idea of the university turns on the concept of "franchise." Despite global reconfigurations and the decline of the liberal welfare state, I do not see the withering away of the nation-state, but rather its retrenchment in enforcing certain perogatives of capital. Most of our universities, after all, are *state* universities, so named and carrying out the explicit mandates of our states. The university speaks precisely to our conception of public welfare, entitlement, and service, and specifically to how we bring citizens into public life.

Franchise, of course, carries two prominent senses: its celebrated sense as attaining a vote and in general a purchase in the public sphere, influence on public policy, and access to public programs, and its more current colloquial sense as a licensed storefront for name-brand corporations (e.g., Kentucky Fried Chicken). While historically there has often been a tension in the man-dates of the university, particularly the American university, between busi-ness and free inquiry (see Barrow 1990), universities are now being increas-ingly conscripted as the latter kind of franchise. This applies not only to public universities based on explicit state charges for public service, but also

15

to private universities, which materially benefit from public funding like the National Institutes of Health (NIH), and which carry out a presumably public mission in educating citizens.

Although this is probably no surprise to any of us working in the university, the recent shift in the idea of the university was brought home to me a few years ago at a faculty convocation inaugurating the school year at East Carolina University (ECU), one of the larger schools in the North Carolina state system.[2] In the midst of the usual round of speeches by various administrators—some announcements (the prodigious new rec center, a couple months behind schedule, will be completed in October, and so on), some ritually conferring a symbolic weightiness upon our academic endeavor, some more in the genre of a pep rally, to get us up for the game at hand—the dean of the College of Arts and Sciences "encouraged" us to "market the college to alumni and friends of the university" and to form "partnerships" with local business, such as Glaxo-Wellcome or Dupont a few miles down the road. While I usually slouch in the back and whisper to friends—such ceremonial events bring out my adolescent defiance, like misbehaving in church—I sat up and took notice. Normally the dean ushered in the new year with the kind of exhortatory if vacuous rhetoric one expects on such occasions; if I recall correctly, the motto of the previous year had been that we should "be the best we could be." Hailing from the literature faculty, the dean had typically been an enthusiastic defender of the values of humanistic inquiry and traditional scholarship, exhorting us to "boost our bibliographies" and thereby to augment ECU's "national prominence." ECU was in a strange position, caught somewhere between flagship and outpost, with ambitions to be the academic jewel of the eastern part of the state, which was undergoing an economic and technological boom (for instance, Glaxo manufactured AZT on the north edge of town through the early 1990s), but with vestiges of a teacher's college (ECTC as the old timers still called it), so the dean's cheerleading toward the vague vista of "being the best we could be" fit consistently with the urge toward national prominence through traditional academic means of distinction.

But this was different and announced a more concrete imperative. Now he seemed to be telling us to get out of our library carrels and start hawking our wares, trading vita lines for a more tangible bottom line. More pointedly, shortly thereafter he instituted a policy to encourage us to seek grants, amending the criteria for our yearly evaluations (determining salary raises) so that, in the English department, we received research publication credit for external grants *submitted,* four grants equalling an article. Not to put too fine a point on it, the dean by fiat seemed to rewrite our professional self-definition, from scholarship to salesmanship.

To be fair, grant-seeking is not necessarily independent of scholarly productivity, but one might speculate without much of a stretch that research on, say, the conjunction of the new science of eighteenth-century geology and literary attention to landscape in Romantic poetry—that one of my current colleagues in English does—would not fare as well under this new dispensation as a proposal in tech writing, so this shift tacitly reconfigures the internal hierarchy of research, what kind of research carries more value, and what research comes to represent the humanities.[3] The sciences and progressively more so the social sciences have been subject to such "market" criteria for some time, but my dean's imperative grafted the protocols of business applicability rather decisively onto the formerly semiautonomous zone of the humanities.

This marketing motivational rhetoric and explicit change in research criteria prompted one of my ECU colleagues to suggest that instead of our being the indirect and occasional conduits for grants and donations, we streamline the process and simply stop, say, every half hour during class to give a minute pitch for the local MacDonald's, or Wendy's, or Hardee's, or Burger King that line the perimeter of campus. We proceeded to draw out the all too viable possibilities for this new form of academic fund-raising, but fortunately my friend has no aspirations to be in administration. This might seem farfetched, but it is not entirely facetious, as evidenced by the advent of corporate advertising and marketing in many public high schools via programs such as Channel One (including those in Greenville, North Carolina, that schooled professors' children), which daily feeds students ten minutes of *Entertainment Tonight*-style news mixed with five minutes of commercials for Coke, corn chips, and Clearasil. The lure for schools, and especially for school administrators, is that Channel One provides "free" television sets—their grant heralded as beneficent support for education, lessening the burden on public funds—in exchange for a contractual guarantee that their programs run every day. The grant, in other words, has strings and is hardly altruistic; if schools decide not to run the Channel One program, then the sets are repossessed (see Kleinfield 1991).

While my recounting of the dean's imperative is admittedly anecdotal, the model of the university it beckons is not a Chicken Little–like millennial prediction but reflects the looming trend in university funding, from public funded to an unabashed imperative to be corporate sponsored, injecting revenue from an amalgam of external, private sources.[4] Further, this imperative is not anomalous, applying only to the person down the hall or across the quad, but has real and significant effects on all of us, on our everyday work life and what counts as academic work. As a counterpart to the stress on grants, unspoken by my dean but manifest especially in the humanities where grants are fewer and where there has historically been less immediate transfer to commercial uses, there is a parallel pressure to cut costs and more "efficiently" administer funding, that is, to generate greater numbers of FTEs with fewer faculty and especially fewer permanent faculty—part-timers, lecturers, and so on, as I am sure is familiar to most of us. The criteria that mandates the garnering of grants—whereby the primary measure of education is taken in short-term, quantitative monetary gains—also generates the conditions of the current job market, by intractable fiscal logic propelling the speedup, outsourcing, and destabilization of teaching labor. Permanent workers are expensive, and an impermanent labor pool also helps to control those who have permanent positions. In other words, the current job crisis stems not from magical or aberrant conditions that the word "crisis" seems to imply, but from the profit criterion that fosters the greater extraction of labor.[5] It bears repeating that the job crisis is not a question of an economic downturn that might right itself magically, like the weather (cloudy today, but we hope for sunshine tomorrow), for the economy has been flush for the past decade if you read the *Wall Street Journal,* nor does it derive from a lessened need for teachers (count the students in your classes), but from the greater extraction of labor from teachers.

Gary Rhoades and Sheila Slaughter succinctly define this shift in criterion to what they call "academic capitalism," observing that "Not-for-profit institutions in the academy are taking on the characteristics and activities of profit-making organizations" (1997, 13). One could amass statistics on this overall trend toward bottom-lining universities—for instance, drastic and disproportionate cuts in the University of California and SUNY systems and the ensuing pressure for private funding, as well as for labor speedup and outsourcing[6] (Richard Ohmann notes the shift from 10 percent to 60 percent part-time labor since the mid-1960s [1995, 231], although most estimates place it at about 50 percent)—and survey the complementary calls for accountability and productivity, but my interest here is the rise of what might be called the new idea of the university, as an accepted and appropriate model by which universities should operate "in the twenty-first century."

As I began, this shift in the dominant prescription for higher education, and especially for public universities, is aptly represented by the two senses of franchise. Universities are now being conscripted directly as training grounds for the corporate workforce, obviously in the growth of business departments but impacting the humanities too, in the proliferation of more "practical" degrees in technical writing and the like.[7] In fact, university work has been more directly construed to serve not only corporate-profit agendas via its grant-suppliant status, but universities have become franchises in their own right, reconfigured according to corporate management, labor, and consumer models and delivering a name-brand product.[8] Related to this, many corporations have been getting into the education business for themselves, as evidenced by Motorola University or Phoenix University. The traditional idea of the university as a not-for-profit institution that offers a liberal education and enfranchises citizens of the republic, not to mention the more radical view that the university foster a socially critical if not revolutionary class, has been evacuated without much of a fight.

II

One can also surmise the tacit expression of the new idea of the university in what might seem an unlikely place, the 1996 blockbuster *The Nutty Professor*. An extraordinarily popular summer release and star-vehicle (hailed as Eddie Murphy's "comeback"), it earned record profits in both initial showings and in video, probably due to its feel-good message that we should be comfortable with our appearances and bodies, whatever shape they take, as well as to its humor. What I find especially striking about it, however, as an inveterate university watcher, is its image of and assumed rationale for the work of the university. The title character played by Murphy, Professor Klump, teaches—inattentively and irresponsibly, missing classes after his transformation to the svelte Buddy Love—but his real work is his research into genetic manipulation for the sake of weight loss. This differs markedly from the original Jerry Lewis version (1963), in which Lewis plays the snaggle-toothed, prototypically geeky Professor Kelp rather than the rotund Klump. After Kelp blows up a classroom full of students during a chemistry class, the dean lectures him: "I will not stand for any members of my staff utilizing the facilities of this university for his or her own *personal* experiments" (my emphasis). In other words, the work of a professor in the earlier popular imaginary is coded primarily as a teacher rather than as a researcher, research outbounded as a "personal" interest or hobby, expressly *prohibited* by university policy! This stands a world apart from the recent version, in which it is taken for granted that Klump's job is in the lab, and from the criteria under which we work, whereby the predominant measure for hiring, tenure, and promotion is precisely our "personal" research—and more and more, the entrepreneurial ability to fund that research.

Further, not only is teaching relegated to a peripheral duty in the recent *Nutty Professor,* but Professor Klump's research is hardly pure or motivated for the advance of scientific knowledge per se, which is the traditional disciplinary rationale for research, nor is it for the sake of the health of mankind, which is the more altruistic, public rationale for research. Rather, his professional prospect is essentially product development, for a techno-miraculous Slim-Fast for the sake of cosmetic change, which would obviously carry enormous commercial potential and profit for his university. In other words, the current *Nutty Professor* assumes without blinking the new commercial profit rationale for research. These popular images from the earlier to later "nutty professors" mark a decided shift in professional definition; modifying Regis Debray's charting of the changing social role of intellectuals in this century from "teacher to writer to celebrity," they project a course from teacher to researcher to entrepreneur.

These images apply largely to the more commercially transferable results of the practical sciences, but one way to see the recent celebration of the figure of the public intellectual in the humanities is as a celebration of the success of an individual academic career—that is, of a symbolic entrepreneur. The public intellectual presents the vista of professional success as transcending the confines of a normal academic career—one is transformed to a successful writer for glossy magazines and commentator for major media. In other words, rather than its putative assertion of our renewed public relevance and power in toto, the public intellectual in this sense poses a model of good old American individualism and a symbolic Horatio Alger–like rise, out of the slums of a four to four or five to five teaching load and transcending the inconsequence of day-to-day life lecturing on *Beowulf* or sitting on the curriculum committee.[9] That the transformation of professional prospect occurs as business as usual in the recent *Nutty Professor* demonstrates how deeply the corporate-cultural norm of the university has been naturalized in the popular imaginary. We have come a long way from Mr. Chips (we do not see Murphy dazzle us with his charisma in the classroom), not to mention Cardinal Newman.

In conjunction with the role of the professor, the portrait of the dean in the recent *Nutty Professor* also marks a precipitous shift in the model and expectation of administration. The dean is uptight, condescending, and sneaky, alternately cajoling and bullying, parodying the stereotype of an anxious white male middle manager and carrying on a long line of film satires of college life. However, previous portraits of deans, most famously in *Animal House* (1978), show their job as that of a stuffed-shirt headmaster, worrying about behavior codes and keeping fraternities in check. The dean in the earlier *Nutty Professor* somewhat more benevolently works with students in organizing a senior dance, pronouncing that "the faculty, as always, is ready to serve the needs of the student body." The dean in the 1996 *Nutty Professor* has only one concern, with which in fact he is obsessed: to garner a donation from a local businessman. His job entails not dealing with students, but in managing—coaxingly or threateningly—faculty toward the goal of dollar signs.

Though bullying, he is remarkably complacent upon discovering Professor Klump has missed a class, delivering an ultimatum that his job—and in fact his life, threatening in lurid detail to strangle him—depends on his research and his success in procuring the grant. (The dean's threat to Professor Klump parodically literalizes the cliché publish or perish, revised now to procure a grant or perish.) This characterization of the dean testifies to the blatant shift in university rationale, for work that directly generates "external" funds, and succinctly represents the reconfiguration of administration as managing faculty rather than serving students, pressing the mandate on faculty to "produce" and holding them accountable to do so. While my former dean was always gracious and encouraging, and to my knowledge has never threatened to strangle anyone, the administrative protocol is one and the same; that the dean's portrait in *The Nutty Professor* seems to come from central casting

ing determinate political power in the university; a recent Association of Governing Boards study, "Renewing the Academic Presidency," rather baldly puts the new administrative imperative: "including faculty in shared governance had been the source of many ills in the modern university" (Perley 1997, A48).

Second, the recoding of faculty not as disinterested researchers in their disciplines for an abstract knowledge production or for the general public good, but as research and development workers and entrepreneurs, to develop more immediately practical, corporately approved, and marketable products that generate funds—or one might literally say profits, given the fattening endowments of many universities (over 270 universities have endowments over $100 million—less than that does not merit a listing, as charted by the 1999 *Chronicle Almanac*). Even in their traditional role as teachers, faculty has been placed in the position of readily replaceable service workers, to process more "products," ascertainable in the accounting of FTEs. In this sense, faculty have been disenfranchised as semiautonomous intellectual professionals—whether in the conservative view as transmitting the canon and extolling Western Civilization in the humanities, or in the progressive view as fostering an oppositional pedagogy and intellectual dissent, or even in a basic labor view as those with rights to a secure job for decent pay—instead taking up a direct service position to those "who pay their salaries," which includes franchise managers and owners (administrators, boards of trustees, and grantors), as well as consumers at the franchise (students and their parents).

Third, although largely invisible in *The Nutty Professor* but consistent with the ethos of the profit-protocol of the new university, students have been unabashedly reinvented as consumers, as shoppers at the store of education, buying a career-enhancing service. This commodification of students' interests manifests itself ideologically, in projecting their experience primarily as a monetary exchange, paying tuition for accreditation necessary to get a professional-managerial class job. This is not necessarily wrong on the part of students—what would we have them do, given the world they find themselves facing?—and in a significant way the opportunity represented by university education, particularly public university education, is precisely to give students a step up the class ladder, especially working-class students. That, after all, represents one real if modest vehicle of the American dream. However, with the present restructuring of labor, a college degree is no longer a guarantee of a secure job, so the gate frequently does not open to the presumed garden on the other side. As the journalists David Lipsky and Alexander Abrams characterize their generation in the subtitle of *Late Bloomers, Coming of Age in Today's America: The Right Place at the Wrong Time* (1994).

This represents a failure not only in terms of citizenship, but one might also say in terms of bad business practice, because even if one accepts the capitalist-prep model of the university, that model does not deliver on its promise on its own contractual terms, thus constituting a kind of false advertising. It fails an economic franchise for many of our young. Further, even if one takes job-training as the primary aim of university education, that training does not exhaust the possibilities of education and its unquantifiable surplus. Not to mention that there might be another basis for the university, perhaps less tangible or quantifiable: a university education might offer a safe space and concerted time for students to imagine other prospects for their lives rather than being a consumer, to examine critically the social world they had no part in making, and to envision a different world they might choose to enter. On the consumer model, students are disenfranchised as future citizens, reconstituted as consumers and potential workers.

In a different way, the commodification of students occurs perhaps most perniciously in the recent and disproportionate rise in college costs and the ensuing restructuring of financial aid—in other words, in what is done to students materially, as objects of banking profit and interests, instead of what is projected ideologically as in their interest (to get a job and middle-class toehold). In a chapter fittingly entitled "Indentured Students" in *Late Bloomers,* Lipsky and Abrams detail the cost—literally and figuratively—of university education, noting that tuition rose exponentially, from the 1970s at more than twice the rate of inflation despite relatively stagnant wages. To pay for it, there has been a massive increase in loan programs like the GSL, about which Lipsky and Abrams state, "In 1978, after thirteen years of the program, a little more than $10 billion had been loaned to students. . . . By the early nineties, more than 62 million student loans had been made through the federal government"—bear in mind that this does not include private or other forms of loans—"ten times as many as the 6 million loans in the GSL's first decade. There had been more than $100 billion borrowed," more than $15 billion a year in the 1990s (1994, 119). Less abstractly, Steven Watt remarks that many current humanities graduate students finish grad school with debts of $25,000 or more (1995, 31; see also Nelson 1997, 173). It is almost impossible for those of us educated before 1985 or earlier, when there was a more active sense of public entitlement, to imagine the costs, real as well as psychic, of entering an unwelcoming workforce while carrying such a burden of debt.

In short, higher education has become a substantial banking franchise, a new domain of extraordinary, low-risk (given federally subsidized and guaranteed loans) profit for Citibank, Chase Manhattan, Marine Midland, and other sanctioned lenders. As the staid *U.S. News and World Report* observed, with some shock, in the 1993 report "Defaulting the Future": "Nearly 8,000 banks, savings and loans, credit unions and other lenders will make an estimated $18 billion in new federally backed student loans in fiscal year 1993" (56). This in turn effectively indentures students for ten to twenty years after graduation and intractably reduces their career choices, funneling them into the corporate workforce in order to pay their loans, which are not only federally guaranteed but federally enforced (if necessary, through wage and property garnishees) and nearly impossible to default (for instance, bankruptcy does not exempt one from student loans). Even if we take the gatekeeping role of universities in the most benign sense, this fails students in not providing them education as a public entitlement to enter a productive workforce, as the G.I. Bill of Rights did for the post–World War II generation, by most accounts with great success not just individually but for the public good of American society. In sum, students have progressively become more disenfranchised, literally kept out of colleges they cannot afford and driven to make career choices based on the bottom line, the bricks in the new pyramid scheme of the corporate franchising of higher education.

IV

Given the advent of the new idea of the franchised university that I have sketched, what, as the saying goes, is to be done? The current restructuring of higher education is one facet of the restructuring of civic life in the United States, whereby previously assured public entitlements such as healthcare, welfare, social security, and so on, along with education, have evaporated or been "privatized," so any solution cannot be separated from a larger vision of what it means to enfranchise citizens of our republic. However, my proposals are less cosmic and speak more specifically to our roles as critics and academic-intellectuals. First, I would advocate a relentless reflexive criticism, that is, one that turns the plentiful analytical tools we have at our disposal to where we work, examining the material effects of the kind of work we do (say, as graders, rather than in our more abstract self-definition, as purveying literature in English), the material institutions that we work in (as labor structures, from housekeepers to provosts), how they govern our work, how they serve the needs of the society at large, and how they bear on students. Of late, a good many of us in the humanities have been calling attention to the embattled state of the university and especially to the horrendous labor conditions of new PhDs, but by and large our analytical tools remain ratcheted to producing new interpretations of the specified objects of our "fields"—in my field, new readings of a circumscribed set of literary and critical texts.

I would especially advocate a concerted examination of the idea and history of the university, not only as the place where we work and that sets the limits of our professional self-definition, but also as one of the few zones in contemporary life that represents the possibility of a public sphere that fosters discussion of public issues and policy and that represents the prospect of public entitlement and opportunity for class levelling. I confess that the story I have sketched of the recent university takes the form of a fall, from the better days of the "Great Society" university and its sense of public welfare. However, my point is not that the university was better in past, glory days—

Clyde Barrow's *Universities and the Capitalist State: Corporate Liberalism and the Reconstruction of American Higher Education, 1894-1928* (1990) and Ellen Schrecker's *No Ivory Tower: McCarthyism and the Universities* (1986), in different ways, make short work of any myth of the halcyon past—but that one can imagine a better future for the university, for those who work there and for those who attend it, than the one that we are witnessing and participating in.

Second, I would advocate attention to the "idea" of the university in what I have called the "cultural imaginary," in movies, general media reports and representations, policy statements, and so on.[11] Most accounts of "the idea of the university," from Kant's *Conflict of the Faculties* (1992) through Readings's *The University in Ruins* (1996), are internal and prescriptive, expressing our self-definition and centering on the disciplinary history of an idea rather than the historical institution. Instead, we should examine how the university is defined by our culture at large, on its own terms and as a response to its needs, as well as the historical and material embodiment of that cultural idea. My point in talking about *The Nutty Professor* is that it represents how we are defined publicly, rather than how we issue our image to a public. As a counterpart to advocating what Michael Bérubé (1995) has called "public access"—to make our work accessible to a larger, less narrowly academic audience—we need to access the public need and expectation of the university. In other words, we need to listen to and read that need, rather than only tell what we do.

Third, I would advocate an unremitting critique of what I have called the profit-protocol governing the new idea of the university. To offer a basic lesson in political economy, we need to distinguish the university as a not-for-profit institution, which serves a public interest, from for-profit organizations, which by definition serve private interests and often conflict with a public interest. What is good for Microsoft or Disney, and for their quarterly stock reports, is not necessarily good for the public interest or for public education. Conceptually, the problem with the university being governed by profit criteria is not the taint of business-mindedness impinging on our tweediness, but that the quantified measure of billable student hours is a noncommensurate criterion by which to measure the more intangible qualitative category of actual education. In practice, the imperative to decrease expenditure through generating more billable hours functions adversely on teachers and students alike (how much attention can a teacher give to a student in a composition class of twenty-six or twenty-seven?).[12] Conversely, the problem with the profit criteria that fosters the increase of funding through grants is that in practice grants channel research to corporately usable results, in effect subsidizing private profit-making corporations with public facilities and staff.[13] In other words, rather than private support for the public interest, grants foster the public support of private shareholders. And the problem with top-down, corporate-modelled administrative mandates is not their presumed drive for "efficiency," but that efficiency in education, again, cannot be measured by profit criteria, that in actuality it results in the greater extraction of labor for unfair wages, and that an administration based on such criteria tends to be beholdened to private interests and not to serve the needs of its workers and students, but instead disempowers them.

Finally, especially for those of us in the humanities, we need to pose new images or fictions, as Richard Rorty might put it, of the university, to reclaim the ground of a public interest, and of higher education to operate for that public interest. We need to reassert the sense of franchise as empowering citizens, as the *Oxford English Dictionary* defines it, offering freedom, immunity, and privilege, rather than the putative freedom of choice of hamburgers or mouse ears. We need to reimagine the rationale of the university, drawing the prospect of education as fostering a public franchise in several ways: for students that they might enter a world that values, to borrow the motto of the Socialist Party, people over profits, granting a genuinely public access to a quality American education, and teaching them the values of an open rather than corporately controlled society; for professors, that our research might further a public interest rather than the more immediate and tangibly quantifiable gains of corporate interests, or for that matter our own narrow professional self-interest; and for administrators, that they might serve the needs of the people within universities, from the bottom up rather than from the top down, toadying to the imperatives of our corporate sponsors. It seems to me that we usher in the future we imagine, and I imagine a different and more convivial future from the present we now have.

NOTES

1. Bill Readings's lauded *University in Ruins* (1996), in my view, overly schematically defines the Kantian idea as reason, and the von Humboldtian idea as the nation. In his *Conflict of Faculties,* Kant directly addresses a political controversy of his day (it is not one of his abstracted philosophical works) and argues to separate the "lower" or what we would call the purer (arts and sciences) faculties, based on the pursuit of knowledge, from the higher faculties, like law, directly integrated with state interests in Germany. In other words, Kant's university was based in part on, and in negotiation with, state interests. My overall point is that the negotiation with state interests has been continuous from Kant up to the present day (most of us teach, after all, in state universities), thus forming one governing component of any idea of the university. While I admire the provocative intervention that Readings's book makes, I think that it elides any historical nuance to construct its narrative of the dereferentialization of the idea of the university; Readings rarely adverts to the actual history of the university, especially the American university, which is the predominant post–World War II instantiation, and is not an idea but an institution with a material history.

2. As they used to proudly announce, the third largest after UNC–Chapel Hill and

North Carolina State. I have since moved to the University of Missouri, where we fortunately do not have such events (in the English department at ECU, we also took a yearly faculty photo), but where one strolls past buildings such as Anheuser Busch Hall (beerology? where the no doubt vehement debate separates the old guard espousing "tastes great" and the new guard declaiming "less filling") and where there has been an active debate over the conditions of recent funding from Monsanto.

3. As Michael Bérubé pithily observes, "the discipline thinks it's going from literature to culture [i.e., cultural studies], and the [job] market tells us we're going from literature to technical writing" (1995, 139).

4. For a dean's rationale of public-private "partnerships" and a concrete breakdown of sources of funding, see Breneman (1997).

5. Lest we think that teaching somehow constitutes a sacrosanct species of work outside the realm of capital and profit, see Karl Marx on surplus labor and the schoolteacher (1977, 644).

6. See Lauter (1995, 212–215); see also Bérubé (1995) and Nelson (1997); on accountability, see Williams (1997, 299–301).

7. See also Watkins (1996) on the role of humanities teachers themselves as "resource managers."

8. For a disturbing and detailed account of the influence of grants, see Soley (1995); for a report on the omnipresence of franchises engulfing one University of California campus, see Brenner (1997). On the recent growth of universities owned by corporations themselves, see Bartolovich (1996, 119–120).

9. See Williams (1995, 69–73).

10. See Rhoades and Slaughter on "managed professionals" (1997, 17–24).

11. For a rare example of this, see Bauer (1998).

12. On the ill effects of downsizing teaching labor, see Reichard (1998).

13. See Rhoades and Slaughter (1997, 13–14); and, in general, see Soley (1995) on the ensuing control engendered by grants.

WORKS CITED

Animal House. 1978. Dir. John Landis; prod. MCA/Universal.

Aronowitz, Stanley. 1995. "Higher Education: The Turn of the Screw." *Found Object* 6:89–99.

Barrow, Clyde W. 1990. *Universities and the Capitalist State: Corporate Liberalism and the Reconstruction of American Higher Education, 1894–1928.* Madison: University of Wisconsin Press.

Bartolovich, Crystal. 1996. "The Work of Cultural Studies in the Age of Transnational Production." *The Minnesota Review* n.s. 45/46:117–146.

Bauer, Dale M. 1998. "Indecent Proposals: Teachers in the Movies." *College English* 60:301–317.

Bérubé, Michael. 1995. "Peer Pressure: Literary and Cultural Studies in the Bear Market." *The Minnesota Review* 43/44:131–144. Report in *The Employment of English: Theory, Jobs, and the Future of Literary Studies.* New York: New York University Press, 1998, 90–111.

Bérubé, Michael, and Cary Nelson, eds. 1995. *Higher Education under Fire: Politics, Economics, and the Crisis of the Humanities.* New York: Routledge.

Breneman, David W. 1997. "The 'Privatization' of Public Universities: A Mistake or a Model for the Future." *Chronicle of Higher Education,* 7 March, B4–B5.

Brenner, Mark. 1997. "McUCR on the Move." *Against the Current* (November–December): 26–28.

Debray, Regis. 1981. *Teachers, Writers, Celebrities: The Intellectuals of Modern France,* trans. David Macey. London: New Left.

"Defaulting the Future." 1993. *U.S. News and World Report,* 21 June, 56+.

Kant, Immanuel. 1992. *The Conflict of the Faculties,* trans. Mary J. Gregor. Lincoln: University of Nebraska Press.

Kleinfield, N. R. 1991. "What Is Chris Whittle Teaching Our Children?" *New York Times Magazine,,* 19 May, 79.

Lauter, Paul. 1995. "Political Correctness and the Attack on American Colleges." In *After Political Correctness: The Humanities and Society in the 1990s,* ed. Christopher Newfield and Ronald Strickland. Boulder, Colo.: Westview.

Lipsky, David, and Alexander Abrams. 1994. *Late Bloomers: Coming of Age in Today's America: The Right Place at the Wrong Time.* New York: Times.

Marx, Karl. 1977. *Capital.* Vol. 1. Trans. Ben Fowkes. New York: Vintage.

Nelson, Cary. 1997. *Manifesto of a Tenured Radical.* New York: New York University Press.

The Nutty Professor. 1963. Dir. Jerry Lewis; prod. Paramount.

———. 1996. Dir. Tom Shadyac; prod. Universal.

Ohmann, Richard. 1995. "After the USSR." In *After Political Correctness: The Humanities and Society in the 1990s,* ed. Christopher Newfield and Ronald Strickland. Boulder, Colo.: Westview.

Perley, James E. 1997. "Tenure Remains Vital to Academic Freedom." *Chronicle of Higher Education,* 4 April, A48.

Readings, Bill. 1996. *The University in Ruins.* Cambridge, Mass.: Harvard University Press.

Reichard, Gary W. 1998. "Part-time Faculty in Research Universities: Problems and Prospects." *Academe* (January–February): 40–43.

Rhoades, Gary, and Sheila Slaughter. 1997. "Academic Capitalism, Managed Professionals, and Supply-Side Education." *Social Text* 51:9–38.

Schrecker, Ellen. 1986. *No Ivory Tower: McCarthyism and the Universities.* New York: Oxford University Press.

Soley, Lawrence C. 1995. *Leasing the Ivory Tower: The Corporate Takeover of Academia.* Boston: South End.

Watkins, Evan. 1996. "The Educational Politics of Human Resources: Humanities Teachers As Resource Managers." *The Minnesota Review* n.s. 45/46:147–166.

Watt, Steven. 1995. "The Human Costs of Graduate Education: Or, the Need to Get Practical." *Academe* (November–December): 30–35.

Williams, Jeffrey. 1997. "Renegotiating the Pedagogical Contract." In *Class Issues: Pedagogy and the Public Sphere,* ed. Amitava Kumar. New York: New York University Press.

———. 1995. "The Posttheory Generation." *Symploke* 3:55–76.

2

Vocationalizing Higher Education: Schooling and the Politics of Corporate Culture

Henry A. Giroux

> Corporate Ascendancy is emerging as the universal order of the post-communist world. . . . Our social landscape is now dominated by corporations that are bigger and more powerful than most countries. . . . Our end of the century and the next century loom as the triumphal age of corporations
>
> —Derber 1998, 3

THE FINAL VICTORY OF
LIBERAL DEMOCRACY?

A recent full-page advertisement for *Forbes 500* magazine proclaims in bold red letters, "Capitalists of the World Unite" (*World Traveler* 1998). Beneath the slogan covering the bottom half of the page is a mass of individuals, representing various countries throughout the world, their arms raised in victory. Instead of workers in the traditional sense, the Forbes professionals (three women among them) are distinctly middle class, dressed in sport jackets, ties, carrying brief cases, or cellular phones. A sea of red flags with their respective national currency emblazoned on the front of each waves above their heads. At the bottom of the picture is a text that reads "All hail the final victory of capitalism." At first glance, the ad appears to simply be a mockery of one of Marxism's most powerful ideals. But as self-conscious as the ad is in parodying the dream of a workers' revolution, it also reflects another ideology made famous in 1989 by Francis Fukuyama (1989a), who proclaimed "the end of history," a reference

29

to the end of authoritarian communism in East Central Europe, the former Soviet Union, and the Baltic countries. According to Fukuyama, "the end of history" meant that liberal democracy has achieved its ultimate victory and that the twin ideologies of the market and representative democracy now constitute, with a few exceptions, the universal values of the new global village.

The *Forbes* ad does more than signal the alleged "death" of communism; it also cancels out the tension between market values and those values representative of civil society that cannot be measured in strictly commercial terms but are critical to democracy. I am referring specifically to values such as justice, freedom, equality, health and respect for children, the rights of citizens as equal and free human beings, as well as "respect for the rule of law, for individual rights for value pluralism, for constitutional guarantees . . . and democratic politics" (Benhabib 1996, 9).

Who are the cheering men (and three women) portrayed in this ad? Certainly not the 43 million Americans who have lost their jobs in the last fifteen years. Certainly not "the people." The *Forbes'* ad celebrates freedom, but only in the discourse of the unbridled power of the market. There is no recognition here (how could there be?) of either the limits that democracies must place on such power or how corporate culture and its narrow redefinition of freedom as a private good may actually present a threat to democracy equal to if not greater than that imagined under communism or any other totalitarian ideology. Fukuyama, of course, proved to be right about the fall of communism, but quite wrong about "the universalization of Western liberal democracy as the final form of government" (Fukuyama 1989b, 2). Before the ink was dry genocide erupted in Bosnia-Herzegovina, Moslem fundamentalism swept Algeria, the Russians launched a bloodbath in Chechnya, Serbs launched genocidal attacks against ethnic Albanians in Kosovo, and parts of Africa erupted in a bloody civil war accompanied by the horror of tribal genocide. Even in the United States, with the Cold War at an end, the language of democracy seemed to lose its vitality and purpose as an organizing principle for society. As corporations have gained more and more power in American society, democratic culture becomes corporate culture, the rightful ideological heir to the victory over socialism.[1]

I use the term corporate culture to refer to an ensemble of ideological and institutional forces that function politically and pedagogically both to govern organizational life through senior managerial control and to produce compliant workers, depoliticized consumers, and passive citizens.[2] Within the language and images of corporate culture, citizenship is portrayed as an utterly privatized affair whose aim is to produce competitive self-interested individuals vying for their own material and ideological gain. Reformulating social issues as strictly individual or economic, corporate culture functions largely to cancel out the democratic impulses and practices of civil society by either devaluing them or absorbing such impulses within a market logic. No longer a space for political struggle, culture in the corporate model becomes an all-encompassing horizon for producing market identities, values, and practices. The good life, in this discourse, "is construed in terms of our identities as consumers—we are what we buy" (Bryman 1995, 154). Public spheres are replaced by commercial spheres as the substance of critical democracy is emptied out and replaced by a democracy of goods, consumer life styles, shopping malls, and the increasing expansion of the cultural and political power of corporations throughout the world.

The broader knowledge, social values and skills necessary for creating substantive democratic participation increasingly seem at odds with, and detrimental to corporate moguls, such as Bill Gates, the new cultural heroes and icons of social mobility, wealth, and success personifying the intersection of greed and moral irresponsibility that has become the hallmark of corporate culture. Gates is envied in the business media for accumulating personal wealth worth 50 billion dollars—"more than the combined bottom 40 percent of the U.S. population, or 100 million Americans" (Derber 1998, 12), but little is said about a society that allows such wealth to be accumulated while at the same time over 40 million Americans, including 20 million children, live below the poverty line. Within the world of national politics, conservative policy institutes along with a Republican Congress incessantly argue that how we think about education, work, and social welfare means substituting the language of the private good for the discourse and values of the public good. At the economic level, the ascendancy of corporate culture has become evident in the growing power of mega-conglomerates such as Disney, General Electric, Time-Warner, and Westinghouse to control both the content and distribution of much of what the American public sees.[3]

Accountable only to the bottom-line of profitability, corporate culture and its growing influence in American life have signaled a radical shift in both the notion of public culture and what constitutes the meaning of citizenship and the defense of the public good. For example, the rapid resurgence of corporate power in the last twenty years and the attendant reorientation of culture to the demands of commerce and regulation have substituted the language of personal responsibility and private initiative for the discourses of social responsibility and public service. This can be seen in government policies designed to dismantle state protections for the poor, the environment, working people, and people of color (Kelley 1997a). For example, the 1996 welfare law signed by President Clinton reduces food stamp assistance for millions of children in working families, and a study by the Urban Institute showed that the bill would "move 2.6 million people, including 1.1 million children into poverty" (Edelman 1997, 43–58). Other examples include the dismantling of race-based programs such as the "California Civil Rights Initiative" and the landmark affirmative-action case, *Hopwood vs. Texas*, both designed to eliminate affirmative action in higher education; the reduction of federal monies for urban development, such as HUD's housing program, the weakening of Federal legislation to protect the environment, and a massive increase in state funds for building prisons at the expense of funding for public higher education.[4]

As a result of the corporate takeover of public life, the maintenance of democratic public spheres from which to organize the energies of a moral vision loses all relevance. As the power of civil society is reduced in its ability to impose or make corporate power accountable, politics as an expression of democratic struggle is deflated, and it becomes more difficult within the logic of self-help and the bottom-line to address pressing social and moral issues in systemic and political terms. This suggests a dangerous turn in American society, one that both threatens our understanding of democracy as fundamental to our freedom and the ways in which we address the meaning and purpose of education.

POLITICS, POWER, AND
CORPORATE CULTURE

Politics is the performative register of moral action, it is the mark of a civilized society to prevent justice from going dead in each of us, it is a call to acknowledge the claims of humanity to eliminate needless suffering while affirming freedom, equality, and hope. Markets don't reward moral behavior, and as corporate culture begins to dominate public life it becomes more difficult for citizens to think critically and act morally. For instance, what opportunities exist within the logic of privatization and excessive individualism for citizens to protest the willingness of the United States Congress to serve the needs of corporate interests over pressing social demands? I am not referring simply to the power of individuals and groups to limit government subsidies and bail outs which benefit corporate interests, but to curtail those forms of institutional insanity that have severe consequences for the most vulnerable of our citizens—the young, aged, and the poor. For instance, with no countervailing powers, norms, or values in place in civil society to counter corporate power how can the average citizen protest and stop the willingness of Congress to fund B2 Stealth bombers at a cost of $2 billion each, while refusing to allocate 100 million dollars to expand child nutrition programs? A political and moral default that appears all the more shameful given the fact that 26 per cent of children in the United States live below the poverty line (Sidel 1996, xiv). In a society increasingly governed by profit considerations and the logic of the market, where is the critical language to be developed, nourished, and applied for prioritizing public over private democracy, the social good over those market forces that benefit a very small group of investors, or social justice over rampant greed and individualism?

As the rise of corporate culture reasserts the primacy of privatization and individualism, there is an increasing call for people to surrender or narrow their capacities for engaged politics for a market-based notion of identity, one that suggests relinquishing our roles as social subjects for the limited role of consuming subjects. Similarly, as corporate culture extends ever deeper into the basic institutions of civil and political society, there is a simultaneous diminishing of non-commodified public spheres—those institutions engaged in dialogue, education, and learning that address the relationship of the self to public life, social responsibility to the broader demands of citizenship, and the development of public spheres that invest public culture with vibrancy.

History has been clear about the dangers of unbridled corporate power (Baran and Sweezy 1966). The brutal practices of slavery, the exploitation of child labor, the sanctioning of the cruelest working conditions in the mines and sweat shops of America and abroad, and the destruction of the environment have all been fueled by the law of maximizing profits and minimizing costs, especially when there has been no countervailing power from civil society to hold such powers in check. This is not to suggest that capitalism is the enemy of democracy, but that in the absence of a strong civil society and the imperatives of a strong democratic public sphere, the power of corporate culture when left on its own appears to respect few boundaries based on self-restraint and those non-commodified, broader human values that are central to a democratic civic culture. John Dewey (1944) was right in arguing that democracy requires work, but that work is not synonymous with democracy.

Struggling for democracy is both a political and educational task. Fundamental to the rise of a vibrant democratic culture is the recognition that education must be treated as a public good and not merely as a site for commercial investment or for affirming a notion of the private good based exclusively on the fulfillment of individual needs. Reducing higher education to the handmaiden of corporate culture works against the critical social imperative of educating citizens who can sustain and develop inclusive democratic public spheres. There is a long tradition extending from Thomas Jefferson to C. Wright Mills that extols the importance of education as essential for a democratic public life. This legacy of public discourse appears to have faded as educational consultants all over America from Robert Zemsky of Stanford to Chester Finn of the Hudson Institute now call for educational institutions to "advise their clients in the name of efficiency to act like corporations selling products and seek 'market niches' to save themselves" and meet the challenges of the new world order (Aronowitz 1998, 32).

In what follows, I want to address the fundamental shift in society regarding how we think about the relationship between corporate culture and democracy. Specifically, I want to argue that one of the most important indications of such a change can be seen in the ways in which we are currently being asked to rethink the role of higher education. Underlying this analysis is the assumption that the struggle to reclaim higher education must be seen as part of a broader battle over the defense of the public good, and that at the heart of such a struggle is the need to challenge the ever growing discourse and influence of corporate culture, power, and politics. I will conclude by offering some suggestions as to what educators can do to reassert the primacy of higher education as an essential sphere for expanding and deepening the processes of democracy and civil society.

EDUCATION AND THE RISE OF
THE CORPORATE MANAGER

In a recent issue of *The Chronicle of Higher Education* (27 March 1998), Katherine S. Mangan reported that there are a growing number of presidential searches "looking for leaders who can bridge business and academe" (1998, A43). According to Mangan, this has resulted in a large number of business-school deans being offered jobs as college or university presidents. The rationale for such actions appears to be that "Business deans are often in a strong position to cultivate corporate contacts . . . [and are] better at translating the academic environment to the outside world" (1998, A44). Mangan's article makes clear that what was once part of the hidden curriculum of higher education—the creeping vocationalization and subordination of learning to the dictates of the market—has become an open, and defining principle of education at all levels of learning.

According to Stanley Aronowitz (1998), many colleges and universities are experiencing financial hard times brought on by the end of the Cold War and the dwindling of government financed defense projects coupled with a sharp reduction of state aid to higher education. As a result, they are all too happy to allow corporate leaders to run their institutions, form business partnerships, establish cushy relationships with business-oriented legislators, and develop curricula tailored to the needs of corporate interests. In some cases, this has meant that universities such as the Massachusetts Institute of Technology and the University of California at Irvine have cut deals with corporations by offering to do product research and cede to their corporate backers the patents for resulting inventions and discoveries in return for ample research money.

Further evidence of the vocationalization of higher education can be found in the increasing willingness on the part of legislators, government representatives, and school officials to rely on corporate leaders to establish the terms of the debate in the media regarding the meaning and purpose of higher education. One typical example can be found in the highly publicized pronouncements of Louis Gerstner, Jr. (1998), who is the Chairman and CEO of IBM. In an editorial in *USA Today* (4 March 1998), Gerstner argues that schools should be treated like businesses because when

U.S. businesses were faced with a stark choice: change or close. They changed. They began to invest in substantial transformation, new methods of production, new kinds of worker training. Most importantly, they continually benchmarked performance against one another and against international competition. . . . And it worked. (Gerstner 1998, 13A)

For Gerstner and many other CEO's, the current success of the capitalist economy is the direct result of the leadership exercised by corporate America. The lesson to be drawn is simple: "Schools are oddly insulated from marketplace forces and the discipline that drives constant adaptation, self-renewal, and a relentless push for excellence" (1998, 13A). Gerstner's argument is instructive because it is so typical, primarily about issues of efficiency, accountability, and restructuring. Corporate organizations such as the Committee for Economic Development, an organization of executives at about 250 corporations, have been more blunt about their interest in education. Not only has the group argued that social goals and services get in the way of learning basic skills, but that many employers in the business community feel dissatisfied because "a large majority of their new hires lack adequate writing and problem-solving skills" (Manegold 1994, A22).

Given the narrow nature of corporate concerns, it is not surprising that when matters of accountability become part of the language of school reform, they are divorced from broader considerations of ethics, equity, and justice. This type of corporate discourse not only lacks a vision beyond its own pragmatic interests, it also lacks a self-critical inventory of its own ideology and its effects on society. But, of course, one would not expect such concerns to emerge within corporations where questions of consequence begin and end with the bottom line. Questions about the effects of downsizing, deindustrialization, and the "trend toward more low-paid, temporary, benefit-free, blue- and white-collar jobs and fewer decent permanent factory and office jobs" (Aronowitz and De Fazio 1997, 193) caused by the reforms implemented by companies such as IBM must come from those democratic arenas that business seeks to "restructure." Mega corporations will say nothing about their profound role in promoting the flight of capital abroad, the widening gap between intellectual, technical, and manual labor and the growing class of permanently underemployed in a mass of "deskilled" jobs, the growing inequality between the rich and the poor, or the scandalous use of child labor in third world countries. The onus of responsibility is placed on educated citizens to recognize that corporate principles of efficiency, accountability, and profit maximization have not created new jobs but in most cases have eliminated them (Rifkin 1995; Wolman and Colamosca 1997; Aronowitz and DiFazio 1994; Aronowitz and Cutler 1998). My point, of course, is that such absences in public discourse constitute a defining principle of corporate ideology, which refuses to address—and must be made to address—the scarcity of moral vision that inspires such calls for school reform modeled after corporate reforms implemented in the last decade.

But the modeling of higher education after corporate principles and the partnerships they create with the business community do more than reorient the purpose and meaning of higher education; such reforms also instrumentalize the curricula and narrow what it means to extend knowledge to broader social concerns. Business-university partnerships provide just one concrete example of the willingness of both educators and corporate executives to acknowledge the effects such mergers have on the production and dissemination of knowledge in the interest of the public good. Lost in the willingness of schools such as MIT to sell part of their curricula to the corporations is the ethical consequence of ignoring basic science research that benefits humanity as a whole because such research offers little as a profit-maximizing venture. Ralph Nader recently indicated in a nationally broadcast speech on C-Span that one result of such transactions is that the universities are doing far too little to develop anti-malaria and tuberculosis vaccines at a time when these diseases are once again killing large numbers of people in third world countries; such interventions are viewed as non-profitable investments (Nader 1998). Research guided only by the controlling yardstick of profit undermines the role of the university as a public sphere dedicated to addressing the most serious social problems a society faces. Moreover, the corporate model of research instrumentalizes knowledge and undermines forms of theorizing, pedagogy, and meaning that define higher education as a public rather than as a private good.

Missing from much of the corporate discourse on schooling is any analysis of how power works in shaping knowledge, how the teaching of broader social values provides safeguards against turning citizen skills into simply training skills for the work place, or how schooling can help students reconcile the seemingly opposing needs of freedom and solidarity in order to forge a new conception of civic courage and democratic public life. Knowledge as capital in the corporate model is privileged as a form of investment in the economy, but appears to have little value when linked to the power of self-definition, social responsibility, or the capacities of individuals to expand the scope of freedom, justice, and the operations of democracy (West 1990). Knowledge stripped of ethical and political considerations offers limited, if any, insights into how schools should educate students to push against the oppressive boundaries of gender, class, race, and age domination. Nor does such a language provide the pedagogical conditions for students to critically engage knowledge as an ideology deeply implicated in issues and struggles concerning the production of identities, culture, power, and history. Education is a moral and political practice and always presupposes an introduction to and preparation for particular forms of social life, a particular rendering of what community is, and what the future might hold.

If pedagogy is, in part, about the production of identities then curricula modeled after corporate culture have been enormously successful in preparing students for low-skilled service work in a society that has little to offer in the way of meaningful employment for the vast majority of its graduates. If CEO's are going to provide some insight into how education should be reformed, they will have to reverse their tendency to collapse the boundaries between corporate culture and civic culture, between a society that defines itself through the interests of corporate power and one that defines itself through more democratic considerations regarding what constitutes substantive citizenship and social responsibility. Moreover, they will have to recognize that the problems with American schools cannot be reduced to matters of accountability or cost-effectiveness. Nor can the solution to such problems be reduced to the spheres of management and economics. The problems of higher education and public schooling must be addressed in the realms of values and politics, while engaging critically the most fundamental beliefs Americans have as a nation regarding the meaning and purpose of education and its relationship to democracy.

CORPORATE CULTURE AS A
MODEL OF LEADERSHIP

As universities increasingly model themselves after corporations, it becomes crucial to understand how the principles of corporate culture intersect with the meaning and purpose of the university, the role of knowledge production for the twenty-first century, and the social practices inscribed within teacher-student relationships. The signs are not encouraging.

In many ways, the cost accounting principles of efficiency, calculability, predictability, and control of the corporate order have restructured the meaning and purpose of education. As I have mentioned previously, many deans are now given the title of CEO, academic programs are streamlined to cut costs, and in many colleges new presidents are actively pursuing ways to establish closer ties between their institutions and the business community. For example, the *New York Times* reports, in what has become a typical story, that at George Mason University, a business-oriented president has emphasized technology training in order to "boost the university's financing (by the state legislature) by as much as $25-million a year, provided that George Mason cultivates stronger ties with northern Virginia's booming technology industry" (Mangan 1998, A44). In other quarters in higher education, the results of the emergence of the corporate university appear even more ominous. James Carlin, a multimillionaire insurance executive who now serves as the Chairman of the Massachusetts State Board of Education, recently gave a speech to the Greater Boston Chamber of Commerce. In a statement that highlights his ignorance of the recent history and critical mission of higher education, Carlin argued that colleges need to be downsized just as businesses have in the past decade, tenure should be abolished, and that faculty have too much power in shaping decisions in the university. Carlin's conclusion: "At least 50 percent of all non-hard sciences research on American campuses is a lot of foolishness" and should be banned (Honan 1998, 33). Pointing to the rising costs of higher education, he further predicted that "there's going to be a revolution in higher education. Whether you like it or not, it's going to be broken apart and put back together differently. It won't be the same. Why should it be? Why should everything change except for higher education?" (Honan 1998, 33) Carlin's "revolution" has been spelled out in his call for increasing the work load of professors to four three credit courses a semester, effectively reducing the time such educators might have in doing research or shaping institutional power.

There is more at stake in university reform than the realities and harsh principles of cost cutting. Corporate culture in its reincarnation in the 1980s and 1990s appears to have little patience with non-commodified knowledge or with the more lofty ideals that have defined higher education as a public service. Carlin's anti-intellectualism and animosity toward educators and students alike signal that as higher education comes under the influence of corporate ideologies, universities will be largely refashioned in the image of the new multi-conglomerate landscape. One consequence will be an attempt to curtail academic freedom and tenure. As one business-oriented administrator admitted to Bill Tierney in a conversation about tenure, "We have to focus on the priorities of the . . . school and not the individual. We must industrialize the school, and tenure—academic freedom—isn't part of that model" (1997, 17). Missing from this model of leadership is the recognition that academic freedom implies that knowledge has a critical function, that intellectual inquiry that is unpopular and critical should be safeguarded and treated as an important social asset, and that public intellectuals are more than merely functionaries of the corporate order. Such ideals are at odds with the vocational function that corporate culture wants to assign to higher education.

While the appeal to downsizing higher education appears to have caught the public's imagination at the moment, it belies the fact that such "reorganization" has been going on for some time. In fact, more professors are working part-time and at two-year community colleges than at any other time in the country's recent history. Alison Schneider recently pointed out in *The Chronicle of Higher Education* that "in 1970, only 22 per cent of the professorate worked part time. By 1995, that proportion had nearly doubled to 41 per cent" (1998, A14). Creating a permanent underclass of part-time professional workers in higher education is not only demoralizing and exploitative for many faculty who inhabit such jobs, such policies increasingly de-skill both part- and full-time faculty by increasing the amount of work they have to do, while simultaneously shifting power away from the faculty to the managerial sectors of the university. Corporate culture has invested heavily in leadership from the top as evidenced by the huge salaries many CEO's get in this country. For instance, Citigroup CEO, Stanford Weill made $141.6 million in direct compensation in 1998 while the CEO of Tyco International, L. Dennis Kozolowski, was paid $74.4 million (Abelson 1998, 1). Michael Eisner, the CEO of Walt Disney, Inc., is estimated to have received over $1 billion dollars since he arrived at Disney fourteen years ago (Bonin 1998, 70). But the price to pay for such a model of leadership appears to undermine even the weakest image of the university as a public space for creating democratic values, critical teaching communities, and equitable work relations.

Held up to the profit standard, universities and colleges will increasingly calibrate supply to demand, and the results look ominous with regard to what forms of knowledge and research will be rewarded and legitimated. In addition, it appears that populations marked by class and racial subordination will have less access to higher education. As globalization and corporate mergers increase, technologies develop, and cost effective practices expand, there will be fewer jobs for certain professionals resulting in the inevitable elevation of admission standards, restriction of student loans, and the reduction of student access to higher education. Stanley Aronowitz argues that the changing nature of intellectual labor, knowledge production, and the emerging glut of professionals on a global scale undermine mass education as the answer to the growing underemployment of the professional classes. He writes:

> Although the media hypes that millions of new jobs require specialized, advanced knowledge and credentials, the bare truth is that technological change, globalization, and relatively slow growth have reduced the demand for certain professionals. . . . And despite the boom of the middle 1990s, chronic shortages of physicians, accountants and attorneys have all but disappeared. In fact, the globalization of intellectual labor is beginning to effect knowledge industries, with Indian and Chinese engineers and computer designers performing work that was once almost exclusively done in North America and western Europe. And do nonscientists really need credentials signifying they have completed a prescribed program to perform most intellectual labor? If jobs are the intended outcome of a credential, there are few arguments for mass higher education. (Aronowitz 1998, 34-35)

Fewer jobs in higher education means fewer students will be enrolled or have access, but it also means that the processes of vocationalization—fueled by corporate values that mimic "flexibility," "competition," or "lean production" and rationalized through the application of accounting principles—pose the threat of gutting many academic departments and programs that cannot translate their subject matter into commercial gains. Programs and courses that focus on areas such as critical theory, literature, feminism, ethics, environmentalism, post-colonialism, philosophy, and sociology suggest an intellectual cosmopolitanism or a concern with social issues that will be either eliminated or technicized because their role in the market will be judged as ornamental. Similarly, those working conditions that allow professors and graduate assistants to comment extensively on student work, provide small seminars, spend time with student advising, conduct independent studies, and do collaborative research with both faculty colleagues and students do not appear consistent with the imperatives of downsizing, efficiency, and cost-accounting (Bérubé 1998, B4–B5).

EDUCATION AND THE IMPERATIVES
OF DEMOCRACY

I want to return to an issue I raised in the beginning of this chapter where I argued that corporations have been given too much power in this society, and hence the need for educators and others to address the threat this poses to all facets of public life organized around the non-commodified principles of justice, freedom, and equality. Challenging the encroachment of corporate power is essential if democracy is to remain a defining principle of education and everyday life. Part of such a challenge necessitates that educators and others create organizations capable of mobilizing civic dialogue, provide an alternative conception of the meaning and purpose of higher education, and develop political organizations that can influence legislation to challenge corporate power's ascendancy over the institutions and mechanisms of civil society. This project requires that educators, students, and others will have to provide the rationale and mobilize the possibility for creating enclaves of resistance, new public cultures for collective development, and institutional spaces that highlight, nourish, and evaluate the tension between civil society and corporate power while simultaneously struggling to prioritize citizen rights over consumer rights.

In strategic terms, revitalizing public dialogue suggests that educators need to take seriously the importance of defending higher education as an institution of civic culture whose purpose is to educate students for active and critical citizenship. Situated within a broader context of issues concerned with social responsibility, politics, and the dignity of human life, schooling should be defended as a site that offers students the opportunity to involve themselves in the deepest problems of society, to acquire the knowledge, skills, and ethical vocabulary necessary for what Vaclav Havel calls "the richest possible participation in public life" (1998, 45). Educators, parents, legislators, students, and social movements need to come together to defend higher education as indispensable to the life of the nation because they are one of the few public spaces left where students can learn the power of and engage in the experience of democracy. In the face of corporate takeovers, the ongoing commodification of the curriculum, a project requires educators to mount a collective struggle to reassert the crucial importance of higher education in offering students the skills they need for learning how to govern, take risks, and develop the knowledge necessary for deliberation, reasoned arguments, and social action. At issue here is providing students with an education that allows them to recognize the dream and promise of a substantive democracy, particularly the idea that as citizens they are "entitled to public services, decent housing, safety, security, support during hard times, and most importantly, some power over decision making" (Kelley 1997b, 146).

But more is needed than defending higher education as a vital sphere in which to develop and nourish the proper balance between democratic public spheres and commercial power, between identities founded on democratic principles and identities steeped in forms of competitive, self-interested individualism that celebrate their own material and ideological advantages. Given the current assault on educators at all levels of schooling, it is politically crucial that educators at all levels of involvement in the academy be defended as public intellectuals who provide an indispensable service to the nation. Such an appeal cannot be made merely in the name of professionalism but in terms of the civic duty such intellectuals provide. Intellectuals who inhabit our nation's universities represent the conscience of a society because they shape the conditions under which future generations learn about themselves and their relations to others and the world, but also because they engage in pedagogical practices that are by their very nature moral and political, rather than simply technical. And at their best, such pedagogical practices bear witness to the ethical and political dilemmas that animate the broader social landscape. The appeal here is not merely ethical; it is also an appeal that addresses the materiality of power, resources, access, and politics.

Organizing against the corporate takeover of schools also suggests, especially within higher education, fighting to protect the jobs of full-time faculty, turning adjunct jobs into full-time positions, expanding benefits to part-time workers, and putting power into the hands of faculty and students. Moreover, such a struggle must address the exploitative conditions many graduate students work under, constituting a *de facto* army of service workers who are underpaid, overworked, and shorn of any real power or benefits (Nelson 1997). Similarly, remedial programs, affirmative action, and other crucial pedagogical resources are under massive assault, often by conservative trustees who want to eliminate from the university any attempt to address the deep social inequities, while simultaneously denying a decent education to minorities of color and class. Hence, both teachers and students bear the burden of overcrowded classrooms, limited resources, and hostile legislators. Such educators and students need to join with community people and social movements around a common platform that resists the corporatizing of schools, the roll back in basic services, and the exploitation of teaching assistants and adjunct faculty.

In the face of the growing corporatization of schools, progressive educators at all levels of education should organize to establish both a bill of rights identifying and outlining the range of non-commercial relations that can be used to mediate between higher education and the business world, and to create the institutional conditions for administrators, teachers, and students to inhabit non-commodified public spheres that expand the possibilities for knowledge-power relations that are not exclusively instrumental and market driven. If the forces of corporate culture are to be challenged, progressive educators must also enlist the help of diverse communities, local and federal government, and other political forces to insure that public institutions of higher learning are adequately funded so that they will not have to rely on corporate sponsorship and advertising revenues. How our colleges and universities educate students for the future may provide one of the few opportunities for them to link learning to social considerations, public life, and the spirit of democratic life.

The corporatizing of American education reflects a crisis of vision regarding the meaning and purpose of democracy at a time when "market cultures, market moralities, market mentalities [are] shattering community [and] eroding civic society" (West 1994, 42). Yet such a crisis also represents a unique opportunity for progressive educators to expand and deepen the meaning of democracy—radically defined as a struggle to combine the distribution of wealth, income, and knowledge with a recognition and positive valorizing of cultural diversity—by reasserting the primacy of politics, power, and struggle as a pedagogical task (Fraser 1997). Such a responsibility necessitates prioritizing democratic community, citizen rights, and the public good over market relations, narrow consumer demands, and corporate interests. At stake is not merely the future of higher education, but the nature of democracy itself. Democracy is not synonymous with capitalism, and critical citizenship should offer young people more than simply the promise of becoming consuming subjects. Higher education is one important site where educators, students, and administrators can address the tensions between corporate culture and democratic civic culture by asserting the primacy of democracy and civic courage over the logic of capital, consumerism, and commodification.

NOTES

1. Stuart Ewen has traced this trend historically to the emergence in the 19th century of the culture of abundance which allowed "for the flowering of a provocative, if somewhat passive, conception of democracy . . . consumer democracy" (1988, 12).

2. The classic dominant texts on corporate culture are Terrance Deal and Alan Kennedy (1982) and Thomas Peterson and Robert Waterman (1982). I also want to point out that corporate culture is a dynamic, ever-changing force. But in spite of its

innovations and changes, it rarely if ever challenges the centrality of the profit motive, or fails to prioritize commercial considerations over a set of values that would call the class-based system of capitalism into question. For a brilliant discussion of the changing nature of corporate culture in light of the Cultural Revolution of the 1960s, see Thomas Frank (1997).

3. There are many books that address this issue, but some of the most helpful in providing hard statistical evidence for the growing corporate monopolization of American society can be found in Derber (1998), Hazen and Winokur (1997), McChesney (1997), Barneouw (1997), and Wolman and Colamosca (1997).

4. For a context from which to judge the effects of such cuts on the poor and children of America, see Children's Defense Fund (1998).

WORKS CITED

Abelson, Reed. 1998. "Silicon Valley Aftershocks." *New York Times,* 4 April, section 3:1.

Aronowitz, Stanley. 1998. "The New Corporate University." *Dollars and Sense* (March/April): 32-35.

Aronowitz, Stanley, and Jonathan Cutler. 1998. *Post-Work.* New York: Routledge.

Aronowitz, Stanley, and William DiFazio. 1994. *The Jobless Future.* Minneapolis: University of Minnesota Press.

———. 1997. "The New Knowledge Work." In *Education: Culture, Economy, Society,* ed. A. H. Halsey, et. al. New York: Oxford University Press.

Baran, Paul, and Paul M. Sweezy. 1966. *Monopoly Capital.* New York: Monthly Review Press.

Barneouw, Erik, et al. 1997. *Conglomerates and the Media.* New York: The New Press.

Benhabib, Seyla. 1996. "The Democratic Moment and the Problem of Difference." In *Democracy and Difference,* ed. Seyla Benhabib. Princeton: Princeton University Press.

Bérubé, Michael. 1998. "Why Inefficiency Is Good for Universities." *The Chronicle of Higher Education,* 27 March, B4-B5.

Bonin, Liane. 1998. Tragic Kingdom. *Detour Magazine,* April, 69-72.

Bryman, Alan. 1995. *Disney and His Worlds.* New York: Routledge.

Children's Defense Fund. 1998. *The State of America's Children—A Report from the Children's Defense Fund.* Boston: Beacon Press.

Deal, Terrance, and Alan Kennedy. 1982. *Corporate Culture: The Rites and Rituals of Corporate Life.* Reading, MA: Addison-Wesley.

Derber, Charles. 1998. *Corporation Nation.* New York: St. Martin's Press.

Dewey, John. 1944. *Democracy and Education.* New York: Free Press.

Edelman, Peter. 1997. "The Worst Thing Bill Clinton Has Done." *The Atlantic Monthly,* March, 43-58.

Ewen, Stuart. 1988. *All Consuming Images.* New York: Basic Books.

Frank, Thomas. 1997. *The Conquest of Cool.* Chicago: University of Chicago Press.

Fraser, Nancy. 1997. *Justice Interruptus.* New York: Routledge.

Fukuyama, Francis. 1989a. *The End of History and the Last Man.* New York: Free Press.

————. 1989b. "The End of History." *The National Interest,* Summer, 3–18.

"GMC CEO Pay." 1998. *USA Today,* 21 April, Section B1.

Gerstner, Louis V. Jr. 1998. "Public Schools Need to Go the Way of Business." *USA Today,* 4 March, 13A.

Hazen, Dan, and Julie Winokur, eds. 1997. *We the Media.* New York: New Press.

Havel, Vaclav. 1998. "The State of the Republic." *New York Review of Books* 45.4: 42-46.

Honan, William H. 1998. "The Ivory Tower Under Siege." *New York Times,* 4 January, Section 4A, 33.

Kelley, Robin D. G. 1997a. *Yo' Mama's Disfunktional: Fighting the Culture Wars in Urban America.* Boston: Beacon Press.

————. 1997b. "Neo-Cons of the Black Nation." *Black Renaissance Noir* 1.2: 134–46.

Manegold, Catherine. S. 1994. "Study Says Schools Must Stress Academics." *New York Times,* 23 September, A22.

Mangan, Katherine S. 1998. "Corporate Know-How Lands Presidencies for a Growing Number of Business Deans." *The Chronicle of Higher Education,* 27 March, A43-A44.

McChesney, Robert W. 1997. *Corporate Media and the Threat to Democracy.* New York: Seven Stories Press.

Nader, Ralph. 1998. "Civil Society and Corporate Responsibility." Speech given to the National Press Club, *C-Span* 2, 25 March.

Nelson, Cary. ed. 1997. *Will Teach for Food: Academic Labor in Crisis.* Minneapolis: University of Minnesota Press.

Peterson, Thomas, and Robert Waterman. 1982. *In Search of Excellence.* New York: Harper and Row.

Rifkin, Jeremy. 1995. *The End of Work.* New York: Putnam.

Schneider, Alison. 1998. "More Professors Are Working Part Time, and More Teach at 2-Year Colleges." *The Chronicle of Higher Education,* 13 March, A14-A16.

Sidel, Ruth. 1996. *Keeping Women and Children Last.* New York: Penguin.

Tierney, Bill. 1997. "Tenure and Community in Academe." *Educational Researcher* 26.8: 17-23.

West, Cornel. 1990. "The New Cultural Politics of Difference." *October* 53: 93-109.

————. 1994. "America's Three-Fold Crisis." *Tikkun* 9.2: 41–44.

Wolman, William, and Anne Colamosca. 1997. *The Judas Economy.* Reading, MA: Addison-Wesley, Inc.

World Traveler. 1998. March, 76.

3

The University: A Place to Think?

Roger I. Simon

The explosion in the use of the World Wide Web has made quite rudimentary the task of accessing basic program information for a very large number of universities across North America. Surfing through a variety of university home pages, one cannot help but notice the wide variation in "imagetexts" (Mitchell 1994), constellations of photographs, graphics, and text, placed on the opening pages of most university web sites. These multimedia designs are clearly efforts at marking and marketing the distinctive character of each university, evident attempts to attract interest from prospective students and their families. Indeed, there is a paper begging to be written that would discuss the historical origins and contemporary inflections of the discourses that structure these exercises in university promotion and public relations. While this is not my intent here, I want to begin with a few contrasting examples of what you might find in such a web search.[1] There are universities whose home pages are brightened by lovely colorful scenes depicting the physical beauty of their campuses. Swarthmore College, for example, depicts a campus scene at dusk; it is a charmingly lit university walkway lined with impressive trees and colorful flowers. A male and female student are seen crossing this pathway. Closer to home here in Ontario, MacMaster University's home page depicts a colorful autumn facade of one of its storied buildings together with a scene showing a cluster of students walking across a well-treed, green campus. The University of Waterloo too, has chosen to emphasize its campus's fall color although the buildings in the image presented are considerably less "classical" than that of MacMaster. Trent University, recently moving away from this scenic emphasis, has chosen a montage of images. In the center of its imagetext is a happy female student playing roller hockey; surrounding this central figure are images of, what appears to me, two faculty members in serious conversation, a keyboard overlain with a newspaper open to the international page, a

45

partial view of the circuitry of a computer chip, and a couple of students reading on the steps of a building. There are many other universities that have chosen the montage approach but the one that actually stopped me "dead in my tracks" was that of Bard College. Bard's home page includes scenes of a student in a library reading room, another either painting or working on a musical score (I cannot tell which), fragments of a building facade, all this overlaid with the text "Bard College: A Place to Think."

Here was a university whose introductory promotional gambit upon opening its home page was the claim that it was "a place to think!" A shallow, empty claim? What else would a university be but "a place to think?" Perhaps because I had, at the time, been reading the late Bill Readings's *The University in Ruins* (1996), this Bard College web page did and still does give me pause, provoking the following sorts of questions: What does it mean to claim the university is a place to think? What forms of thought have universities supported and what changes are a foot in the funding and administration of university-based teaching and learning that might be altering the character of thought at universities? Are the perceptions and investments on the part of those now enrolling in universities congruent with such alterations? In light of these changes, what might characterize the university as "a place to think" in relation to other places where thought takes place? And last but not least, as someone who has been teaching in universities for thirty years, and who still anticipates another decade of such work, in what respect, through what practices, am I committed to helping maintain thought as the center of university life?

I have mentioned Readings not because I necessarily agree with all of the main theses of his controversial book, but rather in acknowledgment that many of his thoughts have influenced the arguments of this chapter. My intention therefore is not a discussion of the central claims of the *University in Ruins*, a book lionized, ridiculed, and at times seriously engaged and critiqued. Rather, I attempt to draw from and work with several of Readings's core concepts, but on my own terms and with somewhat (though not completely) different consequences.

ALIBIS FOR OUR TIMES

To consider the shifting possibilities for thought at "the university" and the mediation and provocation of such possibilities through various pedagogies, we had better recognize that the issues here will not be settled abstractly. The question of thought endemic to a particular social site is less an epistemological matter than it is an institutional and praxeological event. As Readings, citing Jean-François Lyotard, has suggested, "What is called thinking? is never simply a theoretical question" (1996, 161) and therefore it is of limited value to engage in abstract reflection on pedagogy in isolation from a reflection on the institutions within and against which that teaching takes place. What this means is that we cannot begin a grounded discussion of issues of pedagogy and the thought pursuant to its various forms without acknowledging something of the ongoing contemporary (re)structuring of the institutional character of the university. Some readers of this text will be somewhat, if not intimately, aware that the social forms within which university educators work are in a certain degree of flux. These include administrative language practices, practices for the distribution of financial and material resources, the functional division of knowledge central to the organization of any given university, the teaching program and collegial affiliations, practices of recruitment and selection, modes of application of information technologies, and methods of assessment.

This flux is being influenced by a variety of specific factors whose impact on higher education needs to be better understood. This includes the fiscal crisis of state (itself related to economic globalization) and the decision of federal government, several years ago, to substantially reduce the Canada Health and Social Transfer payments to provinces with the consequence of years of university under funding, tuition increases, and an increasing student debt load. Coincident with this has been the neoliberal political populism of conservative provincial governments to rearticulate university teaching and research around its role in stimulating and supporting business and industry and offering a "client" a consumer-driven "product" that provides training and career preparation. All of this, no doubt, means that the traditional humanistic disciplines, the disciplines least likely to help extract surplus value from the production and circulation of the information and skills that are their central concern (and hence least likely to attract donations or contracts from the private, corporate sector), are increasingly less central to the life of the university. As Samuel Weber suggests, "what seems to be involved is a fundamental and political redefinition of the social value of public services in general, and of universities and education in particular" (1999, 3). Eroding is the university's mandate for "educating" rather than "training" the citizen, as well as the privilege of setting a research agenda through the free pursuit of curiosity. In saying this, I do not want to forget that in Canada, at least since World War II, if some saw higher education as a route to truth and beauty, more were drawn (or financed by their parents) in hope of earning substantially more than the mass of Canadians who barely finished primary school (Morton 1997). In neither Canada nor the United States has the university ever been solely a site for the free pursuit of ideas without expectations of utilitarian benefits accruing in exchange for ones' time and money. But what is shifting is the degree to which governments are willing to intervene in the articulation of university programs of training and research in regard to specific economic interests in support of particular agendas for "growth" as defined by a specific set of social elites.

This is a familiar analysis and my intention is not to dwell on it, however, it cannot be stressed enough that those of us working and studying in universities can ill afford to ignore the social, economic, demographic, and technological factors that are provoking the alteration of the institutional form of the university. All the more so, for university staff reviewing their educational policies and contemplating program revisions. No doubt, since we live, work, and study at our universities, our attention to the institutional form of the university will be neither dispassionate nor disinterested, but will force us to surface our basic commitments. The notion of commitment I have in mind here is the particular allegiance to and responsibility for a distinct "idea of the university," not as a philosophic abstraction, but an organizing logic for one's work in one's institution.

We need not see any given commitment as an appeal to the "true nature of the university," as if such a thing existed. There never has been one single, unifying idea effectively informing the institution of the university. This does not mean, however, there are not claimants who seek to stabilize its meaning. We can get some sense of these claims by examining a few statements that offer those of us working in universities, what Readings called "alibis" (1996, 160). In using the word "alibi," Readings understood that those who teach and study in universities, particularly in secular, capitalist economies, if not accused, are very much under suspicion. This was clearly and constantly illustrated to me by my father, a dress manufacturer with little formal education. He always wondered in amazement that anyone would actually pay me to teach and write as I have been doing throughout my career and in this regard, he never ceased having me attempt to justify the value of my work life. Indeed, in Readings's terms, he was asking for my alibi, a narrative that provides a reasonable justification of what I, or rather "we" university educators do. But an alibi is not just a rhetorical device to placate inquiries from outside the university, more importantly, alibis serve as rationalities that are called upon in the organization of institutionalized knowledge and the realization of practices intended to instigate study and knowledge acquisition. Thus, while alibis are simultaneously a declaration of legitimacy, a defense, and a vindication of one's practices, they also serve to structure and regulate those practices. As a consequence, what more precisely a university might be "as a place to think" is to a large part a function of the alibis of its faculty.

I want now to contrast three alibis, that is, statements regarding one's teaching within very particular conceptions of university education and explore what each implies regarding the university as a "place to think." The first of these alibis stands in the long tradition of university education as a "useful uselessness" (Young 1992). Here, the university is *in* but not *of* the social world. Literally then a world apart, thought in a university on the terms of this alibi must attempt to preserve the university as "a place of incubation where the most profound human needs and longings are released, formed and matured by exposure and initiation" into the culture of the academy (Emberley 1996, 18). Committed to thought on these terms, our alibi would be the renewal of "a sacred trust . . . between the genuine teacher and a student," a trust fulfilled "in the stewardship each participates in as they go through the process of understanding and renewing the world of culture" (18–19). This is nothing short of facilitating an adventure of self-knowing and the making of the autonomous subject understood as "a spiritual journey, one whose goal is understanding of the self and of the worlds that surround us" (19). On such terms, the university would clearly be a place to think particularly as this thinking enters into a process of self-formation.

The second alibi, one also familiar to most us, completely reverses this agenda. It is an alibi that takes full measure of the words of Michael Harris, the premier of Ontario. I quote from Premier Harris's speech to the Council of Ontario Universities "Summit" on November 19, 1997:[2]

> A skilled and highly educated workforce is central to our ability [to make Ontario the best jurisdiction in North America to live, work, invest and raise a family]. Aside from benefits to our province, students themselves are in a much better position economically and intellectually, with the security of a post-secondary education. . . . [In this context,] are there . . . questions of system-wide service, value, and efficiency that you [in universities] can address? Who in the university system will decide to reduce enrollments or close programs when there are few jobs available in a profession? . . . Who is responsible for opening or expanding programs in fields where there are significant shortages, like computer science and software engineering? Our government respects the autonomy of universities in our educational system. But I suggest that there are no avenues for change to rule out as we face the challenges of the next century. Decisions must be made about ensuring good value for students and taxpayers in their investment in post-secondary education. (2)

Good value for students on these terms means clearly ensuring capacities that fit existing opportunity structures for the creation and accumulation of wealth generated by contemporary capital. One's teaching alibi and the consequences of regarding thought on these terms is quite straightforward. It is well articulated by Heather McIvor (1997), a faculty member of the University of Windsor.

> The campus is a place of commerce, it has always trained workers for the economy. That is my job. My responsibility is not to reproduce myself, that is to produce more scholars, but rather to train my students in the skills they will need both for their future careers and the enjoyment of culture in their leisure time. Most students come to university to acquire marketable skills, and why shouldn't they? . . . If we forget that an undergraduate education is the biggest investment our students have ever made, that most will go deeply into debt while in our care, and that we have a responsibility to teach them skills which will help

them to pay off that debt, it is little wonder we've lost the support of the paying public. . . . How do we help people learn? . . . By creating logical and predicable structures within which we expose students to course material [with the consequence they acquire new information and skills]. (604–606)

A place to think? Surely, but with thinking as an activity subordinate to the acquisition of new information and skills.

The third alibi articulates yet again a very different position. Here, the university is both in and of the social world but not on the terms Premier Harris often describes. So alternatively, in the words of Leon Botstein, the president of Bard College, first and foremost, universities

> should avoid becoming dominated by commerce and a narrow definition of utility. Their primary goal should be to reinvigorate the link between education and democracy and to spur the creation of services to the public and the cultural life of communities. They should orchestrate a resurgence of interest . . . in pursuing careers in science and scholarship, and inspire new arenas and methods of inquiry. . . . Universities should ensure a citizenry that is neither thoughtless nor speechless. (1997, 10)

To do this, a university must "become [a] society's center of cultural activity, creativity, debate, service and political exchange" (12). As a place of thought, the university would rearticulate the relation between educational practice and the social life of our communities, particularly so as to enhance the prospects for such ideals as democracy.

So here are three alibis, three logics of rationalization and justification with each implying very different things regarding the university as a place of thought. We should indeed recognize these as the very common terms of the ongoing debate about the function of the university. Indeed, it might be argued that a university requires all three teaching practices and the forms of thought they inculcate in ways that neither diminish nor exacerbate the tensions between these practices. And if you were to argue this, I would be prepared to join you in the detailed discussion of what sort of programs and policies might encourage this productive tension. However, my concern in this chapter is not to engage arguments for and against any given configuration of these three positions. It is rather to explore the possibility of yet another position beyond these three.[3] A position with a very different ordering of pedagogic action, one that is less heroic, less dependent on the demand that it perform a unified ideological function. In doing so, I do not want to displace the concerns of value for money in the face of horrendous debt loads Canadian students are accumulating; neither do I want to dismiss expectation that one's university education enhance one's social and/or economic standing, nor equate educational value solely with advantage that might accrue to an individual forms of capital accumulation.[4] Nor do I think the question of the university's service to the state

irrelevant in a society where higher education is predominantly state supported. So given these caveats let me briefly open another option.

A UNIVERSITY WITHOUT HEROES?

As I have just suggested, the three alibis I have presented are each rationalities
underscoring particular forms of pedagogic action; rationalities that articulate
heroic subject positions as essential to their successful enactment. The traditional scholastic alibi requires of students interpellated into its logic, that they
be classical pedagogic heroes, having the courage and fortitude to embark on
an arduous, obstacle-filled voyage of self-discovery, a voyage that is ultimately
redemptive in that, if successful, realizes the reward of self-possession and the
mastery of knowledge (Taylor 1999). The teacher who both motivates and
facilitates this journey is likened to an apostle who seeks to awaken one to possibilities of a redeemed future state (this mode of pedagogic logic is a favorite
plot device of classic "teacher films," for example, *Educating Rita, Stand and
Deliver,* and *The Dead Poets Society*). The modernist liberal alibi that positions
the university as necessary to the democratic and cultural well-being of society, also requires heroic pedagogic action, but this time the primary hero is
the teacher who is able to help secure the future of the nation through the
making of the ideal citizen, one who will participate in public life to the full.
The economic utilitarian alibi, obviously, requires a very different kind of hero,
a bureaucratic hero, the antihero as hero, the technical servant who provides
the appropriate knowledge and procedures to not only make the complex
mechanism of wealth accumulation work well, but also to facilitate one's participation in this process of wealth accumulation.

It is no surprise that the various heroic enactments required by each of
these pedagogic rationalities all reference education as a redemptive promise,
that thought situated within the framework of each rationality will function
as a corrective, a Heideggerian "bringing forth" of a not yet realized potential.
Now I am not going to disavow the promissory character of pedagogy,
despite the many problems associated with any given pedagogic promise, this
disavowal would be neither possible nor desirable. However, I must raise at
least one general problem inherent to teaching alibis structured within a
redemptive promise, justifications of the details of any given university curriculum and its associated course syllabi (including its readings, sequence,
lectures, and evaluative methods). Promise is inherent to the activity of curriculum and course planning. Indeed, when we hand our students a course
outline at the first meeting of a course, we are promising not only to "cover"
particular topics and to use particular evaluative methods, but also that this
plan will be worthwhile, that it will bring the receptive student to a new,
enhanced state of redeemed potential in regard to some combination of stu-

dent knowledge, understanding, and skills. The problem that concerns me, however, is the possibility that something precious is lost amid the practicalities of our promissory practices, a deflecting of attention away from what (increasingly) I think should be preserved as unique to the social geography of "the university."

To make evident what is at stake in this deflection, I ask: How might we think thought in the university on terms not totally subsumed within the terms of its promissory curricular structures and their requisite heroic narratives? To take up this question requires radically reframing the very terms of what is accomplished in a university, perhaps allowing, for a moment, a discussion of the university not as it already appears to be (an existing institution with defined traditions, roles, procedures, and purposes) but as something far more emergent. As Readings suggested, the question of the possibility of thought within the university will not be settled "by a program of reform that either produces knowledge more efficiently or produces more efficient knowledge. Rather, the analogy of production itself must be brought into question: the analogy that makes the University into an (increasingly bureaucratic) apparatus for the production, distribution, and consumption of knowledge" (1996, 163). So I beg your indulgence. Let me for a moment turn the notion of "the University" inside out, considering it, not as an agency of production, not as an already existing institution, but rather a particular effect of the pedagogic actions of the members of an institution (not yet a university) gathered together to produce various pedagogic scenes, various instantiations of a unique space/time within which thinking is first and foremost a social activity, something that takes place between people through active interchange. As such, the university is, as Readings suggested, "one site among others where the question of being-together is raised" (20), raised with an urgency that proceeds from an erosion of institutional forms (like the political forums of the nation-state) that increasingly have served to mask that question.

If we take the specificity of this question seriously, this question of what forms of "being-together" pedagogic actions initiate, the university as a "place to think" can be characterized not so much in terms of what it redeems (the self, the social, or the checkbook), but rather, in terms of the specific obligations it engenders, precisely the obligations of thought-in-relation. This requires the reimagining of the university as an emergent "dissensual community" (Readings 1996, 127) relinquishing the regulatory idea of communicational transparency in which the unity of thought can be realized. On these grounds, "what is called thinking is never simply a theoretical question, one that a fully grounded epistemology might answer" (161). As Readings suggests, reflections on teaching as a practice must insist on "a pedagogic scene structured by a dissymmetrical pragmatics, and this unequal relation must be addressed in terms of ethical awareness. The scene of teaching belongs to the sphere of justice rather than truth: the relation of student to teacher and teacher to student is one of asymmetrical obligation, which appears to both sides as problematic and requiring further study" (161). Within such a community, the condition of pedagogical practice is what Emmanuel Levinas (1991)[5] would call an "an infinite attention to the other," a practice that draws out of the otherwise of thought through an undoing of the pretension to self-presence, an undoing that always demands further study.

What I am arguing, albeit perhaps too abstractly, is that teaching-learning relationships be understood not simply as sites for the transmission of knowledge and skills, but as sites that encumber participants with responsibility and accountability in regard to sustaining thought-in-relation. Furthermore, what the substance of these responsibilities are and in what ways we can be accountable to them cannot be fully addressed through detailing our curricular promises and devising performance indicators that might tell us how well we have met these promises. Thus, teaching-learning relationships embody the ethical challenge of acknowledging and responding to the emergent specificity of others, something only available as the substance of thought-in-relation is enacted.

Now what is crucial in this position is that taking the ethics of obligation seriously means that the question of "being-together" within the university, "being-together" within pedagogic relationships, cannot be decided entirely in advance of its enactment. This is a rather simple statement, but one with enormous consequences. It suggests that redemptive claims for education cannot be made without attention to what I wish to preserve as the core idea of a university: that it is a space/time in which being together on the terms of thought-in-relation can be held open as a question. This implies several very important perspectives in regard to the practice of teaching. First, on such terms, what it means to do justice to teaching means turning to the question of accountability on grounds other than those evaluative schemes that ignore the contingent character of thought in the university. Second, it also means that the legitimation of the teacher's discourse is not immanent to that discourse but is always dependent— at least in part—on the context of its reception. And third, it means that teaching is not exhausted in the achievement of intersubjective communication. The goal of education is not fulfilled in the achievement of a mimetic identity by the student, either as a replication of the professor as model of rigorous thoughtfulness, or as a replication of a cluster of specific knowledge and skills assumed required to take up one's place in socioeconomic systems of production and exchange, but in precisely our ability to hold open the question of education itself while substantively and productively engaging students in new concepts, ideas, perspectives, and modes of thought.

The quickest way to bring all this down to earth is to consider how the contingent, ethical character inherent to teaching that initiates thought-in-relation might impact on procedures for the allocation of faculty merit pay or, if not this, what is considered relevant data regarding one's teaching for the purpose of promotion and tenure reviews. For anyone who has wrestled with the question of how to make faculty assessments responsive to the contingent character of university teaching, you know that we will need much time for such a discussion. Rather than pursing this policy discussion, I want instead to provide a brief curricular example that illustrates the implications of what I have been arguing. To do so I return to Bard College. At Bard, all first-year students are required to take two seminars, one in the fall and one in the spring. These seminars are courses in which students are introduced to the literary, philosophical, and artistic legacies of several interrelated cultures. Readings are chosen to represent a wide range of intellectual discourse. For several years now, the fall semester of the first-year seminar has been devoted to the study of education. As first-year students embark on the project of university education, within this seminar they are asked to make themselves aware of the assumptions they have held about this process and to consider various ways education has been defined by different thinkers at different points in history. Some of the texts studied include Niccolò Machiavelli's *The Prince,* Jean-Jacques Rousseau's *Discourse on Arts and Sciences,* Mary Wollstonecraft Shelley's *Frankenstein,* Paulo Freire's *Pedagogy of the Oppressed,* W.E.B. Du Bois's *The Souls of Black Folks,* and Sigmund Freud's *Civilization and Its Discontents.* I find this a rather extraordinary idea. That university students are required, as part of their introduction to study in an institution of higher education, to actually discuss and debate the meaning and significance of education and thought it might encompass. This seems to me an example of a curricular intervention with the potential of affecting an attentiveness to the thought initiated in the scenes of pedagogic action in which faculty and students participate, and hence a tremendous resource for encouraging and facilitating holding open thought as something central to pedagogic relationships.

CYNICISM OF FACULTY AND THE
COUNTERCONDITIONS OF THOUGHT

I have been arguing about commitments, the commitments we make to certain teaching alibis and the commitment we might make to an idea that locates the core of the university in the emergent quality of how the obligations of the scene of teaching and of thought-in-relation might be enacted. There is a need, however, before I finish to take one step backwards and recognize that for many faculty, particularly, young new faculty, the question posed to the university is not "how to turn the institution into a haven for thought but how to think in an institution whose development tends to make thought more and more difficult, less and less necessary" (Readings 1996, 175). Both in regard to either the heroism required by one's teaching alibi or the idealism of the pedagogic scene as a network of obligations, there is a cynicism being bred in our universities that stems from the contradiction between what is often characterized as the "romanticized scenarios of teaching and thought" and the real conditions of work in the university. I am talking here very mundanely about the intertwined issues of class size, teaching resources (teaching assistants, rooms, time slots in a schedule, and so on), the time demands of multiple faculty responsibilities, and the evaluation procedures faculty are subject to, particularly early in their careers. This cynicism, no doubt, is structured by underfunding and the bureaucratic turn in administrative policy making that—in the final analysis—does not really want to hear what new faculty are saying about their experiences of teaching. It is with no small sense of irony then, given the penchant of at least my university for establishing program and university-wide performance indicators, that I suggest that we might usefully put our minds to devising a new performance indicator: a "cynicism index." Such a measure might be extremely useful as a warning of the erosion of any sort of commitment to an idea of a university on the part of its participants, for indeed the erosion of commitment is the countercondition to thought, the countercondition of the university as a "place to think." One indication that a university has a low cynicism index would be evidence that its faculty were actually taking time to seriously argue over the character of thought in the university.

NOTES

Presented at a university-wide conference: "Undergraduate Education: Understanding the Experience?" Wilfred Laurier University, Waterloo, Ontario, October 15, 1999.

1. As universities shift their Internet-based marketing strategies, web page designs are in flux. The images reported here "were up" on university home pages in the fall of 1999.

2. The text of Premier Harris's speech was posted to the Internet newsletter *Addressing the Academy,* which was founded and edited by the late Ioan Davies. An indefatigable defender of centrality critical thought to university life, he will be sorely missed.

3. In exploring another position, I am in effect offering another alibi, one that is surely open to deconstruction. In the *University in Ruins,* Readings calls for a teaching "without alibis . . . ceasing to justify our practices in the name of an idea from 'elsewhere,' an idea that would release us from responsibility for our immediate actions. Neither reason, nor culture. Neither excellence, nor an appeal to a transcendence that our actions struggle to realize, trying as we may to justify our deeds and absolve ourselves" (1996, 129). Contra to Readings, I doubt that one can ever teach "without alibis," that will be a complete absence of an appeal to transcendence even in a alternative position that emphasizes the contingent and problematic character of thought-in-relation as the fundamental question of pedagogy.

4. On what might constitute educational value in the eyes of prospective students, Samuel Weber offers the following thoughts: "To what extent the humanities are able to sell themselves as providers of potentially profitable information is very much an open question, one that will determine their future in a world of global capitalism. For the humanities, much will depend on the ways that the established disciplines define

their future practices. Disciplines that continue to conceive of their activity in terms of self-contained and sovereign fields will, I think, find themselves faced with increasing difficulties, both in terms of their attractiveness to outside donors, and also in terms of finding an internal constituency among incoming students. This is not merely because of the largely pragmatic considerations of acquiring marketable skills, although such considerations are more than justified in the face of a job market in which the number of qualified, reasonably well-paid positions is rapidly decreasing. Rather, the justified expectation of students that the university will provide them with an opportunity of understanding the world in which they must not merely work, but also live, may well require a revision of the cognitive model that has long dominated university teaching and learning: the professionalized model of a closed, self-contained area or field in which one can establish a relative degree of mastery through learning and scholarship. The very notion of scholarship tends to take for granted the enabling exclusions and limits through which any field of knowledge is constituted as a closed and self-contained area" (Weber 1999, 4).

5. This infinite attention to the other Levinas (1991) terms "proximity." See chapter 3.

WORKS CITED

Botstein, Leon. 1997. *Jefferson's Children*. New York: Doubleday.

Emberley, Peter. 1996. *Zero Tolerance: Hot Button Politics in Canada's Universities*. Toronto: Penguin.

Harris, Michael. 1997. "Summit Speech." November 19. Can be found at: <www.yorku.ca/faculty/academic/idavies/ata/issue2/harris.htm>. Last accessed: December 2000.

Levinas, Emmanuel. 1991. *Otherwise Than Being or Beyond Essence*. Dordrecht: Kluwer.

MacIvor, Heather. 1977. "Castles on the Cortex; or, Medieval Scholasticism Revisited." *University of Toronto Quarterly* 66.4 (Fall): 601–613.

Mitchell, W.J.T. 1994. *Picture Theory*. Chicago: University of Chicago Press.

Morton, Desmond. 1997. " 'The University' Is Theory: Universities Are Facts." *University of Toronto Quarterly* 66.4 (Fall): 593–600.

Readings, Bill. 1996. *The University in Ruins*. Cambridge, Mass.: Harvard University Press.

Taylor, Catherine. 1999. *University Education and the Struggle for a Freer Future: Impasses and Passageways in Contemporary Discourses of Lesbian Studies and the Liberal Arts*. Ph.D. diss., University of Toronto.

Weber, Samuel. 1999. *The Future Campus: Destiny in a Virtual World*. This article can be found at: <www.hydra.umn.edu/weber/text1.html>. Last accessed: October 2000.

Young, Robert. 1992. "The Idea of a Chrestomathic University." In *Logomachia: The Conflict of the Faculties*, ed. Richard Rand. Lincoln: University of Nebraska Press.

4

Literary Theory and the Role of the University

Peter Baker

One goal of my title is to provoke a certain response. Don't you have things turned around? Shouldn't it be *the role of literary theory in the university?* I want to argue here that for complex reasons literary theory—not a unitary concept by any means, but a heuristic term covering many different, and sometimes conflicting, critical projects—has become a discourse able to say some things about the purpose of the university, what the role of the university in society is, what the university can, does, and should look like. Most arguments today concerning the university utilize a positivist discourse, often economics- or business-oriented, talking about delivering services and training workers to compete in the global marketplace. Literary theory, by contrast, maintains important links with the intellectual and philosophical reasonings associated with the creation of the modern university. Far from occupying an isolated intellectual sphere, these theoretical issues continue to speak to the realities faced by the entire university community. The discourses of literary theory cross disciplinary boundaries and are thus able to elicit the responses of people engaged in other types of activity within the university. Theory, first under the guise of deconstruction and lately in association with gender and multicultural studies, has even entered into press and media accounts of the university. Paradoxically, those writings on so-called political correctness that identify literary theory as the enabling agent for change in the university community—always a negative change for the professed enemies of P.C.—are right to some extent about the role of theory in creating a climate for change.[1] As the American university of the late twentieth century increasingly changes to represent the gendered and multicultural realities of its citizens, for example, literary theory has something to say about *why this should be.*

The modern university system is of relatively recent historical formation. Though the European universities trace their origins back hundreds of years (twelfth century for Oxford and the Sorbonne, eleventh century for Bologna), and American universities like Harvard and William and Mary date back to the seventeenth century, the modern university that is, at least in principle, both of democratic access and structured around a polyvalent curriculum is less than two hundred years old.[2] Jean-François Lyotard has discussed some of the founding arguments for the modern university and their continuing influence, or lack thereof, in his provocative and controversial *Postmodern Condition.* Lyotard is concerned to investigate what he calls the *grands récits* or metanarratives that philosophers develop to give a coherent ideational structure to the way we should think about historical developments. He traces two metanarratives back to the German Romantics (Schiller and others) in their arguments concerning the role of the modern university. On one side there is the high Romantic argument, with its roots in Kant's theory of enlightenment, that each individual has an innate potential and that university education should enable individuals to reach that potential.[3] On the other side, there is what we might call the social progress argument, associated with Hegel and later with Marx, that democratic access to education helps eliminate local prejudices and ignorance as a key element in promoting the progress of society as a whole. Lyotard argues that our "postmodern condition" is characterized by the "failure" of these two metanarratives, *not* as he is most commonly understood as saying because of their inherent flaws, but because they no longer compel a working consensus at the level of the larger social or political level that we call "society."[4] Given the breakdown at the level of social consensus of these explanations for the value of education to society, we are left with "empty" technocratic arguments concerning the necessity of specialized knowledge and training, delivery of services, and competitiveness in the global marketplace.

Lyotard's study takes as its point of departure the idea that philosophy has traditionally been the discipline that sees itself as providing the rationale for the constitution of other fields of discourse. This is clear in the omnipresent references to the German Romantic philosophers in the debate over the purpose of the university. Philosophy as the study of "pure" knowledge lends its prestige to the other disciplines, which are then seen as applications of philosophical models. One need only think of Aristotle's inquiries into what we would now call physics, natural sciences, and ethics to recall a time when the realm of the philosopher was the whole of human knowledge and endeavor. Philosophy, in Lyotard's terms, thus provided the metanarratives for the other fields of inquiry, that is, the guiding ideas concerning *why* someone would pursue such an inquiry, how it related to "pure" knowledge, and in a less examined way, how it was useful for practical applications. There are many reasons for the declining role of philosophy in providing the guiding ideas for the pursuit of knowledge in general. For example, philosophy's turn toward neo-Kantianism and positivism in the late nineteenth and early twentieth centuries emphasized the "practical" dimension—previously the least important rationale for deciding the validity of different kinds of inquiry. This allowed philosophy to be viewed as supporting both a scientific and social "can do" pragmatism.[5] The austere analytical philosophy of the Anglo-American tradition in the twentieth century leads into language and areas of inquiry that, for the most part, leave aside real-world connections, even to other disciplines within the university. The phenomenological tradition associated primarily with continental philosophy of the twentieth century, on the other hand, has allowed for a continuation of those kinds of questions that make sense to other people in non-specialized language. The most useful philosophical approach to emerge recently in support of the kind of argument I am making here might be the feminist epistemology represented in the works of Elizabeth Kamarck Minnich, Sandra Harding, and others.

Richard Rorty has offered what we might call a liberal assimilationist account for understanding how literary theory has come to occupy the role previously played by philosophy in answering the larger questions about the reasons for studying a particular field, how it relates to knowledge in general, and its practical applications. As someone hired in the 1980s, when English departments in American universities scrambled to hire people to teach "literary theory," I feel somewhat chastened by this next step of addressing the historical contingency by which literary theory became the name for studying the theories of Kant, Hegel, Marx, Freud, and Lyotard, in addition to the latest critical work on Shakespeare, Jane Austen, Gustave Flaubert, Gabriel García Márquez, and Toni Morrison, plus the emerging fields of structuralism, deconstruction, feminism, gay and lesbian literature, and postcolonial and multicultural studies. Although Rorty's liberalism prevents him from escaping a certain paternalizing valuation of Western civilization, I think his account of literary theory deserves recognition, if only because it was so influential in establishing the general understanding of the role of "theory" in the university. As he says:

> Once the range of literary criticism is stretched that far there is, of course, less and less point in calling it *literary* criticism. But for accidental historical reasons, having to do with the way in which intellectuals got jobs in universities by pretending to pursue academic specialties, the name has stuck. So instead of changing the term "literary criticism" to something like "culture criticism," we have instead stretched the word "literature" to cover whatever literary critics criticize. (81)

Those with some training in philosophy will recognize this as a classic nominalist argument, that is, words and concepts have the meaning we assign them and not any kind of immanent truth.[6] In teaching a Modern Literary Theory course this semester, I invoked a version of this argument to try to explain why the range of material we were studying this semester could just as easily be taught as Modern Intellectual History or Twentieth-Century Philosophy.

Moreover, Rorty's narrative—his story of how "literary criticism," or what I am calling theory, became associated with a range of philosophical, cultural, and political ways of thinking—can be pushed further than he himself might want to go in order to explain how literary theory has become an enabling condition for the sudden rise of variously related disciplines in literary and cultural studies.[7] In fact, there are many scholars who are urging that we change the nomenclature as well, and recognize that literary studies should now be more appropriately identified as cultural studies (see Easthope).

To understand how literary theory has come to occupy this position, it may help to undertake a brief review of the role of literary criticism in the social formation.[8] As Gerald Graff's institutional history of teaching literature shows, English literature was not even a field of study in American universities until the late nineteenth century, and separate attention to "American" literature, as such, had to await the early twentieth century. In the English tradition, poets and writers historically were placed in a defensive posture of justifying their interest in literature rather than more active and heroic pursuits, at the same time as they learned rhetoric and oratory from texts in the Classics rather than works in their native language. So, we have famous essays with titles like "A Defence of Poetry" (Shelley) and Sir Philip Sidney's "An Apology for Poetry." Sidney's argument relies principally on an invocation of the authority of classical models characteristic of Renaissance humanism. Finding his models in classic Greek and Roman verse and in the poetry of the Bible, Sidney praises the literary qualities of the Psalms of David, for example, particularly "his notable *prosopopeias,* when he maketh you, as it were, see God coming in His majesty, his telling of the beasts' joyfulness, and hills' leaping" (112). While a footnote in my edition of the "Apology" says that *prosopopeia* is a synonym for "personification," the primary meaning listed in the OED is, "A rhetorical figure by which an imaginary or absent person is represented as speaking or acting." This rhetorical figure provides a tantalizing link to current theory and the work of Paul de Man, who has called the figure of *prosopopeia* "the master trope of poetic discourse" (48). De Man's interest in this figure is understandable in the context of the propensity within deconstruction—the style of criticism de Man was largely responsible for bringing to a wider audience in the United States—to seek the absent center that structures or organizes a literary work or an argument. And before I am charged with anachronism in comparing Sidney to Paul de Man, let me recall that Sidney's cleverest and most-often remembered move in his defense of poetry is to claim that poetry can never be accused of misleading people by falsifying reality. As Sidney says, "Now, for the poet, he nothing affirms, and therefore never lieth" (132).

Sidney's stance on poetry and the role of criticism in the social formation is far from being the dominant mode, however. The dominant mode of criticism in the English tradition was set in the eighteenth century, using antecedents in Aristotle, Longinus, and Horace, as what I will here be calling "normative" criticism.⁹ Samuel Johnson's "Preface to Shakespeare" may be taken as representative of this mode, particularly as it relies for its primary authority on the critical precepts of the ancient authors just mentioned. Johnson sets the standards for what counts as literary value in a way that is now recognizable in the debate over the literary canon, saying in part: "What mankind have long possessed they have often examined and compared; and if they persist to value the possession, it is because frequent comparisons have confirmed opinion in its favor" (221). Dr. Johnson's position here varies from Sidney's in not merely invoking but reifying its obeisance to received authority, reflecting the workings of eighteenth-century ideology that encouraged strong obedience to church, monarch, and state. The ideological character of Johnson's position becomes clearer when he examines the critical grounds for valuing the work of Shakespeare. He particularly values Shakespeare's depictions of nature, and when there are cases of doubt that arise concerning the validity of Shakespeare's work, Johnson urges "there is always an appeal open from criticism to nature" (225). But as recent feminist theory has emphasized, "nature" is likewise not a neutral term, but also encodes elements of the dominant ideology. My own position would be just opposite to that of Dr. Johnson: I would say, rather, that we need to move from "nature" to "criticism," in order to establish criticism as an oppositional discourse.

The question is whether criticism need always be "normative" as Dr. Johnson implicitly urges, or whether there is such a thing as a "non-normative" criticism.¹⁰ A non-normative poetics would lead to a role for criticism far different from that envisioned by Dr. Johnson, what we might call *literary criticism as an oppositional discourse.*¹¹ Within the social formation, criticism can either serve as a means of reproduction of what Italian theorist Antonio Gramsci terms cultural hegemony or criticism can oppose this hegemony. There are still quite active critics who view the role for criticism as the reproduction of others like themselves who will occupy similar roles in the social formation. Bové quotes literary critic Frank Kermode declaring, in an address to members of the profession: "Yet it must be obvious that the formation of rival canons, however transient, is very dangerous; that in allowing it to happen we risk the death of the institution. Its continuance depends wholly upon our ability to maintain the canon and replace ourselves, to induce sufficient numbers of young people to think as we do" (*Mastering Discourse* 51). Kermode's major premise here is the place of the canon within academic institutions, but the view he expresses of the educator's role extends well beyond the field of literary criticism to raise important questions about the purpose and role of professional educators and the educational institution as a whole within our society.

One issue raised by the concept of non-normative criticism as an oppositional discourse is whether literary studies and university education generally can be seen as "cultural capital," in the term proposed by Pierre Bourdieu. When I teach courses at the state university on the history of literary criticism

and modern literary theory, students often raise serious questions concerning the sheer difficulty of the language in the material they are being required
to read. I turn this question of specialized languages into a way of addressing
"cultural capital," since a major part of what a university education has always
been designed to accomplish is to teach students various specialized languages—no longer simply Greek and Latin. This is one of the ways that teachers of theory can allow students to use theory to conceptualize their own
experience as university students and members of a class-based society. Students who come from different geographical areas of the country are said to
speak different "dialects"; students who come from different social classes,
which usually means different educational backgrounds, can be said to speak
different "sociolects." Clearly, something Kermode and I have in common in
our goals for teaching students about literary criticism is to give them a certain training in the specialized language of criticism that is one aspect of the
sociolect of university-educated persons generally. Teachers defending the
liberal arts curriculum have been saying for some time now that it doesn't
matter so much *what* students major in, as long as they learn how to think
critically, while the more cynical view is that these students are being trained
to make the right noises. One way to view this apparent contradiction is to
ask if training in the sociolect is aimed primarily at passing on cultural capital in order to reproduce the social-class structure as a part of university training generally; or, are students being *trained in those "critical" skills necessary to recognize, analyze, and change those institutions responsible for
maintaining the class structure and its corresponding cultural hegemony?*

Michel Foucault's work on mental health, prisons, and even sexuality, as
what he calls "disciplinary" environments, offers critics ways of theorizing
the role of educational institutions in inculcating social values to reproduce
both the social hierarchy and individual social roles. Bové makes the connection between Foucault's theorizing on the university and Gramsci's idea
of hegemony in a way that leads to the following contradiction, one that all
of us who work in higher education must deal with sooner or later:

> The intellectual operation of the hegemonic organization requires a broad-based,
> humanistic education. But it also requires an elaborate structure of testing and
> tracking to elaborate "top intellectual qualifications" to distribute workers and
> rewards. The effect of this structure is to deny in practice what is claimed in the-
> ory: namely, the illusion of democratic access to and control of technology and
> high culture. (*Wake of Theory* 35)

These are strong words and may be seen to present a deterministic view of
the university, the culture, and the larger social formation of which they are
a part. The power of this passage stems at least in part from the way Bové
invokes the metanarratives Lyotard identifies as informing the foundations of
the modern university system. Indeed, all left oppositional discourses rely in

some measure on the metanarratives of liberation and/or social progress: that's why they are oppositional.[12] The educational system, embodying a "hegemonic organization," which Bové sees as operative here, denies the "liberatory" aspect of individual enlightenment at the same time as it seems to block any vision of social progress—and this is why such characterizations, like those following Bourdieu that invoke "cultural capital" in a limiting sense, are so threatening to our sense of what we think we do. Some of the questions might be posed as follows: do literary and cultural theorists propose any ways of reinvigorating metanarratives of individual enlightenment and social progress? or do these models need to be replaced by something new? how do we go about establishing either local or social consensus for the goals of equality, empowerment, progress, and change? and are these the right goals?

Bové claims that, "Were literary critics to take Gramsci seriously, they would carry out a thorough critique of the basic paradigms of literary education and especially its relation to the university. They would, in addition, attempt to reconstruct that education along different lines" (*Wake of Theory* 37). This vision of the task of the contemporary critic, which Bové casts in the conditional mood, is what many of those engaged in the various and sometimes conflicting activities of literary and cultural theory are attempting to actualize. This is also the change that those who are lamenting the rise of "political correctness" and the decline of "cultural values" are engaged in fighting against.[13] My own view is that such change is normal, desirable, and even inevitable, and that the stridency of multiculturalism's opponents on the cultural right is merely a sign of their failing rearguard effort. This does not mean, however, that they are in no position to cause harm. Despite what high-minded defenders of cultural values across the whole political spectrum may intend, it is surely no accident that the "culture wars" were making news during the same period as the widespread defunding of higher education. This is the connection that Bérubé makes when he argues that "what we miss, if we continue to construe multiculturalism only as a set of intellectual options and curricular imperatives, is the necessity to articulate multiculturalism to the economics of school funding and school policy" (235). As we need to insist repeatedly, debates over the curriculum are also *always* debates about ethics, critical responsibility, and political accountability. Bérubé makes this point to counter P.C. pundits who claim educators have abandoned "values": "It follows, therefore, that we are being attacked over these *exigencies* of value not because we have vacated the terrain on which critics interrogate cultural values, but precisely because we have *not* vacated this terrain" (108). The radical relativism of Stanley Fish or the political quietism of Richard Rorty makes theory an easy target (for critics on both the left and the right), but we need to maintain an awareness of the real-world context in which the critical debate is conducted and its all-too-real effects on our students' lives.

The local scene of conflict where I encountered resistance to the project of literary theory was a department curriculum committee meeting, when I proposed a course in Contemporary Literary Theory that I had been led to believe was the main course I had been hired to teach. At this meeting one of my colleagues began by questioning whether a course in recent theory, since it covered material from roughly the past thirty years, was even deserving of being represented in the curriculum at all. Since the course in History of Literary Criticism covered a period of more than two thousand years, a course with only thirty years' material seemed relatively insignificant. Another colleague went on to say that recent experiences at academic conferences, and what people were saying to her privately, led her to believe that literary theory was being repudiated by members of the profession and that such a course risked being outdated even by the time it was approved as part of the curriculum. The discussion then moved to the appropriateness of teaching this material at a mid-level state institution such as ours. Would the students have enough preparation before they took this class to be able to distinguish between what was valid and what was not in the current approaches? Perhaps, it was suggested, such a course would be better suited to a large research institution with an active graduate program. What possible use could "our" students have for this kind of material, anyway?

I was caught completely unprepared for this sustained attack on the legitimacy of literary theory as a discipline. I had never encountered this kind of objection at my previous school, though it has a nearly identical profile as a metropolitan university with a high percentage of first-generation college students. The most serious objection anyone had ever raised there was that I would have a hard time getting students interested in the material. Since I knew from my previous experience that this was not true, I was prepared to argue this point and give supporting examples. But I was not prepared to mount an impromptu defense of literary theory as material deserving college credit. I fell back on the weakest possible defense—that some of our students did go on to graduate school and the GRE in English had an increasing number of questions on theory and criticism. I also said that when and if our students arrived in graduate school they would be expected to have some background in theory. I received some eleventh-hour support from my colleague teaching the History of Literary Criticism course, who said that her course already contained too much material and she felt it entirely reasonable to introduce a new course to take some of the burden off this already overloaded course. The compromise that was eventually reached was to rename the course "Modern Literary Theory" and to include material on literary formalism on the syllabus so students would be able to see exactly what the newer approaches were "departing from." I did receive support from the department chairperson who told me that once the course had been approved on the university level I should teach whatever I deemed appropriate.

I am tempted to see this experience of local conflict along the lines of the newer form of censorship that Jacques Derrida sees as operative in the modern university. There is very little direct top-down censorship of what one can actually teach, but there remains a variety of methods by which such control can still be exerted. As Derrida says:

> Today, in the Western democracies, that [overt] form of censorship has almost entirely disappeared. The prohibiting limitations function through multiple channels that are decentralized, difficult to bring together into a system. The unacceptability of a discourse, the noncertification of a research project, the illegitimacy of a course offering are declared by evaluative actions: studying such evaluations is, it seems to me, one of the tasks most indispensable to the exercise of academic responsibility, most urgent for the maintenance of its dignity. Within the university itself, forces that are apparently external to it (presses, foundations, the mass media) are intervening in an ever more decisive way. ("The Principle of Reason" 13)

Derrida's statement links the internal pressures on what one can teach and study to the external pressures that I have been identifying with the cultural right's recent attacks on multiculturalism. This was certainly one of the features of my experience. Derrida also calls for the study of these kinds of incidents as one of the tasks that we must undertake in order to maintain the integrity of the academic institution, and here I agree as well. The question of literary theory as a body of material deserving study at the university has special poignancy in the atmosphere of the "culture wars," in which theory has been widely demonized as a leading force behind ongoing (negative, politically motivated) changes at the university, curricular and other. This idea of the pernicious effect of theory also underlies, I think, the curious suggestion that theory is in the process of being repudiated by the scholarly community. The more important question, which I think still bears asking, is why the mid-level state university curriculum should be any different from the private liberal arts college or state research institution when it comes to teaching theory. Whom or what did my colleagues see themselves as protecting?

My colleagues insisted fairly emphatically that "our" students simply did not have the necessary background to weigh effectively the approaches that would be presented in a course on contemporary theory. But what does this mean? It could mean that "our" students are less intelligent than students at private colleges and larger (and better-funded) research institutions, but this I have come to disbelieve. It is true they often do not make the right noises, but I have argued that this reflects primarily lack of training in the sociolect. Once they become engaged with the texts, I have found that "our" students, because they are less reverent of authority in general and of printed texts in particular, can often be tougher and more insightful readers of theory texts than students at more prestigious institutions, where a sense of entitlement can often lead to a kind of knowing superiority. It may be that we are still dealing with a model wherein theory is seen as a kind of rarefied criticism that should ultimately be subservient to the primary text and students are thought not to have enough background in these primary sources. If the students lack this necessary background, they may also be overly swayed by trendy theories that are ultimately unfounded, in the view of my colleagues. My sense is that this argument for the "tradition" usually serves rather as a way of enforcing the practice of "normative" criticism.

The prominent feature in all of these arguments for shielding state university students from theory is the question of authority. Students at the state university where I teach do have the potential to raise real questions about the underlying metanarratives for university education. For these students, as I have experienced repeatedly, questions of enlightenment and social progress are not simply pleasing noises, background music to fast-track jobs or intriguing problems to be worked out by means of bloodless abstractions. I think my colleagues who are worried about the effects of teaching theory at my school are right to be worried. Theory can have real-world effects. Importantly, it can affect how one views the vested authority of texts, teachers, and institutions generally. I believe students at mid-level state universities are actually more likely than their more privileged peers to welcome criticism as an oppositional discourse that legitimates many of the progressive curricular changes they see as too long in coming. The tough time I had going through institutional channels to get a course in literary theory approved had as one result that I was reintroduced to some of the real stakes involved in the debate over theory. I am more likely to see what I do as raising real questions about the institutional power structures within which academics operate. And when the students in Modern Literary Theory ask their tough questions, I am more likely to see they not only don't need our protection, but that they are seeking to use theory as a means to engage in a process leading to the solidarity necessary to bring about change in their real-world communities.

Whereas most members of earlier generations of literary scholars might have assented to R. P. Blackmur's dictum, "Criticism, I take it, is the formal discourse of an amateur" ("A Critic's Job of Work," qtd. in Bové, *Wake of Theory* 72), the current climate in literary studies is much closer to what Edward Said has urged under the heading of "secular criticism." In Said's definition: "criticism must think of itself as life-enhancing and constitutively opposed to every form of tyranny, domination and abuse; its social goals are noncoercive knowledge produced in the interests of human freedom" (29). Here, in Said's terms, is a definition of what I have been calling oppositional criticism, one that develops an aversive stance to the cultural hegemony through developing notions of what critical discourse terms subjectivity and empowerment. This is the kind of empowerment, for example, that women and traditional minorities are seeking through the further democratized access to higher education. From the perspective I have been urging it should be clear that the only group for whom the pursuit of knowledge is "free and disinterested" is the one that has the economic, social, and ideological power to control what constitutes knowledge in the first place. As Elizabeth Minnich argues: *"it is precisely that which is claimed to be most inclusive because most general (that is, most abstract) that is most skewed by the old errors. And that means that what is supposedly most neutral, disinterested, objective, is most, not least, reflective of past exclusions and their rationalizations and mystifications"* (172; italics in the text). These are not simply questions of "special interests," but a paradigm shift in what constitutes knowledge. Sandra Harding argues in her recent work in feminist epistemology and the history of science that so-called objective viewpoints that embed traditional white male prejudices produce tainted results, and that feminist science, for example, is demonstrably better science.

The question becomes: what kind of pedagogical institution do we support and what are, or should be, the aims of the university? The role of literary criticism in the social formation can take the form of a "normative" criticism, but normative criticism has as one of its goals to reproduce structures of power and domination characteristic of a class-based society. The obedience to received authority that traditional criticism implicitly urges underlies the argument in favor of a fixed canon reflecting immutable cultural values. When we raise the question of what should be, instead of seeking ways to justify what is, we are engaging in an imaginative activity that Sidney argued was typical of the poetic figure of *prosopopeia*. The faculty for making present what is absent can extend to reflecting on what kind of learning environment we would seek to have, rather than finding ways to make do with what we have now. This positive orientation toward what is not (but should be) relates to what Derrida, in his recent work on contemporary European politics, has claimed is the necessarily aporetic character of "a democracy that must have the structure of a promise" (*The Other Heading* 78).[14] Instead of accepting the dominant technocratic ethos for the university, literary theory insists on ideals of enlightenment and social progress that are historically inextricable from the founding arguments for the modern university and that remain as powerful guiding ideals even when they are unfulfilled or no longer provide the basis for a broad social consensus. Contemporary literary theories present multiple possibilities for developing non-normative, oppositional approaches to criticism that are "life-enhancing" (Said) and carry the aporetic promise of "a democracy to come" (Derrida). This is one way to view the claim that literary theory is an enabling condition for the ongoing changes taking place within the university community.[15]

NOTES

1. Michael Bérubé argues in *Public Access* that these P.C. pundits have been all too successful in setting the terms of the public debate, so rather than respond to them I urge that we develop the terms of the debate within the discourses about the university that are no less traditional but that maintain the radical potential associated with terms like enlightenment and liberation.

2. Gerald Graff, while restricting his purview to literary studies, has described this history in the American university in his *Professing Literature*. He also restricts his supposedly broad-based study to a completely undemocratic, as well as unrepresentative, study of elite institutions—"research-oriented departments of English at major universities" (2). Even if Graff's study is addressed primarily to an academic audience, only seven percent of college-level professors actually teach at the kind of institution his study surveys, although more than ninety percent received their training at such institutions.

3. One recalls the opening of Kant's "What is Enlightenment?": "Enlightenment is man's release from his self-incurred tutelage" (263). To correct the gender bias here is tempting, but that would be to undertake a change in Kant's thinking, which did not admit of the possibility of enlightenment for women, as a subsequent sentence in the opening goes on to state explicitly (cf. Minnich, *Transforming Knowledge* 76–77).

4. That we have lost our faith in the value of every individual is confirmed by the intractability of what gets called "homelessness." The demise of the social progress argument in the United States is expressed in pithy form by Bérubé, as when he says, "No doubt, whatever else Reaganism has done to the nation, it has left us almost incapable of thinking about the 'common good,' whether in education, health care, housing, or taxation" (240 n.16). Anyone concerned with democratic access to higher education should be very much aware of the "defunding" of public higher education, specifically the massive shift in federal money from federally insured student loans to "research" grants—which are often a form of crypto-military funding—that allowed George Bush to claim plausibly during his 1992 campaign that his administration had actually increased funding for higher education.

5. Cornel West argues against this practically oriented appropriation of pragmatist philosophy in his *Prophetic Thought in Postmodern Times* (31 ff.).

6. Much of the divisive infighting among theorists could be eliminated or at least productively channeled if we used some of the nominalist precepts. Diana Fuss's important contribution to the debates over feminism, which presents essentialism and constructivism as necessarily implicated in each other's structuring arguments, is, from one perspective, a nominalist argument.

7. Edward Said has historicized this connection (the same connection, of course, that the cultural right bewails) in *Culture and Imperialism:*

> The newer currents in the academy, and the force of what is called theory (a rubric under which were herded many new disciplines like psychoanalysis, linguistics, and Nietzschean philosophy, unhoused from the traditional fields such as philology, moral philosophy, and the natural sciences), acquired prestige and interest; they appeared to undermine the authority and the stability of established canons, well-capitalized fields, long-standing procedures of accreditation, research, and the division of intellectual labor. That all this occurred in the modest and circumscribed terrain of cultural-academic praxis simultaneously with the great wave of anti-war, anti-imperialist protest was not fortuitous but, rather, a genuine political and intellectual conjuncture. (57)

8. I agree with Jeffrey Williams when he says: "the history of criticism is not a neutral or innocent category, but has a polemical significance and legitimates a certain line of criticism and a particular direction of doing literary work" (282).

9. For a recent example, see Altieri, who repeatedly cites a passage from Longinus' treatise *On the Sublime* in which the classical philosopher says we should learn how to act by comparing our acts to the great actions of those who cross the stage of the past. This relates to Altieri's claim that "The major influence of aesthetic theory here is on how we choose to specify what holds a community together so that we internalize its role as a normative ground in our acts of judgment" (249).

10. I locate a version of such a criticism in the work of the contemporary poet, Charles Bernstein, as in *his* recent "defense" of poetry, *A Poetics*. Bernstein says, for example: "I'm advocating a poetics that is not adjudicating, not authoritative for all other poetry, not legislating rules for composition. But rather a poetics that is both tropical and socially-invested: in short, poetic rather than normative" (158).

11. Paul Bové argues that "A counterhegemonic or oppositional criticism has certain minimal requirements: a historically specific research project oriented by autonomous developments elsewhere in culture and guided by a political program that avoids, as far as possible, the suppression of memory and the division of labor that are the hallmarks of the academy's general subservience to the hegemony. In other words, radical critical intellectuals must understand the historical specificity of the cultural practices of their own period with an eye to bringing their own practice and discourse in line with other oppositional forces in a society struggling against hegemonic manipulation and state violence" (*Mastering Discourse* 93).

12. This includes even the most left-oriented or contestatory discourses, such as that of Mas'ud Zavarzadeh and Donald Morton, when they argue, for example, that "The ideological project of the humanists is very similar to that of their neoconservative allies outside the academy, and their strategies have evolved around renewed emphasis on certain kinds of courses and the use of established institutional and bureaucratic channels to block radical change in the academy" (15). The goal of "radical change," as it is expressed here, owes at least some of its force to the metanarrative of social progress.

13. Michael Sprinker's analysis of the anti-P.C. right has relevance here, as in his claim that "The defense of Western culture is characteristically, when one peels away the thin veneer about 'maintaining standards,' a racist (and not infrequently sexist and class-biased) reaction to the democratization of American higher education over the past quarter century" (109).

14. This characteristic use of *aporia* in a catachrestic manner to point to something which as yet has no name or cannot be defined within our current thinking also relates to Derrida's recent writings on justice in "Force of Law." I deal with these complicated questions in some depth in my forthcoming study, *Deconstruction and the Ethical Turn.*

15. This essay was delivered as a university lecture at Towson State University, sponsored by the Faculty Research Committee. I want to acknowledge here the crucial support from my colleagues at the university—especially Sara Coulter, Elaine Hedges, and Dan Jones—and from other friends in the teaching community, including Henry Majewski and Gene Miller.

WORKS CITED

Altieri, Charles. *Canons and Consequences: Reflections on the Ethical Force of Imaginative Ideals*. Evanston: Northwestern UP, 1990.

Bernstein, Charles. *A Poetics*. Cambridge: Harvard UP, 1992.

Bérubé, Michael. *Public Access: Literary Theory and American Cultural Politics*. New York: Verso, 1994.

Bourdieu, Pierre, and Jean-Claude Passeron. *Reproduction in Education, Society and Culture*. Trans. Richard Nice. Beverly Hills: Sage, 1977.

Bové, Paul. *In the Wake of Theory*. Hanover: Wesleyan UP/UP of New England, 1992.

———. *Mastering Discourse: The Politics of Intellectual Culture*. Durham: Duke UP, 1992.

De Man, Paul. *The Resistance to Theory*. Minneapolis: U Minnesota P, 1986.

Derrida, Jacques. "Force of Law: The 'Mystical Foundation of Authority.' " Trans. Mary Quaintance. *Deconstruction and the Possibility of Justice*. Ed. Drucilla Cornell et al. New York: Routledge, 1992. 3–67.

———. *The Other Heading*. Trans. Pascale-Anne Brault and Michael B. Naas. Bloomington: Indiana UP, 1992.

———. "The Principle of Reason: The University in the Eyes of Its Pupils." Trans. Catherine Porter and Edward P. Morris. *Diacritics* 13 (1983): 3–20.

Easthope, Antony. *Literary into Cultural Studies*. New York: Routledge, 1991.

Fuss, Diana. *Essentially Speaking: Nature, Feminism and Difference*. New York: Routledge, 1990.

Graff, Gerald. *Professing Literature: An Institutional History*. Chicago: U Chicago P, 1987.

Harding, Sandra. "Rethinking Standpoint Epistemology: What Is 'Strong Objectivity'?" *The Centennial Review* 36.3 (1992): 437–70.

Johnson, Samuel. "Preface to Shakespeare." 1765. Eds. Charles Kaplan and William Anderson. *Criticism: Major Statements*. 3rd ed. New York: St. Martin's, 1991.

Kant, Immanuel. "What Is Enlightenment?" *Philosophical Writings*. Ed. Ernst Behler. New York: Continuum, 1991. 263–69.

Kaplan, Charles, and William Anderson, eds. *Criticism: Major Statements*. 3rd ed. New York: St. Martin's, 1991.

Lyotard, Jean-François. *The Postmodern Condition*. Trans. Georges Van Den Abeele. Minneapolis: U Minnesota P, 1986.

Minnich, Elizabeth Kamarck. *Transforming Knowledge*. Philadelphia: Temple UP, 1990.

Rorty, Richard. *Contingency, Irony, and Solidarity*. Cambridge: Cambridge UP, 1989.

Said, Edward W. *Culture and Imperialism*. New York: Knopf, 1993.

———. *The World, the Text, and the Critic*. Cambridge: Harvard UP, 1983.

Sidney, Sir Philip. "An Apology for Poetry." 1595. Eds. Charles Kaplan and William Anderson. *Criticism: Major Statements*. 3rd ed. New York: St. Martin's, 1991.n.

Sprinker, Michael. "The War Against Theory." *The Minnesota Review* 39 (1992/1993): 103–21.

West, Cornel. *Prophetic Thought in Postmodern Times*. Monroe: Common Courage, 1993.

Williams, Jeffrey. "Packaging Theory." *College English* 56.3 (1994): 280–99.

Zavarzadeh, Mas'ud, and Donald Morton. "Theory Pedagogy Politics: The Crisis of 'the Subject' in the Humanities." *Theory/Pedagogy/Politics*. Urbana: U of Illinois P, 1991. 1–32.

II

CULTURAL POLITICS AND THE STRUGGLE OVER CURRICULA

5

Curriculum Mortis: A Manifesto for Structural Change

Ronald Strickland

Since the early 1980s, in the wake of the paradigm shift from New Criticism to the politically self-conscious postmodernism and poststructuralism currently dominant in English studies, teachers of literature have been under attack from conservative academics and journalists.[1] The terms of this attack, and of the counter-critiques mounted by politically and theoretically oriented scholars, are by now quite familiar. Conservatives and liberal humanists charged that radical English teachers were ignoring traditional canonical texts in favor of indoctrinating students in an alternative canon of "politically correct" texts espousing Marxist, feminist, and "multicultural" agendas. Theorists and radicals responded that the traditional canon itself constitutes a "politically correct" set of values of a different sort, and that the focus of English studies should be critical interrogation of cultural texts and other discursive systems rather than uncritical appreciation of "great" literature.

My sympathies in this debate lie entirely in the theorist/radical camp. In this essay, however, I want to take up a question that has not been sufficiently addressed by either side of the debate over the English curriculum: what is the role of English studies in an increasingly technical-vocational academy? In relation to this question, I think the conservatives who are concerned that theoretically self-conscious and politically oriented approaches will mean the death of literature have been barking up the wrong tree. In the current postmodern, postindustrial academy, quasi-professional and vocational courses rub shoulders with traditional arts and sciences courses. Workers, not just managers, are now trained in colleges and universities. Traditional literary study—conceived in post-Romantic terms as an escape from economic and political concerns—is fast becoming an expendable luxury in universities whose primary function is the training and credentialing of the growing technical-professional-managerial work force. In this climate market pressures, not critical theory, will doom the study of literature.[2] Yet if conservatives have, for the most part, misread the symptoms of literary study's current "dis-ease," radical scholars and teachers have been too often distracted by the conservatives' rear-guard attacks. We have not yet developed the kinds of institutional structures and practices necessary for engaging the challenge to democratic education posed by the technical-vocational mission of the academy.

Most of us are complicit in this technical-vocational mission. We maintain the luxury of teaching literature or literary theory in relatively comfortable conditions at least partly by appropriating resources generated by "service" programs attached to English departments. These programs—composition, technical writing, English as a second language, etc.—are disproportionately staffed by graduate assistants and non-tenured faculty, and they are typically marginalized within English departments in a variety of contexts such as office space, departmental committee representation, curricular offerings, and graduation requirements. Within the larger professional arena, we have a scholarship publishing structure that tends to reward those whose specialized research is most remote from the concerns of these "service" courses. This hierarchy of privilege needs to be dismantled not merely because it is unfair for our colleagues who teach technical-vocational courses, but also because it limits the critical scope and effect of literature teachers as well.

We need to meet the challenge of the growing technical-vocational hegemony in the academy within our own departments, in our curricula. The most promising models for curricular change currently on the horizon are the "cultural studies" and "textual studies" models, in which both elite and popular texts are taken as objects of study, in which the traditional canon is opened up to include more texts by women and people of color, and in which critical literary and cultural theories are given primary emphasis in the curriculum and in individual courses. These innovations are necessary and valuable, but they don't go far enough toward redressing the narrow parochialism of traditional literary studies because they don't engage and contest the values and assumptions of the technical-vocational training courses in the university at large and, often, in English departments themselves. In the following pages, I will explore some possible models for an English curriculum more directly engaged in a contestatory dialogue with the technical-vocational mission of the academy in a postmodern, postindustrial society.

THEORETICAL FRAMES:
TRANSDISCIPLINARITY AND
CULTURAL STUDIES

One of the means by which New Criticism and its narrowly aesthetics-oriented approach to literature has continued to fend off political and theoretical challenges in the classroom (if not in the scholarly journals) is the well-entrenched field coverage model of literary study. As Gerald Graff has demonstrated in *Professing Literature,* this model produced an ostensibly pluralist literary curriculum in which specialists in particular literary-historical periods were encouraged to do narrowly focused research and teaching, each in his or her own narrow specialization, each blithely ignoring the larger assumptions about literature that set the boundaries of the profession. For some time now over-specialization has been recognized as counterproductive by politically engaged teachers both on the right and the left. Compare, for example, the following observations:

> Each department or great division of the university makes a pitch for itself, and each offers a course of study that will make the student an initiate. But how to choose among them? How do they relate to one another? The fact is they do not address one another. They are competing and contradictory, without being aware of it. The problem of the whole is urgently indicated by the very existence of the specialties, but it is never systematically posed. The net effect of the student's encounter with the college catalogue is bewilderment and very often demoralization. (Bloom 339)

> Unless one fudges the definition of intellectuals in terms of purely formal and statistical educational criteria, it is fairly clear that what modern society produces is an army of alienated, privatized, and uncultured experts who are knowledgeable only within very narrowly defined areas. This technical intelligentsia, rather than intellectuals in the traditional sense of thinkers concerned with the totality, is growing by leaps and bounds to run the increasingly complex bureaucratic and industrial apparatus. Its rationality, however, is only *instrumental* in character, and thus suitable mainly to perform partial tasks rather than tackling substantial questions of social organization and political direction. (Piccone 116)

The first passage was written by Allan Bloom, and the second was written by Paul Piccone—two writers who hold diametrically opposed conservative and progressive views on university education but who share an increasingly widespread dissatisfaction with the myopic over-specialization of most academic disciplines. Despite the wide range of disagreement between conservatives and progressives in the academy, the undesirability of over-specialization is one thing that both sides can agree on. The university curriculum should be a site in which different perspectives—political and intellectual positions—can confront one another. One result of over-specialization is that political and intellectual conflicts among faculty and students are displaced to the level of administration. Instead of a situation in which colleagues with different political, intellectual, and institutional positions debate specific issues, the power struggles are hidden behind closed doors as administrators negotiate funding levels. The net effect of this displacement is a systemic retardation of intellectual vitality.

I came face to face with just this sort of crippling effect of over-specialization in my own institution recently when one of my English department colleagues submitted a new course proposal for a graduate level cultural studies course—Introduction to Cultural Theory—to the university curriculum committee. The Communications department protested the proposal, and a committee of four English faculty, including myself, met with a committee of four Communications faculty in a special meeting, chaired by a member of the university curriculum committee, to see if we could amicably work out the objections to the course. At the meeting I was surprised to learn that the Communications department objected to the English department offering such a course because, they argued, "literature" was our proper area, and "media"—which they took to be the purview of cultural studies—was theirs. We should stick to "literature," they suggested, and they would teach "media." We explained to our colleagues from Communications that we see our field as somewhat wider than that of "literature," that we're not sure what "literature" is anyway, and that, in any event, we think it's necessary to read what is not "literature" in order to understand what is "literature." Furthermore, we argued, since cultural studies is by definition a field that crosses disciplinary boundaries, the courses should be taught in more than one department—we would have no general objection to cultural studies courses offered by the Communications department. They responded that this sort of intellectual quibbling was fine for the amusement of faculty arguing in coffee rooms or writing in scholarly journals, but that what was really at stake here was a real-world academic turf battle—and "cultural studies" was their turf. So neither side gave any ground, and this conflict was bumped upstairs to be settled by the university curriculum committee. The university curriculum committee eventually decided in our favor. Nonetheless, I think it's unfortunate that our institutional structures discourage public debates on these kinds of curricular conflicts. In this particular instance, the objection rested on such flimsy intellectual grounds that it probably wouldn't have been made in a forum open to a general audience of faculty and students. This is "academic politics" with a vengeance. The flimsiness of the objection itself is merely a symptomatic effect of a sloppy pluralistic institutional structure that discourages the political conflict of serious intellectual debate.

If a curriculum based on liberal pluralism seems inadequate to the development of critical literacy from a left perspective, it is no more attractive to the right. The neoconservative response to the problem of over-specialization was inaugurated several years ago by William Bennett's call for limiting pluralism and establishing a coherent, traditional curriculum based on the classic texts of Western civilization—a version of the "great books" curriculum. Bennett assumes that the most important function of humanities education is to pass on a common legacy of Western civilization to all college students. He describes this canonical tradition, in terms adapted from Matthew Arnold, as "the best that has been thought, written, or otherwise expressed about the human experience" (3). Some obvious objections to this goal are that this legacy isn't, in fact, "common" to all American citizens, that it leaves out a good deal of human experience, and that to subject students from oppressed social groups to an unqualified celebration of this tradition amounts to cultural imperialism. On the other hand, the classics of Western civilization represent an important body of cultural capital to which all students should be given access. The more urgent question may be not *what* should be taught, but *how* it should be taught. As Gerald Graff has pointed out, "a Shakespeare text taught by Bennett would bear small resemblance to the same text taught by [Terry] Eagleton" ("What Should We Be Teaching" 193). At its best, that is, critical theory requires a rigorously critical approach to whatever is taught. Similarly, cultural studies specifically attempts to promote a critical, oppositional engagement with traditional culture, often by juxtaposing texts and perspectives of non-Western and suppressed cultural traditions to those of the European canonical tradition.

The main obstacles to a unified, coherent curriculum, as the conservatives see it, are "politicized" transdisciplinary movements that often have the effect of breaking down the walls between traditional disciplines: feminism, with its primary focus on gender as a category that is more significant than any particular discipline, and multiculturalism, which seeks a curriculum that would be more reflective of and responsive to the experiences of minorities. But women's studies and ethnic studies programs actually tend to work against over-specialization by enlarging the area of general interaction among disciplines. Here the neoconservatives have a blind spot that corresponds to their blindness to the true source of the crisis facing traditional literature. The most serious obstacle to a unified traditional curriculum is the proliferation of and increasing importance given to technical, professional, and vocational education within the university, though this development is almost always unnoticed by the conservative critics. Among radical teachers, on the other hand, the presence of technical and vocational programs within the university, and the presence of such courses within English departments, should be seen as opportunities and institutional contexts for challenging the corporate-sector values and practices that characterize these programs. We need to develop curricular structures within our departments in which a debate among positions representing different value-systems and social and professional paradigms can be carried on.

Amid the ongoing controversy about the ways that intellectual and political forces like critical theory, feminism, and multiculturalism are changing the English curriculum, one of the most powerful forces for change has received the least attention—the students. In demographic and economic terms, the academy is being asked to educate different students, and for different purposes, than was the case forty or even twenty years ago. More of our students are non-traditional college students—minority students, recent immigrants, first-generation college students from working-class backgrounds, and older, returning students. English departments are being called upon to provide a wider variety of services—including training in critical thinking, writing and rhetoric, and exposure to traditional cultural values—to students whose main purpose for attending the university is to gain specific and directly applicable training for employment. Thus, in addition to the benefits in intellectual rigor and political accountability to be gained from an ongoing critical engagement between faculty teaching technical-vocational and service courses and faculty teaching traditional humanities courses, these courses offer us access to groups of students—particularly working-class students and African-American students—who often shun the humanities majors in favor of majors offering more immediate and more lucrative career opportunities.

There are some formidable obstacles to a critical engagement between literature faculty and faculty teaching technical-vocational and service courses in English departments. Cross-disciplinary interaction is always difficult to achieve and maintain in the academy because of the institutional forces for specialization that I mentioned earlier. But in this situation that problem is compounded by the overlay of institutional status hierarchy. There is a persistent attitude among literature faculty that those who teach rhetoric, composition, technical-professional writing, or English for speakers of other languages are people who would rather be teaching literature but don't "have what it takes" (whatever that is). This attitude is generally reinforced by the uneven distribution of institutional resources, rewards, and prestige among the different subdisciplines of English studies. The professional environment strikes me as a close parody of a feudal society—the literature teachers are the "aristocrats," living off the appropriated surplus labor of the "peasants"— teaching assistants, part-time and temporary faculty, and teachers of marginalized courses. And "literature" performs some of the same functions for us that it performed for the feudal aristocracy—it confirms (for us) that our exalted professional status is the natural result of our cultural superiority.

The first move toward changing this crippling status hierarchy is to begin to treat our marginalized colleagues with more respect. By this I don't mean that literature faculty should accept uncritically the value or credibility of the marginalized positions. Quasi-professional technical and vocational programs in the universities valorize themselves as academic disciplines precisely on the basis of their association with traditional academic disciplines. Too often, we have allowed them to enter that arena without demanding the price of admission—an engaged participation in the ongoing intellectual debate over social and cultural values. Any course of study within the university should be held accountable for its fundamental aims and purposes in relation to the aims and purposes of other disciplines and programs within the university and in relation to the general aims of education in a democratic society. Departmental and disciplinary boundaries are not easily crossed, but the multi-disciplinary structures of many English departments offer viable starting points for transdisciplinary work. If literature teachers can begin to engage seriously the too-frequently ignored teachers and students of technical and vocationally oriented courses in our own departments, eventually, perhaps, we can develop ways to interact more directly with those in other departments as well.

My use of the term "transdisciplinary" instead of the more familiar term "interdisciplinary" marks an important distinction. "Transdisciplinary" scholarship and pedagogy goes beyond a common practice of "interdisciplinary" work that merely appropriates knowledge produced in one discipline for use in another discipline without questioning the basic assumptions, or conceptual frameworks, of either discipline. "Transdisciplinarity," as it has been described by Mas'ud Zavarzadeh and Donald Morton,

> is aware of the status of knowledge as one of the modes of ideological construction of reality in any given discipline; through its self-reflexivity, it attempts not simply to accumulate knowledge but to ask what constitutes knowledge, why and how and by whose authority certain modes of understanding are certified as knowledge and others as para-knowledge or non-knowledge. (10)

Transdisciplinary pedagogy is not a matter of ignoring existing disciplinary knowledge, or of merely substituting some other body of knowledge for, say, an existing literary canon. Instead, it constitutes what Dominick LaCapra calls a "transformative endeavor" that requires an "intimate knowledge of the disciplines and the related canons or disciplinary practices one is criticizing and attempting to refashion, including the sometimes valid resistances to change that they may pose." The goal of such work "is not to valorize 'blurred genres' in general," but to explore connections that appear blurred only from within narrow disciplinary frameworks (5). What LaCapra terms the "transformative endeavor" identifies what I see as the theoretical challenge to open literary study up to transdisciplinary and counter-disciplinary paradigms. We need to break down disciplinary barriers that have the effect of trivializing the work of the scholar/teacher by narrowing the range of questions that can be addressed. This will require teachers and students habituated to the narrow specializations of our discipline to make a deliberate and concerted effort to broaden their perspectives, but the rewards—both political and intellectual—will be worth the effort.

CHANGING THE CURRICULUM

The English department at Illinois State University, where I teach, is a large, multi-purpose department. In addition to traditional literary studies, courses in literary theory, film, cultural studies, children's literature, women in liter-

ature, and African-American literature, we offer a specialization in English
education for secondary teachers; we offer technical and professional writing courses at both the graduate and undergraduate levels; we offer linguistics courses and courses in English as a second language at both the undergraduate and graduate levels with an optional master's degree emphasis in
TESOL; and we have a large composition-rhetoric program. Yet our undergraduate curriculum remains literature-centered. Our writing courses, our linguistics courses, and our English education courses are relegated to the margins of the curriculum, while the core of traditional literature remains
relatively undisturbed. All students are required to take two introductory
courses in literary genres and a senior seminar designed as a "capstone"
course, looking back at the courses the student has taken. Students are
encouraged to take a chronologically distributed sampling of six courses in
English and American literature. This leaves room for two or three electives,
which could be in literary theory, rhetoric, creative writing, technical writing, or linguistics. The English education majors, training to be high school
teachers, are routinely exempted from the full complement of English and
American literature in order to make room for required education courses.

In respect to this curriculum, I think the opposition of theory vs. literature
is largely irrelevant—just a family squabble among a fairly narrow sector of
the department. What the current curriculum suppresses are oppositions like
literature (including literary theory) vs. rhetoric, literature vs. composition,
literature vs. linguistics, literature vs. technical writing, etc. My department's
curriculum, and the problems that attend it, are typical and symptomatic of
curricula and problems found in many other English departments. The literature-centered focus of our curricula and our departmental organizational
structures inhibit our theoretical self-consciousness and our ability to engage
each other in serious debate. This affects our scholarship as well as our teaching. For instance, among all of the excellent work in postcolonial criticism
and theory from literary and cultural studies scholars in the past ten years or
so, I haven't encountered any mention of the ongoing effects of cultural imperialism reproduced in our ESL programs. I have read many brilliant critiques
of colonialist ideology focusing on canonical works, non-literary documents,
and popular culture, but none of the postcolonial critics is thinking about the
issue of cultural imperialism in ESL. The work published in *TESOL Quarterly,*
meanwhile, tends to be positivistic and apolitical, though there have been
some recent efforts to bring the insights of literary theory and cultural studies to bear on TESOL issues, and the newsletter *TESOL Matters* provides an
informal forum for geopolitical issues.[3] But teachers of literature should be
putting pressure on teachers of ESL, and vice versa. If the emergence of postcolonial and subaltern criticism in literary studies has no relation to the teaching of ESL in the academy, how can we expect such developments to have
any impact beyond the academy? As long as ESL remains a marginalized and

often ignored "service" function of English departments—or worse, a service program functioning autonomously apart from the English department—we are missing an opportunity for a productive critical engagement with these colleagues and students. Similar critiques can be—and have been—made of the relationship of composition and technical writing to literature in English departments. The point I want to emphasize here is that the ill effects produced by our traditional professional hierarchies go beyond the widely acknowledged problem of exploitation of graduate teaching assistants and adjunct faculty. The marginalization of these subdisciplines limits the scope of our critical and theoretical awareness as well.

To counter this intrinsic parochialism and elitism, we need curricula that would require all students to take a representative sample of the broader field of English Studies and that would systematically require students and faculty to think through the interrelations of various functional divisions (rhetoric, literature, cultural studies, applied and theoretical linguistics, technical and professional writing, etc.) and philosophical orientations (humanism, Marxism, aestheticism, logical positivism, feminism, etc.) within our departments and the discipline at large. Such conditions aren't reflected even in the course catalogs of departments that are often hailed and reviled as leaders in the theory revolution—Duke University, Brown University, and the University of California at Santa Cruz, for example—because the undergraduate English curricula at these institutions remain firmly literature-centered. In the curricula of these progressive elite institutions theory courses and literature courses coexist in an unproblematized pluralistic framework that can only be maintained in an environment uncontaminated by have-nots: classrooms free of students determined to get access to social power through the mastery of writing, technical communication, or language skills.

Some English departments have consciously restructured their curricula in attempts to limit the trivializing effects of pluralism, however. An interesting model is that of Carnegie Mellon University. From Carnegie Mellon's English department students can take degrees with emphases in creative writing, literary and cultural studies, and rhetorical studies, and the department offers separate majors in professional writing and technical writing. All of the students in these programs are required to take a core of four courses (Creative Writing students take a core of five courses). According to the university's undergraduate catalog, the core is designed to "include work in all three disciplinary areas of the department: creative writing, literary and cultural studies, and rhetoric" (192). The catalog recommends that all students take courses called "Survey of Forms" (fiction or poetry) and "Discursive Practices, Language, Structure, Signs" during their first semester in the major. In subsequent semesters students take courses entitled "Discourse and Historical Change" and "Reading Twentieth-Century Culture." Creative writing majors take both fiction and poetry courses in the "Survey of Forms" category.

At the time the new curriculum was established Gary Waller (then Head of Carnegie Mellon's English department) described it, in a somewhat self-consciously ironic parody of advertising hype, as "the first poststructuralist literary curriculum" (6). Waller's "packaging" of the curriculum as the latest-up-to-date-new-model English studies prompted Donald Morton and Mas'ud Zavarzadeh to characterize the change as a "recuperative, complicit curriculum":

> As befits his technocratic audience, Waller's rhetoric is that of an efficient manager concerned with the "application" of ideas (produced by others) and with "dovetailing" their various parts so that he can achieve a "breakthrough," producing the first (post)structural curriculum for (consumption in) the profession. Waller's proposed curriculum is purely and safely cognitive; the students are taught to "understand" but not to "intervene." (23)

This critique was not unwarranted, particularly in view of the way Waller was capitalizing on the "new and improved" image of Carnegie Mellon's curriculum while down-playing the potential political implications of the change. Nonetheless, there are some significant gains here. By requiring all students to be familiar with a variety of discursive strategies, Carnegie Mellon's curriculum displaces literary formalism from its center. And it seems designed to give all students some exposure to skills of ideology critique in courses such as "Reading Twentieth-Century Culture" and "Discourse and Historical Analysis." One wonders, however, whether the students experience the discursive paradigms of the different required courses as discrete bodies of knowledge or as transdisciplinary fields of discourse that often overlap and contest each other.

One way of restructuring a curriculum to foreground contestatory relations among various discursive fields is that of the new English and Textual Studies major at Syracuse University, where I was formerly a graduate student. The department's course catalog description of the new curriculum bears quoting at length:

> The new curriculum is organized not by coverage of a literary or critical canon but by a focus on the problematics of reading and writing texts. Such a curriculum attempts to distinguish between a traditional pluralism, in which there are many separate viewpoints and each exists without locating itself in relation to opposing viewpoints, and a multiplicity of positions, each of which acknowledges its allied or contestatory relation to other positions. The purpose of a curriculum based on the latter model is not to impose one way of knowing on everyone but to make the differences between ways of knowing visible and to foreground what is at stake in one way of knowing over and against another. The goal is to make students aware of how knowledge is produced and how reading takes place and thus to make them capable of playing an active and critical role in their society, enabling them to intervene in the dominant discourses of their culture.

The Syracuse curriculum can be schematized as a triangle with groups of courses clustered under three distinct modes of inquiry: historical, political, and theoretical. Students begin by taking two introductory courses, entitled "Reading and Interpretation I: From Language to Discourse," and "Reading and Interpretation II: Practices of Reading." Then they are required to take two courses each from two groups, one course from the remaining group, and three courses of electives that can be from any of the groups, or chosen from creative writing or advanced expository writing courses that are not in any group.

What is particularly valuable about the Syracuse curriculum, in my view, is that it self-consciously attempts to place different intellectual positions in contestatory relation to each other. One aspect I find disappointing, however, is that the Syracuse program remains entirely literature- and culture-focused. The composition and rhetoric program was separated from the English department as part of the transformation from "English" to "English and Textual Studies." The technical writing program was always small and marginalized at Syracuse, and it seems to have been entirely left out of this new curriculum, as does the creative writing program. I don't know the exact reasons for these exclusions, though I know enough of the departmental political battles at Syracuse to suspect that the story is much too long to go into here. Instead, humbly acknowledging that it's much easier to propose a curricular change than to get one approved by an entire department, I want to sketch out a variation of the Syracuse triangle as it might be adapted for the department I teach in at Illinois State:

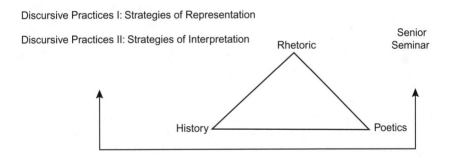

Discursive Practices I: Strategies of Representation

Discursive Practices II: Strategies of Interpretation   Rhetoric   Senior Seminar

History   Poetics

The corners of the triangle represent "history," "rhetoric," and "poetics," respectively. Each student would enter the major by taking two required introductory courses of three credit hours each: Strategies of Representation and Strategies of Interpretation. In these introductory courses attention should be given to a full range of discourses practiced in the English department—linguistics, literature, rhetoric, technical communication, etc. Then students would proceed into the triangle: here each student would take 18 hours on one corner and six hours each on the other two corners. All students would be required to sample from each of the three major divisions. Finally, all students would take the senior seminar, as is now required, for a total of 40 hours.

The broad categories of history, rhetoric, and poetics are intended at once to correspond to and in some ways to disrupt our current divisions. Some existing courses could be adapted to fit in these divisions. Our current genre courses and creative writing courses might fit under poetics, while the composition, rhetoric, and technical writing courses would generally go under rhetoric. Conventional period surveys of literature might ordinarily fit under the history rubric. Literary theory courses would go under the poetics category; rhetorical theory courses would go under the rhetoric category. But a key goal of this curriculum would be to displace literature from its center in order to allow new conjunctions and juxtapositions of such fields as technical writing, cultural studies, and literature. Hence, such a curriculum would require a rethinking of the goals and assumptions of existing courses.

All course syllabi should be self-conscious about the paradigms of knowledge and value that frame and enable their construction, and all courses should acknowledge their boundaries and boundary-crossings in relation to the discursive paradigms of other courses. My hope would be for the emergence of new courses designed specifically to engage the particular problems and issues that constitute two or more categories. For instance, I recently team-taught a course entitled "The Concept of Authorship and the Problems of Literary Authority" with a member of our technical writing faculty. We investigated issues of authorship and authority in ways that foregrounded the conflicts among various historical, political, and theoretical perspectives. At least partly because of the inclusion of a technical writing perspective in the course, we gave considerable attention to changes in the material conditions of authorship arising from the transition from manuscript culture to print culture and from the uneven but steady growth of literacy over the past few centuries in England. In addition, we attracted an unusually diverse mix of literature-oriented and technical writing-oriented students who came to the class with conflicting assumptions and expectations. This required constant adjustments of emphasis and produced a heightened sense of perspectival limits for both the students and the teachers. Or, for another example, we have a special topics course entitled "The Rhetoric of History and the History of Rhetoric," team-taught by a member of our rhetoric faculty and a colleague from the History department. I can envision a course exploring the consequences and parameters of English as an "international" language that would examine international uses of English in different economic, political, and cultural contexts, and that could put the values and assumptions of ESL, technical writing, and postcolonial subaltern theory in productive interaction with each other. Such courses should aim to address the potential conflicts and interrelationships among different discourses within the broader field of English studies.

In the triangulated curriculum, courses specifically designed to investigate the interrelationships of different discourses would be encouraged, but regulated. In these instances I would have the professor(s) develop a syllabus that demonstrably addresses the cross-sectional implications of the course, and have such courses certified as counting either way for students. The department's curriculum committee (constituted in a way that includes faculty who identify themselves as representatives from the various corners of the triangle) would arbitrate the designations. My intention here would be to reward cross-sectional courses by making such courses more attractive to students. Finally, I would set up an ongoing colloquium series on topics of broad interest among the various subdisciplines of English studies, and require students from the introductory sections and the senior seminar to attend and participate in these colloquia each semester.

In addition to the aim of requiring students to be exposed to a broader cross-section of English studies and encouraging them to consider the interrelations of various positions and orientations within the field, another goal of this curricular model would be to encourage us as faculty to interact more directly with each other. There would still, of course, be room for professors who prefer not to interact to teach in relative isolation, on one corner of the triangle. But there would also be expanded opportunities (and a sort of informal intellectual reward in the form of a heightened atmosphere of collegial discussion) for those who wish to teach in the interactive model.

This, of course, is just one of many possible patterns and many different rubrics for the various subdisciplines within an English curriculum that could be devised for different local situations. The number of subdisciplines and their names is not as important as is the need for them to be put in productively interactive relationship to each other. The teaching of literature, rhetoric, and cultural studies should be viewed as a discursive arena in which intellectuals can develop a sustained critique of existing social values through which a critical literacy can be produced. Above all, the study of literature as the uncritical cultivation of aesthetic appreciation or the unreflective transmission of values—whether progressive or conservative—should be avoided.

I know from discussions with colleagues in my own department and other departments that the kinds of curricular changes I am calling for will encounter resistance and skepticism from those—including theorists and many radicals and progressives—who are comfortable with the current dominant hierarchy of privilege within the discipline. After viewing my Illinois State triangle plan one of my colleagues observed that such a change would leave him, as a literature teacher, completely out of the department's mission. When I pointed out to him that the curriculum I am proposing still gives primary emphasis to literature in at least two-thirds of the curriculum (the history and poetics corners of the triangle) he was genuinely surprised, though not exactly persuaded. The fact is, in his mind the department's mission is the teaching of literature, and everything else we do is just incidental. Or literature is the center around which various satellites such as technical writing, composition, and linguistics orbit. Yet this model for the department marginalizes about one-third of the faculty—of approximately forty-five tenured and tenure-track members of our department, only thirty or so teach literature.

Nonetheless, I must acknowledge, the curriculum I have outlined is really only a very modest beginning toward the development of an open-ended critique of values and power relations that could resist the considerable pressures for the human sciences to serve uncritically the changing needs of the late capitalist global labor market. Juxtaposing subdisciplinary discourses as I have suggested will not necessarily lead to a critique of what we are being asked to do. The changes I am recommending could produce a public, institutional arena for literature teachers to talk with teachers of composition, rhetoric, technical and professional writing, ESL, English education, etc., about our interrelated roles and responsibilities in the production of educated citizens. However, we would still face the difficult task of learning how to talk to each other, and, yet more difficult, how to critique each other's positions.

The task at hand for English teachers of all specializations is to recognize that our work is already highly politicized and to exploit that condition. Conflicting political demands are being made upon us in the form of the neoconservative call for us to guard the gates of traditional high culture, and in the form of the corporate labor market pressure for us to give students skills training without critical consciousness-raising. Our success in resisting these pressures will be limited unless we can change our curricular and other departmental structures to allow, even to require, full participation in the academic life of the department by all faculty, including those teaching the presently marginalized and devalued "service" courses. It is up to us to find new ways to engage all students and faculty in the debate on culture and social values at as high a level of sophistication and intellectual rigor as possible.

NOTES

1. See, for example, Bennett, Bloom, Hirsch, Kimball, and Sykes. Many literary scholars have observed (and some have documented extensively) the extent to which the claim that literature transcends politics supports a conservative political agenda. See, for example, Widdowson et al.; Baldick; Eagleton, *Literary Theory* (esp. Ch. 1) and "The Subject of Literature"; Stimpson; Graff, *Professing Literature;* and Zavarzadeh and Morton.

2. The one neoconservative writer who has given most attention to these economic pressures against traditional literary study is Alvin Kernan, in *The Death of Literature.* Yet, even after a detailed and informative analysis of the social and economic forces arrayed against traditional cultural values, Kernan returns to attack deconstruction and poststructural theory in a highly oversimplified critique at the end of his book.

3. See, for example, Peirce; Pennycook, "The Concept of Method"; and the ex-

change in *TESOL Quarterly* between McCall and Pennycook, "The Author Responds."
In addition, the newsletter *TESOL Matters* provides an informal forum for debate on
geopolitical concerns.

WORKS CITED

Baldick, Chris. *The Social Mission of English Criticism.* Oxford: Oxford UP, 1983.
Bennett, William. *To Reclaim a Legacy: A Report on the Humanities in Higher Edu-
cation.* Washington: NEH, 1984.
Bloom, Allan. *The Closing of the American Mind: How Higher Education Has Failed
Democracy and Impoverished the Souls of Today's Students.* New York: Simon
and Schuster, 1987.
Carnegie Mellon University. *Undergraduate Catalogue,* 1990–91.
Eagleton, Terry. *Literary Theory: An Introduction.* Minneapolis: U of Minnesota P, 1985.
———. "The Subject of Literature." *Cultural Critique* 2 (1986): 98–110.
Graff, Gerald. *Professing Literature:* Chicago: U of Chicago P, 1988.
———. "What Should We Be Teaching—When There's No 'We'?" *Yale Journal of
Criticism* 1 (1987):
Hirsch, E. D., Jr. *Cultural Literacy: What Every American Needs to Know.* Boston:
Houghton Mifflin, 1987.
Kernan, Alvin. *The Death of Literature.* New Haven: Yale UP, 1990.
Kimball, Roger. *Tenured Radicals.* New York: Simon and Schuster, 1989.
LaCapra, Dominick. "On the Line: Between History and Criticism." *Profession 89.*
New York: MLA, 1989.
McCall, Martha. "Comments on Alistair Pennycook's 'The Concept of Method, Inter-
ested Knowledge, and the Politics of Language Teaching': A Reader Reacts." *TESOL
Quarterly* 25 (1991): 745–48.
Peirce, Bronwyn Norton. "Toward a Pedagogy of Possibility in the Teaching of English
Internationally: People's English in South Africa." *TESOL Quarterly* 23 (1989): 401–20.
Pennycook, Alistair. "The Concept of Method, Interested Knowledge, and the Politics
of Language Teaching." *TESOL Quarterly* 23 (1989): 589–618.
———. "The Author Responds." *TESOL Quarterly* 25 (1991): 749–53.
Piccone, Paul. "Symposium: Intellectuals in the 1980's." *Telos* 50 (Winter 1981–82).
Stimpson, Catherine. *Where the Meanings Are: Feminism and Cultural Spaces.* New
York: Routledge, Chapman and Hall, 1988.
Sykes, Charles. *Profscam: Professors and the Demise of Higher Education.* Wash-
ington: Regnery Gateway, 1988.
Syracuse University English Department. Unpublished departmental announcement.
Fall 1990.
Waller, Gary. "Working with the Paradigm Shift: Poststructuralism and the College
Curriculum." *ADE Bulletin* 81 (Fall 1985): 6–12
Widdowson, Peter, et al. *Re-Reading English.* London: Methuen, 1982.
Zavarzadeh, Mas'ud, and Donald Morton. "Theory, Pedagogy, Politics: The Crisis of
the 'Subject' in the Humanities." *Theory Pedagogy Politics: Texts for Change.* Ed.
Zavarzadeh and Morton. Urbana: U of Illinois P, 1992.

6

Brown v. Higher Education: Pedagogy, Cultural Politics, and Latina/o Activism

Ralph E. Rodriguez

In the landmark decision of *Brown v. Board of Education, Topeka, Kansas* (1954), the Supreme Court unanimously declared school segregation unconstitutional, striking down the "separate but equal" precedent set in 1896 with *Plessy v. Ferguson.* The Court's opinion on this case notes the important connections between democracy and education. The author of the opinion, Chief Justice Earl Warren, declared that,

> Today, education is perhaps the most important function of state and local governments. Compulsory school attendance laws and the great expenditures for education both demonstrate our recognition of the importance of education to our democratic society. It is required in the performance of our most basic public responsibilities, even service in the armed forces. It is the very foundation of good citizenship. Today it is a principal instrument in awakening the child to cultural values, in preparing him for later professional training, and in helping him to adjust normally to his environment. In these days, it is doubtful that any child may reasonably be expected to succeed in life if he is denied the opportunity of an education. Such an opportunity, where the state has undertaken to provide it, is a right which must be made available to all on equal terms. (1954)

Chief Justice Warren makes patently clear two issues key to educational theory. First, schools serve as institutions of social reproduction (of the making of disciplined and responsible citizens) and second, the fulfillment of democratic ideals hinges on access to a quality education. The tension between these two ideals—reproducing citizens and promoting democratic principles—seems to be lost on the Court, but this does not immediately concern

us. The Court's clear acknowledgement of the bonds between educational
access and the realization of democracy is the crucial point here. Although
economic impediments too often structure who will have access to and be
able to succeed in college, these encumbrances do not categorically defy
being successfully negotiated. Indeed, the barriers Latina/os face in the university system[1] and the strategies they employ to negotiate these obstacles
form the focus of this chapter. While some scholars of Latina/o life and culture have directed their attention to these pedagogical and political matters,
the persistence of a racial achievement gap among Latina/o students mandates that we pursue venues to improve the education of these students.

The "Brown" in my title refers, then, not to Linda Brown of Topeka, Kansas,
but rather metonymically to the collective U.S. Latina population. In this case,
the "Board of Education" is not the defendant, but rather higher education in
general. Latina/os (Puerto Ricans and Chicana/os in particular) find themselves chafing against the strictures of higher education in this particular
courtroom drama. Nearly a half century has passed since the Supreme Court
mandated that schools realize their democratic potentials, yet we still find
Latina/os struggling to gain access to a college education, fighting to have
their histories and cultures represented in the curricula, and encountering
numerous hurdles on their quest for self-determination. While that renowned
1954 Supreme Court decision ruled educational segregation unconstitutional, "We are," to quote Dorothy in *The Wizard of Oz,* "a long way from
Kansas now, Toto."

Reporting for the *Chronicle of Higher Education* on a study of Hispanics in
higher education, for instance, Scott Carlson (1999) employs a rhetoric that
suggests that Latina/os choose to go to the least selective universities or community colleges.[2] Too frequently, the author (perhaps adopting language from
the study itself) uses phrases like "tend to enroll in the least selective colleges"
or "are not keeping up with white or Asian Americans in enrolling in competitive colleges and universities." Statements like these rhetorically shift the
onus away from institutional impediments and onto Latina/o students. The
rhetoric bears, in other words, that far too common strategy of blaming the
victim. Paragraph after paragraph, the article questions not the institutional
and economic structures that bar Latina/os from pursuing college degrees, but
rather implies that students lack the motivation to attend prestigious universities or community colleges. Only in the final paragraph does the article
briefly address the racial, gender, and socioeconomic biases in standardized
testing. It, however, never makes an attempt to account for the scarcity of
resources for inner-city schools, the continued assaults on bilingual education,
and/or the complexity of urban politics and how these factors impinge on the
elementary and secondary education of Hispanic students.[3] Finally, the article's argument implicitly degrades the value of a college education at anyplace
except the most elite campus. The article's arrogance and absences remind us

that for Latina/o youth education remains, to borrow a phrase from Stanley Aronowitz and Henry Giroux (1993), under siege.

As Giroux (1996) and other radical pedagogists and cultural theorists have eloquently argued, the current state of transnational capital and of the corporatized educational system has shifted education from a public to a private good. Under a market-driven education, courses in Latina/o Studies are often devalued because they do little to train students for the corporate marketplace. Or in a worse case scenario, when these courses steer away from fulfilling their radical democratic potential, they may serve as little more than training grounds for corporations.[4] They help produce more efficient managers capable of dealing with an ethnically diverse workforce or cosmopolitan entrepreneurs prepared to transact business with international clients. When multicultural courses neglect to articulate their subject matter to the larger socioeconomic structures and material conditions of the communities' lives they study, they often simply provide students with the false sense that they have mastered the community they are examining. This complacency offers an arrogant comfort that suggests the students now understand how "those people" live. Thus, students may presume they can now relate to, work with, and/or more efficiently manage these "others."

We must not, however, surrender ourselves to the corporate university, the precipitously high drop out rate of Latina/o high school students,[5] or the ill-informed critiques that Hispanics "choose" to go to the least selective universities. Nor, however, should we uncritically accept all proposed solutions to the current crisis in Latina/o education or prepare to raise the flag of victory. Hard times await us. Notwithstanding thirty plus years of Latina/o activism, we find ourselves struggling for social justice in the public sphere, and I suspect that most of us find ourselves embroiled in struggles with our respective universities not only to increase efforts to recruit Latina/o students, but also to retain them. While recruitment efforts have improved some over the years, universities typically have problems retaining Latina/o students. These matters must be taken seriously, for education, as Chief Justice Warren so poignantly observed, underlies the foundation of a radical democracy, capable of providing opportunities for all. To achieve these goals, educators and students must find a "language of possibility," not of defeat and cynicism. "We invent," assert Aronowitz and Giroux, "a language of possibility that proposes extensive philosophic and programmatic changes in education only if we can imagine a public sphere within which alternatives are seriously considered. Epistemologically, the challenge of critique turns in on itself and loses its emancipatory character when political imagination has disappeared" (1993, 24). To maintain that political imagination and to achieve an egalitarian public sphere requires a clear understanding of the obstacles encountered along the way.

In struggling against these obstacles, student activist organizations such as

El Movimiento Estudiantil Chicana/o de Aztlán (MEChA), I will argue, can play a key role. I have now been a member of or faculty mentor to MEChA at three different institutions, with quite distinct student populations. Those universities include University of Texas (UT) at Austin (where I did my graduate work and first really became active in MEChA), Oregon State University (OSU), and Pennsylvania State University (PSU) (where I have served as an informal faculty advisor to these schools' MEChA chapters). Rather than merely celebrate these student activists' efforts, I want to examine the general success and failure of various strategies these activists have deployed to ensure educational self-determination. With the aim of enhancing successful strategies and abandoning less fruitful ones, I want to identify and analyze the tactics Latina/o student groups use to build community on campuses and to combat institutional attacks. We must seriously consider the changing political and educational environments in which we work and study, for they affect our own organizing strategies. This chapter attempts to abet our struggles.

CULTURAL STUDIES, CRITICAL PEDAGOGY, AND THE RACIAL ACHIEVEMENT GAP

Aiming to reclaim and democratize higher education, we may find it instructive to look not only at the history of various Latina/o social movements, but also to draw on the lessons of cultural studies and radical pedagogy. As many readers will recall, the Center for Contemporary Cultural Studies (CCCS) in Birmingham, England, had its roots in adult education. Many of the founding members—Richard Hoggart, E. P. Thompson, and Raymond Williams— began their critical work offering classes to folks who had been, as Lawrence Grossberg points out, " 'blocked from' any higher education" (1997, 375). In educational and class terms, these academic/activists served populations that were not unlike the Chicana/o and Latina/o student base discussed in this chapter. Thus, adopting some of the strategies and lessons of this cultural studies model and understanding how educational theorists and cultural critics have adopted and refined it can ultimately prove beneficial in understanding and challenging the barriers Latina/os face in the university system. As Stuart Hall enjoins us, however, we must remember that "theory is only a detour on the way to something more important" (quoted in Grossberg 1997, 385). We must be able to theorize our positions in order to work expeditiously and critically, but we can never lose sight of the prize. To theorize in the absence of a concrete project will never get us to that critical juncture, where we might realize the radical potential of education and democracy. However, we must also bear in mind that a critical theory, informing and informed by a clearly defined project, remains invaluable.

Richard Johnson argues that a student-centered and self-reflexive pedagogy has long been key to cultural studies in Britain. He maintains that there has been "a strong tradition, within the teaching of Cultural Studies in the academy, of encouraging students to work on issues which are important to them personally, with which the are already engaged, which 'bug them' " (1997, 53). This desire to study personally relevant subjects sparked the student blowouts in Los Angeles in 1968. Led by Sal Castro, a number of Chicana/o high school students went on strike because the curricula at their high schools failed to consider Chicana/os' history and contributions to American culture. The very issues Johnson highlights, that is, comprised the core of various Latina/o social movements during the civil rights era. Foundational documents of the Chicano movement such as *El Plan Espiritual de Aztlán* or *El Plan de Santa Barbara*[6] anticipate and resonate well with Johnson's feelings about student-centered learning. In the 1960s and 1970s, Latina/os and Chicana/os struggled for self-determination and an education they could find relevant to their daily lives.

El Plan de Santa Barbara makes manifestly clear the importance of education in the struggle for self-determination: "We recognize that without a strategic use of education, an education that places value on what we value, we will not realize our destiny. Chicanos recognize the central importance of institutions of higher learning to modern progress, in this case, to the development of our community. But we go further: we believe that higher education must contribute to the information of a complete man who truly values life and freedom" (Muñoz 1989, 192). Then as now, Latina/o student activists have made and continue to make successful inroads into higher education. While these social movements have dramatically impacted education at all levels, however, we need to understand a key problem Latina/o students faced and continue to face, namely, the way education can rupture as well as empower.

Until we appreciate this dilemma, we cannot fruitfully analyze the roles student activists can play in reshaping higher education. In his essay "Troublemakers," Rolando Romero details the contours of this educational double bind:

By providing a way out of the barrio, it [education] also furnishes the tools of detachment from the community. And herein lies the ambivalence towards education, the Latino source of both desires and fears. Unfortunately universities have traditionally played into this ambivalence in their inability to understand the dynamics and metaphors of representation within their own institutions. Time and again the cultural academic text continues to provide a receptacle for the projection of everybody's fears: Latinos' fear of "losing" their identity, the dominant culture's fear that its "standards" will be diminished by their ambivalent Other. As long as the institution denies access, then Latinos will appropriately reject the educational institution. (1997, 217)

Many primary and secondary school teachers' racist attitudes compound these students' ambivalence. Latina/o students find themselves pinned between their own cultural fears and the xenophobic anxieties of the dominant school culture. Well before Latina/o students get to college, many educators and counselors have clearly signaled to them that they feel these students are inferior to their white middle- and upper-class counterparts. In "Disparities Demystified," for instance, Pedro A. Noguera and Antwi Akom (2000) illustrate how teachers' lowered expectations for students of color keep them from receiving a rigorous high school education, an education that would unequivocally prepare them for college.

> A large body of research has shown that students of color are more likely to be excluded from classes for those deemed gifted in primary school, and from honors and Advanced Placement (AP) courses in high school. The Education Trust has shown, through its research on science and math education, that even students of color who meet the criteria for access to advanced courses are more likely to be turned away based on the recommendation of a counselor or teacher. (30)

Not only are they turned away from courses that would guarantee them a strong start in college, but as Noguera and Akom note, "They are also more likely to be placed in remedial and special-education classes, and to be subject to varying forms of school discipline" (30).

Despite statistical evidence that demonstrates these students' strong intellectual capacities, racist conceptions of them cloud many educators' minds. Rather than see these students as capable and engaged, educators often view them as problems. Rather than push them ahead, they pull them down. The students' ambivalence about schooling combined with their teachers' lowered expectations help to create a racial achievement gap. Consider, for example, the case of Montclair, New Jersey, a city generally celebrated for its harmonious race relations and progressive politics. Nevertheless, even in this ostensible Eden the racial achievement gap strikingly manifests itself. "Despite their parents' financial success and advanced degrees," declares Lise Funderburg, "many black children are still testing lower than whites" (2000, 26). Citing a study of Montclair's public schools, Funderburg notes that "only 54 percent of black ninth graders scored above half of the total test-taking population on a recent standardized reading test, compared with 95 percent of white students. Math scores were only slightly closer" (26). The students' ambivalence, the teachers' lowered expectations, and the racial achievement gap that we witness time and again in the primary and secondary school system must be born in mind as a key context for discussing the role of pedagogy, cultural politics, and student activism at the university. Each of these factors influences the performance, attitude, and success of students of color in college.

Notwithstanding, or perhaps because of these obstacles, we must continue to struggle for and with our students of color to democratize schools and universities. Now is not the time to resign hope. Since I want to speak in as specific terms as possible, the remainder of this chapter will draw on my experiences as a student, educator, and activist at the university. Though the university comprises the focus of this chapter, I trust some of my arguments will resonate with the situation in secondary and primary schools. Indeed, much of my work has engaged directly with elementary and high schools. I begin with my experiences at UT Austin, where I was a graduate student from 1992 to 1997.

FROM THEORY TO ACTION

In the fall of 1992, I began work toward my doctoral degree in English with a specialization in Ethnic and Third World literatures. Louis Mendoza, a fellow graduate student and active member of the Texas Chicana/o community, encouraged me to attend a MEChA meeting with him. After that meeting, I became a more or less a regular member of MEChA as well as the Chicana/o Graduate Student Association (CGSA). Having read actively for several years in left cultural politics, these groups taught me about organizing and fighting for education as a public good and a democratic sphere. As I recount these struggles, I attempt to capture them as accurately and honestly as possible; they remain, however, my recollections. Other participants in these groups (and there were plenty) may remember them differently. I do not pretend to have the final insights on the events I recount nor a transparent access to them. I was one participant among many in these struggles and as such my recollections are located in and informed by my own experiences and subject formation.

Over the course of five years, both MEChA and CGSA participated in a number of educational and political campaigns. For the purpose of this chapter, I will focus on one protracted struggle around the formation of an educational resource center, which I believe represents well the types of struggles we engaged in as well as addresses the organizing strategies of a group of Chicana/o students in the Southwest. This example from Texas provides a valuable counterpoint to the subsequent examples that come from the Northwest and Northeast. The comparisons and contrasts among these three examples illuminate the benefits and drawbacks of certain strategies, the way geographic location influences student tactics, and, among other things, the difficulty and necessity of forming coalitions.

The Center for Mexican American Studies (CMAS) at UT Austin was founded in 1970 with Américo Paredes as its director. It was one of the first of its kind in the nation, and it represented the struggles of a number of student and faculty activists. This is not the time to recount the lengthy history of the center. Suffice it to say that by the time I arrived in Austin in 1992, the CMAS had already established its presence on campus, a presence that in 1992 felt vexed and conflicted. The seeds of discontent had been sown before I arrived, and they were about to bear fruit. A number of students undeniably felt that the Center and its then director were not as actively involved in the local Mexican

American community as the students hoped them to be. Since I entered at just about the climax of the strife, I am not in a position to make insightful assessments about the Center's or its director's involvement in the community, nor do I find it especially helpful in this instance to make that judgment. What remains critical here is that certain students and community members felt that the university and the Center needed to be more engaged with its Mexican American neighbors, neighbors separated from the college by Interstate 35, a dividing line, if you will, between the halls of academe and the community it purported to serve. Consequently, two student groups, MEChA and CGSA, came together in the spring of 1993 to develop a resource center in the heart of East Austin. This area houses a large population of African Americans and Mexican Americans, most of whom are from the working class.

Through the generosity and commitment of some local neighbors, we acquired the Quintanilla House, a historic landmark in East Austin.[7] After several meetings to determine the mission and the name of this new project, we transformed the Quintanilla House into the Barrio Student Resource Center (BSRC). To announce our presence and solicit the support and input of our new neighbors, many students, fluent in both English and Spanish, made door-to-door visits in the neighborhood. We also used more conventional publicity measures such as leaflets and brochures, and on May 1, 1993, we hosted an open house celebration to continue to forge clear alliances with the community and to help build bridges between the community and the university. Our brochures detailed the purpose of the BSRC as follows:

> The BSRC will be a site that will link the East Austin Community and the local universities. One of the purposes of the BSRC will be to facilitate communication and interaction between university students and members of the East Austin area in order to enrich both communities. The BSRC will provide college students with an opportunity to enhance their education by broadening their academic experience through community work. The Center's programs will contribute to the intellectual, cultural, and social growth of local students and community members.

The pedagogical drive of the Center was to help students not traditionally represented at universities prepare for and gain access to a college education. To that end, the Center conducted workshops on preparing for the Scholastic Assessment Test (SAT) and sessions about how to fill out financial aid forms. In addition, we hoped to allay any anxiety about higher education and to dispel myths about who could attend and succeed in college, so we visited local schools to discuss our experiences and to answer any questions students might have about higher education. The BSRC was well received, and I like to believe it helped a number of students find and pursue educational outlets that might otherwise have been closed off to them.

Within approximately two years, the BSRC lost the Quintanilla House to other community members who wanted to use the space for different ends. Members from the BSRC group attempted to identify and garner outside funding sources to keep the project going, but the Center soon folded. Even this particular project's limited life span (and again it bears noting that these student groups operated on multiple fronts and engaged with various other projects outside of the BSRC) can teach us much about student activism and the successes and failures of particular strategies.

In a geographic location such as Texas and at a university as large as UT Austin (approximately forty-five thousand students), students can organize and strategize in ways simply not possible in other locations. The examples from OSU and PSU that follow will make this clear. At UT Austin, a large population of Latina/o students, though by no means proportionate to the state's population, could be simply assumed. Consequently, students at the university could organize around professional, social, cultural, and/or political matters without necessarily having to engage with others whose interests fell outside theirs. For instance, the Hispanic Business Association could count on a significant membership that did not necessarily have to draw on the members of more politically oriented groups such as MEChA. Indeed, these groups could work quite successfully without any interactions between them. Thus, while some professional organizations maintained a much larger student base, there were still enough Chicana/o students to keep MEChA and CGSA active.

Even when groups like MEChA and CGSA work together on a project like the BSRC, one must consider the complications this coalitional work involves. While the two groups shared similar ideological beliefs about self-determination, social justice, and a commitment to drawing clear ties between the university and the local Mexican American community, they often found themselves at odds. MEChA, for instance, drew most of its student base from the undergraduate population, while the CGSA was exclusively a graduate student group. From time to time, then, concerns arose over whether the graduate students would co-opt the undergraduates' labor for their own ends, despite that we were working on a common project. In fact, I recall that a number of these power struggles arose around framing the mission and purpose of the BSRC. A ready answer does not exist to prevent these intragroup struggles from arising, yet recognizing up front that working collectively requires much care and trust helps build better group bonds. The aim is not to wipe out intragroup differences, for these often lead to productive conversations and help to revise outmoded organizational strategies. The point is to note that even in groups that share ethnic and political ties there are going to be ideological differences to iron out, so that everyone feels s/he shares a stake in the struggle. To mask these differences or to ask people to assume positions predicated on an essentialist ethnic or political identity prove deleterious to the group. These maskings pull things apart rather than together. If we are to learn anything from past struggles, we must remember, as Angie Chabrian-Dernersesian (1994) points out that the Chicana/o movement often asked a number of different Latina/os to efface their ethnic identities to advance the Chicano cause.[8] While what Gayartri Spivak calls a strategic essentialism may be necessary at times to advance a political agenda, too often fictitious or constructed scenarios lead to fictitious solutions, solutions that frustrate because they have not addressed a particular problem in all of its complexity.[9] What, then, can we learn about the strategies employed around the BSRC project?

First, it must be acknowledged that the folks involved in this project provided critical information to a secondary student population, whom our educational system has all too often neglected. Certainly students who took advantage of the tutoring hours at the BSRC received individual attention not available in school and became better critical thinkers. Further, financial aid and SAT workshops helped these students better understand how to negotiate much of the bureaucracy involved in receiving a college education. In bridging the racial achievement gap, none of these accomplishments should be trivialized. What, however, were some of the shortcomings of this particular project?

In the first place, the BSRC never intended to force structural changes in the educational system. Rather than question the very validity of standardized testing, for instance, we accepted the tests on their own terms and sought to help students improve their test-taking skills. Rather than force the issue about teachers' lowered expectations for students of color or question why schools with a limited property-tax base often provide substandard education relative to wealthier school districts, the BSRC sought to assist students with their homework and their oral and written communication skills. In short, the BSRC was not the revolution; it was a student- and community-run educational resource center. This is not to say that we never sought legislative changes through our elected representatives at the local, state, and federal levels, but to recognize that we had a limited goal of assisting a particular student population in a very local context. Driven by personal and political goals that a number of us learned from our studies in cultural politics, Chicana/o history, and rhetorical analysis, we sought to use our critical tools to have a material impact at a local level.

While the project achieved limited ends, it was well worth pursuing and proved mutually beneficial to the organizers and the students assisted. The implementation of similar resource centers throughout the country coupled with grassroots efforts to reform the very structures of our secondary and primary schools may very well help to narrow or perhaps close the racial achievement gap. Student activists attending universities such as UT Austin with significant numbers of students of color and progressive white allies are well positioned to launch these types of campaigns. What happens though to Chicana/o organizing when the home base moves away from traditional centers of Chicana/o student activism? What happens when we find ourselves not in Austin, San Antonio, Albuquerque, San Diego, Boulder, but in, say, Corvallis, Oregon, a town not known for its booming population of Chicana/o students.

My first professional job transplanted me from Austin to Corvallis, where the Department of English at OSU hired me as a nineteenth- and twentieth-century Americanist with a subspecialty in Mexican American literature and culture. I was fortunate to come in that year (1997) with Erlinda Gonzales-Berry, who was hired to head the recently established Ethnic Studies department. I also joined a number of very progressive faculty members already at OSU including, but certainly not limited to, Patti Sakurai, Linc Kessler, Laura Rice, Jenny Cornell, Tracy Daugherty, Jon Lewis, Marjorie Sandor, Kurt Peters, Rich Daniels, Matt Yurdana, Michael Ingramm, and Joan Gross, to name only a few. I hesitate to list more names because these lists can never be exhaustive, and thus someone is invariably slighted. These colleagues, many of whom had a very long institutional history with OSU, made invaluable mentors and allies. Despite their support and the close bonds we formed around political issues, I found myself in a location where the politics and constituencies varied dramatically from those in Texas. Perhaps a good friend's question encapsulates the experience best, "What are you doing teaching outside of Aztlán?"

With the move from Texas to Oregon, the Chicana/o student population shifted from the thousands to below five hundred. Even proportionate to the overall student body, the decrease was a dramatic one. The move from Austin to Corvallis also registered as a move away from a relatively large urban area to a town of fifty thousand, built more or less around the university; the only other major employer of note was Hewlett Packard. Finally, as the town's adumbrated French name implies, it is located in the "heart of the valley," and valleys are frequently prime agricultural sites. Thus, despite its geographical remove from the Southwest, it is no surprise that throughout the valley one finds a number of immigrants from Mexico, especially from Michoacan. Agribusiness has long built its success on the backs of immigrants.

As I would come to discover over my two years in Corvallis, though its numbers were limited, a very active Chicana/o and Latina/o student population thrived at OSU. The limited numbers of Latina/o students make this example and the following one at PSU productive contrasts to the UT, for when student numbers are limited, the organizational strategies must necessarily be revised. Chicana/o and Latina/o organizations at schools with relatively small numbers of Latina/os cannot afford not to work with one another on political projects. I shift here to the term "Latina/o" from "Chicana/o" because unlike at Texas, where groups could form themselves around a specific Latina/o identity, namely "Chicana/o," "Latina/o" better represents the diverse population of students at OSU. It also foregrounds the need for these students to come together under a larger umbrella term like "Latina/o." Latina/os at schools like OSU and PSU must emphasize coalitional work both within the Latino community and with other community organizations. While better cohesion among leftist groups in general is a desirable goal, it is absolutely imperative when there are only a few hundred Latina/o students on campus. Most of us recognize this need to build coalitions among Latina/o students, but forming these alliances proves much harder in practice than in theory. At times, it felt impossible to bring the Latina/o students at OSU together for a common cause.

At OSU, seven different university-recognized student groups draw on the Latina/o student base. These groups include the Society of Hispanic Professional Engineers, the Centro Cultural Cesar Chávez, Calmecac, Estudiantes Indigenas de las Americas, Baile con Mexico, MEChA, and Mixtitlan Danza y Teatro de OSU. As the groups' titles suggest, they are organized around professional, educational, political, and cultural themes. Moreover, many of the students participate in more than one of these groups. It would be naive, given the broad spectrum of interests these groups cover, to think that they could all unite in a common cause or causes. One would hope, however, to create solidarity among the groups and to effectively mobilize as many of them as possible in times of crisis. I maintained closest relations with MEChA, Calmecac (an educational outreach program), and the Centro Cultural (a headquarters more or less for the Latina/o student groups as well as a cultural center designed to promote interest in and educate others about Latina/o lives and cultures).

Since many of the Latina/o students felt embattled, they welcomed Professor Gonzales-Berry and me rather enthusiastically, if cautiously, in some quarters. Professor Gonzales-Berry came to head the Ethnic Studies department, whose formation in 1996 had been a contested one. I entered into an English department that had never offered a course exclusively in Chicana/o or Latina/o literature, though colleagues had offered courses in literature of the Americas. Consequently, students—Latina/os and non-Latina/os—were hungry for the courses Professor Gonzales-Berry and I would be able to offer. In the spring of 1999, for instance, I offered an English course, cross-listed with ethnic studies, in Chicana/o literature, and three times my chair had to raise the maximum enrollment figure. Enrollments closed only when the room's fire-safety limit had been reached. Professor Gonzales-Berry was crucial in generating this enthusiasm. Jim García, the coordinator of the Casa Educacional Education Office, had also been key in supporting Latina/o students at OSU. Other faculty and staff such as Loren Chavarría and Juan Trujillo had worked closely with these students as well. What really captured my attention at OSU and what I think accurately characterizes successful organizational strategies at schools with relatively small numbers of Latina/os was the openness of MEChA to a diverse constituency.

Unlike MEChA chapters I had been in elsewhere or had come to know through friends at other universities, I found OSU's Mechistas (the members of MEChA) unusually open to a number of Latina/o and non-Latina/o students. Though a Chicana/o student organization, MEChA had, for instance, a Peruvian student as its president. Even a few self-identified white students participated in and were welcomed by MEChA. The chapter welcomed anyone who embraced its beliefs. This openness struck me as a particularly strategic swerve around constraining authenticity politics and a critical awareness of the measures necessary for a group like MEChA to survive and prosper at OSU. To push forward a critical agenda requires a critical mass; short of that mass, one must make adjustments such as working with a range of people who share one's ideas but not necessarily one's ethnic ties.

By contrast, if anything revealed the shortcomings of crude identity politics, it was the Latina/o students' inability to come together as a whole. The boorish idea that because a group of people shares an ethnic bond they will necessarily support one another or work harmoniously together manifested itself in the sheer animosity that existed between a number of the Latina/o groups. While MEChA, for instance, welcomed anyone into its fold who shared its philosophy, the group often failed to find a common bond with other Latina/o groups, just as other groups often vilified MEChA. The goal here is not to assess blame in these squabbles but to analyze how these tensions limit students' ability to democratize higher education. At a university with limited resources for student programming and with a limited number of Latina/os, Latina/os need to be able to mobilize for a common cause. This is not to say that each group needs to embrace every event sponsored by the other, but that in times of crisis (e.g., when diversity requirements face being cut, when racist attacks are brought to light, or when diversity becomes an empty corporate slogan) these students should have the groundwork already in place to work together.

For example, Calmecac, an organization committed to educational outreach, should have been a locus where students from various Latina/o organizations could have come together to support one another. Though more limited than the BSRC, Calmecac performed similar functions. Whereas, however, the members of MEChA and CGSA at UT Austin could provide enough students to run the organization, the Mechistas at OSU could not count on such hearty numbers, though they were the students who alone ran Calmecac. Ideological differences and strained turf relations hindered the participation of a broader Latina/o student coalition in Calmecac. This strain ultimately jeopardized this group's success. Perhaps with a broader base of support, the students could have prevented the cutting of Calmecac's university funding in 1997. Again, I use MEChA and Calmecac as illustrative examples. I speak only from my vantage point of familiarity with these groups over a two-year period. Their history predates my arrival at OSU, and their future proceeds after my departure. I understand that Professor Gonzales-Berry and Jim García have worked indefatigably with the students to bridge some of these tensions and that the Casa Educacional and El Centro Cultural Cesar Chávez have proven instrumental in working out these differences.

I shift now to my current position at PSU. Since in many ways the experi-

ences at OSU and PSU are similar, I will highlight only those points that further this discussion. In 1999, I accepted a job offer from the Department of
English at PSU, as did my colleague Jane Juffer, to develop an undergraduate
and graduate concentration in Latina/o Studies. Similar to OSU, only a limited
number of Latina/o students attend PSU. As of the fall of 1998, there were
1,706 Latina students in the entire PSU system; 1,110 of these students were
enrolled at the University Park campus, the location where Professor Juffer
and I teach. Note as well that with the shift to the Northeast, the numerically
dominant group of Latina/os is not Chicana/os, but rather Puerto Ricans.
Some of the political concerns motivating these students differ from the Chi-
cana/o issues I had grown accustomed to in the Southwest and even in Oregon. For instance, military bombing runs in Vieques remains a hot topic
regarding Puerto Rico and the United States, while it has only limited play in
the Chicana/o community. Political differences aside, however, these groups
share in common a racial achievement gap in education.

In working to develop Latina/o Studies at PSU, Professor Juffer and I have
visited and been in contact with a number of the Latina/o student groups. I
have also served as an informal advisor to MEChA and the League of United
Latin American Citizens (LULAC). The very development of a Latina/o Studies
concentration is the topic for yet another chapter, so I am going to limit my
discussion here to the joint functioning of two particular Latina/o student
groups at PSU. The MEChA and LULAC chapters provide an interesting example, for they meet together and essentially function as one group. Whereas the
MEChA chapter at OSU welcomed anyone who supported its philosophy, the
joining of MEChA and LULAC chapters at PSU represents a movement across
political boundaries. Founded at the student conference in Santa Barbara in
1969, MEChA has always maintained a commitment to self-empowerment and
self-determination through grassroots efforts as one of its foundational principles. MEChA is an on the ground political organization committed to an
activist politics long associated with the student movements of the 1960s. By
contrast, LULAC, founded in 1929, has long been associated with pushing for
political change through the electoral process. The two groups may share
some fundamental beliefs about Latina/os, but their strategies and political
philosophies could not differ more. In addition, the MEChA and LULAC chapters at PSU also come together as representatives from diverse Latina/o communities, predominantly Mexican American and Puerto Rican. Consequently,
to witness these two groups collaborating piqued my curiosity. Working with
a very limited student base, these two groups have managed to raise awareness about Latina/o cultural values at the campus. In conjunction with other
Latina/o student organizations such as the Puerto Rican Student Association,
these groups have managed to use Hispanic heritage month to educate their
classmates and the campus about Latina/o culture. MEChA and LULAC have
also hosted compelling Día de los Muertos (Day of the Dead) celebrations. The

interesting thing with the students I have met so far at PSU is that while they are very proud of their cultures, many of their interests stop there. They are not as critically aware of Latina/o politics as they might be. In large part, I think this is a matter of exposing them to the issues and working with them to better educate themselves about these matters. There are, of course, very politically astute Latina/os on campus. In one year, I can hardly say that I have met all of the students interested in Latina/o Studies.

Political awareness aside, the willingness of these two historically distinct Latina/o groups (MEChA and LULAC) to come together in a common bond interests me most. Their collaborative work highlights what I believe will continue to be a trend in Latina/o Studies and Latina/o activism, comparative and coalitional work, respectively. As Juan Flores (1997) notes, these are new times for Latina/o Studies. The shift to comparative Latina/o Studies and away from single national or ethnic communities (e.g., Chicana/o Studies and Puerto Rican Studies programs) "coincides with the more transnational and global character of Latino ethnic groups" (208). Shifting migration patterns, as a result of transnational capital and free trade, bring more and more diverse Latina/o communities into contact. While these communities each have different political ties to their home countries, much can be learned and gained through studying them together and fostering political alliances among them. The example of MEChA and LULAC represents a microcosm of a much larger coalitional effort that will need to take place if the quest for social justice will prove to be successful. These groups will, of course, have to work out mutually beneficial strategies and commitments if their alliances are to survive. They cannot be entered into blindly or naively.

CONCLUSION

In reflecting on these examples of Latina/o student activism, I am reminded of Homi Bhabha's (1998) thoughts on political empowerment and cross-cultural alliances. He writes that

> Political empowerment, and the enlargement of the multiculturalist cause, come from posing the questions of solidarity and community from the interstitial perspective. . . . Social differences are not simply given to experience through an already authenticated cultural tradition; they are the signs of emergence of community envisaged as a project—at once a vision and a construction—that takes you "beyond" yourself in order to return, in a spirit of revision and reconstruction, to the political *conditions* of the present. (3; emphasis in the original)

All the projects I discussed require precisely what Bhabha refers to as the "emergence of community," an emergence that requires group efforts and coalitional work. To imagine oneself not working from an already given historical position or tradition, but rather coalescing around projects that will foster collective identity, provides a powerful means for building a coalition aware of its history and cognizant, too, that it is forging new bonds and treading new ground.

Confronted by structural impediments in the educational system, students and faculty can come together in this spirit of invention and collaboration to work toward democratizing education for Latina/o students and revitalizing radical democracy as a concrete ethical referent for their struggles. As Giroux reminds us, "By addressing radical democracy as a political, social, and ethical referent for rethinking how citizens, especially youth, can be educated to deal with a world of different, multiple, and fractured public cultures, educators confront the need for constructing a new ethical and political language to map the problems and challenges of a newly constituted global public" (1996, 134–135). In organizing around educational equity for Latina/os, we would do well, then, to ground our project in the common cause of achieving a radical democracy, one capable of overcoming the sundry inequities in our current democratic state.

While it may have been slightly myopic for the activists at Texas not to press harder for structural changes needed in the educational system or not to consider carefully enough in advance the long-term viability of a resource center like the BSRC, we can learn from that example how to implement and improve similar programs in the future and how they might be better articulated to systemic changes at the university. Similarly, while MEChA and CGSA maintained strong enough numbers to ensure their livelihood, there should still be an effort to build common cause among various progressive groups. Prior to my arrival at UT Austin, a number of Latina/o student groups briefly formed a coalition called Todos Unidos. These coalitions point the way in the future, as I believe the examples at OSU and PSU make clear. Indeed, the more that I work on campuses with restricted numbers of Latina/o students the more convinced I become that coalitions are absolutely necessary to insure a successful college experience for Latina/os. By building alliances, these students feel they have a stake in their colleges and communities, and this experience helps mitigate feelings of alienation so common among Latina/o students, especially Latina/os attending colleges outside of large Latina/o communities.

In these times in which education remains under siege for Latina/os, faculty, administrators, and students need to work together to ensure that Latina/os can come together around a common cause. Laying the foundation for supportive relationships means being able to see past ideological differences. It means reaching out in advance to another group and asking it to share in the organizing of an event. It means working together to promote change. It means invoking radical democracy as a concrete referent for our social projects. Faculty can assist both as advisors to these Latina/o organizations and as educators willing to address issues of student organization. They can work with students, through informal reading groups or directly in the classroom, to learn more about Latina/o history and culture, so the students will better understand the challenges they face. Additionally, administrators, from departmental chairs to university presidents, need to recognize that at almost all campuses across the United States, students of color feel embattled. When the curriculum fails to recognize their cultures' contributions to the arts, sciences, and so on, or when students of color find themselves threatened by acts of overt and structural racism on campus, this only exacerbates their feelings of isolation and rage.

Further, universities do often serve as tools of social reproduction, but that does not mean that activists (student and faculty alike) cannot find resistive venues for challenging and changing debilitating and prejudicial trends of thought. As Raymond Williams notes, education is not an "autonomous system." It is articulated to other institutions: "It is then reasonable, at one level, to speak of a general educational process as a key form of cultural reproduction, which can be linked with that more general reproduction of existing social relations which is assured by existing and self-prolonging property and other economic relations, institutions of state and other political power, religious and family forms. To ignore these links is to submit to the arbitrary authority of a self-proclaimed 'autonomous' system" (1981, 186). Since the educational system is only monolithic and autonomous in its own self-aggrandizing pronouncements, we can disarticulate its normalized relations of power and find more progressive articulations. Drawing on these connections, we can identify those sites that help promote change. We can and must, in the idiom of Aronowitz and Giroux, find a "language of possibility" for fostering social change and advocating social justice. The stakes are too high and struggles too important to buy into the politics of cynicism, a politics founded on the notion that there is no outside to the circle of domination. Overcoming the racial gap means balancing out the resources so that the relationship between Latina/os and universities does not have to be as contentious as my title, "Brown v. Higher Education," suggests. Latina/os need not feel embattled at the university, but until some racial justice is meted out, there is a battle.

NOTES

I would like to thank Jo Nutter, Jane Juffer, and Henry Giroux for their thoughtful feedback on this chapter. I, of course, remain responsible for its contents.

1. By "university system" I mean to denote not only the classes these students attend, but also the entire system of higher education they encounter, including, but not limited to, filling out applications for financial aid, preparing to take standardized tests, and so forth.

2. I refer here to Scott Carlson's report, "Hispanics' Success Stymied by the Types

of Colleges They Attend, Study Finds" (1999). He is reporting on the Educational Testing Service and the Hispanic Association of Colleges and Universities jointly authored study of Hispanics in higher education.

3. The article's use of the umbrella term "Hispanic," of course, masks significant differences between the various groups this label identifies. That is, the access to education and the general educational level among the various groups labeled "Hispanic" varies dramatically. As Juan González notes, for instance, those fleeing Cuba after Castro's revolution brought with them "perhaps the highest educational levels of any Hispanic immigrant group in U.S. history. At a time when only 4 percent of Cubans on the island had reached the twelfth grade, more than 36 percent of the refugees had college degrees, or at least some college education" (2000, 111). This differs sharply with the educational experience of many Chicana/os and Puerto Ricans who found themselves living in the barrios and ghettos of the United States. We should be as specific as possible when discussing the educational experience of the various communities who are labeled "Hispanic" or "Latina/o." This specificity is especially important when analyzing the failure of the educational system to address the needs of these populations. Since, however, my argument relies in part on the coalitional work of these groups in effecting change for all Latina/os, I make use of the umbrella term. In my broader claims and certainly in my case studies, I try to be as specific as possible.

4. I found Jane Juffer's paper, "From Criticism to Cartography: Latina/o Studies, Multiculturalism, and the Corporate University" (2000), helpful for thinking about these issues. Her arguments go beyond those I have outlined here.

5. From 1972 to 1993, the high school drop out rate of Latinos has only marginally declined. In 1972, it was just under 35 percent; in 1993, it was recorded at 28 percent, according to the president's Advisory Commission on Excellence in Education for Hispanic Americans.

6. In March 1969, Mexican American youth from across the country came together in Denver for the National Youth Liberation Conference hosted by Corky Gonzales and his Crusade for Justice. At this conference, they drafted *El Plan Espiritual de Aztlán*. Approximately a month later the students met again in Santa Barbara under the auspices of the Chicano Coordinating Council on Higher Education. At Santa Barbara, the student activists who had been members of various Mexican American youth organizations decided to create a united front and form El Movimiento Estudiantil Chicano de Aztlán (MEChA). They codified that unity in *El Plan de Santa Barbara*, a manifesto calling for Chicana/o self-determination. For a more detailed account of these events and the Chicana/o movement in general, see Gómez Quiñones (1990) and Muñoz (1989). For various feminist critiques of the movement, see García (1997).

7. Some of the others involved in this project included Louis Mendoza, Sandra Soto, Raúl Coronado Jr., María Cotera, Manolo Callahan, Marco Iniquez Alba, Rebecca Gámez, Jacqueline Frausto, Toni Nelson Herrera, Carla Mendiola, Dianira Salazar, Chito Vela, Rafael Melendez, Dennis Medina, María Loya, Lorenzo Blanco, and Karla Mancha.

8. See Chabram-Dernersesian (1999) for more on the authenticity politics involved in the Chicana/o movement.

9. I take my lead here from Wallace (1994), who questions the function of unrepresentative fictions.

WORKS CITED

Aronowitz, Stanley, and Henry Giroux. 1993. *Education Still under Siege.* 2nd ed. Westport, Conn.: Bergin and Garvey.

Bhabha, Homi. 1998. *The Location of Culture.* 1994. Reprint, New York: Routledge.

Brown v. Board of Education of Topeka, Kansas, 347 U.S. 483 (1954).

Carlson, Scott. 1999. "Hispanics' Success Stymied by the Types of Colleges They Attend, Study Finds." *Chronicle of Higher Education,* 30 September. Can be accessed at: <www.chronicle.com/daily/99/09/99093004n.htm>. Last accessed: June 28, 2000.

Chabram-Dernersesian, Angie. 1994. " 'Chicana! Rican? No, Chicana-Riqueña!' Refashioning the Transnational Connection." In *Multiculturalism: A Critical Reader,* ed. David Theo Goldberg. Oxford: Blackwell.

Flores, Juan. 1997. "Latino Studies: New Contexts, New Concepts." *Harvard Educational Review* 67.2 (Summer): 208–221.

Funderburg, Lise. 2000. "Race in Class, after Integration." *The Nation,* 5 June, 26–29.

García, Alma, ed. 1997. *Chicana Feminist Thought: The Basic Historical Writings.* New York: Routledge.

Giroux, Henry. 1996. *Fugitive Cultures: Race, Violence, and Youth.* New York: Routledge, 1996.

Gómez Quiñones, Juan. 1990. *Chicano Politics: Reality and Promise, 1940–1990.* Albuquerque: University of New Mexico Press.

González, Juan. 2000. *Harvest of Empire: A History of Latinos in America.* New York: Viking.

Grossberg, Lawrence. 1997. "Bring It All Back Home: Pedagogy and Cultural Studies." In *Bringing It All Back Home: Essays on Cultural Studies,* ed. Larry Grossberg. Durham, N.C.: Duke University Press.

Johnson, Richard. 1997. "Teaching without Guarantees: Cultural Studies, Pedagogy, and Identity." In *A Question of Discipline: Pedagogy, Power, and the Teaching of Cultural Studies,* ed. Joyce E. Canaan and Debbie Epstein. Boulder, Colo.: Westview.

Juffer, Jane. 2000. "From Criticism to Cartography: Latina/o Studies, Multiculturalism, and the Corporate University." Paper presented at the Disciplinary Diagrams/Political Fields Conference, Durham, North Carolina, March 30–April 2, 2000.

Muñoz, Carlos. 1989. *Youth, Identity, Power: The Chicano Movement.* London: Verso.

Noguera, Pedro, and Antwi Akom. 2000. "Disparities Demystified." *The Nation,* 5 June, 29–31.

President's Advisory Committee on Excellence in Education for Hispanic Americans. 1996. "Our Nation on the Fault Line: Hispanic American Education." September. Can be accessed at: <www.ed.gov/pubs/FaultLine/>. Last accessed: June 26, 2000.

Romero, Rolando. 1997. "Troublemakers." In *As We Are Now: Mixedblood Essays on Race and Identity,* ed. William S. Penn. Berkeley and Los Angeles: University of California Press.

Wallace, Michelle. 1994. "The Search for the 'Good Enough' Mammy: Multiculturalism, Popular Culture, and Psychoanalysis." In *Multiculturalism: A Critical Reader,* ed. David Theo Goldberg. Oxford: Blackwell.

Williams, Raymond. 1981. *Culture.* Glasgow: Fontana.

7

Culture, the Academy, and the Police; or, Reading Matthew Arnold in "Our Present Unsettled State"

Jerry Phillips

[T]he encroachments of the rich are more destructive to the constitution than those of the people.

—Aristotle 1993, 100

Never did people believe anything more firmly than nine Englishmen out of ten at the present day believe that our greatness and welfare are proved by our being so very rich. Now the use of culture is that it helps us, by means of its spiritual standard of perfection, to regard wealth as but machinery, and not only to say as a matter of words that we regard wealth as but machinery, but really to perceive and feel that it is so. If it were not for this purging effect wrought upon our minds by culture, the whole world, the future as well as the present, would inevitably belong to the Philistines.

—Arnold 1993a, 65

I think people believe that the only strategy we have is to put a lot of police officers on the street and harass people and make arrests for inconsequential kinds of things. Well, that's part of the strategy, no question about it.

—Gates 1988

I

In his study of "the Arnoldian tradition" in American culture, John Raleigh observes that

109

> Matthew Arnold's writings, literary, social, religious, and cultural, have enjoyed
> and still continue to enjoy an extensive vogue in the United States. . . . No other
> foreign critic, and perhaps few native ones, have acquired such a reputation and
> exercised such a palpable influence on American culture. What criticism needed
> at his time he provided. What it still needs he provides. (Raleigh 1961, 1)

Raleigh penned these words in 1961, and what strikes one today, in our present troubled times, so full of uncertainty, is Raleigh's absolute faith in the abiding cultural utility of Arnold's ideas. This chapter leans on Raleigh's tribute in order to assess the contemporary ideological significance of the Arnoldian tradition. A large question looms over the landscape of issues explored here: is it the case that Arnold still "provides" what we humanists most assuredly need (Graff 1987)?[1]

One way to answer the above-question is through self definition—that is, we identify ourselves, and in the same process identify our needs.[2] Another way of investigating the controversy of Arnold's contemporary relevance is to interrogate the social world in which the humanities exist. The latter methodological approach—the line of vision informing my argument—is based on the assumption that the needs of humanists are shaped from without: thus, the question of whether or not Arnold still ministers to them, cannot be properly answered if we do not know why such needs exist in a certain (social) form. The interrelationships obtaining between culture, the academy, and the police form the objective criteria for evaluating the lasting promise, or growing irrelevance, of Arnoldian cultural imperatives in the contemporary moment. In my view, the latter measure of growing irrelevance is more eloquent of Arnold's status today. I suggest that "the Arnoldian program" (Raleigh 1961, 99) of making citizens through the genius of the liberal humanities has run aground on the hard, jagged rock of neoliberal society—a society whose principal agent of social discipline is less the educator than the police officer, less the school than the prison.

Our present unsettled state is causing the ground to shift as regards the very meaning of what it is to be a citizen.[3] Even as his cultural influence declines, Arnold can still help us to understand this profound geological activity. For as noted by Barry Cooper, Arnold's concept of "culture" is in one sense "an Aristotlean political science," which keenly serves as "a rational standard for political judgment as well as a motive for public conduct" (1976, 25, 35). Arnold's work offers us the challenge of thinking through a seminal contradiction: his "political science" holds value for both *projects of social control* and *projects of freedom*. As a discourse of social control, the Arnoldian text lends support to conservative notions of a monumental culture, allegedly our common heritage, which must be handed down from above (Bloom 1987). However, as a discourse of freedom, the Arnoldian text makes it possible to conceive of the liberal arts as a pedagogy of hope and moral courage. From this perspective, culture is not something we merely imbibe, it is *something we do*—"in the interest of creating critical rather than 'good' citizens," observes Henry Giroux (1990, 121). Before embarking on an exploration of Arnold's key ideas, we need to consider the contemporary versions of those forces of social discipline—culture, the academy, and the police—whose combined activity forms the ground for Arnold's thought.

The contemporary social scene is characterized by the long reach of the commodity-form into all areas of life. The general tendency therein is the colonization of "society" by the prerogatives of the market (Herman 1995). In the realm of culture this has led to an inauspicious situation. For example, consider the fact that, with the decline of governmental support,

> museums have increasingly felt the need to obtain more corporate sponsorship for exhibits, and thus to adjust their overall orientation to attract this primary source of funding. Corporate expenditures on the arts rose from under $100 million in 1970 to more than $500 million in the early 1990's. One curator noted that "most corporate sponsors finance exhibitions based on centrist ideals and uncontroversial subject-matter." (Herman 1995, 9)

The colonization of "society" by "the economy" has also left its mark on the internal culture of the liberal academy. Lawrence Soley observes that "Government actions have promoted . . . increasing ties between business and universities. Although universities have always pandered to wealthy patrons, universities' toadyism intensified after President Reagan slashed spending on domestic programs. Reagan's cuts to students loans and funding for grant-giving agencies put the pinch on universities" (Soley 1995, 9). Leonard Minsky writes in the preface to Soley's book that "The past role of universities to serve the public has been hopelessly compromised. The cynical role now played by corporatized universities has made them untrustworthy arbiters of the public good" (1995, 11). The degree of truth in Minsky's assertions is of course debatable; but, nonetheless, his comments oblige us to take seriously the real social forces now confronting the Arnoldian program of citizenship through humanistic education.

The steady march forward of commodification has led to the wholesale dismantling of the welfare state. The welfare state—which places regulations or fetters on the drive for profit in the regions of health care, income, housing, and education—was born out of the struggle of workers to keep alive fundamental values of "society" (Piven and Cloward 1979, 264–361). Said values (expressive of the need for dignity and community) originate in what Kees Van Der Pijl terms "the social, reproductive substratum" of the economic order, the non-commodified sphere of "authentic joy, love and friendship" (1997, 38). The collapse of welfare statism under the pressure exercised by "the despotism of capital" (Marx 1976, 793) threatens to exhaust the capacity of the social substratum to generate human values; and to this extent it facilitates what Jurgen

Habermas calls a "legitimation crisis"—a crisis in the ability of a society to integrate (normatively) its various political elements (1975). Despotic capital (i.e.,
neoliberalism) brings on crisis because in its rending of the diverse "safety nets"
attendant to welfare statism, it reduces large numbers of people to the status
of "disposable human material" (Marx 1976, 785–86). But a population deemed
"redundant" does not simply disappear; and so in order to control its menacing
social presence, despotic capital gives over much of society to the logic of the
police. This, to be sure, is the complex of forces which forms the background
for President Clinton's assertion that "We need to put more police on the
streets and more criminals behind bars" (Clinton and Gore 1992, 71). As culture and the academy go the way of corporatization, and as society falls under
the omnipotent eye of the police, the "Aristotelian political science" of
Matthew Arnold comes into its own.

II

Arnold's political science is expressive of "the liberal imagination" in action
(Trilling 1950). Thus, in adjudging Arnold's contemporary relevance, one is
actually considering the place of liberal values in a society that is born out of
the rule of despotic capital. The crisis of legitimation is at bottom the crisis
of liberalism. The following questions are therefore unavoidable. What
import the liberal academy in a social order based squarely on the operations
of private capital, which entail, as Marx points out, "the free exploitation of
man by man" (1976, 875)?[4] What purchase liberal culture in a state system
that increasingly reduces itself to the terms of the police? Finally, where
should the self go to escape the hegemony of the Philistines, to commune
with what Arnold called "the inmost impulse of . . . being" (1993b, 9)? Richard
Ohmann writes that Arnold had "high hopes for literary culture"; he envis-
aged it as a means of holding at bay the colonization of society by economy
(1987, 3). However, in our time, which bears witness to the strong rule of the
market, the social structures necessary for the realization of liberal (and "literary") values are increasingly robbed of ideological authority. As Terry
Eagleton remarks, "It is the logic of late capitalism to breed a more fragmen-
tary, eclectic, demotic, metropolitan culture than anything dreamt of by
Matthew Arnold—a culture which is then a living scandal to its own firmly
Arnoldian premises" (1992, 34–35). In this respect, the question of whether
or not Arnold still provides what the humanities need, is more properly an
issue of can he provide what they need, given the larger social context.[5]

   Arnold's writings demonstrate that culture, the academy, and the police are
wedded together into a single social complex by the contradictory energies of
liberalism: on the one hand, we meet in Arnold's prose a language of human
values beyond the marketplace, still relevant to our times; but, on the other

hand, Arnold devotes a small river of ink to the problem of disciplining workers. He strongly believed that "the excess of the working class in its present state of development" was synonymous with "anarchy" (1993a, 92). Insofar as Arnold's political science is addressed as the problem of "anarchy" from below, he lends considerable cultural authority to the class interest of capitalists.

As "the self-appointed apostle of culture" (Raleigh 1961, 37), Arnold advanced both disciplinary and liberatory values. On the one hand, he viewed the liberal educator as a propagandist against the workers' revolution: "the lovers of culture," wrote Arnold, "are unswervingly and with a good conscience the opposers of anarchy" (1993a, 182). But, on the other hand, Arnold was sharply critical of unfettered, despotic capitalism: its denial of community in the name of economic profit, and its generation of "our ever accumulating masses of pauperism" (1993a, 175) were, for Arnold, intolerable assaults against the "social substratum," the realm of moral community. In the spirit of Arnold (against "the diseased spirit of our time" [1993a, 168]), and in league with the argument developed in Aristotle's *The Politics,* I contend that the need to place ethical limits on the social influence of the marketplace is a matter of the utmost exigence, for without such limits, culture, in the Arnoldian sense of "becoming something rather than having something," the idea of "growing towards some measure of sweetness and light," cannot even begin to elicit "our best self, or right reason" (1993a, 62, 103, 100). Consequently, the democratic body politic (and its concomitant notion of community) is degraded therein.

If one accepts Lionel Trilling's dictum that culture "is not a flow, nor even a confluence; its form of existence is struggle, or at least debate" (1950, 20), then one is obliged to seek out, in the present moment, a language of culture that resists the totalitarian monologism of the marketplace. To quote Henry Giroux, liberal educators, the would-be purveyors of cultures, need to link the liberal arts "to the imperatives of a critical democracy, [so that] the debate on the meaning and nature of higher education can be situated within a broader context of issues concerned with citizenship, politics, and the dignity of human life" (1990, 121). It is my view that the fate of liberal education (whatever the character of the curriculum) rests in the balance between values of "humanity" and values of social discipline. I submit that if the latter prevail over the former, we shall enter a political era (characterized by cities and suburbs of the dead) where the basic human decencies—"openness and flexibility of mind" (Arnold 1993b, 25), the "love of our neighbor, the impulses towards action, help and beneficence" (1993a, 59)—will be rare birds, indeed.[6]

III

Arnold's writings are often informed by a fundamental conflict between binary and dialectical modes of social inquiry. Couplings like "Hebraism and "Hellenism," "culture and anarchy," the "State" and the "individual," "curiosity" and "machinery" behave on occasion like binary oppositions, the first term simply canceling out the second in a hierarchically organized discourse. However, one also finds conceptual pairings in Arnold's work that exist in a dialectical rather than antithetical relationship: in this scenario the first term feeds into the second and vice versa, in a volatile rhetorical economy of charged signifiers.

Thus, in his dialectical mode, Arnold argues that one should not "hellenise" or "hebraise" to the total exclusion of the opposing principle; one should plot one's course with a view to what Aristotle called "the realization and perfect exercise of excellence" (1993, 174)—in Arnold's terms, the cultivation of "our best self" in "the world of ideas, not the world of catchwords and party habits" (1993d, 34). If the "governing idea of Hellenism is spontaneity of consciousness," while that of Hebraism, "strictness of conscience" (1993a, 128), then Arnold, in the words of Vassilis Lambropoulous, is "able to preserve the tension between his two main terms without sacrificing one to another, without banning totally the joy of self-affirmation from the process of salvation" (1989, 172). Arnold's dialectical tendency can be seen as a stand against the waste of human energies in the adventure of history. For just as Marx is able to preserve the progressive aspect of capitalism in the notion of the liberatory potential of the productive forces, so Arnold (as a committed Christian) is able to preserve the moral value of pre-Christian civilization.[7]

The binary mode of inquiry commits Arnold, as a political commentator, to a logic of social closure, whereas the dialectical mode implies an open ethics of imaginative "becoming." The ideological controversy of social closure ranged against imaginative becoming translates into values of "discipline" ranged against values of "humanity." No coupling has greater impact on this ideological controversy than that of capitalism and democracy. This is a coupling that is thematically implicit in many of Arnold's prognostications; it is, one might say, the logos that organizes all else into theoretical principles ("culture and anarchy," "criticism" and "policy," "right reason" and "fetishism," etc.).

As fellow travelers on that treacherously winding road we call modernity, the measures of capitalism and democracy provide key insight into the language of liberalism, and its contradictory being in the world: democracy implies community, the public square, and "the Rights of Man"; whereas capitalism implies class division, the marketplace, and private property. Now Arnold does not accept one or the other but accepts both in piecemeal fashion. This accounts for the twin allegiance of his texts—to discipline and closure on the one hand, to human felicity and "becoming something" on the other. The crux of the matter, for Arnold, as a liberal educator, a man who spent much of his practical life as an inspector of schools, is the quality of social power invested in the institutions that make up the State. Should the State serve democracy or capitalism? To what degree can it serve both? Here lies the rub for progressive liberalism: as regards "the action of the State" on a contested body politic, can the State bring about a "collective and corporate character" (1993b, 13, 23)? Is there a social arena where "the bond of a common culture" (1993b, 3) might come into its own, with a view to resolving class struggle in nationhood? One immediately recognizes the general social mission of the public school and the liberal academy in the modern world. But before I speak of the politics of education, I must describe that ethos of the State which supports the cultural hegemony of the liberal educator.

Throughout his writings Arnold characterizes the liberal bourgeois State as the guardian of our collective becoming on the open road of ethics: the State institutionalizes "high reason and right feeling" and forms "a rallying-point for the intelligence, and for the worthiest instincts of the community, which will herein find a true bond of union" (1993b, 15). The State encourages us "to rise above the idea of class to the idea of the whole community . . . and to find our center of light and authority there" (1993a, 93). In short, Arnold conceived of the State as preserving human values against the dehumanizing tendencies of "the mechanical and material civilization" that increasingly dominated the nineteenth-century social scene (1993a, 63). However, Arnold also spoke of the bourgeois state in its other guise, as an engine of class power—the power of "merchants and master manufacturers" (Smith 1986, 201) over workers. Arnold was cognizant of the fact that "many Englishmen, perhaps [the] majority," opposed "strengthening the hands of the State," even in the name of "democracy," because they feared the despotic tendencies of statism per se (1993b, 1, 16). Arnold met such "fanatics" head on: he would have them know (especially the middle classes) that there is an excess on the political horizon to be greatly feared, more feared than the excesses of the typical state—namely, the excess of "anarchy," the political conceit of the working class. As Arnold put it:

> I propose to submit to those who have been accustomed to regard all State-action with jealousy, some reasons for thinking that the circumstances which once made that jealousy prudent and natural have undergone an essential change. I desire to lead them to consider with me, whether, in the present altered conjuncture, that State-action, which was once dangerous may not become . . . the means of helping us against dangers from another quarter. (Arnold 1993b, 2)

The values of discipline and the logic of social closure reign supreme in this passage. The State is accorded the office of counterrevolutionary agent par excellence: as imagined by Arnold, it is a complex of moral and physical force which negates the "dangers" offered to the body politic by the "Populace," that "vast portion . . . of the working class which, raw and half-developed, has long lain half-hidden amidst its poverty and squalor, and now is issuing from its hiding-place to assert an Englishman's heaven-born privilege of doing as he likes, and is beginning to perplex us by marching where it likes, bawling what it likes, breaking what it likes" (1993a, 107). Lest we forget, the Victorian liberal reformer was genuinely concerned with matters of social justice, but rarely could he or she identify with workers as complex social agents. As pointed out by Richard Johnson, in his study of Victorian educational policy as social control (1970), the militant worker was routinely identified with political anarchy, thus committing liberal reformism to a conception of political stability that necessarily favors the interests of merchants and master-manufacturers.[8]

Arnold's disdain for workers bespeaks more than mere snobbery. His portrait of the Populace (or more accurately, his caricature) plays on an ideological myth that seeks to direct moral force against proletarian activism: the myth of the dangerous classes.[9] Here the politics of metaphor is crucial: Arnold's language exploits the stereotypical notion of the Populace as "the Great Beast," the supreme exemplar of "the plain faults of our animality" (1993a, 69). Thus the Populace issues forth "from its hiding-place" like a savage predator, "untamably" bent on blood and destruction. Arnold refuses to consider seriously such demands as the right to the franchise, the right to the shorter working day, the right to organize unions, and the right to better wages—all volatile issues of the day. Instead, he advances the myth of the dangerous classes, in a language of blatant moral prejudice about those who are "raw," uncivilized, insolent, envious, and ignorant, those whose actions in the public square can never rise above "anarchy," whose nature is properly conveyed by an alleged propensity for "sheer violence" (1993a, 109).

In large measure, we labor in "the immense field of life and literature" in the shadow of Arnold (1993d, 51). The statist concern with social order embraced by Arnold, which typically sidelines the question of social and economic justice, has been a key factor in the praxis of liberal education, in the school and the academy. It has accorded the liberal educator a definite conservative function. As Richard Ohmann suggests, the humanities have been used within the universities "to harden class lines and teach the skills and habits of mind that will serve the industrial system" (1976, 334).

Arnold would have us believe that the supposed beastliness of the working class—namely, its attraction to "bawling, hustling, and smashing," and its love of "beer" and "gin"—is really "the eternal spirit of the Populace" (1993a, 109). That is to say, his democratic sensibility does not preclude his giving voice to elitist pieties. We learn in his essay "Democracy" that "the bulk of . . . persons . . . need to follow an ideal, not set one" (1993a, 14). Elsewhere he contends that "the mass of mankind will never have any ardent zeal for seeing things as they are; very inadequate ideas will always satisfy them" (1993d, 41). Arnold's elitism should not only be seen as the unfortunate and unnecessary by-product of middle-class, Victorian reformism; instead, one should approach the deep philosophical investment in what Arnold called "the scale of humanity" (1993b, 7) as singularly expressive of "the will to power" on the part of the liberal educator. In other words, the inegalitarian anthropology of the liberal educator is integral to a self-aggrandizing discourse.[10]

Arnold assures us that "religion comes to a conclusion identical with that which culture . . . likewise reaches. Religion says: the kingdom of God is within you; and culture, in like manner, places human perfection in an internal condition, in the growth and predominance of our humanity proper, as distinguished from our animality" (1993a, 61–62). Note that religion has long performed the office of naturalizing social relations—God, the angels, the monarch, the nobles, and the commoners was, for centuries, a normal gradation. In the post-feudal world of Victorian England, culture becomes a "secular religion," a moral solar power, as it were, which aims to transform "the raw masses" into well-done viands that can be incorporated into the body politic and subsequently broken down into harmless elements. This, to be sure, is a fantasy scenario, where the political reality of the working class simply disappears. What role does the liberal educator play in this (ideal) hegemonic process?

If the "mass" of the Populace is a beast that must be led into the sunlight of "our humanity proper," then the liberal educator becomes a tamer of the wild, a missionary. To be sure, nineteenth-century colonialism and the rhetoric of "progress," based increasingly on evolutionary principles, played central roles in widely disseminating the motif of "the civilized man" bravely confronting the "darkness" of "savagery" and "ignorance." As evidenced by the political tone and "theological" bent of his discourse, Arnold seeks to profit from the symbolic capital associated with the figure of the missionary. If the missionary brings "sweetness and light" to the "natives" in the overseas economy of colonialism, then the liberal educator performs the same office, with respect to workers, in the domestic economy of capitalism. Thus we arrive at a controversial juncture in the liberal reformer's political being, which might be clarified as follows: Arnold certainly recognizes that industrial capital traduces democracy and generates social conflict; but his political science is aimed at curbing the activities of workers rather than masters.[11] As a consequence of this emphasis, Arnold can only imagine the preservation of democratic values— ethical ideals that unambiguously bespeak "a general humane spirit" (1993a 110)—, not so much in the practical sphere of mundane "life," but in the ideal sphere of "culture, with its disinterested pursuit of perfection" (89). In the sphere of "culture," the liberal educator will undertake the progressive task of binding classes into nationhood. Indeed, liberal educators are "the true apostles of equality"; their mission is simply "to make the best that has been thought and known in the world current everywhere" (79).

Brian Doyle has written that "the impulse towards a conception of the national culture seen in terms of an organically unified whole national way of life, promoted a related view of education as the central mechanism for the reproduction of this national culture" (1982, 23). As opposed to the divisive notion of socioeconomic class, "Englishness," for Arnold (as for other Victorian reformers), was a cultural category endowed with considerable synthesizing powers. Under the aegis of the "English nationhood," the contradictions of the liberal bourgeois state gave way to an ideal "spiritual" democracy, involving "reading, observing, and thinking" (Arnold 1993a, 97). Thus the contentious issue of the effect of private property on democracy can be put aside in favor of a gentler controversy—the debate over "a public and national culture" (184). Note that as culture attains real practical value as a "mechanism" for social control, its ideal existence—as a spiritual adventure of "growing and becoming" (95)—is morally degraded. For the subject (particularly the militant worker who can be nothing but a "popular rioter" in bourgeois discourse) is explicitly accorded a definite social destination, a final resting place for being: the law-abiding citizen. I consider this to be a moral degradation of the "high" version of culture because it makes "order" rather than "justice" the prime concern of the state educational system.[12]

One might say that, in our time, we are witnessing the agonistic passage of culture from being a force for "order" to a force for "justice." However, the move toward the consideration of justice in the culture of educational thinking occurs at a time when the objective conditions for the realization of social justice are fast disappearing. The so-called culture wars between those who advocate a culturally diverse curriculum and those who advocate a curriculum based on the Great ("Western") Books are best understood as political debates about the past, present, and, most especially, the future direction of nationhood. Will the nation include more or fewer of its citizens in the public conversation that underlies the institutional form of the humanities? That is the question. Thus, the struggle for a just curriculum is part of a wider struggle for critical democracy. As Henry Giroux writes:

> the various questions that have been raised recently about either defending, reconstructing, or eliminating a particular canon in higher education can only be understood within a broader range of political and theoretical considerations that bear directly on the issue of whether a liberal arts education in this country should be considered a privilege for the few or a right for the vast majority of citizens. (Giroux 1990, 113)

The contradictory value of liberal education is made plain here: on one side, we have the liberatory vision of a participatory democracy, a culture of all citizens; on the other, we have the disciplinary vision of elitism, a culture of the privileged few. What is at stake in both visions is the meaning of public culture.

The culture wars amply demonstrate that the very notion of a public culture involves contested claims about the real nature of the public and the culture most appropriate to it. These are no small matters in a country as racially and socially divided as the United States. I suggest that public culture is less a monumental or institutional field than a complex set of social narratives which describe, prescribe, and proscribe ways of thinking, feeling, and dreaming our being in the world. In the context of capitalist class relations, where public culture is increasingly infused with anti-proletarian values, liberal educators have played a crucial role in consolidating what can be thought, felt, and dreamt about the status quo.

Consider the fact that Arnold reduces the Populace to the category of "animality." The reduction of the worker to the gross, uncivilized body (and the corollary elevation of the liberal educator to the supreme civilized mind) is wholly consonant with the factory ideology of the master manufacturer, who feels obliged, by the logic of capitalist production, to show the "hands" and the "operatives" how to employ the machines. In both situations—the educational and the industrial—the worker is the ward of a paternal figure, in a "pedagogy of the oppressed."[13] The Faustian bargain between liberal educators and the masters of capital goes to the heart of the relation between the liberal body politic and the profit-driven marketplace.

IV

In the peculiarity of his political and philosophical outlook, Arnold was a man of his time. But it is worth noting that his model of liberal pedagogy is in many ways our own.[14] We moderns have made of *Culture and Anarchy* a key reference text for any serious debate about the place of "art and letters" in relation to the art of politics and the "art of wealth-getting," as Aristotle termed it (1993, 12). Lambropoulous has succinctly described the pervasive influence of Arnold's great treatise:

> No other work in the Anglo-American canon of criticism and aesthetics has enjoyed its popularity. Successive generations of scholars, theorists, and teachers wishfully succumb to its seductive advocacy of beauty, reason, and letters, or at least feel obliged to address themselves to the same issues. Every discussion of literature, art, or culture in general will take it under serious consideration and acknowledge the continuing relevance of its critical vocabulary . . . Our political understanding itself is indebted to his social philosophy, and consequently our culture has been largely Arnold's. (Lambropoulous 1989, 172)

If our culture has been "largely Arnold's," what, then, of our State—the organ of our best collective self, "the much wanted principle of authority" that counteracts anarchy (Arnold 1993a, 89)? Since 1869, the date when *Culture and Anarchy* was first published, liberal democratic statism has undergone some impressive transformations. Consider, for instance, the bourgeois State in modern U.S. history. In this period the State has been shaped by: the extension of the franchise to the adult male, and, subsequently, to the adult female, populace; the enfranchisement of historically oppressed "racial" minorities; the establishment of specific governmental bodies, some of which place fetters on the activity of private capital in the marketplace (e.g., anti-trust legislation); the expansion of the ideological and repressive State apparatuses (e.g., schools, prisons, police forces, etc.); and, finally, the development of social welfare bureaucracies to insure certain necessities of life (such as housing), and to administer resources to that needy "residium" of the working class that the masters of capital cannot or will not employ. This broad sketch of the modern experience of the democratic State should be borne in mind as we enter further into our discussion of the collapse of liberalism.

My point is simply this: liberalism has historically served as a buffer between the ideals of democracy and the realities of a capitalist marketplace. Capitalism, when unfettered, tends to become a systematic violence against the democratic body politic, because the question of human community (not to be answered solely on the terms of *homo economicus*) is necessarily voided by the profit-motive, which cannot avoid commodifying and alienating activity, desire, and creativity. To be sure, the liberal body politic has helped to stabilize capitalist social relations, but in saying "no" to some of capital's more egregious practices (consider, for instance, the outlawing of child labor, a fairly common feature of the nineteenth-century industrial scene), it also helps to keep on the negotiating table issues of human welfare, not reducible to the logic of the marketplace. In short, as a philosophy of the State (and human community), liberalism makes of the relationship between capitalism and democracy a *dialectic rather than a binary,* and, in this respect, it keeps politics alive as an art of the possible.

As an ethical entity, the liberal State is based on a timeless moral sentiment: the notion of what Arnold termed "the essential unity of man" (1993a, 136). According to Arnold, "democracy is a force in which the concert of a great number of men makes up for the weakness of each man taken for himself" (1993b, 10). In this definition, democracy is synonymous with the values of solidarity and compassion; indeed, one might say that the spirit of democracy is only realized in relations of mutual dependence. Thus, no matter the actual letter of the law, the State that violates the principle of mutual dependency will necessarily fall short of the democratic ideal. Democracy recedes: when men and women are "separate, personal, at war" (99); when men and women come "to value machinery [primarily wealth and technology, but generally anything foreign to the pursuit of inward human perfection] as an end in itself" (1993a, 83); when social ties are treated as unjust fetters on "our strong individualism" (63); when "our maxim of 'every man for himself' " (63) is left ideologically unchallenged in the public square and the marketplace; and finally, when large numbers of the working class, "this class pressed constantly by the compulsion of material wants," are made economically redundant and herded into urban slums (84). In short, what Arnold calls "the vital impulse of democracy" (1993b, 6) is dialectically tied to the sense of ethical community brought into the world by "culture."

The rhetoric of democracy as mutual dependency explicitly denies the monopoly on moral values claimed by the capitalist marketplace. In a treatise on the subject of "equality," which he published in 1878, Arnold severely questioned the moral propriety of limitless wealth-getting, and he denounced the doctrine of the inevitability of enormous social inequality. His notion of the authentic ethical community must be read, then, as a timeless critique of "the mere unfettered pursuit of the production of wealth, . . . [which] threatens to create for us, if it has not created already, those vast, miserable, unmanageable masses of sunken people" (1993a, 175). Arnold regarded the laissez-faire market (the linchpin of the neoliberal dogma that reigns today) as naught but "a mere fetish," a gross ideal that imprisons us ever more deeply in the "one-dimensional" world of "our ordinary selves" (150, 99). Far from being a force for human progress, the laissez-faire market is as much an agent of "anarchy" as the brutal Populace.

Liberal educators—"persons who are mainly led, not by their class spirit, but by a general humane spirit, by the love of human perfection," according to Arnold (1993a, 110)—promote a spiritual democracy of the rational, inquisitive mind and the considered aesthetic sense that serves as a stark moral corrective to those masters of capital, who vulgarize the body politic and marginalize "the world of ideas" (1993d, 33) in the name of increased production and ever-greater profits. The challenge to the liberal educator is to "lift us out of [the] vulgarity and brutality" of our ordinary lives (1993c, 237), in order to bring us to a true appreciation of human creativity, human intelligence, and human potential (237). The authentic education, however, does not reside in "merely toying with poetry and aesthetics" (1993a, 100), or in mere technical know-how; liberal pedagogy must concertedly aim at the development of the active social consciousness on the part of the student, the existential and ethical recognition that "because men are all members of one great whole, and the sympathy which is in human nature will not allow one member to be indifferent to the rest or to have a perfect welfare independent of the rest, the expansion of our humanity, to suit the idea of perfection which culture forms, must be a general expansion" (62). *We must school ourselves in culture and school ourselves for being in the world.*[15]

When the student—by leave of a sustained engagement with the "great civilizers," art and letters (Arnold 1993c, 229)—has fully come to terms with the transcendent message of culture, that "we are indeed, as our religion says, members of one body, and if one member suffer, all the members suffer with it" (1993a, 174), then the liberal educator can be regarded as having fulfilled his or her spiritual mission: to cast "the day of general humanization" into greater relief (1993c, 235). Thus, the liberal academy is more than simply "a recognized authority in matters of intellectual tone and taste," as Arnold defined it in his essay "The Literary Influence of the Academies" (1968, 52). It is also a putative moral center, where the anti-capitalist value of "a desire after the things of the mind simply for their own sakes" (1993a, 59) may not be perfectly realized but can at least be entertained, if only in abortive form. Which is to say, the liberal academy emerges as a key liminal space for analyzing the dialectical politics of "order" versus "justice," "closure" versus "becoming", "capitalism" versus "democracy". I believe that the well-being of the public square is intrinsically linked to the "free-play of thought" in the liberal academy (148). Then again, the well-being of the liberal academy is directly related to the effectivity of the barriers placed around the public square to protect it from the encroachments of despotic capital.[16] For in the absence of a liberal State, the adjective "liberal," as affixed to the nouns "culture," "education," and "academy," would surely be robbed of substantive meaning. This, in my view, is the process we are already witnessing in the increasing hold of the commodity on everyday life.

V

For all that it fell short of accepted international standards in the provision of health-care and the institutionalization of unemployment and social insurance programs, the U.S. Welfare State still symbolized the traditional liberal axiom—key to the logic of social contracts—that the masters are, in some measure, responsible for the well-being of the impoverished strata of the Populace. The political advent of Ronald Reagan, in 1981, set in motion a propaganda machine, dedicated to the singular task of convincing the public that the claims of liberalism were so much sentimental hogwash.

We can see today, in the complex of homelessness, drug abuse, chronic violence, and fearful immiseration that confronts the individual in a thousand settings spread across the entire United States, that the machine wrought for its masters an infamous victory. I recall that at one point in the 1980s ex-British Prime Minister Margaret Thatcher was quoted as saying that there was "no such thing as society"; there was only "the market" and free-floating individuals. This extreme "Lockean" fiction (in Arnold's terms, the acme of Philistinism) was derided by many, but it also had its believers, thus indicating that the propaganda of the masters had gained considerable cultural ground in post-imperial Britain. The situation in the United States is no less disastrous.

Immanuel Wallerstein points out that of the three nineteenth-century ideologies that sought to make sense of the relationship between capitalism and democracy— "conservatism, liberalism, and socialism"—it was liberalism "that emerged triumphant. . . . For it was liberalism that was best able to provide a viable geoculture for the capitalist world-economy, one that would legitimate the other institutions both in the eyes of the cadres of the system and, to a significant degree, in the eyes of the mass of populations, the so-called ordinary people (1994). The masters and their intellectual servants claim that socialism is morally and historically exhausted. But what of contemporary liberalism and conservatism in a public square that has suffered, in the last two decades, an unusually aggressive infiltration of marketplace values?

The dissolution of civic and social structures that stand for "the essential unity of man" severely undermines what Arnold called "the social idea" embodied in social contracts (1993a, 79); the likely outcome of this process is truly inauspicious. Doug Henwood observes that "As all the welfare state buffers that once softened the market's discipline are being dismantled, we're being returned to the savage rule of pure nineteenth century capitalism" (1997, 29). In other words, the last days of liberalism bespeak the advent of a morally devitalized society: a society that claims "the end of ideology"; a society of managers, consultants, and accountants; a society of elite workers, "contingent workers," and those who don't work at all; a society of the masters; a society of the masters' intellectual servants; a society given over to the police. In the following pages I shall endeavor to make plain the fundamental, nay, the necessary, link between the study of "art and letters" in the liberal academy and the political status of the police.

In July 1868, 60,000 British workers converged on London's Hyde Park to demand the franchise. The Home Secretary, however, closed the park, with a view to neutralizing "the mob." Most in the crowd took note of the sanction of the law, but some destroyed fences and pitched stones at the palatial homes surrounding Belgravia. The entire episode entered the historical record as the so-called Hyde Park Riots. The Hyde Park Riots were the representative anecdote for Arnold's *Culture and Anarchy*. Arnold regarded "outbreaks of rowdyism" (1993a, 85) as perfectly illustrative of his essential argument: that where culture is not, liberty degrades into mere libertarianism (i.e., the barbarism of "doing as one likes").[17] As stated above, *Culture and Anarchy* played no small role in formulating that ideology of the humanities which we know so well as our own: namely, that the study of "art and letters" is key to the perfection of oneself, to the development of what Arnold called "the whole spiritual man" (1993e, 200), from the starting-point of "the raw person" (1993a, 64). Note that if "rawness" is a synonym for anarchy, then culture, as a synonym for order, is necessarily on the same side of the fence as the police. In other words, the cultivation of the liberal self harbors a disciplinary commitment to the law, however unjust. The cynical bargain struck between liberal educators and the masters of capital, concerning the propagandistic function of education, turns, then, on the moral capital withheld from the Populace but, in the same gesture, invested in the police.[18]

As linked to the ruling-class interest in political closure, culture helps to consolidate the ideological conflation of political becoming with social anarchy. Arnold contends that the study of arts and letters strengthens the social contract by contributing important values to the idea of national community; but he concedes that culture requires "a principle of authority" to supplement its work (1993a, 89). He writes: "whatever brings risk of tumult and disorder, multitudinous meetings in their public places and parks—demonstrations perfectly unnecessary in the present course of our affairs—our best, or right reason, plainly enjoins us to set our faces against. It enjoins us to encourage and uphold the occupants of the executive power, whoever they may be, in firmly prohibiting them" (100). One easily comprehends that the prohibitive force imagined here is none other then the metropolitan police, "the Cerberus of society," says Charles Christian in his 1812 treatise on policing New York City, whose "constant vigilance" secures all social relations, particularly those based upon the unequal distribution of private property (1970, 30). For Arnold, where culture fails to bond the community, the police (i.e., the law) must step in. Arnold's model of the smoothly functioning polity combines liberal paternalism with a conservative concern for social order. Contemporary events, however, suggest the increasing irrelevance of the Victorian reformer's model of social control.

The passage of the extraordinary "Violent Crime and Law Enforcement Act of 1994" (better known as President Clinton's "crime bill") presages the advent of postliberal governance. The Act encompasses, among other things: the "three strikes" provision (i.e., anyone convicted of three Federal felonies automatically receives a life sentence, without parole); sixty new categories of Federal capital offenses; enhanced mandatory sentencing in Federal courts; the termination of Pell grants which enable Federal prisoners to receive higher education; the criminalization of street gang membership; and finally, the funding of the recruitment of 100,000 extra police officers, across the nation (Cockburn 1994).[19] Aristotle noted that "poverty is the parent of revolution and crime" (1993, 31). Historically, class-divided societies have dealt with the threat of revolution from below and the "anarchy" of widespread criminality by mixing brute repression with subtle modes of social discipline. But societies have also dealt with the offspring of poverty by imposing ethical and political limits on "the encroachments of the rich" against the integrity of the body politic. Thus Aristotle condemned "the unlimited acquisition of wealth," and he denounced those "who turn every quality or art into a means of getting wealth" (13-14, 14). Like Arnold, Aristotle regarded laissez-faire economics as utter barbarism, a savage assault upon the human spirit.

In writing *The Politics* Aristotle was moved by a question that cannot be fully explored in a society totally dominated by the masters: "What is the right use of property and wealth—a matter which is much disputed" (1993, 163). We cannot explore this question with the seriousness that it deserves because where Aristotle argued that "extreme poverty lowers the character of democracy. . . . [Thus] the proceeds of the public revenues should be accumulated and distributed among the poor" (150) to secure their general welfare, our society looks to dismantle public assistance programs, and seems intent on casting large numbers of the poor to the winds of fate. Then again, Aristotle argued that "all trade should be excluded" from the public square, because the preeminent concerns of the marketplace—the selling of goods with an eye to profit, and the need to advertise one's wares to the prospective customer—are in many ways antithetical to the values of democracy. In contrast, our society freely allows the cries of the traders in the public square to drown out the full range of voices on which democracy depends.

We seem to have lost the historical memory that the "anarchic" or despotic conduct of the rich has always been an abiding concern of any society that aspires to "civilization." Alexander Cockburn notes that "for almost 800 years [1025 to 1844] the economic behavior that creates . . . [today's social problems] . . . were [*sic*] generally considered illegal and sinful. But religious institutions that once monitored engrossers [speculators, usurers, etc.] have disappeared as a force for social equity" (1994). In the nineteenth century, as regards a moral force that might monitor wealth accumulation, Matthew Arnold proposed "culture" as the substitute for religion. But in our time culture is increasingly inadequate to the job. In the coming postliberal society which is not easily avoidable, now that "the United States has become the most economically stratified of industrial nations," reports Keith Bradsher (1995); in the coming postliberal society where "the internal canker of *publice egestas, privatim opulentia* ['public poverty and private opulence']" (Arnold 1993a, 71) eats daily at the "social substratum," the ethical backbone of the democratic body politic, culture, in the Arnoldian sense of spiritual becoming, will struggle to find a meaningful role in the national political discourse. This because: society itself will struggle to hold onto values—of community, leisure, and creativity—that are not reducible to the logic of the unfettered marketplace.

In my view, the worthy ideal of "the whole spiritual man" and "the whole spiritual woman," is seriously threatened by the totalitarian universe—of buying and selling—ushered in by the wholly liberated commodity. Arnold accords culture a strong utopian significance: it "seeks to do away with classes" (1993a, 79). No doubt, the ideal of a classless education does much to advance bourgeois hegemony; however, historically, it has also afforded a context in which voices from below might struggle with, and even negate, the hegemonic narratives of culture which reduce "the public" to various constituencies of elites. In our time, the counterhegemonic potential of liberal education is increasingly undermined by dystopian social forces which work to segregate the poor (especially, poor people of color). Such forces— homelessness, unemployment, anomie, etc.—render "culture" irrelevant, reducing life to a Darwinian struggle for survival.

Arnold argued that "lovers of culture" should not ignore the plight of "our fellow men, in the East of London [a notoriously impoverished region in Victorian England] and elsewhere"; he strongly emphasized that "we must take [them] along with us in the progress towards perfection, if we ourselves really, as we profess, want to be perfect" (1993a, 174). To do otherwise is to do violence to our common humanity. To do otherwise is also to make of culture *a vulgar ethics of those who have enough to eat*—a hopeless travesty of the ideal of "sweetness and light." I think it certain that the misery of those considered "the underclass" corrupts us all to a degree that we accept it as "inevitable." "No individual life can be truly prosperous," writes Arnold, "passed . . . in the midst of men who suffer" (1993c, 224). I unequivocally reject the normative and elitist aspects of Arnold's model of culture; but I regard the notion that culture is a principal means of making community as a valuable ideal that ought to be keenly defended in the liberal academy and elsewhere. I submit that without that spiritual mission, the modern humanities are lost.

VI

Ronald Reagan and Margaret Thatcher have reminded us that "merchant and master manufacturers" and their intellectual servants typically conduct class war with more venom than the Populace. The callous treatment of the poor, normalized in everyday social *praxis,* in my view, signals a Faustian descent toward real barbarism. One can envisage the day when society will be no more, and individuals will uneasily confront each other in a veritable Hobbesian universe, made safe only by a massive increase of the police. "This is the era of the police," said a Los Angeles councilman in 1988 (Davis 1988, 39). The zeitgeist of our time was perhaps illumined in a comment made by Senator Joseph Biden, with respect to the congressional debate on President Clinton's crime bill: "If someone came to the floor and said we should barb wire the ankles of anyone who jaywalks, I think it would pass" (Wright 1995, 36). When Charles Christian penned his treatise on law enforcement in the early nineteenth century, he imagined the police as "guarding from danger every man's door, protecting from oppression the innocent and helpless" (1970, 30). Can we honestly say that such sentiments are the moral measure of the police in poor communities today, particularly those poor communities in the inner city that are overwhelmingly Latino or African-American?[20]

Culture, in the higher sense of ethical becoming, was not able to prevent the slave trade, World War I, the Nazi Holocaust, or the dropping of the nuclear bomb. In all these instances of human barbarism, dread worldly forces prevailed. I take it for granted, however, that without culture—as an engine for "detaching ourselves from our stock notions and habits" (Arnold 1993a, 186) and as "a force for social equity"—things would yet have been worse. According to Arnold, culture "saves the future, as one may hope, from being vulgarized, even if it cannot save the present" (65). To this extent culture keeps our eyes on the prize of Utopia: the perfection of "the social idea," the completion of men and women as excellent social beings. "Culture," says Terry Eagleton, "can be defined in one sense as that which is surplus, excessive beyond the strict material measure; but that capacity for self-transgression and self-transcendence is precisely the measure of our humanity" (1992, 40). Yet the masters would have us believe that our present "Philistine" society is the only Utopia possible, whatever society one might dreamily imagine. In other words, they seek to convince us that the present set of social arrangements is decisively fixed, possibly for eternity. It is, of course, in the masters' interests that we accept the myth of the eternal present, for current property relations are then beyond question. The danger of the eternal present is felt everywhere today: in the extreme social commitment to the police, in "the end of ideology," in the marginalization of culture, in the collapse of civic life, and even in the theoretical edifice of "the postmodern condition."[21]

The closure implicit in the myth of the eternal present is, perhaps, the most serious threat to the integrity of the human spirit; for when the principle of "becoming something" is absent, the values of hope, regeneration, and "self-transformation"—all dependent on "the movement of ideas" (Arnold 1993a, 91)—are difficult to entertain. Thus Arnold warned against the delusion of treating social arrangements as "part of the order of nature, that [can never] come to an end" (1993b, 12). Like Marx, Arnold believed that the sense of the eternal present must always be questioned in the name of a better human world that lies in the historical future.

The profound tension between capitalism and democracy, between the marketplace and the public square, between economy and society, between industry and the inner life, basically, the tension between the forces of "anarchy" and the forces of "culture," has been the key fact of the modern social experience. Arnold wrote that the divide between the individual and the State (the mundane reality of capitalist democracy) is the result of "one irresistible force, which is gradually making its way everywhere, removing old conditions and imposing new, altering long-fixed habits, undermining venerable institutions, even modifying national character: the modern spirit" (1993b, 25). The triumph of "the modern spirit" (as expressive of the promise of culture) is the fact that it shows men and women that history is theirs to make, that "human thought, which made all institutions, inevitably saps them" (25). Postmodernists tell us that "the narrative of progress," a key ingredient of liberalism, is no longer relevant to our times. Certainly, at this juncture in the historical process, in "our present unsettled state, so full of the seeds of trouble" (1993a, 138), it would seem a radical project even *to hold onto* mainstream Enlightenment values, particularly, the ideals of Liberty, Equality, and Fraternity. Having said this, however, I firmly believe that we can ill afford to relinquish the concept of a morally-charged, historical narrative.

For are we to make peace with the misery daily visited upon millions of people, here and everywhere? Can we accept that "the due fruit of mankind's centuries of painful schooling in self-conquest" (Arnold 1993a, 133) is a society squarely based on what Adam Smith termed "the vile maxim of the masters":

"all for ourselves and nothing for anyone else" (1986, 512). I believe that in both cases our common humanity obliges us to say "no!"; indeed, it enjoins us to explore, on a daily basis, the concept of "becoming something" and the value of struggle.

NOTES

I would like to thank the following people for the helpful criticisms that they made of earlier drafts of this paper: Mary M. Gallucci, Nancy Churchill, Leigh Binford, and Fred Pfeil.

1. Gerald Graff criticizes "the humanist myth" which proffers "the delusion that academic literary studies at some point underwent a falling-away from genuine Arnoldian humanism" (1987, 5). Graff points out that "commercial and corporate interests" made laughable "the pretensions of the literary elite to cultural leadership" (12). I agree with the tenor of Graff's remarks; however, the Arnoldian tradition in American culture is not reducible to a single history of spuriousness. Each age remade Arnoldian humanism in its own image. Thus however spurious it may be as a project for empowering "the literary elite," Arnoldian humanism is always a vehicle for genuine social concerns. Its status as a powerful moral ideal can help clarify the distance between the theory and practice of liberal education.

2. This was the strategy adopted by the American Arnoldian W.C. Brownell in the early decades of the twentieth century. Brownell noted that criticism in the United States was "routine" and provincial vis-à-vis the criticism of Europe. Brownell sought to remedy the situation by stressing the need of "the Academy" to give "more *standing* to our criticism" (1924, 92). Like Arnold, Brownell outlined "the traits of the ideal critic" (93), and then advanced the academy as the place where the critic's voice comes into its own. See Kuklick (1990, 195–206), and Parker (1967, 339–51), for astute observations on the institutional birth of the humanities.

3. For a pointed critique of this development, see Eisenstein (1982, 567–88).

4. "We are asking for trouble," contends Anthony Platt, "if we simply pretend that the university can become an island of inclusion and equality in a society that is obsessed by race and divided by class and becoming more so each day" (1993, 77).

5. Compare Raleigh's nervous conclusion: "But, of course, although we know that Arnold asked the right questions, we cannot be sure he supplied the right answers. History, despite some portentous rumblings, has not finally spoken, and we still do not know whether Arnold's work and that of his followers is an augury of the future or a monument of the past" (1961, 265).

6. My thinking here is strongly influenced by Paulo Freire: "Within history, in concrete, objective contexts, both humanization and dehumanization are possibilities for man [sic] as an uncompleted being conscious of his incompletion. But while both humanization and dehumanization are real alternatives, only the first is man's vocation." (1990, 27–28).

7. If Arnold's dialectic preserves human creations against the cynical profligacy of history, then, it must also be admitted that this work of preservation takes place in a primarily idealist realm. Unlike Marx, Arnold has nothing substantial to say about the abiding material reality of human history since the Fall into class-divided soci-

eties: what Fredric Jameson has called the "scandalous fact of mindless alienated work," which has been the lot for innumerable generations of people (1988, 162). That Arnold could celebrate "the Greeks" as "the great exponents of sweetness and light united" (1993a, 141), but nowhere mentions the economy of slave labor that underpinned "Greek civilization," is itself an eloquent testimony of the abstract idealist bias which consigns the real contributions of the despised "masses" to the historical margins.

8. Adam Smith noted that the question of "political stability" is invariably answered on the terms of the masters, that law is an expression of class power. "Whenever the legislature attempts to regulate the difference between masters and their workmen," Smith observed that "its counselors are always the masters" (1986, 246). One wonders what it would take to demystify the workings of the law, as based on class power, when so much social energy is invested in the spectacle of working-class crime. As Jeffrey Reiman has written, "the criminal justice system [makes] it look like crime is the work of the poor. And it does this in a way that conveys the image that the real danger to decent, law-abiding Americans comes from below them, rather than above them, on the economic ladder. This image sanctifies the status quo with its disparities of wealth, privilege, and opportunity, and thus serves the interests of the rich and powerful in America" (1979, 5).

9. For an historical overview of this specter which comes and goes with the nature of economic times, see Morris (1994).

10. Richard Johnson argues that educational policy in early Victorian England was shaped by the need "to create powerful systems of control, centering upon the teacher as social missionary and the school as a functioning center of sound influences" (1970, 116). Johnson points out that the teacher was imagined as a "substitute parent," while the school became a substitute family. This because working-class culture was viewed by liberal reformers as being pathologically incapable of supporting the proper family structure. Thus, the victims of capitalist exploitation were made responsible for the evils that beset them. Johnson clarifies the moral motivation of this strategy: "by blaming the poor for their poverty (and much else besides) the educationalist was *enabled to believe* that his was a humane, an adequate and an essentially Christian response to potentially removable evils" (105).

11. Arnold proffers the notion of intellectuals as a class unto themselves; however, his claim cannot stand so long as the statist tendencies of the intellectual class render it a useful servant to the masters of capital. I am reminded of the critique of intellectuals advanced by W.E.B. Du Bois in the context of global exploitation: "the educated and cultured of the world . . . receive their training and comfort and luxury, the ministrations of delicate beauty and sensibility on condition that they neither inquire into the real source of their income and methods of distribution nor interfere with the legal props which rest on a pitiful human foundation of writhing white and yellow and brown and black bodies" (1986, 197). In their worst instrumentalist moments, the heirs of Arnold's legacy are surely vulnerable to Du Bois's critique.

12. Compare Freire: "The pedagogy of the oppressed, animated by authentic, humanist (not humanitarian) generosity, presents itself as a pedagogy of man. Pedagogy which begins and ends with the egotistic interest of the oppressors (an egoism cloaked in the false generosity of paternalism) and makes of the oppressed the object

of its humanitarianism, itself maintains and embodies oppression. It is an instrument of dehumanization" (1990, 39).

13. The pedagogue as paternal missionary is a true proponent of what Freire calls "the banking concept of education," in which "knowledge is a gift bestowed by those who consider themselves knowledgeable upon those whom they consider to know nothing. Projecting an absolute ignorance onto others, a characteristic of the ideology of oppression, negates education and knowledge as processes of inquiry" (1990, 58).

14. Compare Raleigh: "In the academic world it seemed—to some anyway—that Arnold had become the preeminent English critic and that to be a professor of English meant being, by definition, an Arnoldian" (1961, 193).

15. Authentic humanist education opposes over-specialization to the degree that the latter functions as a form of what Donaldo Macedo calls "the illiteracy of literacy." In this scenario, according to Macedo, "we develop a high level of literacy in a given discourse while remaining semiliterate or illiterate in a whole range of other discourses that constitute the ideological world in which we travel as thinking beings" (1994, 27).

16. In a persuasive analysis of "teaching and research as economic problems," Patrick Hogan has noted that there is "no antagonism between teaching and research. There is, however, very serious, even debilitating conflict between both of these and capitalism" (1993, 24). See Soley (1995) and Honan (1994) for eye-opening accounts of the corporate advance on academic culture.

17. We should not allow Arnold's seductive eloquence to blind us to the fact that his analysis of working-class activism is redolent with tabloid vulgarities. As Raymond Williams has observed:

Calm, Arnold rightly argued, was necessary. But now the Hyde Park railings were down, and it was not Arnold's best self which rose at the sight of them. Certainly he feared a general breakdown into violence and anarchy, but the most remarkable facts about the British working-class movement, since its origin in the Industrial Revolution, are its conscious and deliberate abstention from general violence, and its firm hold in other methods of advance. . . . I think it had more to offer to the "pursuit of perfection" than Matthew Arnold, seeing only his magnified image of the Rough, was able to realize. (Williams 1982,133)

Williams reminds us of how easy it is for liberalism to slip into "bad faith," to fail to live up to its own promises.

18. The liberal self has long served as the model of "the gentle reader" in literary culture. To this extent, the implied reader of many literary texts is accorded the moral capital that liberal culture denies to working-class collectivities. In short, the reader is asked to align him or herself with the disciplinary politics of the police. For detailed analyses of literature's complicity with the police, see Bendient (1986), Miller (1988), and Lentricchia (1988).

19. For cogent explications of this appalling legislation, see Lusane (1994, 14–22) and Wright (1995, 3–17).

20. For telling discussion of policing in the racialized inner city, see Davis (1994, 21–27), Bierma (1994), and DeSantis (1994).

21. In his study of "the Black Atlantic," Paul Gilroy notes that "it may be possible to argue that what is increasingly perceived as the crisis of modernity and modern values is perhaps better understood as the crisis of intellectuals whose self-consciousness

was once served by these terms. . . . Reformist and revolutionary leftists alike are now being challenged to defend the protocols of secular reason and the ideal of human and social perfectibility" (1993, 43). In my view, "the crisis of intellectuals" is intrinsically tied to the decline of welfare state liberalism under the impact of despotic capital. The theoretical moment of "the postmodern condition" might well be regarded, then, as the expression of a kind of *resentment*. A society that sidelines its critical intellectuals, will, according to intellectuals, want for myths to live by. This reading warrants further study.

WORKS CITED

Aristotle. 1993. *The Politics*. Trans. B. Jowett. Cambridge: Cambridge University Press.

Arnold, Matthew. 1968. "The Literary Influence of Academies." In *Matthew Arnold's Essay in Criticism: First Series*, ed. Sister Marion Hoctor. Chicago: University of Chicago Press.

————. 1993a. *Culture and Anarchy and Other Writings*. 1869. Reprint. Cambridge: Cambridge University Press.

————. 1993b. Democracy. In *Culture and Anarchy and Other Writings*. 1861. Reprint. Cambridge: Cambridge University Press.

————. 1993c. Equality. In *Culture and Anarchy and Other Writings*. 1878. Reprint, Cambridge: Cambridge University Press.

————. 1993d. The function of criticism at the present time. In *Culture and Anarchy and Other Writings*. 1864. Reprint, Cambridge: Cambridge University Press.

————. 1993e. Preface to *Culture and Anarchy and Other Writings*. 1869. Reprint, Cambridge: Cambridge University Press.

Bendient, Calvin. 1986. *He Do the Police in Different Voices: The Wasteland and Its Protagonist*. Chicago: University of Chicago Press.

Bierma, Paige. 1994. Torture behind bars. *The Progressive* 58, 17 (July): 21-27.

Bloom, Allan. 1987. *The Closing of the American Mind: How Higher Education Has Failed Democracy and Impoverished the Souls of Today's Students*. New York: Simon and Schuster.

Bradsher, Keith. 1995. Gap in wealth in U.S. called widest in the West. *New York Times,* 17 April.

Brownell, W.C. 1924. Criticism. In *Criticism in America: Its Function and Status*. New York: Harcourt.

Christian, Charles. 1970. *A Brief Treatise on the Police of the City of New York*. New York: Arno Press.

Clinton, Bill, and Al Gore. 1992. *Putting People First: How We Can All Change America*. New York: Times.

Cockburn, Alexander. 1994. Beat the devil. *The Nation,* 17 January, 42-43.

Cooper, Barry. 1976. Culture and anarchy: The politics of Matthew Arnold. In *Prospects for Constitutional Democracy: Essays in Honor of R. Taylor Cole*. Ed. John H. Hallowell. Durham: Duke University Press.

Davis, Mike. 1988. Los Angeles: Civil liberties between a hammer and a rock. *New Left Review* 170 (July-August): 37-60.

DeSantis, John. 1994. *The New Untouchables: How America Sanctions Police Violence*. Chicago: Noble Press.

Doyle, Brian. 1982. "The Hidden History of English Studies." In *Re-reading English.* Ed. Peter Widdowson. London: Methuen.

Du Bois, W.E.B. 1986. "To the World: Manifesto of the Second Pan-African Congress." In *Pamphlets and Leaflets.* ed. Herbert Aptheker. 1921. Reprint. White Plains, NY: Kraus-Thomson.

Eagleton, Terry. 1992. "The Crisis of Contemporary Culture." *New Left Review* 196 (1992): 34–35.

Eisenstein, Zillah R. 1982. "The Sexual politics of the New Right: Understanding the 'crisis of Liberalism' for the 1980s." *Signs* 7.2: 567–88.

Freire, Paulo. 1990. *The Pedagogy of the Oppressed.* Trans. Myra Bergman Ramos. New York: Continuum.

Gates, Daryl. Chief, Los Angeles Police Department. 1988. Quoted in Mike Davis, Los Angeles: "Civil Liberties between the Hammer and the Rock." *New Left Review* 170 (July-August): 37–60.

Gilory, Paul. 1993. *The Black Atlantic: Modernity and Double Consciousness.* Cambridge: Harvard University Press.

Giroux, Henry A. 1990. "Liberal Arts Education and the Struggle for Public Life: Dreaming about Democracy." *South Atlantic Quarterly* 89: 1 (1990): 113–38.

Graff, Gerald. 1987. *Professing Literature: An Institutional History.* Chicago: University of Chicago Press.

Habermas, Jurgen. 1975. *Legitimation Crisis.* Trans. Thomas McCarthy. Boston: Beacon Press.

Henwood, Doug. 1997. "Talking about Work." *Monthly Review* 49: 3 (July-August): 18–30.

Herman, Edward S. 1995. *Triumph of the Market: Essays on Economics, Politics, and the Media.* Boston: South End Press.

Hogan, Patrick. 1993. "Teaching and Research as Economic Problems." *Education and Society* 11, 1: 15–25.

Honan, William. 1994. "Business and Universities as Partners." *New York Times,* 27 February.

Jameson, Fredric. 1988. "Marxism and Historicism." In *The Ideologies of Theory: Essays 1971-1986. Vol. II, The Syntax of History.* Minneapolis: University of Minnesota Press.

Johnson, Richard. 1970. "Educational Policy and Social Control in Early Victorian England." *Past and Present* 49: 96–119.

Kuklick, Bruce. 1990. "The emergence of the Humanities." *South Atlantic Quarterly* 89: 1: 195–206.

Lambropoulous, Vassilis. 1989. "Violence and the Liberal Imagination: The Representation of Hellenism in Matthew Arnold." In *The Violence of Representation: Literature and the History of Violence.* Ed. Nancy Armstrong and Leonard Tannerhouse. London: Routledge.

Lentricchia, Frank. 1988. *Ariel and the Police: Michel Foucault, William James, Wallace Stevens.* Madison: University of Wisconsin Press.

Lusane, Clarence. 1994. "It's a Crime Bill." *Covert Action Quarterly* 50: 14–22.

Macedo, Donaldo. 1994. *Literacies of Power: What Americans Are Not Allowed to Know.* Boulder: Westview Press.

Marx, Karl. 1976. *Capital, Vol. I: A Critique of Political Economy.* Trans. Ben Fowkes. 1867. Reprint. New York: Vintage.

Miller, D. A. 1988. *The Novel and the Police.* Berkeley: University of California Press.

Morris, Lydia. 1994. *Dangerous Classes: The Underclass and Social Citizenship.* London: Routledge.

Ohmann, Richard. 1976. *English in America: A Radical View of the Profession.* Middletown: Wesleyan University Press.

———. 1987. *Politics of Letters.* Middletown: Wesleyan University Press.

Parker, William Riley. 1967. "Where Do English Departments Come From?" *College English* 28: 5: 339-51.

Piven, Frances Fox, and Richard Cloward. 1979. *Poor People's Movements: Why They Succeed, How They Fail.* New York: Vintage.

Platt, Anthony M. 1993. "Beyond the Canon with Great Difficulty." *Social Justice* 20: 1-2: 72-81.

Raleigh, John Henry. 1961. *Matthew Arnold and American Culture.* Berkeley: University of California Press.

Reiman, Jeffrey. 1979. *The Rich Get Richer and the Poor Get Prison: Ideology, Class, and Criminal Justice.* New York: John Wiley and Sons.

Smith, Adam. 1986. *The Wealth of Nations, Books I-III. 1776.* Reprint. Harmondsworth: Penguin.

Soley, Lawrence. 1995. *Leasing the Ivory Tower: The Corporate Takeover of Academia.* Boston: South End Press.

Trilling, Lionel. 1950. *The Liberal Imagination: Essays on Literature and Society.* Garden City: Doubleday.

Van Der Pijl, Kees. 1997. "The History of Class Struggle: From Original Accumulation to Neoliberalism." *Monthly Review* 49: 1 (March-April): 28-44.

Wallerstein, Immanuel. 1994. "The Agonies of Liberalism: What Hope Progress?" *New Left Review* 204 (March-April): 3-17.

Williams, Raymond. 1982. *Culture and Society, 1780-1958.* Harmondsworth: Penguin.

Wright, Paul. 1995. Federal Crime Bill. *Z Magazine* 8, 3 (March 1995): 3-17.

8

Timescapes for Literacy: Time in Academic Communities

John Lofty

CENTRAL STANDARD TIME

Students enter the academy from different sociolinguistic backgrounds. In our students' language we hear dialectal differences, and in their writing we see varying degrees of familiarity with the normative conventions of so-called Standard American English. Many teachers recognize the richness in the varied forms and uses of their students' languages as they help students to broaden their linguistic repertoire to encompass formal English. In *The Five Clocks,* Martin Joos, using the clock as a symbol for language, argues for the legitimacy of a range of styles of spoken and written English from "frozen" to "intimate."

> It is still our custom unhesitatingly and unthinkingly to demand that the clocks of language all be set to Central Standard Time. And each normal American is taught thoroughly, if not to keep accurate time, at least to feel ashamed whenever he notices that a clock of his is out of step with the English Department's tower clock. (4)

To show that time, like language, comes in different forms or varieties, I want to use Joos's symbol to explore the different conceptions of time that we find in higher education. Although the Central Standard Time of academic life will be a familiar measure to many students, it will be a new metron for some and one actively resisted by others. Students and teachers often do not keep the same time.

Much less understood by teachers than language variation is the way in which students entering English classes have learned time codes different from those that shape our own expectations about how academic work is produced.

135

Differences between our time values and those of students might be expressed by students giving lower priorities to paper deadlines than to social commitments, by their not recognizing the need to complete readings before class discussion, or by their failing to read the signals marking the end of a conference.

Our student body is becoming more diverse as increasing numbers, for example, come from multicultural backgrounds, enter college as first-generation students, and reenter schooling as mature students whose time available for academic studies is likely to compete with time for work and family. The time demands on the lives of the latter group will be very different from those made on more traditional students whose lives can revolve around study. Consequently, the diversity of our student populations confronts us with differences in academic preparation and varying attitudes toward allocating appropriate time for study.

Research on the culture of the classroom suggests the probability not only that people from different cultures experience time differently, but also "that disparate times coexist in the same social formation" (Rutz 1). Students who have internalized the norms of time that regulate institutional life and who can adhere to them are likely to have an educational advantage over those we judge as not yet "disciplined," those who do not know or accept the various etiquettes of academic time.

Standard American English assumes a set of benchmarks against which we can—if we so choose—measure our own forms of language to establish shared expectations for how language will be used for specific purposes in particular communities. By studying semantic conventions and rules of usage, we adjust the clocks of our language to a single metron. A comparable normalizing process occurs, I will argue, in how teachers and administrators structure, regulate, and value time in the academy.

To show that time, like space, has contours and dimensions other than the line of time's arrow, I will use the term "timescape" to refer to contrasting temporal structures, such as the class hour or a student-teacher conference. Timescape will encompass also the movements and extensions of time, its rhythms, pacings, and patterns that differ in a small-group discussion, for example, from those of a lecture. I distinguish here between a time frame and a timescape to focus on how we experience the interiorities of time. Different temporal values are associated with these structures and rhythms, such as students being free to take the floor in a discussion but respecting the lecture-hall code of holding questions until the end. Because the timescapes of our work have been shaped by people with particular interests, we need to observe how their sociopolitical dimensions variously serve the needs of students, teachers and the institution itself.

My purpose, then, will be to examine how timescapes influence reading, writing, and discussion with reference both to composition and literature courses. We often organize and teach each course in different ways, varying the frequency of papers, workshops, conferences, and sometimes the length of classes. Much can be learned here by comparing our teaching practices as well as by examining how students respectively read, write, and discuss texts in each course. Given our need to understand how we can promote a full range of academic literacies that connect different courses, to explore the temporal dimensions of teaching may illuminate an area that has received as yet only scant attention. As student populations change, however, teachers will encounter the varied conceptions of time that students bring into the academy. How teachers recognize and respond to these variations will affect students' entry into and ability to succeed within academic communities.

In public education, the need to document fully the relationships between time and learning has been recognized already by the formation of The National Education Commission on Time and Learning. The Commission's 1992 report to Congress opens by observing that "Our schools and the people involved with them—students, teachers, administrators, parents and staff—are prisoners of time, captives of the school clock and calendar" (4). In *Discipline and Punish,* Michel Foucault argues that students in school, like inmates in a prison, have learned to regulate and monitor their own temporal behaviors. Students do so by internalizing such time frames as the daily schedule, which functions panoptically to normalize a centralized set of codes and practices. "[The panopticon's] three great methods—establish rhythms, impose particular occupations, regulate the cycles of repetition—were soon reduplicated in the organization of schools, workshops, and hospitals" (149). If educational institutions unwittingly have created a prisonhouse of time, then it is exclusively through human agency and its sociopolitical systems. The politics of time will be discussed after I have first shown some of its effects on teaching and learning.

The hegemonic influence of cultural time values on our learning lives is expressed by the kind of linear thinking represented in *time = distance multiplied by speed,* an equation that has permeated our whole society in the form of emphasizing how far and how fast we have traveled. The time values derived from this particular formula further identify speed with efficiency and distance with productivity. In the context of learning, these twin measures of time become functions of intelligence. Furthermore, our culture maintains the speed/time metaphor of intelligence. For example, television quiz shows invite individuals or panelists to hit the buzzer and "beat the clock." We can read electronic books whose pages appear only long enough to be scanned once before disappearing.

Efficiency expressed as units of production, of course, has been a major concern of American industry, particularly since the early years of this century when Frederick Taylor's time and motion studies made possible precise measurements of a worker's productivity. As public institutions, schools have been regarded as instruments of the corporate state whose mission, in part, has been to prepare a labor force. Schools therefore have attempted to reproduce in their students the time management skills and attitudes toward work that productive enterprises require. Joel Spring has argued that the content, structure, and delivery in cellular units of the school curriculum are responses to such needs of the business community.

The relationship between different sets of cultural time values and the quality of social life has been documented fully by sociologists such as E. T. Hall, Jeremy Rifkin, J. T. Fraser, and Michael Young. My interest here is to explore the effects of monolithic time values on our attempts to create and sustain a full literacy in diverse academic communities. A cultural interpretation of the timescapes of English departments will need to focus on how students experience time as they read, write, and talk and to consider the consequences for learning when we accelerate each mode. Given their connections, I will briefly explore each rather than offer extended discussions of any one. Believing that pedagogical theories need to emerge from and be grounded in students' actual learning experiences, I will draw on conversations with my own students as well as with colleagues.

CONFERENCING: TIME TO TALK

Jay Robinson and Patricia Stock view literacy as a series of conversations on the written word that offer students potential access to social, academic, and professional communities:

> What is real in student learning is the emergent text that is constructed and drawn upon by students as they learn. The emergent text is composed by the interactions of members of the classroom community and from their transactions with written texts, and it is written in memory. To some extent the text that emerges will be a common one for all members of the community, but each will have a personal version; such commonality as does come to exist will do so only through negotiation in classes over the meanings and values of the texts that are emerging. We use the term emergent text to distinguish it from the texts that students and teachers bring with them to the course—prior texts that have been constructed in other domains. (185–86)

If students' motivation to enter such discourse communities is shaped partly by the qualities of how we talk about language and literature in the academy, then we need to show students how to begin and sustain such conversations. To understand how the temporal rhythm of conferences affect learning, I asked students at an urban university in Colorado how their awareness of time affected the questions they would pose, the issues they would raise, and the scope of ideas they would attempt to explore. The conferences referred to here include those that serve both literature and composition classes.

Students described conference time in two sharply contrasting ways: what they termed academic or professional time in contrast to what they referred to as social or personal time. Students' talk about each quickly clarified that their distinction pointed less to the extent to which conversation was "on" or "off" task than to the degree to which conversation encouraged an open and exploratory exchange of ideas. Professional time conversations were defined as those that solved writing or reading problems by answering questions; in contrast, personal time allowed more conversational space for student and teacher working together to generate issues as well as to reach answers.

Andy, a graduate student of literature, reports that students can experience professional time as mechanical and unconducive to promoting complex thinking because of its accelerated pace:

> I respect professional time. I understand and sympathize with a lot of the people who are masters of the five-minute conference. Sometimes I admire it as a skill, and I wish I could get to that but at other times I feel cheated by it. Eight times out of ten I feel like professors want to hurry up and get the conversation over to get you out of the door. It's like how people complain about doctors and their lack of a bedside manner. The prof might convey haste with physical agitation, hurried answers that you can tell right away are not very substantial or by turning the tide of the conversation to answer something else that the prof knows will end the conversation more quickly than a full answer to your real question. Conversation is manipulated to a quick end.

Students repeatedly expressed concern about not having enough time for their questions to be answered.

> [The professor] will start talking, and I can think of a million follow-up questions to ask her about what she is saying, but I'll just hold off asking them because I know it will lead to more. I know I don't have that time with her. I feel anxious that I am not getting what I need from the conference. I am thinking about too many things at one time and not concentrating on what we are doing at that moment. I am thinking ahead to the next question I want to ask. (Inga, graduate student of literature)

Perceived limits to available conference time influenced both the number and the scope of questions that some students would ask. Before preliminary discussion about ideas for their papers even began, several students felt defeated when they did not believe they could raise topics requiring substantial discussion.

Contrasting with the accelerated rhythms of professional time, a few students described the experience of talking with their teachers as expansive or timeless. "While we're talking," Mary, an undergrad, explains, "I'm not really aware of time until the next person arrives. I'm more interested in getting subjects talked about, questions answered, new goals set." Students described this experience as personal time because within it they could experience themselves both as person and student, a fusion of roles that supports both learning and the learner.

> People are not just coming to you for nuts and bolts answers to their questions especially because we are dealing with a liberal art, whether it's discussing literature or writing. Part of students just wants contact, self-assurance about themselves as learners, or as creative minds, or as knowledgeable people. Some of this is wrapped up in self-esteem, and students want someone who will listen to them. (Andy, graduate student)

Students value personal time because it allows them meaningful communication such as Anna needs to motivate her to learn. "Personal time is time when you feel like you are a human being, when you are not just this student to this person. You don't feel like you are just part of a job. You still feel like a student, but you feel like someone cares about you." If we conceptualize teaching literature or composition as transmitting content—knowledge and skills—from teacher to student, then affirming students by providing "contact" and "self-assurance" might be valued for humanistic reasons but not regarded as central and essential to the task of teaching.

Since teachers and students often have only limited time for conferences, mini-conferences appear efficient because they meet many students' immediate needs for direction. When conference time is limited, conversational patterns are likely to be characterized by students asking questions and teachers giving answers; we find, then, a much narrower range of language functions than found, for example in a small-group discussion. Questions and answers serve extremely important functions in almost any communication. When this one use of language becomes the dominant conversational model, however, it can easily discourage students from increasing their range of linguistic competence by restricting their practice in using several different kinds of talk. My concern with using mini-conferences either for conferences in a literature or a composition course is that the pressure of time directly influences possible kinds of talk.

When I asked Kevin, one of my own composition students, if he thought he had enough conference time with me, he replied:

> A longer period of time would be more beneficial for me so that I could get some of my more elementary problems addressed. Time drags to a crawl before our meeting. I sit outside your door waiting, like I have spent time in the past waiting to discuss something that I will never be good at. Visions of me when I was in grade school flash back into conscious memory. Doubt fills my mind. I fight not to shut down. Then it's my turn.

His response reminded me that I needed to give back to students the time that my professors in Ann Arbor had given to me. When I came to talk with Professor Ralph Williams, for example, knowing that I would need to wait, I brought a book or chatted with fellow students outside his office. No student tapped nervously on his door to interrupt conversation. We reassured each other that Williams was still in there talking with a student for a conference that seldom lasted less than half an hour and often much longer. The time and space that regulated the lives of graduate students ceased to exist once we were engaged in conversation. The walls of an office overstuffed with faded leather spines and open volumes resting atop piles of papers and articles expanded to take us to fifth-century Greece, Renaissance Italy, or the Age of Reason. I was never aware of him checking his watch. His responses to my first comments were as full and deliberate as to my last. His pointed and expansive responses to what I thought then were simple questions taught me how complex answers evolve over time. Students took advantage of office hours that filled his days and were punctuated only by classes or by retreats to the library, or a meeting. He seldom spoke of time itself. Time, nevertheless, was the medium in which he thought and had his intellectual being.

In Colorado, Maria, an Hispanic graduate student of literature, described the quality of conference time that she most valued in terms of a seamless tapestry of talk woven from professional and personal time. Maria described the temporal context for this kind of conference as Chicano time: "You talk until you are done." Maria's words, that "The key to this sustained conversation is that we developed a personal relationship," seriously challenge those who believe that we can best serve our students by sharply separating personal and professional domains. Although we must be concerned with how best to manage the relationship between professional and personal time, students and teachers alike will understand the connections and distinctions more fully only as we discuss publicly what teaching and learning mean.

The shifts in conversation between the personal and the professional when discussing writing signals more than getting down to business. The transition often marks the move from grounding or making references to subjective experience in a conversation to attending to what some formalists might describe as the "objective characteristics" of a text. This critical position assumes that such features are independent of the reader's responses and also of the cultural milieu of our reading. On the other hand, if we want our students' interpretations at least to make reference to their personal, affective experience of a text, then our conferences need to preserve something of the conversational rhythms of personal time. Critics such as Louise Rosenblatt, David Bleich, and Kathleen McCormick argue convincingly for the role of personal experience in theoretical and practical criticism.

In *The Call of Stories,* Robert Coles describes one of his literature students reminding him that conversation is a two-way exchange that involves personal time. " 'Doesn't this time count too, for both of us? You never know where the conversation will take you.' Further, he let me know that the 'you' could mean me, hence the possibility that my 'office hours' might really be part of my 'living hours' " (91). Because personal time provides opportunities for students and teacher to assimilate reading and writing experiences into their lives, personal time is highly functional and more than a concession to the need for phatic talk. But under time limits that constrained many writing conferences, students often would only ask questions and suppress the reflective and exploratory talk likely to support such practices. Blurring the sharply drawn lines between personal and academic time does not solve the problem. Rather, we must rethink how we use conference time so that students can develop personal responses that incorporate the kind of pointed critical scrutiny of ideas associated with professional time. Students will need to learn that conversational rhythms are not antithetical to critical thinking. To articulate intelligibly personal responses to literature demands rigor both in exploring thinking and feeling.

Because literacy allows us to shape, reshape, and communicate our world views, students will need extended chunks of time to discover and clarify their ideas. Increasingly, graduate students arrange informal group meetings to discuss readings and share their writing, but the practice seems much less common among undergraduates. Teachers can facilitate the formation of such groups by describing their value and allowing class time for students to get to know and work with each other. Professor Williams provided what he called "quod libetal hours," open times for students at their pleasure to discuss issues and ask questions that emerged from the lectures—a time for students to extend, by talking, the boundaries of their reading and writing.

As a new assistant professor, Williams's teaching style modeled for me a set of time values that I believed could serve my own students as well as those values had served me. By proceeding deliberately and giving my students the time they needed, I attempted to imbue my own teaching with his unspoken precepts. But my efforts failed to create for my students the experience of learning now entrusted to me. Although my college students did not depart midsentence at the bell and more than five minutes opened between classes to talk with colleagues, the accelerated rhythms that characterized our work together continued to frustrate me. We often talked, read, and wrote as though double-parked on a conveyor belt. Largely unable to recreate the gift of time that can transform education into a near mystical experience, in conferences I caught myself glancing at my wrist, thinking about the next paper that I needed to publish, and mentally preparing tomorrow's class.

To risk a generalization, many composition teachers now confer with students about their work in frequent and extended conferences. Thomas Carnicelli argues convincingly for the pedagogical value of such conferences in *Eight Approaches to Teaching Composition* (1980). On the other hand, many literature professors see fewer of their students frequently or confer with them less extensively. Conference time often is limited to two or three hours a week. In rare cases, four or more hours are offered. Although an increasing number of universities now emphasize the importance of teaching as much as research, departments have traditionally valued research time for literature professors more highly than teaching time. And students themselves are variously motivated and often reluctant to attend office hours. Consequently, both students and teachers need support with the difficult task of creating chunks of time for prolonged, focused conversation. Making time to talk with one's departmental colleagues can be even more difficult.

TIME TO WRITE

The writing process, like all processes, occurs in and over time. With clock and calendar, we monitor and regulate precisely when students will write, how frequently, and how much time we will allow. When we study the writing process, however, we have focused primarily on the visible activities that characterize the stages of drafting, conferencing, and revising. In our time-conscious society, time values are diffused through every aspect of our work. Time's givenness or apparent objectivity, though, has until recently made it largely invisible on the margins of our research interests. Consequently, we have overlooked how the temporal dimensions of the process are themselves critical elements to understand. Because these dimensions constitute part of the process, we need to know how they determine the quality of writing.

When asked to explain the role that writing played at the invention stage, Nina replied, "My ideas evolve as I write. Writing is extremely illuminating. Reading opens doors, but writing turns on the lights." To understand the roles that time might play in turning on those lights, I asked students to describe how the timescapes, the temporal features of the contexts in which they wrote, enabled them to discover and shape ideas, engage subjects fully, and take risks. My first question explored different ways in which student writers were conscious of time.

Most students talked about time in terms of its passage. Typically, they noted it by using technological markers that predictably included the clock, the CD player running out, and the computer recording new pages written. A few students, like Shawna, noted time passing with reference to natural time markers. "I prefer writing in a natural light, so a growing inability to see ink on paper as the sun went down has more than once been my only cue that time has passed at all." Students' ability to move from the experience of time as measured duration to time as the act of writing itself was directly influenced by how well their writing was going, the degrees of difficulty they were encountering, and their engagement with the topic. When these writers were struggling, they became increasingly conscious of time, an awareness that in turn hindered their writing.

Like any other intellectual activity, writing has the power to generate states of consciousness described by the psychologist Mihaly Csikszentmihalyi as "flow" or optimal experience. Such states are occasions when people report feelings of deep concentration, understanding, and enjoyment, an experience known also as the fugue state. Sustained concentration causes the writer's awareness of clock time to fade against the intense involvement in writing. For Brooke, "Sometimes hours went by like the rain on a pane of glass in a spring storm." She does not keep a clock near her computer and is often amazed "that what seemed like forty-five minutes of writing was actually three hours." Although students' varied experiences of writing on a computer cannot be addressed in this essay, how computers and related technologies are reshaping time will be a rich area of research.

As we might predict, awareness of calendric time increases dramatically for many students as they approach deadlines. But the time marker had two sharply contrasting effects on my students' thinking and writing. First, the due date motivates the physical stage of writing. I assume that ideas might well have been incubating prior to writing. Many students claim, though, that they cannot begin serious writing until a few days, hours in some cases, before the paper is due: "I am always painfully aware of time when I write. I am a procrastinator in the extreme. It seems I cannot get started on a writing project until I have the stress of a deadline looming over my head" (Ann, undergraduate).

If deadlines stimulate some students to begin writing, how do they see this prompt affecting the quality of their composing? Pauline, an undergraduate reports, "Ironically knowing that I've only got a few hours to wrap up a paper, my mind can also go into overdrive and pull me through with words and thoughts I never dreamed possible." The stress and pressure of time constraints for these students transforms time into the driving force that enables them to "concentrate," "remember ideas," "focus," "think critically," and "make connections" among different texts. Until some students' anxiety level had reached a critical threshold, they believed they could not attain the mood or "writer's high" needed to engage such mental operations.

Other students claimed that deadlines had the opposite effect; that they "hinder the clarity and focus of my writing," "drain my concentration away," and cause me to "come up with abbreviated ideas." These writers also believed that short-term time limits encouraged safe formulaic writing and thus inhibited creativity. The writer who took risks that proved unsuccessful would not then have the time to begin a paper again. Timelines are an efficient, and to a degree, an essential way for students and teachers to manage writing time. At issue is not whether due dates are functional. At stake are the many students who have become disempowered by the conditioned belief that without externally imposed limits they can be motivated neither to begin nor complete the writing. For some students, this is a near pathological dependency on a particular reification of time.

I next asked students to describe how they used the time allocated for their writing. They gave two contrasting accounts: one group preferred to allow time for ideas to incubate and develop over several weeks, while the other group chose to write their papers within days or even hours of the due date. Barbara begins writing early so that "I can think about it at other times besides when I am doing the writing. I need several days so that I can keep coming back to the project—give it another look." Leanne needs "time to mull things over and put down preliminary ideas. As the weeks moved on, I began to jot down different ideas as they came to me, and I began to narrow my focus."

Although Leanne valued "open time" so that her ideas could develop, she budgeted her time by counting the hours for the physical act of writing. Based on her experience with various kinds of writing, Leanne had discovered that she must allow approximately six to seven hours for a five-page personal reaction paper, sixteen to eighteen hours for a research paper using five sources, twenty minutes for a business letter, and one hour for a personal letter. While other students reported counting hours for writing, none set limits so rigidly.

Many students begin writing close to the deadline because they prefer to begin and complete their projects within short time periods. Cornelia, a graduating senior, explains:

> I prefer taking an entire day or two as necessary from morning to night and doing my research, as well as writing, all at once. It is most effective for me to work in this way because my ideas are the freshest. As each day lapses, I tend to forget my points, so it is best for me to concentrate and get the task accomplished in one day.

Cornelia had been able to write her way very successfully through her undergraduate education using this method. Her telescoped approach would have caused problems, though, had she been required to submit drafts in progress, and it would appear to limit severely the possibility of using writing to develop her ideas. In contrast, Inga, the graduate student of literature recognizing that writing needs time, began early but then found it difficult to develop momentum without pressure.

> When I start a paper way before the deadline, I'm not very productive and tend to procrastinate. But once I sit down and know that it has to be written, I start to put ideas together and think critically about texts. I always learn something new about literature or what I am writing about as I am writing, and then I wish I had given myself more time to explore the topic further.

Whenever possible, I encourage my own students to monitor the pace of their writing, to organize their own schedules, and to be responsible for the times they will hand in their work. Together we negotiate a calendar of due dates that builds in sufficient flexibility for students to have extra time when they need it, but that in turn allows teacher and students to know when papers are ready for reading. Coordination of schedules enables students to understand the time demands of reading from readers' perspectives and avoids a term-high stack of papers. At first, many students resist this practice and say, "Just tell me when it's due, and I'll do it." Gradually, though, the same students accept that if they are ever to become autonomous learners, they need to be weaned from depending on the teacher as time-setter and to internalize a new set of time values consonant with valuing their responsibility for the whole writing process. When students enter the academy, they need to learn how to translate what presents itself as an external professional discourse into a personal and professional one.

What might students learn when they internalize a set of time values consonant with their own personal and professional growth? To answer such questions, we need to consider the varied kinds of symbolic subjects and practices that engage writers in literature as well as in their general writing classes. In both classes, we ask students to invest time in the process of making meaning by representing their experience of reading and of topics that we ask them to write about. I would argue, though, that students often understand their investment of time—and sense of self—to be for pedagogical and political purposes that are strategically different in each course. When asked to write about literature, many of my students anticipate an engagement with course content that will be exclusively text-based; in contrast, my composition students expect that much writing will be self-referential. In both courses, however, a dual focus obtains.

Yet each course—whatever else we might want it to accomplish—has the potential to provide comparable opportunities for students to engage in what Paulo Freire calls praxis, political actions resulting from individual awareness of the need for social reconstruction. For example, after reading Chicano literature, students could write protest letters to American-owned companies who exploit and endanger their labor force. Composition students do write about child abuse and disenfranchised, marginalized people such as the unemployed and homeless. Students seldom appear to value in the same way, though, the time that they spend writing for each course.

One arguable reason for the different valuation is that students have not learned (have not been taught?) that both courses require them to internalize, or own, the symbolic practices and products they produce by writing. To achieve such ownership, students must acquire time values that support their own personal growth. One such value that I encountered in my own education was the belief that a liberal arts education, versus skills-based training, could not be measured in credit hours. Another value would be the need to reread works over time. Whether teaching literature or composition, we need to help students make authentic investments of time in the work at hand.

TIME AND READING

As overseers of our students' academic lives, we tend to focus more on whether we have enough time than on how our conceptions of it affect students' study of language and literature. Kirk, an English department chair, explains to me that a hazed awareness of time informs our assumptions about how students read.

> We can say that we need to read this novel by next week so that we can talk about it. The whole idea of [anticipating such student questions as] "Well, how do I read a novel? How do I pace myself? Do you read every word, or do you skim and slow down and scan and read in depth? Or do you read it all through to get the idea then read it again?" Reading strategies have to do with students' conceptions of how to use time. But we don't deal with that.

To understand students' beliefs about the role time plays in how they read, I asked how teachers' instructions and expectations for reading affected students' reading strategies. I wanted to identify the influence of different timescapes on the act of reading. Since critical approaches to teaching literature varied within the department, students' answers reflected the range: a focus on comprehending subject, situation, and theme, an emphasis on understanding how language and culture shape meaning, and attention to the subjective experience of readers. I wanted to understand the roles that time plays in promoting reading experiences that students themselves value.

As we saw with both conferencing and writing, students described a tension between states of full engagement in the activities themselves and situations in which students' attention was distracted by time constraints. Students marked one kind of reading experience by watching the clock and counting the pages, in contrast to one they described as "timeless." Although all activity is in time, our perception of its rhythms and duration change with the nature and quality of an experience. Using words like "immersed," "submerged," and "absorbed," some students described their awareness of time as being only a peripheral constraint on their reading. In contrast, other students described time by the clock, in the foreground of reading, with words such as "skimming," "flying," and then "forgetting the content." One recurrent metaphor students chose to describe both experiences was time as a surface or plane beneath which readers descend. Riel's words represent this view well:

> I tend to read for extended periods of time, say three to four hours straight. During a reading session, I find that I slip toward and away from awareness of time as if I were allowing myself to be submerged and then coming up for air again. If a writer is very engaging and forces me to think creatively, I may become immersed even while reading in a noisy and potentially disruptive situation.

Seymour Chatman draws an important first-order distinction between time for reading and the time of the text. "There is reading time and there is plot time, or, as I prefer to distinguish them, discourse-time—the time it takes to peruse a discourse and story-time, the duration of the events purported" (62). For students to enter "story time," their reading time needs to be disassociated from clock time. Kath, an undergrad, writes: "Time is the cage in which I live. It represents the rules and boundaries of society that I must obey. When I read a piece of literature, it is necessary for me to ignore the rules and read at my leisure." Words like "leisure," "relaxed," and "comfortable" might connote uncritical or inattentive reading. But many students believe that when reading, less is more. Slow-paced reading allows them to enter a text as actively engaged subjects who shape meaning, pose questions, and relate and compare readings. These students also wanted to engage literature on a personal level—in Debra's words, "by identifying with or reacting to the thoughts, words and deeds of the characters."

When I have attempted to teach all of the readings on a syllabus, my students typically reported that by trying to cover so much material we had lost detail. On rare occasions, students argued that by giving too much time to each they lost adequate coverage. Curriculum development turns on the axes of range and depth. Teachers therefore continually balance students' needs to become aquainted with a range of periods and movements against student's need to understand and appreciate key works in detail. As the breadth of canon and criticism increases exponentially, the cost of striving for "cultural literacy" often is an accelerated pace of reading that threatens depth of understanding and retention of knowledge. If we want optimal reading experiences—ones that allow students to inhabit works long enough to understand and respond to what they might offer, demands for coverage need to be balanced by a reading list that makes a full engagement with texts possible.

As custodians and supervisors of institutional time, college teachers, like their high school counterparts, are attuned to clock and schedule—although usually to a much lesser degree than are students. Students' responses to the pace they think they need in order to meet teachers' reading schedules can undermine their connections with material even before they can respond to it. Kate, an undergrad, confesses, "I chronically fear that I will not be able to finish my reading on time and consequently I procrastinate out of fear—a sense of being overwhelmed by too much work in too little time."

Many readers claim that when pressed for time, they attended less to making meaning through the rhythm of engaged thinking than to getting through pages in time for class. This strategy severely curtails the complexity and range of readers' possible responses to a text:

I recently had to read *Dombey and Son* and *Middlemarch*. The size of both and the time allotted by the professor threw me into a slight panic. I needed to read fairly fast, so I let much of the text fly by in a blur without much concentration. The formation of the language lost its meaning in my effort to race to the end.

To develop ideas after reading, students need what Maureen, a graduate student, describes as "soaking time":

> I want to read and read and read, and then I want to carry it around. Some of the reading will steep on itself like a big compost heap. But a lot of it will fall outside the chicken wire and never get on the garden. You find what interests you, and you saturate yourself in it, explore it how you want. But still the class has ended, and I am into another course just as I was beginning to define what I was interested in.

While there is a logic to dividing and then presenting knowledge into discrete course-length chunks, such segmentation prohibits Maureen from following her own learning rhythms. While she can "make time" to reread by arranging a less intense course schedule, she is under economic and academic pressure to push ever forward. Graduate students who protract their programs often are seen as less competitive than those who complete their studies on or ahead of time.

We see especially within urban institutions a group of students increasingly diversified by age, ethnicity, parental, and work responsibilities. Kirk, department chair, observes that the increasing numbers of nontraditional students who currently enter his classes read less than those from a decade ago. "The old style of the monastic academic who can sit in his room all day and read has gone. Our students have to get children off to school, deal with the orthodontist. When does the reading get in?" When I put this question to Mary, a single parent, she replies: "Usually later in the evening after dinner is over and my two kids are in bed, I read anywhere from a half to two hours. I treasure my reading time, which I have to plan."

How might a professor reply, for example, to students' protests of not enough time to read? Ford argues:

> I think it is perfectly reasonable to assign a book in a seven-day period. A thousand pages of Fielding would be fine; a three hundred and fifty page book of Foucault is not unreasonable. Students are moaning and groaning about reading slowly. "I need more time." That's your problem. In terms of the reading lists, I have already factored in the issue of your job and your family—the demands of your personal life. If we have got a problem with time for the assignment, then I want you to speed up. I want you to learn how to handle that load. It's like going from here to New York. I don't care whether you go in a Porsche or a Volkswagen bus. I don't care whether it takes you three hours or thirty-five—just as long as you get to New York. I can't be responsible for how fast my students read.

If Ford presents an extreme position, his stance nevertheless enables us to construct from it the viewpoint of the professor who, while setting reasonable expectations, also works hard to assess the changing demands of students' personal lives and their experience as readers.

SOCIAL CONSTRUCTION OF MEANING

In recent years, social construction has been influential as one model of teaching English that has gained popularity in composition and literature courses. Many teachers of college English have shifted from conceiving of reading and writing as discrete linguistic skills to be taught in isolation from learners' social contexts. Instead, many have begun to recognize that meaning is generated from the interaction between readers of student texts or literature and language only when readers are active in an interpretive community.

In part a reaction to cognitivism, this diverse group of theorists argues that thought does not precede language in the privacy of individual minds, and that language is the medium in which social groups generate and realize their thoughts. Meanings are not self-contained, waiting-to-be-discovered and recorded entities. Meanings are created as readers respond to texts in "interpretive communities." (The precise influence and constitutive roles of a reading/writing community are weighted differently, however, among literary theorists such as Stanley Fish, who originated the term, David Bleich, and Norman Holland.) Writing about how theorists of social construction influence composition, Robert Connors and Cheryl Glenn observe:

> The concept of *discourse communities* is perhaps the central idea in social construction as it appears in composition studies. According to their belief that all knowledge is socially constructed, Bruffee, Bizzell, and David Bartholomae have each asserted that the academic disciplines of the university can be viewed as particular discourse communities whose knowledgeable peers, through their consensus, sanction the topics and the methods of inquiry, the resulting knowledge and the appropriate forms of its presentation. (140)

Such a viewpoint depends then on collaborative work and particularly on textual meanings being negotiated in interpretive communities.

Interpretation is a temporal process that occurs in and over time. By situating interpretation in time, we see that Stock and Robinson's "emergent texts" evolve in the collaborative work of a discourse community. Emergent texts are themselves constituted in part by the prior texts that individual readers draw from memory. The dynamic relationship between emergent and prior texts is seamless and overlapping. Past readings are appropriated into and occupy the site of the ongoing interpretation. Conversely, as T. S. Eliot argues in "Tradition and the Individual Talent," emergent texts redefine and resituate prior texts within a tradition. The twin processes, in turn, prepare readers for future interpretations. For teachers and students of a discourse community to negotiate meanings, they need to understand reading time as complex and nonlinear.

POLITICS OF TIME

A growing body of literature documents time not only as a social and cultural construct. The literature also documents time as a primary way to demarcate and establish power relations and hence to control people's work lives. Henry Rutz defines the field's interest:

> A politics of time is concerned with the appropriation of the time of others, the institutionalization of a dominant time, and the legitimation of power by means of the control of time. And above all, a politics of time is focused on the struggle for control and forms of resistance or acquiescence. (7)

If we are not accustomed to thinking about the political implications of how we use time, we might well question Rutz's use of terms such as "appropriation," "institutionalization," and "legitimation." If, on the other hand, we routinely consider the political dimensions of institutional practices, then Rutz's critique, if not his perspective, will be familiar. Rutz's purpose is to critique practices that, though normalized, express political values over which individuals historically have had little if any control.

Students' resistance to and attempted disruption of the temporal control of their school lives is more often documented at the secondary level (Willis; Lofty) than at the college level. Students who do not challenge such control are perhaps more likely to succeed and go on to college than those who do resist. Community-college students are one group that does resist the temporal regulation of their learning lives. Sue Kuykendall observes of her own students:

> [C]ommunity-college students are more resistant to academic time schemes than any other kinds of students—they are, generally (the generalization is just that, though, of course), the students who could not or would not acquiesce to mainstream academic time . . . [T]hey are bolstered in their resistance by more years of experience than high school students have to support their refusals to go along with teachers' appropriations of their time. Many community-college students lack confidence, but the confident community-college student is a very powerful force against the reproduction of linear professional time.

The politics of time that governs institutional life seldom reflects that such students not only enter college voluntarily but also do so paying for their higher education. In other words, students are subject to levels of regulation that we might not anticipate for clientele in other contexts, such as business.

Students in four-year colleges, in contrast, certainly in recent years have often acquiesced to forms of institutional control. In my own experience, students usually conform to and accept the timescapes of academic life until specifically asked to critique how time shapes the quality of their learning. Time may also play a role in retention and recruitment issues, a role masked by students' option to quit school. Some students can accommodate to academic timescapes more easily than others. We saw, for example, that the time constraints faced by a single, working parent are very different from those of the full-time student on financial aid.

Students need to know the time values and practices of academic life, but their difficulties accommodating to the timescapes of the academy can become good reason for their exclusion. Such moves assume political and historic significance as the academy assesses underrepresented student populations segregated along lines of class, ethnicity, and gender. Less apparent, though, is the role of time in constructing these lines. That colleges admit, retain, and exclude students in terms of their temporal identities has been scarcely recognized. Temporal identities become visible typically only when students transgress our time codes, for example, by talking during instructional time or by handing in "late work." Less visible to teachers is the source of such transgressions in students' temporal identities, which encompass behaviors relative to how time is used and valued. Both temporal and linguistic identity have been shaped by home, community, and prior schooling.

Students' own statements about conferencing, reading, and writing document particular instances when their time values differ from their teachers'. Those differences, however, only become visible and politically significant when held against theoretical positions that appear to anticipate very different classroom practices. If our theoretical context assumes that teachers should control all aspects of the task environment—from determining what texts mean to setting deadlines—then what these students report about how time effects learning might not seem to be the problem of teachers. Such statements would be heard as evidence that students are unable to cut the mustard or are unwilling to commit themselves to a life of the mind. If, on the other hand, our theoretical context assumes work toward a model of the classroom as a democratic community, then students' statements alert us to the need to integrate our time values with those of our students.

To interpret the politics of time in English departments, we need to explore not only how students experience time as they read, write, and talk but also how our own work as professors is shaped by time, for example, by the tenure clock. As a new assistant professor at a small urban university in the West, I was asked by the department chair how many different things I could do well at one time. To get tenure, he continued, I would need to publish in refereed journals, present at national conferences, read widely to stay current within my field, serve on various committees, and collaborate with the public schools. Each term I would teach two or three classes, meet frequently with students, and advise about fifty students. My chair concluded with well-intended advice: "You will need to budget your time carefully."

My ability to reproduce meritoriously this particular set of cultural practices would be the grounds for tenure. An inability or unwillingness to do so, for example by slighting research to concentrate on teaching, would strongly risk forfeiting tenure. The values and attitudes informing institutional practices are themselves shaped by mainstream society's particular concept of efficient production. Many English departments traditionally measure productivity in terms of scholarship and publication. As important as this work is to sustain the intellectual life of the academy, the demands of teaching and service compete legitimately for their share of the finite resource of time. Although we set priorities and monitor closely how we allocate time for each, maintaining an equitable balance can be difficult. The assumption that balance can ever be achieved is itself problematic. One promising solution that some departments have adopted is for individual faculty to set their priorities over a contracted period: a professor might allocate time primarily to teaching for two years or to conducting a research project. The professor would continue to work in the other areas but would allocate proportionately less time to them. This priority might also be reflected in a variable teaching load.

In my introduction, I noted that the form and content of schooling has reflected the needs of the business community. With the example of Frederick Taylor's time and motion studies, this observation now deserves further comment relative to the politics of time. Taylor organized labor by a rational model of scientific management that related output to the efficient use of time given to a task. Michael Apple argues:

> Taylorism is significant not just because of its widespread application to labor in general, with the growth of time and motion studies and atomistic strategies to separate conception from execution in factories and offices in the early years of this century. It is also of considerable consequence in education. As Kliebard has demonstrated, for instance, the most widely accepted models of curriculum planning still in use have their roots originally in Taylorism. Furthermore, many of the techniques now being proposed in or standing behind the reports for evaluation and testing, for standardized curricula, and for "upgrading" and rationalizing teaching, e. g. systems management and management by objectives, competency-based testing and curriculum development, reductive behavioral objectives, and so forth, come from similar soil. (140)

The extent to which the precepts and practices of Taylorism have influenced higher education will vary across institutions and departments within them. The academy is no longer an ivory tower, if indeed it ever was, detached and protected from the ideologies of the marketplace. As we acknowledge the legitimacy of this influence, we also need to recognize how the politics of time affect the quality of research and teaching, often in invisible yet profound ways.

Teachers continue to be asked to account for how they are using their class-room time. Potentially they might gain one useful perspective on their educational practices by applying time and motion studies to their work. Understanding the utility and limits of such studies for education requires us to remember that because time is not homogenous, several *different* kinds of time are always shaping our work. Miriam Ben-Peretz and Rainer Bromme offer one important classification: instructional time, curricular time, sociological time, and experienced-personal time (64). The first two are the time of credit hours and carnegie units; the second two are context-bound and grounded in qualitative descriptions. Ben-Peretz and Bromme go on to define "instructional time" as "classroom time, allocated and prescribed by teachers and engaged in and used by teachers." "Curricular time" they define as "time allocations and specifications for time use prescribed by curriculum developers" (67). My concern is what we lose by focusing primarily on instructional and curricular time while overlooking the importance of "sociological time," which regulates the lives of social entities, and "experienced-personal time." Ben-Peretz and Bromme define the latter as "the perception of the temporal order by individuals [who] perceive time in different ways and may be viewed as assigning personal meaning to time" (73). Experienced-personal time is the least studied form of time but nevertheless relevant to our understanding of the values that students attribute to reading, writing, and discussion.

Time and motion studies can show in some useful ways how we use instructional and curricular time. For example, to achieve balance, we can note the weeks we give to one period, writer, or genre in relation to another, the hours we allocate for lecture in relation to discussion, and how we use our conference time—number, frequency, and length of conversations. Because such studies quantify time, however, they are unlikely to reveal students' sociological and experienced-personal time: how students experience the varied qualities and meanings that time has in their work or to reveal how different socio-temporal contexts affect learning. To explore the interiority of temporal experience, case-study descriptions and narrative accounts will be more appropriate than numerical studies. In education, we have often attended primarily to what we can immediately track by "objective measures," which do provide valuable information. Without using such measures in conjunction with participant descriptions, however, we severely limit our understanding of complex phenomena.

TIME, INTELLIGENCE, AND ASSESSMENT

Our whole educational system is driven by and in turn drives a culture that regards the ability to think, talk, read, and write quickly as primary markers of intelligence. Silence and studied speech can easily be equated with slow-wittedness rather than as markers of reflection. As I observed earlier, intelligence itself is often defined as and identified with the rapid performance of problem-solving tasks. At every level of education, we see this value reflected in time-trial evaluations of students' performance. In a matter of days and often hours, teachers are expected to assess learning that has grown over the years but whose content, shape, and expression now have to be confined within the temporal boundaries of a sit-down exam.

Even for doctoral qualifying exams, many of our English departments use versions of the four-hour exam. One justification often given is that time limits bring intellectual rigor but that take-home exams produce burdensome volumes of writing that protract assessment and the students' anxieties. Yet my own reading of exams written under both conditions has shown the quality of writing, and the exploration and development of ideas possible under take-home relative to four-hour exams not surprisingly to be very different in quality. Because the former offer time for sustained thinking and revision—features of writing that we value—the exam has the potential to move the student beyond comprehensive evaluation toward reflection, synthesis, and original thought. The exam itself then becomes a powerful opportunity for learning.

Finally, the question is not which system is better, but how time factors shape performance and assessment. This question has been addressed in part by elementary and secondary school teachers who have moved away from time-trial testing in favor of cumulative record keeping. The practice of continuously assessing performance and evaluating language growth over time as documented by a portfolio of work is restricted largely to public schools. Because continuous assessment is time-consuming, the criticism has been made there that it is inefficient.

One major function of education is to promote democracy by enabling each person to participate meaningfully in social and political life. Effective participation is predicated on an educated populace with the linguistic abilities to interpret what they read and are told and able to act on the basis of their understandings. Yet access to higher education and professional life continues to be made on the basis of an exam system that relies largely on timed assessments. Such assessments select those most successful under this type of condition.

I would argue that to measure an individual's potential for additional learning by such a system is counterproductive to maintaining a democracy. The issue here is the democratic function of the educational system itself. The democratic value of equal access to education is undermined by our failure to recognize how the identification of intelligence with fast performance can work against equitable assessment. The many who cannot demonstrate their intelligence under this assessment are more likely to be advised toward job training than toward additional formal education. We have a gatekeeping system, then, that effectively excludes many people from participation. Because their pursuit of formal education is restricted, they are less likely to regard themselves as being as empowered in the broad political sense as those who have been accepted.

To make visible the politics of time will be new work for many of us. Several major tasks lie ahead. We need first to examine institutional and classroom practices to discover their embedded time values; then we will be able to consider their implications for the missions of our English departments and more broadly for a democracy. To define and implement optimal conditions for students' education, we shall want to select and affirm those practices that are in line with our chosen values and to restructure the time values and practices that work against us. We must also study the local timescapes of the communities from which our students come and help students to understand their relationship to the larger time codes into which we initiate them by their work in the academy—codes that regulate our own production and consumption of texts.

THEORY INTO PRACTICE

The belief that literacy potentially confers a place and voice to members of marginalized discourse communities has one set of roots in politically repressive cultures (Freire). The various forms of this movement applied to American education have been influential because their principles are consonant with preparing students to participate in democratic versus totalitarian forms of social life. Predictably though, because our perception of time values is restricted, we have not yet fully examined how they are implicated in political systems. We have not yet accepted that systems of time are social constructs dependent on context rather than monolithic structures. While investing in constructivist theories of pedagogy, many teachers, myself included, have continued to retain features of practice not only at variance with such theory but broadly indebted to positivistic traditions.

An exact correspondence between theory and practice is unlikely. Discontinuities disrupt not only the likely success of practice but also point to the need for constructivist theory to provide a more complex account of social context by addressing time's constitutive roles for building community. One step toward addressing the slippage between theory and practice would be to reconsider classroom procedures and policies that are out of step with theory. As teachers, how can we apply these insights about time to our theories and practices of teaching college English?

College teachers typically require students to sign up for several conferences each term. Some students will need to experience the value of a successful conference before they will attend voluntarily. I prefer, however, to encourage by inviting rather than by requiring attendance. Adult students can assume this responsibility and will do so once they experience for themselves or hear fellow students talking about the value of office hours. If time con-

straints require one to choose, regular short fifteen- to twenty-minute conferences can more usefully promote ongoing conversations about students'
writing than infrequent but longer ones.

Late papers are another issue that bedevil some teachers' lives. To solve the
problem, Connors and Glenn offer the following much-quoted piece of practical advice.

> It is often better to announce a harsh and unyielding policy initially and then
> adjust it than it is to announce a liberal policy, see it abused, and then try to estab-
> lish a harder line. If you do receive a late essay that has not been explained in
> advance, one common way of dealing with it is to mark the time and date when
> it came into your hands, write "late essay" on it, and deduct from it one or sev-
> eral grade levels for lateness. (40)

College students will be very familiar from high school with their teachers
deducting points for late work. Yet if we claim to grade students' work solely
on features of their writing and then make time a factor in evaluation, we
introduce an extraneous criterion, one that belongs to the process of textual
production. If we are grading the whole writing process, considering time is
appropriate. But then such teachers will need not only to penalize students
who fail to meet the time criterion, but also to reward those with extra points
who hand in their work on time or early. An important question to consider
here is on whose time do we base our rewards and punishments?

As a teacher who follows a process approach to teaching writing, I do not
punish students for late work. Instead, I involve the class whenever possible
in setting due dates because, like ourselves, students deserve to have their
time needs considered. For example, when possible we consider when major
assignments in other classes are due. With mature and working students, the
schedules of their own children and job responsibilities need considering. To
negotiate due dates is not a concessionary move but rather a central feature
of democratic process in classroom communities.

If students need extra time and can show me work in progress, I will routinely
give "extensions." Because I am reading student writing throughout the term—
journal-entries, response papers, revisions, final projects, etc.—and would seldom read an entire set of papers over one weekend anyway, receiving so-called
late papers is seldom a problem. I still expect students to do their best to get
work to me and to student readers by the agreed due date so that we can all
begin reading. The majority of students in my classes do meet our due dates
because they need to complete papers to have time for other course work.

We need to consider how our uses of time affect the quality of college
English, from the conference, to the structure of courses and higher education, to the paths that an increasingly diverse student body take through the
system. As our ideas change about what it means for students to read, write,
and talk about texts, our reform initiatives will need to exceed such revisions

as extending conference time, negotiating deadlines, or shortening reading lists to promote more deliberate reading. Reform initiatives will need to address epistemological questions of how we construct knowledge about literature and to address questions about our purposes of schooling in a fast-changing society. Institutions at every level already are exploring alternate ways to organize learning time. Believing that teaching and learning are more effective when teachers and students work together intensively on a limited number of subjects, Colorado College offers courses in a block plan featuring sequential modules of several week's duration.

At the secondary-school level, under the impetus of the Coalition of Essential Schools led by Theodore Sizer at Brown University, an increasing number of schools now schedule classes into extended blocks of time to avoid the fragmentation of learning that occurs in a seven-period day. If you have never taught high-school English or been friends with its teachers, you will have difficulty imagining teaching or studying in the confines of such a school day. After meeting college students for hourly lectures three times a week, Bob Johnson decided to try teaching for a year in a public school:

> [I]n higher education, teaching comes along in neat little sixty and seventy-five minute bundles. You escape to your own world, the office or library stacks for a few hours before any more teaching shows up. You have to. Committee assignments and writing and keeping up on the "literature" around your subject all demand this ritual of privacy reclaimed. The average professor probably goes half the day without seeing anybody. Not so, the lowly, unsung highschool teacher. Arriving at a highschool in the morning and walking in the doors leaves you breathless. Highschool surrounds you! There is never a break, not all day! Noisy, animated, swarming human bodies will confront you, demanding interaction, every minute of your labors. (87)

We do well to remember that our students' high-school years have been in a very different temporal environment from that of a college or university. Yet even at the college level, the "class hour" continues to determine how we package much of our instruction and thereby influences how students attune themselves to its own particular rhetoric.

In my own English department, we recently combined two separate courses into a year-long seminar. The synthesis creates a more encompassing classroom timescape for relating materials, allowing previously separate discussions of teaching writing and teaching literature to be integrated. The seminar also develops closer working relationships among students than are usually possible in term-length courses. The seminar provides several opportunities to work recursively through concepts and practices, thereby encouraging students to achieve depths of understanding harder to reach in a single term. Although work is not assigned during the term break, students have ample opportunity to reflect on their previous term's work and to plan future projects. Since the course continues over a year, rhythms of learning can be sustained that provide more continuous learning time than when students take the two courses separately.

A further time issue was raised when the seminar was scheduled to meet for one three-hour session each week in contrast to two shorter classes. Many students preferred the rhythm of the longer class valuing a longer block of learning time to explore topics in detail. Others, however, thought that the time between classes was too long, and we lost some of the momentum of learning that comes from more frequent but less extended contact, a problem that a quod libetal hour solved in part. Another challenge for students was that they had to learn how to distribute some of their reading time over the week to avoid skim reading the night before class. As teacher, I thought the longer class allowed us to inhabit the work more fully but found knowing my students and community building more difficult.

The minor change in course structure led our faculty to discuss not only logistical scheduling problems but also the more profound issue of how institutions traditionally format learning in credit hours. Such discussions remind us that because time is socially constructed and because the structures we create have political implications, we need to structure time to the current and future needs of students as well as of teachers. As we think about the effects of time on learning, we need to resist the notion that there ever can be a fully successful one-size-fits-all plan. We need to develop our own timescapes for English studies within the context of individual colleges and classes that respond to the changing needs of the student populations that we serve.

NOTE

Former students and colleagues in Colorado deserve my first thanks for their extended conversations about time. Ellen Westbrook, from the Delahaye Group, helped me think through and write about these issues. Sue Kuykendall, from the Humanities Department at Parkland College, Champaign, Illinois, drew my attention to the particular situation of community-college students and provided sharp commentary on my work. My colleagues Tom Carnicelli, Bob Connors, MeKeel McBride, and Paula Salvio helped me greatly with their thoughtful questions, insights, and arguments.

WORKS CITED

Apple, Michael W. *Teachers and Texts: A Political Economy of Class and Gender Relations in Education.* New York: Routledge and Kegan Paul, 1986.

Ben-Peretz, Miriam, and Rainer Bromme, eds. *The Nature of Time in Schools: Theoretical Concepts, Practitioner Perceptions.* New York: Teachers College, Columbia University, 1990.

Bleich, David. *Subjective Criticism.* Baltimore: Johns Hopkins UP, 1978.

Carnicelli, Thomas. "The Writing Conference: One to One Conversation." *Eight Approaches to Teaching Composition.* Ed. T. R. Donovan and B. W. McClelland. Urbana, Ill.: NCTE, 1980.

Chatman, Seymour. *Story and Discourse: Narrative Structure in Fiction and Film.* Ithaca: Cornell UP, 1978.

Coles, Robert. *The Call of Stories: Teaching and the Moral Imagination.* Boston: Houghton Mifflin, 1989.

Connors, R., and C. Glenn. *The St. Martin's Guide to Teaching Writing.* New York: St. Martin's, 1992.

Csikszentmihalyi, M. *Flow: The Psychology of Optimal Experience.* New York: Harper Collins, 1991.

Donovan, Timothy R., and Ben W. McLelland, eds. *Eight Approaches to Teaching Composition.* Urbana, Ill. NCTE, 1980.

Fish, Stanley. *Is There a Text in This Class? The Authority of Interpretive Communities.* Cambridge: Harvard UP, 1980.

Foucault, Michel. *Discipline and Punish: The Birth of the Prison.* Trans. Alan Sheridan. New York: Vintage, 1979.

Fraser, J. T. *Time, the Familiar Stranger.* Amherst: U of Massachusetts P, 1987.

Freire, Paulo. *Pedagogy of the Oppressed.* New York: Continuum, 1970.

Freire, Paulo, and D. Macedo. *Literacy: Reading the World and the Word.* South Hadley: Bergin and Garvey, 1987.

Hall, E. T. *The Dance of Life: The Other Dimensions of Time.* Garden City: Anchor, 1983.

Johnson, R. "High School As Science Fiction." *Teacher Education Quarterly* (Winter 1991): 87.

Joos, M. *The Five Clocks: A Linguistic Excursion into the Five Styles of English Usage.* New York: Harvest/HBJ, 1961.

Kuykendall, Sue. Personal Correspondence.

Lofty, John S. *Time to Write: The Influence of Time and Culture on Learning to Write.* Albany: SUNY, 1992.

McCormick, Kathleen, and Gary Waller, with Linda Flower. *Reading Texts: Reading, Responding, Writing.* Lexington: Heath, 1987.

National Education Commission on Time and Learning. Annual Report Fiscal Year 1992. Washington, 1993.

Rifkin, Jeremy. *Time Wars: The Primary Conflict in Human History.* New York: Henry Holt, 1987.

Robinson, Jay L. *Conversations on the Written Word: Essays on Language and Literacy.* Portsmouth: Heinemann, 1990.

Rosenblatt, Louise M. *The Reader, the Text and the Poem.* Southern Illinois UP, 1970.

Rutz, Henry J., ed. *The Politics of Time.* American Ethnological Society Monograph Series, Number 4, 1992.

Spring, Joel. *Education and the Rise of the Corporate State.* Boston: Beacon, 1972.

Willis, P. *Learning to Labor: How Working Class Kids Get Working Class Jobs.* New York: Columbia UP, 1981.

Young, M. *The Metronomic Society: Natural Rhythms and Human Timetables.* Cambridge: Harvard UP, 1988.

III

THE RESPONSIBILITY OF
LITERATURE AND THE
POSSIBILITY OF POLITICS

9

The Political Responsibility of the Teaching of Literatures

Paul Smith

The title with which I begin is not of my own choosing: except for the "s" at the end of "literatures," this was the title of a session in which I was one of the speakers at the 1989 MLA meetings[1]—meetings where, not for the first time, and no doubt not for the last, an urge within our profession to estimate (or sometimes affirm) our relation to "the political" emerged in many sessions marked by what I read as an anxiety stronger than it has been for some while. That anxiety is, by and large, a self-lacerating one: an endless registration of the guilt of bourgeois intellectuals and teachers who fear that our political will and even our liberal goodwill might not be directly exercisable within the confines of the academy; who suspect our distance from some putative "real world" where "the political" exists but where we ourselves somehow don't; who will too easily imagine the very material of our enterprises to be always already marginal to "larger issues." That set of fears and apprehensions about our role appears to have a new intensity right now, when the profession of literatures can be perceived to be under attack from within: when, that is, literature as a topic for our teaching and writing seems to be losing a good deal of its privilege; when literatures are apparently under threat of being displaced by theory, by the promotion of other cultural texts such as film and television, and by the increasingly prevalent will to cultural studies; and when the handy and compact reading lists of the various European and American literary traditions are being revised to include the cultural productions of excluded minorities. And often enough, to make matters worse, these recent influences on the profession of literatures parade openly beneath the banner of "politics," constituting an unmistakable accusation against the way things have chronically been.

So to ask now specifically about the political responsibility of the teaching of literature is in a definite way to risk rubbing salt in the wounds, or at the very least increasing the anxieties. These I'm happy to risk—partly because it can surely be no bad thing to have any of the institutions we inhabit continually on their toes in relation to basic manners, assumptions, and epistemologies; but also in part because I've long been susceptible to my own kind of distress when faced with what we might call the flight from politics in whatever discipline or activity. That flight is most often taken by way of simple disavowal or a reactive dismissal of what I take to be an obvious condition of our profession, and it might be as well to begin by reaffirming that condition.

That is, there can be no question but that to teach literatures is to engage in a political act. It is an activity which, like any other teaching, takes place in the arena of political and social relations. Evidently the function of universities, colleges, and schools within the cultures we inhabit is crucial for the production and reproduction of social relations and power, and thus is already highly politicized even before one considers the action of the state upon the processes of education. Equally, it is an activity which takes as its object of study particular discourses that are and have chronically been of considerable moment in the realms of ideology and culture. These are clearly and obviously political matters, and one could readily add to them what might be considered the micropolitical relations subsisting between students and teachers, among students, among teachers, between teachers and administrators, and so on.

The precise political character of any particular act of teaching is obviously dependent upon many circumstances and variables: the place or institution where instruction is carried out; the nature of the students (their diversity in terms of class, race, gender aptitude, motivation); the teacher him/herself; the topic and aim of the teaching; and so on. But in all cases, the production and transmission of what we call (shorthand) "knowledge" always comports a relation to the *polis* and to the *oikos*—in our contexts, a relation to the political economy of an apparently ever-expanding capitalist entity, to which our knowledge is always related, in which it is always implicated, and which defines and is defined by it. In this sense I don't think that a version of Pierre Bourdieu's well-known metaphor of "cultural capital" is an outrageous one to describe what it is that we aid in transmitting: if we agree that as teachers we are agents in the circulation and accumulation of particular forms of cultural capital, we move immediately toward a definition of teaching that begins to grasp teaching in its inescapably political aspects.[2]

Bourdieu in fact has a special term for what sort of capital we deal in: "educational capital." Educational capital can be said to be constituted most broadly in the endowments that agents receive from their familial and educational cultures, and it becomes part of those agents' cultural capital. Bourdieu's observation on the nature and the form of the capital we help to circulate locates it deeply in the complexities of a social life based on exchange, surplus-value, and capital accumulation. While his use of Marxist economic terms here is probably still best considered metaphorical, it is nonetheless a useful attempt to dialecticize superstructural and base elements of social life (rather than seeing one as determining the other) and has the not inconsiderable virtue of foregrounding and analyzing some of the ways in which agents take social and political advantage of their largely class-bound cultural formations.

For Bourdieu it follows that teaching—a profession that usually inhibits its practitioners from holding economic capital but that tends to encourage their continuing accumulation of cultural capital—is part of the system of reproduction[3] for a society highly dependent upon its agents' abilities to hierarchize and discriminate by way of recognizing, reading, and "appreciating" various legitimated cultural marks and symptoms. In that sense, our teaching as such is irrefutably political: it is supposed to play a maieutic role in the transmission, preservation, and exploitation of cultural capital. Additionally, we teachers in the humanities have historically held special responsibilities in relation to cultural capital. The subject matter of traditional humanities departments—the culturally sanctioned texts of always factitious and usually ethnocentric traditions—can be thought of as an especially rarefied set of markers of social distinction and cultural discrimination. As forms of cultural capital, the literatures or particular literary texts we deal in are especially highly valued and almost unproblematically legitimated. If there were any doubt on that score, it would be enough to consider how often the selection of texts in humanities curricula has at its inception the question, "What do our students need to have read in order to go out into the world and be x?"— where "x" names some kind of more privileged set of social relations to which we imagine they will then have access.

To pose the activity of "the teaching of literatures" in this way is, of course, only one way to express what I take to be the obvious: that it is scarcely intelligent to try to disavow or repress the political implication of that work. But again, the precise nature of all this is contingent, depending upon what we understand by "literatures." Literature is itself an immensely variable term, as we teachers know full well. Even if we've been avoiding or ignoring the debates of the last few years concerning "the canon," we can assess its variations just by recalling the simple empirical fact that we don't take to the classroom all the literature or even all the types of literature that we are familiar with. The politics of literature is in a way a function of this its variability as a form of cultural capital. Part of our task in relation to it, then, is to be aware of and to investigate, and to have our students investigate, this variability of the forms of cultural capital: that is (and to carry on the metaphor), to investigate the relation between cultural capital and cultural value.

It is important to remember here that literature is not value in itself, not the concretization of value. As Marx reminds us in the economic realm, value is not a concrete term, but only an abstract medication that enables the accumulation and circulation of capital. Indeed, for Marx value is fundamentally hidden, representable only as a function of commodity differentiation in the circuits of exchange. The demystification and calculation of that process in the realm of literatures—the way in which literatures come to be instantiations of value—ought perhaps be a major focus of our attention as teachers. Thus we might become involved not so much in the teaching of literatures, but in the teaching of the function and uses of literatures within the *polis* and the *oikos* where we find ourselves, the function and uses of literatures in the establishment of largely hidden affirmations and assumptions of cultural value.

But as we have often been assured by those of our profession who love literatures, literatures function on many levels. A literary text can be understood in several senses, then: not only as an element of cultural capital itself, but also as a more familiar kind of commodity. That is, although "literature" as a term of cultural capital is necessarily circulated and exchanged (as in classrooms), and although it might be argued that a literary text might have its own kind of use value (as, say, when the professor reads mystery novels on the beach, as it were "in private"), equally importantly it is also a commodity in the everyday sense: we buy it and sell it, and we act as specific agents in and for the literature industry. At this level literature is a commodity that plugs our teaching directly into the industrial circuits of this capitalist economy in which we live. It seems to me self-evident that the place of the literary text in those circuits is intrinsically part of its significance, its meaning. Thus a consideration in the classroom of that meaning ought perhaps to be a crucial element in the teaching of literatures. For instance, I think that it is an enlightening exercise to ask students to investigate the economic details, of, for example, Penguin's publishing and pricing of the "Penguin Classics" series— texts for which the publishers do not have to pay the same residuals as they would have to pay for something like Nancy Reagan's memoirs; or to ask students to research why you can no longer buy Samuel Delany's science fiction from shopping-mall bookselling chains; or to ask them to consider the economics of the kinds of library (public, college, and so on) to which they have access (or don't); or perhaps most tellingly, to ask where they themselves get the money to buy their classroom texts. I'm suggesting here, then, that part of the "political responsibility of the teaching of literatures" is to recognize that we do not simply read and teach texts but that we are involved with what I've called elsewhere commodity-texts.

This stress on the fact that the literary texts we study and teach are in fact commodity-texts, and on the investigation of the relation between the literal and the metaphorical constructions of literatures as forms of capital, both seem to me to be intrinsic to what it might mean to teach literatures politically. Both literatures and teaching itself are also institutions in and around which particular social and economic relations are established, upheld, and indeed enforced. It thus makes sense to me to entertain the proposal that our first pedagogical task is to allow students to think those relations; to think what are the political, social, and economic contexts of literatures; to think the place of literary teaching itself; and to think the uses of literatures or the uses to which literatures and their teaching are put.

II

It might well seem that so far I have merely been stating the obvious, making my argument at an unnecessarily basic level, by underlining the necessarily political nature of our acts as teachers of literatures. And a while ago I would have thought so too. But it strikes me more and more that it is necessary to keep reminding ourselves of the centrality of the political to our work. And I say that even though the program in which I myself teach (though I won't say I often or eagerly teach "literatures" in it), the Literary and Cultural Studies program at Carnegie Mellon, is supposedly (and in the end I would argue *is*, in fact) in the vanguard of progressive English departments—where matters of the politics of curriculum and pedagogy are foregrounded in everyday practice; where theory, history, and cultural texts of all varieties are taught with as much emphasis as literature itself; and where all those texts that we could or can teach in order to combat the reification of literature and the mystification of its value may take a turn in the classroom. But—to become anecdotal for a moment or two—even there we are affected by the continual debates about the place canonical texts should hold in a newly expanded and differently orientated curriculum. We have, for instance, recently had long disputes about how many Shakespeare courses we should offer in a given year—proponents of "as many as possible" arguing that it is ungodly to teach three gender-studies courses but only on Shakespeare. We've heard African-American courses dismissed by lovers of literature as "unnecessary" and as "exoticism." We've had long debates about whether or not our graduate students should be trained in a traditional literary period. We've heard fears that a potential hiree trained in media studies would be unable to teach properly in an English department. And so on.

These are just anecdotal moments, of course, and seen through my own peculiar lenses. But they suggest to me that what is at stake here in a broader frame is the question that is implicit in the name of our program and others like it: "literary and cultural studies." That is, in many of the new programs of the sort that we have established, a major pedagogical and theoretical problem is what ought to be the relation between these two terms, the literary and the cultural, where what is still implicit is the idea that literature should be preserved as an especially privileged artifact of culture. In some ways it seems to me an unnecessary and even obfuscatory question, since to think culture is surely to think literature as a part or subset of culture (whereas the converse is by no means the case—as we know from the work and attitudes of many in our profession, to think literature is not necessarily to think culture at all).

Here I am, of course, treading very close to the edges of ongoing debates about canons (or perhaps a more descriptive term for canons, systems of norms) and the concomitant debates about values—debates whose only and somewhat insufficient virtue, in my view, is to underscore the inescapably political nature of what we do. Because of my distaste for these debates and my sense that they ought to be unnecessary, I do not intend quite to enter the lists. But it has been remarkable (and, indeed, distressing) to me that among the consequences of these debates has been the increasingly legitimated role of what I'd call a liberalist medication. Briefly, that mediation thinks to counter the multifarious challenges to the system of norms, and the charges against systems of values, by importing the notions of cultural context and/or historical contingency—in the hope, I'm sure, of ultimately maintaining the privilege of literatures and the privilege of class-bound values.

That is, the continued championing of literatures often articulates itself by way of a supposed concern for history and context. The "thick description" of histories and contexts becomes then the preparatory gesture before literature is once again installed at the center. The current fetishization of histories and contexts thus often lands up being merely a diversion from the real fetishization of the literary. The central importance of literatures is attested to anew by the tendrils that they can be shown to throw out into other aspects of society and culture. In most cases it is entirely clear that the project is still the hermeneutics of literatures, rather than what we might call the sociology of literatures and cultures. Histories and contexts are used merely to help update the view of literary texts, in much the same way as some in our profession now deploy "theory" to cast new light on the text: new critical methods (which are presumed to represent progress and growth of a sort) will illuminate the text in a new way. (The whiff of the liberal ideology of enlightenment here gets more and more oppressive as it comes to seem more and more wrong-headed.)

The new liberal mediators seem to locate themselves willingly within a very special kind of contradiction which is perhaps well exemplified in E. D. Hirsch, Jr's contention that the consolidation of "cultural literacy" should be considered a necessary part of the continued progress and growth of industrial society. The contradiction lies in the fact that the ideology of endless capitalist progress and growth is articulated alongside a cultural ideology which has recourse to a fixed thesaurus and which thus authorizes itself to try to establish a kind of gold standard. In other words, the terms and the objects of cultural *values* are posed as it were chiasmatically with the terms and objects of capitalism's *value*. What gets hidden by this chiasmatic maneuver is once again the whole system of social relations that underpins both values and value. Social norms, and what Marx called the juridical relations among agents, are safeguarded in the installation of both values and value, and thus one goal of a politically responsible teaching of literatures would be to historicize the conflicts and contradictions that the system of literatures suppresses between its norms/canons and its value.

This is by no means the same operation as hermeneutically historicizing the literary text. Perhaps the point can be made by suggesting that we refloat the archaic verb "to historize"[4] to dub those procedures which tend to conceal their own special cultural capital interests in the aim of prolonging them; this would leave the word "historicize" to the investigation of exactly those cultural capital interests. At any rate, one inevitable measure is the immediate and unceremonious impeachment of what can probably be accurately described as the canonical *method*—and along with it a whole series of other politically significant, politically motivated elements and effects (the notion, implied or overt, of genius; popular culture/high culture distinctions; the systematic or professionalized suppression of students' own cultures and reading experiences; and so on). The refusal of the canonical method, its overthrow, needs to be complete. it is not merely a question of opening our study to more texts, to more kinds of texts (a move that is more often than not just a supplementing or a complementing of the canon—repressive tolerance in action), but rather of installing a whole different view of texts in their relation to the activity of social life, a whole different view of the uses to which texts are, have been, or could be put, and so on—even if (especially if) that means exposing the bank and its gold standard to a kind of ruinous run. Literatures, traditionally understood, could well supply instances of texts, but within our dealings with cultures no text can remain privileged over any other, and the ideological construct of "Literature" itself cannot be taken for granted.

III

If my essay has started off at too basic a level and then has moved to the anecdotal, I've risked compounding my sins by shifting to the theoretical level. Some of the impetus for the latter comments has been derived from a variety of texts by pedagogical theorists and teachers, as well as from Bourdieu's sociology of taste and, more silently, from Alain Touraine's attempts to formulate a "sociology of action."[5] Some impetus, too, has been drawn from one of Gayatri Spivak's most impressive and suggestive essays—her work on Mahasweta Devi's short story "The Breast Giver." Although that essay is dealing with what Spivak proposes as a very specific situation—wherein Devi's "subaltern" literary text might be negotiated in a foreign (that is, first-world) pedagogical situation, and in my terms is potentially made available for assimilation into the cultural capital of the North—I've found much of what Spivak says here suggestive in thinking about the necessities and potentialities of teaching literature in a politically responsible way in any context at all. That is, I think that some of the propositions Spivak makes from her "teaching strategy" (241) for this text in that context are perhaps generalizable.

In the pedagogical situation, Spivak proposes to look at Devi's text form the point of view of the (cultural) historian and the (literary) critic/teacher. These two personae "must critically 'interrupt' each other, bring each other to crisis" in their different dealings with the text (241). One effect of this interruption, or of what I like to call the "interlection" between differing subject positions of readers, is to reconstellate the text and to help make explicit its use (actual or potential) in different contexts. Without underplaying the particularity of the text and context Spivak addresses, one might easily extrapolate from what she proposes the notion that any text at all, when it is brought into the classroom, is necessarily alienated (it is drawn into foreign arguments, "other" concerns, contexts, and arenas of discourse than the ones to which it ostensibly addresses itself). This process of alienation seems to me to be what happens to literary texts in any pedagogical situation; and indeed the recognition that any text is not at home in this sense is a prerequisite for "understanding" it.

This necessary interruption/interlection of the text and the drawing out of its uses is a process that is akin to a kind of *durcharbeiten,* a working-through with and by the text. The psychoanalytical reference here is partially intended to point to the way in which a pedagogy involving interlection and a working-through of interruptions would necessarily make use of a notion of resistance. That is, the dialectics of subject positions brought to the fore or deployed in the practice of reading is itself productive of resistance: resistance to the text, resistance to the codes that inform it, and resistance to the subject positions themselves. This resistance I call agency,[6] and think of as the productive process in any form of subjectivity whereby the "subject" interrupts and interlects interpellations and social codes.

One purpose of resistance or of encouraging interruptive/interlective resistance to the text would be to inhibit us from giving privilege to any particular voices or groups as bearers of knowledge and shapers of history; instead it would enable us to return the text to students' lives. This entails an engagement of student voice (not only its responsibility or its ability to respond, but its suggestive and agential ability) and to student experience in a way that encourages students' understanding of the discursive systems of exploitation and domination that surround them. At the same time, it seems necessary to begin or rebegin the process of privileging student writing as creative act or interaction in relation to the cultures that produce texts.

At the same time, too, it seems to me that however difficult this may be, it is the teacher's responsibility to submit to a continual reworking of his or her authority in the classroom. It is no use to put authority into play merely in the shape of the text's codes and the explanatory codes of our culture. We have, that is, to recognize that our own authority as teachers is constituted in and by those very same and other codes. These too need to be interlected. This is akin to the radical reshaping or reworking of texts, insofar as we must count ourselves among those texts. The authority of our explanations of the cultures we deal with is necessarily coded, and students therefore necessarily "read" us.

In another essay Spivak has proposed that "the pedagogy of the humanities [be seen] as the arena of cultural explanations that question the explanations of culture" (117). Taking this seriously would immediately present the task of unmaking and remaking our own methodologies, our own explanations (of which the canonical argument is perhaps a hegemonic one at the moment and thus should be the least sheltered from attempts to "explain" it). The classroom can become an arena of interruptions, a dialectic of interlections that will work through and work toward the perpetual consideration of the uses to which texts can be and are put.

IV

All this is probably (definitely) somewhat wishful and even willful at this point. It is even too early to say that the canonical method is impeached; indeed, it daily gets further impetus and support from the crisis mentality that has overtaken the official purveyors and administrators (the conservators) of educational integrity, and we are surrounded by the melancholia of those who still want to talk about the literature they love and about the importance of their feelings in relation to what they fear will become a lost object. In that context (at some moments, a laughable and pathetic one, at others a gravely serious one), the would-be politically responsible teacher is forced to make a strategic choice: a choice, broadly, between some form of complicity with the politics of values and value and an unquestioned role in the transmission of cultural capital on the one hand; or on the other hand, a refusal of such complicity, an ongoing and ruthless critique of the transmission of gold-standard culture. My own choice is this latter, as excessive and even loutish as it might appear in our day. I want to be able to conclude that we have a political responsibility *not* to teach literatures wherever literatures are deployed in a way that eradicates and elides the social relations in which we live and obfuscates the norms and values that are the instruments of those social relations. Perhaps we now have a political responsibility *not* to teach literatures in any context where literatures, teaching itself, and the teaching literatures are understood as not political—that is to say, wherever our colleagues do not promote the questioning of the very notion of the system of "Literature"; wherever students are not made aware of the unearned income they garner when literatures are perceived as a preeminent part, and not simply a subset, of cultural and political production; wherever students are encouraged to think of loving literature as something more than the melancholic perversion that it is; wherever it is in fact considered irresponsible to historicize literatures as forms of cultural capital in the way sketched out above. Political responsibility is in our hands as teachers; and I see it as part of our responsibility right now to intensify the challenges that the profession is currently feeling and to decide whether we will be teachers of literatures or not.

NOTES

1. The present text is a revised and expanded version of my talk at that session. I thank John Clifford for inviting me to speak there in the distinguished company of Richard Ohmann and Jane Tompkins. I also thank the audience, especially Louis Kampf, for their provocative questions.

2. See Bourdieu and Passeron, and Bourdieu, *Distinction* and "Aristocracy."

3. Bourdieu and Passeron's analysis of schooling as reproduction of existing class distinctions and forms of social life has been seen by many as somewhat flawed and inflexible. See, for a thorough critique, Giroux. My own view is that the variety of forms and provenances of everyday cultures is not accounted for in Bourdieu, and that processes of agential and collective resistance (potential or actual) to reproduction are largely ignored. At the same time, it's obviously difficult not to take seriously the socially and ideologically reproductive insistence of institutions such as schooling.

4. Of the *OED*'s three definitions of "historize," the third seems apt: "To act the historian."

5. Particularly, I have been drawing on Aronowitz and Giroux, Freire and Macedo, Scholes, and Sharp. See too Giroux et al. On Bourdieu, see note 2 above. Touraine's work is perhaps best approached through *Return.* Some of my formulations above depend on his; see especially pp. 53–55 on the issue of values and norms.

6. See *Discerning* for my argument about the production of agency from multifarious interpellations and subject positions.

WORKS CITED

Aronowitz, Stanley, and Henry Giroux. *Education under Siege: The Conservative, Liberal, and Radical Debate over Schooling.* Granby: Bergin and Garvey, 1985.

Bourdieu, Pierre. "The Aristocracy of Culture." *Media, Culture and Society* 2 (1980): 237+.

———. *Distinction: A Social Critique of the Judgment of Taste.* Trans. Richard Nice, Cambridge: Harvard UP, 1984.

———, and Jean-Claude Passeron. *Reproduction in Education, Society and Culture.* Trans. Richard Nice. London: Sage, 1977.

Freire, Paulo, and Donaldo Macedo. *Literacy: Reading the Word and the World.* Granby: Bergin and Garvey, 1986.

Giroux, Henry A. *Theory and Resistance in Education: A Pedagogy for the Opposition.* South Hadley: Bergin and Garvey, 1983.

————, David Shumway, Paul Smith, and James Sosnoski. "The Need for Cultural Studies: Resisting Intellectuals and Oppositional Public Spheres." *Dalhousie Review* 54.2 (Summer 1984): 472-86.

Scholes, Robert. *Textual Power: Literary Theory and the Teaching of English.* New Haven: Yale UP, 1985.

Sharp, Rachel. *Knowledge, Ideology, and the Politics of Schooling: Towards a Marxist Analysis of Education.* New York: Routledge, 1980.

Smith, Paul. *Discerning the Subject.* Minneapolis: U of Minnesota P, 1988.

————. "Pedagogy and the Popular-Cultural-Commodity-Text." *Popular Culture, Schooling, and Everyday Life.* Ed. Henry A. Giroux and Roger Simon. Granby: Bergin and Garvey, 1989. 31-46.

Spivak, Gayatri Chakravorty. "Explanation and Culture: Marginalia" and "A Literary Representation of The Subaltern: A Woman's Text from the Third World." *In Other Worlds: Essays in Cultural Politics.* New York: Methuen, 1987. 103-107, 240-68.

Touraine, Alan. *Return of the Actor. An Essay in Sociology.* Trans. Myrna Godzich. Minneapolis: U of Minnesota P, 1988.

10

The Case for Jameson; or, Towards a Marxian Pedagogy of World Literature

Christopher Wise

> The Third World is still very much alive as a possibility. It is not a matter of cheering for Third World countries to make their revolutions; it is a dialectical matter of seeing that we here are involved in these areas and are busy trying to put them down, that they are a part of our power relations.
>
> —Jameson, Interview

Since the publication of Fredric Jameson's "Third World Literature in the Era of Multinational Capitalism" in *Social Text* (1986), a number of critical commentaries have appeared in opposition to this essay, most notably Aijaz Ahmad's "Jameson's Rhetoric of Otherness and the 'National Allegory'" (1987). In particular, Ahmad's essay has contributed to a growing impression among U. S. academics that Jameson's approach to Third World texts may now be safely circumvented rather than closely analyzed on its own merits. In fact, the complexity of Jameson's Marxism often renders it vulnerable to suspicion and precipitous negation, usually before one has sufficiently situated many of his more problematic assertions within the larger context of his collected writings. For this reason, Douglas Kellner in *Postmodernism/Jameson/Critique* (1989) rightly reminds us that "to understand any of Jameson's texts one needs to grasp their place in the history of the Jamesonian oeuvre, as articulations of a relatively stable and coherent theoretical project" (5, my emphasis). Regrettably, this is precisely what Ahmad and other recent critics of Jameson have failed to do in presenting his position.[1]

While one cannot expect Ahmad to provide commentary on the entire trajectory of Jameson's published writings, especially in a short journal article, it is nevertheless unfortunate that he seems unwilling to acknowledge the provisional nature of Jameson's approach, the way in which the various conceptual formulations in Jameson's criticism, from his earliest writings to the present, are not to be understood *absolutely* but "as moments and figures, tropes, syntactical paradigms of our relationship to the real itself" (Jameson, *Marxism and Form* 374). Secondly, one cannot help but regret the fact that many critics of Jameson, especially following the successes of his writings on postmodernism, have now found it expedient to unmask for us Jameson's hidden "imperialistic" agenda. In a recent issue of *PMLA,* for example, Jonathan Culler has similarly observed that we must rethink current institutional demands for controversy and novelty that require young critics to distort and misrepresent their precursors to gain a hearing (534). In "Jameson's Rhetoric of Otherness," Ahmad not only distorts and caricatures Jameson's theoretical position, he also adopts the persona of the wounded and betrayed comrade, a rhetorical strategy that is both offensive towards Jameson and patently unfair.

Hence, while we may not doubt that Jameson's approach to literature of the Third World is not without its failings and insufficiencies, especially in its tendencies towards macrological oversimplification, no *merely* critical assessment of his various contributions to the problematic of the Third World, like Ahmad's essay, will wholly satisfy the overriding urgency of the political and economic questions that presently demand our attention. Among other reasons, Jameson's writings on the Third World require our careful consideration because they are both informed and validated by one of the most technologically advanced methods of cultural analysis presently available, historical materialism.[2] In this sense, the refusal to export Euro-American theory into the Third World, or even Third World literature into Western academies, is tantamount to condoning a prolonged and systemic underdevelopment of the Third World—the superstructural replication of the economic at the level of cultural production. Of course, Jameson's Marxism is also (and unavoidably) an embarrassment of riches at the present historical moment of unequal development and distribution between First and Third Worlds, but there is also a sense in which the systemic contradictions of late capitalism do not invalidate Jameson's position as much as they tend to verify it.

We may no more refuse to deploy the technological advances represented by Jameson's Marxism in the context of the Third World than we may refuse to deploy any other technology in the Third World on the basis of its historical and geographical development from within a former or even on-going colonizing power. Another way of saying this might be that, while "form" itself may be *inherently* ideological (in the bad sense), we must also seek to develop a "positive conception of ideology as a necessary function in any form of social life" (Jameson, *Postmodernism* 416). Jameson's theoretical position has both pragmatic and epistemological value in both the First and

Third World. It is important not only for the illuminating insight that it provides, but also for its liberating potential, or for its ability to motivate praxis that may contribute towards altering the most pressing issue of our time: the systemic underdevelopment of the Third World.

Additionally, because the study of Third World literature has become more common in English and Comparative Literature departments in the United States since the early 90s, Jameson's highly sophisticated criticism has much to offer the college classroom. Despite the difficulty of his theoretical writings, they offer a certain theoretical coherence and provide a variety of practical, specific, and relatively simple strategies both to facilitate the teaching of non-Western texts in the First World and to enable the increased production of literature in underdeveloped nations on a global scale, especially through its promotion in Western academies. Jameson's practical methodology, as outlined in *The Political Unconscious* (1981) and numerous journal articles on pedagogy, constitutes one of his most important legacies to the Marxist tradition.

PEDAGOGICAL MARXISM

Despite popular misconceptions, Jameson has consistently maintained that critical theory represents only one opportunity for praxis among many others available to scholars, teachers, and students in the academy today. "(T)o teach Marxism and tirelessly to demonstrate the nature of capitalism and its consequences is a political act which needs no apologies," Jameson has written ("Notes" 37). But while the university remains for Jameson a viable place where intellectuals may continue to have an impact on contemporary society, he harbors no illusions about the relatively *small* impact university teaching makes on culture at large. "(I)t would be fatuous," Jameson has stated, "to imagine that we are able to use the university without a keen sense of the way in which, in return, it uses us" (39). Though Jameson has been criticized for readily accommodating academic "pluralism," as Samuel Weber has charged, or for "retreat(ing) into the theoretical fortes," as Warren Montag has complained (90), there is a sharply polemical thrust to his pedagogical writings that complicates such dismissals of his position.

"The first business of a Marxist teacher," Jameson has consistently asserted, "in whatever field, the humanities or social sciences—is clearly to teach Marxism itself" ("Marxism and Teaching" 31). In fact, Jameson's larger theoretical position is predicated upon his conviction that, within the university system, the Marxian teacher should seek to "make converts" or "form Marxists" (32).[3] In this sense, it may well be the emphatically orthodox nature of Jameson's Marxism, rather than his theoretical "complacency," that is more vulnerable to critical scrutiny. For example, Jameson has repeatedly insisted on defining the larger task of a Marxian pedagogy in terms of Lenin's dictate that "the two nec-

essary (but not sufficient) preconditions for social revolution are a class-con-
scious proletariat and a revolutionary intelligentsia" (33; see also Interview).
However, in the mid-1990s, especially in the aftermath of recent developments
in Eastern Europe and the former Soviet Union, it might well be asked if Lenin's
historically dated and "revolutionary" mandates adequately continue to address
the complexities of contemporary, late capitalist society, a question Jameson
himself has raised in *Postmodernism* (1991).[4] Nevertheless, Jameson has
insisted that Marxism as a collective political entity, or unified group project,
must seek to establish itself as "an unavoidable presence" within the academy
and, similarly, as "a distinct, original and unmistakable voice in American social,
cultural, and intellectual life" ("Marxism and Teaching" 33). In this sense, the
creation of a Marxian culture, wholly *through* the resources of institutional and
reified culture, may be said to constitute for Jameson the "supreme mission of
a Marxist pedagogy and a radical intellectual life today" (33).

But rather than a merely elite or esoteric form of Marxism, Jameson's work
must be understood in the larger context of any number of developments in
American society after the sixties, including the rapid diminishment of public
space, the historical disappearance of the intellectual (in the old-fashioned
Sartrean sense), and the ever-greater apportionment of specialized disciplines
within the university system. While theory has always been for Jameson an
area of vital concern, he has never advocated that Marxian thinkers wholly
give over their time and energy to issues of strictly theoretical significance:
"My own particular contributions," Jameson has stated, "mainly lie in showing
the capacity of Marxism to engage the most advanced currents of 'bourgeois'
thinking and theory; but that is only one task among others" (Interview 73).

For teachers in the field of literary and cultural studies, Jameson has singled
out a number of key areas in need of transformation within the American university, including (but not limited to) the following: (1) the analysis of pedagogical activity itself, along with the larger institutional and administrative
structures of the academy, the individual disciplines, their separate histories
and ideological preconditions; (2) constant critique and revision of the
canon, which includes calling into question existing definitions of the canon,
as well as exposing its ideological criteria. (Jameson does not rule out elimi-
nation of the very notion of the canon as a pedagogical construct); (3) insistence upon the recognition of institutionally oppressed literary traditions,
such as women's, minority, radical, Third World, and working-class texts, as
well as facilitating educational reform at all levels within the academy in all
these crucial areas; (4) the establishment of an influential and decisive oppositional voice in the spheres of literary theory and criticism, including the
maintenance and further development of a strong alliance between critics of
Marxian, feminist, minority, gay, and Third World orientations; (5) the support of conventions and professional conferences for literary teachers and
critics in all of the above mentioned areas; (6) the broadening of existing dis-

ciplinary fields of literary study so that the whole range of "signifying practices," such as film, television, advertising, and popular culture, may be
included in university curricula (Jameson and Kavanagh 5–6; see also Interview, esp. 74–75). Lately, Jameson himself has contributed to the broadening
of the traditional disciplinary boundaries of literary study through his analyses of science-fiction and popular film, as well as Third World literature.

Hence, while cautious about the transformative potential of political activity
within the academy, Jameson nevertheless outlines a far-ranging radical program that may contribute to the deconstruction of the more overtly imperialistic aspects of the university system. In fact, one might argue that Jameson is
unnecessarily pessimistic about micropolitical activity today, or, more specifically, about the potential impact of university education upon society at large.
Indeed, as many contemporary theorists have suggested, what is needed today
is sustained political activity on a local basis, performed not by a leftist or cen-
trist vanguard, but by a broad-based coalition of individuals and groups committed to dismantling the hegemonic structures of late capitalist imperialism,
including the legacies of patriarchy, homophobia, racism, and class exploitation. Hence, Jameson rightly reminds us that we must adopt "a very long-range
view of the function of Marxist pedagogy" ("Marxism and Teaching" 32).

A PEDAGOGY OF "CONTENT"

"The problems of human culture," Jameson has argued, "are no less complicated than those of inorganic matter" (James and Kavanagh 9). Consequently,
he has advocated a bifurcation within his own pedagogical approach between
undergraduate and graduate studies, a strategy that he himself describes as a
"practical double standard" (Interview 72). Jameson roughly characterizes this
distinction in terms of a *pedagogy of content,* which is more suitable for
undergraduate students, and a *pedagogy of form,* which better suits the needs
of graduate students (72). While graduate study for Jameson is comparable to
scientific research, involving the equivalent of laboratory experiments that are
conducted within a controlled environment (73), in undergraduate study he
maintains that students never directly confront a cultural artifact, or the
unmediated *ding-an-sich,* as much as they must first come to terms with the
various levels of preexisting interpretation, or even "prejudice" in Gadamer's
sense, which already inform and determine their individual reading experience. "(I)n undergraduate work," Jameson argues, "one does not really confront the 'text' at all; one's primary object of work is the *interpretation* of the
text, and it is about interpretations that the pedagogical struggle in undergraduate teaching must turn" (73, Jameson's emphasis).

Rather than immediately encountering the cultural document as such, the
undergraduate then only experiences "an illusion of contact," normally involv-

ing the reaffirmation of one's already well-established interpretive codes or
"ideological" preconceptions. Jameson's pedagogical theory in this regard is
consistent with his argument in the preface to *The Political Unconscious* that
we never really experience a cultural document or literary text as a "thing-in-
itself," mainly because we bring to the document any number of preexisting
interpretations that have already shaped our own worldviews. "(W)e never
really confront a text immediately," Jameson asserts, "(rather) we apprehend
it through sedimented layers of previous interpretations, or if the text is brand-
new—through the sedimented reading habits and categories developed by
those inherited traditions" (9). Within such a context, the role of the teacher
therefore involves making transparent the various levels of preexisting interpretation, or, as Althusser would have it, the "toujours-déjà-donné" (always-
already-given), and thereby render visible to students the means by which they
normally register (or conceptually reconstruct) a cultural artifact.

In the undergraduate classroom, Jameson identifies two distinct strategies
that the teacher may profitably employ: (1) the strategy of *historical reconstruction* and (2) the dialectical (or reflexive) strategy of the *critique of contemporary interpretations* ("Marxism and Teaching" 33). Both of these
strategies are intended to challenge the individual student's interpretive prejudice in the above sense, or the various attitudes and forms by which a student will conceptually process, and thus legitimate, a largely unconscious
social perspective. Another way of saying this is that Jameson seeks to reveal
to students the "political unconscious" that unavoidably determines their
individual reception of a cultural artifact. No attempt then is made to defend
the clearly privileged activity of studying literary texts within an institutional
setting, especially given the context of more obviously immediate needs that
face society at large, such as the plight of the homeless, the spread of racism
and homophobia, or, as Mike Davis complains, the "new class polarization
taking place in the United States" (81), though Jameson *does* defend the pragmatic and political value of alerting students to the means by which they normally legitimate and thus reproduce the kind of society that first brings into
existence any number of the above social ills (Interview 73). In opposition
then to Eagleton's criticism of *The Political Unconscious* that "a Marxist-
structuralist analysis of a minor novel by Balzac (will hardly) shake the foundations of capitalism" (65), Jameson suggests that, by rendering transparent
the ways in which a student unconsciously validates a particular social order,
the teacher significantly challenges the student and thereby performs a political act of clear value and productiveness (Interview 73).

The strategy of historical reconstruction is therefore an attempt both to cancel and preserve (*aufhebung*) the orthodox Marxian approach of evaluating
texts according to their base-superstructure relations, and according to a text's
progressive or reactionary elements ("Marxism and Teaching" 33–34): Jameson does not necessarily advocate that we abandon "old-fashioned" ideologi-

cal analysis, nor even the classical Marxist notion of "class struggle" as generally constitutive of human history, though he does argue that past Marxist criticism is insufficient insofar as it has historically failed to grasp both the complexity and ambivalence of most cultural phenomena (34). Like Ernst Bloch, Jameson argues then that within *all* cultural documents there exist utopian impulses for meaningful community life, or yearnings for authentic social existence beyond current forms of alienation.[5]

Conversely, Jameson has maintained that even the most progressive literary works will unavoidably commit reifying violence by virtue of the fact that they exist as historical forms within a social context. For example, in "Marxism and Teaching" Jameson articulates what later becomes a major theme in *The Political Unconscious,* namely that "(t)here has never been a work of art in human history which was purely progressive or revolutionary, without entertaining some kind of ideological complicity with domination" (33). Obviously, Jameson is influenced in this regard by Walter Benjamin's great thesis that "there is no document of civilization which is not at the same time a document of barbarism" (*Illuminations* 256).[6] However, Theodor W. Adorno's notion of the inherently baleful concept has also influenced Jameson's own sense of ideological critique, probably even more than Benjamin's thesis, especially insofar as Adorno dialectically theorizes the inevitability of reification in late capitalist culture.[7]

One example of Jameson's approach to cultural documents may also be noted in his essay "Modernism and Imperialism," which is an attempt to demonstrate how the very forms of modernist novels like E. M. Forster's *Howard's End* or James Joyce's *Ulysses,* regardless of their individual content, are significantly influenced by the larger cultural contradictions of imperialism. Thus even largely apolitical writers like Joyce or Forester may ultimately have more to teach us about imperialist ideology than writers like Rudyard Kipling or Rider Haggard, who are obviously colonialist authors in their subject matter. In the writings of Kipling or Haggard, for example, the reality of British colonialism often constitutes the content of their prose, but the generic form of their writings more closely approximates established realist modes of writing that dominated the literary marketplace in the era of mercantile capitalism (43–44). In Joyce's *Ulysses,* on the other hand, Jameson will argue that the very structure of imperialism may be said to have more deeply left its mark upon the "inner form" or generic structure of the novel (44).

Jameson's pedagogical approach then turns upon the dual notion that "the cultural monuments of the past are always and necessarily, although in varying proportions, progressive *and* reactionary all at once, or . . . Utopian *and* ideological simultaneously" (43–44, Jameson's emphasis). Kellner has aptly termed this duality in Jameson's methodology a "double hermeneutic" and also has argued that the utopian and ideological dimensions within Jameson's writings constitute the key operations of his larger theoretical position (15). Conversely,

Jean-François Lyotard has applauded the "uneasiness" of Jameson's method of interpretation, especially insofar as Jameson's position implies that "the critical task is not only endless; it might even be without fixed criteria" (73). In either view, Jameson is appreciated insofar as he exhibits a keen sensitivity to the ambiguity of cultural phenomena in general, as well as the complexity involved in the reconstruction of any given historical context. By approaching cultural documents in this way, Jameson maintains that we are able to "recreate the living and ambivalent, concrete situation of social struggle from which they emerge," which may then enable us to respect such documents as both human praxis and symbolic action ("Marxism and Teaching" 34–35).

Nevertheless, Jameson is also aware that the American academy offers unique challenges for any teacher who would attempt such a complex pedagogical strategy, given the general hostility to both historical and critical thinking that exists among undergraduates today. Jameson suggests then that the teacher begin *not* by elaborately reconstructing the social and historical situation of any particular writer or text but rather by analyzing existing contemporary interpretations of a text in an effort to reveal their various contradictions and insufficiencies (35). This is Jameson's dialectical or "reflexive" strategy involving "the critique of contemporary interpretations," in which the teacher proceeds not by foisting her own dogmatic position upon the hapless student but rather by carefully examining the standard approaches of contemporary criticism, from the myth-critical to the New Critical and structural.

However, Jameson does not necessarily attempt to reveal these various critical positions as intrinsically flawed or ridden with contradictions as much as he seeks to reveal the ways in which they are largely incomplete, or the ways in which Marxian criticism is "both appropriate and necessary as a solution to their contradictions" (35). The task of Marxism in the undergraduate classroom for Jameson, then, does not involve philosophical exposition as such, nor even a defense of the truth-value of Marxism, though it does involve an attempt to dislodge the various resistances and defense-mechanisms that often prevent undergraduate students from arriving at anything approaching a socio-political appreciation of a text. In short, the teacher attempts to alert the student to the various "deformations" of a text, or the ways in which a text is often rewritten to conceal many of its most significant aspects.

Literary study for Jameson proves useful insofar as it serves "to disrupt or reconstruct our experience, imagination, and ideas about social reality" (Jameson and Kavanagh 2–3). By demonstrating the interpretive mechanisms operative in the act of receiving and registering any cultural artifact, students may begin to appreciate how they themselves have unconsciously come to occupy a position within a larger social order. Or, borrowing from Althusser's terminology, Jameson argues that the student begins to grasp how she has come to accept as natural or inevitable what is often better characterized as an "imaginary relation to the real means of social reproduction" (2).

A PEDAGOGY OF "FORM"

In "State of the Subject" (1987), Jameson proposes three new organizing concepts in his own approach to graduate studies, or his own "pedagogy of form" (19): the first of these is the concept of the *situation,* as developed by Jean-Paul Sartre, and which is a "code word" of sorts for the Marxian organizing heuristic of the mode of production.[8] Second, Jameson endorses the concept of the *pensée sauvage* as formulated by Claude Lévi-Strauss. Third, the hermeneutical method of *question-and-answer* is recommended by Jameson, as developed in the writings of Hans-Georg Gadamer and R. G. Collingwood.[9] While many Marxists today have found in phenomenology an intolerable contempt for both history and rational analysis, Jameson has chosen to adapt it to his purposes (not unlike his use of structuralist and poststructuralist theory), especially in *Marxism and Form* (1971), where he defends Sartre's phenomenological hybrid of existentialism and Marxism. Hence, we should not be surprised to find Jameson borrowing terminology from phenomenological hermeneuticists like Gadamer in an effort to simultaneously "preserve and cancel" (*aufhebung*) a number of useful non-Marxian concepts.

In the graduate seminar then, Jameson attempts to reconstruct creatively the actual historical *situation* to which any cultural document responds, but the procedure is more self-conscious (or perhaps more "metacritical") than in the undergraduate setting. Approaching a cultural document as an active response to a social *situation,* or as a symbolic human answer to a question posed by historical and material necessity, involves for Jameson a two-part process: first, one must reconstruct the situation and, second, one must reconstruct the text as an active resolution of its problems and contradictions, including crises in the ecological system (earthquakes, droughts, famine), or a breakdown in the economic system due to systemic overproduction, periodic wars, and so on ("State" 20). Reconstruction of the situation then involves first establishing the historical context "not as some inert landscape with various features or contents, but rather as an urgent problem-field of some kind, as a social field dominated by some central contradiction." If history consists of the "struggle to wrestle a realm of freedom from the realm of necessity," as Marx has asserted (qtd. in *The Political Unconscious* 18–20),[10] the cultural document therefore functions as a symbolic "question" posed to history in a creative effort to resolve the on-going dilemmas of material necessity, or the problems posed to various peoples by the particular environment that they inhabit.

In this regard, Jameson finds Lévi-Strauss's notion of the *pensée sauvage* particularly helpful insofar as even "primitive" peoples will ordinarily create their own abstractions and associative systems that may be said to parallel modern or scientific conceptualizations in the developed world. In *Late Marxism,* Jameson also comments that "functionally the primacy of the concept (in Western philosophy) is not so different after all from the elaboration of magical names (in primitive societies), since both are forms of 'enlightenment' in the sense in which they secure domination over nature, and organize the 'blooming, buzzing confusion' of the natural state into so many abstract grids" (20). In both cases, abstraction operates as human praxis, or as an active intervention within a concrete situation or dilemma. It is important to note, however, that such responses, be they the most "primitive," ritualistic works of art, or the most abstract forms of Western conceptualization, are never entirely severed from the material world, as in some free-floating Möbius strip or New Critical verbal icon. Rather *all* cultural artifacts or documents are always and necessarily "allegorical," especially insofar as they may not transcend the a priori limits of the concept of society, or that "supreme class under which all other classes must be subsumed" (*The Political Unconscious* 292–96).[11]

Though theoretically distinct, Jameson's discussion of the first two "horizons" (or interpretive "levels") of the *historical* and *social* in his tripartite hermeneutic in *The Political Unconscious* may help clarify his pedagogical methodology. The first interpretive horizon of the "narrowly political or historical" roughly corresponds with Jameson's initial pedagogical strategy of reconstructing the historical situation as "an urgent problem-field . . . dominated by some central contradiction" (20). Conversely, at the second level or horizon of the social, Jameson focuses on the way the object under scrutiny necessarily performs an allegorical as well as an ontological function, or the way the document must be considered not as a pure, isolated phenomenon, but as only one *parole* (or "utterance") within "the great collective and class discourses" (76).

Hence, at the horizon of the social, one of the primary critical objectives is the reconstruction of the *ideologeme*, or "the smallest intelligible unit of the essentially antagonistic collective discourses of social classes" (76), and, in addition, to artificially reconstruct the voice(s) to which the ideologeme was necessarily opposed. When treating ancient cultural documents, the analysis of dominant/subordinate class interests may occur through a careful reconstructive study of the various fragments, *pseudoideas,* or *protonarratives* to which the working scholar still has access. Jameson specifically recommends a survey of the various "subcultures, folk-songs, fairy tales, popular festivals, occult (practices), magic, and witchcraft" (85–86).[12] Within modern society, the same process may be performed through an analysis of those subcultures and peripheral groups traditionally excluded from dominant culture, such as ethnically- and class-marginalized groups, women, the mentally ill, the sexually "deviant," and so on (85–86).

COMPARATIVE STUDIES IN SITUATION

Dismissing old-fashioned, Eurocentric models of Comparative Literature, Jameson proposes instead a pedagogy of situational comparison that, ironically, emphasizes both difference and the arbitrariness of cultural comparison. To avoid confusion, however, it is important to keep in mind the rather obvious point that Jameson is *not* proposing a comparative study of cultural texts but rather a comparative study of two different historical situations. In this sense, Jameson's object of study does not really exist at all, or Jameson is proposing a "gestalt organized around some central emptiness" or absence (*Prison-House* 35). Not unlike Einsteinian physics then, Jameson's pedagogical theory is predicated upon his belief that contemporary objects of study in the human sciences are "no longer things or organisms which are isolated by their own physical structures from each other, and which can be classified in various ways" (14). History itself is rather an "absent cause": it "can be apprehended only through its effects, and never directly as some reified force" (*The Political Unconscious* 102).

While the cultural document or artifact may be defined as one such "effect" of history, history itself as a kind of "ideological Heisenberg principle, can never be present to the mind or the naked eye" (*Signatures* 228). Or, borrowing from Walter Benjamin, Jameson compares his situational hermeneutic to a nightmarish visit to the "scene of a crime" (195). Paradoxically, Jameson's method may be said to succeed insofar as he is able to dissolve the cultural document back into history, now "reconceptualized in an exceedingly 'complex and overdetermined' way" (181). As we would expect, then, Jameson's pedagogy of situational comparison differs from his "pedagogy of form" in that the tensions between history and theory, our various conceptual wrestlings *with* history, will now be revealed to us as even more problematic and complex than we had originally anticipated ("State" 22). Far from ignoring the inevitable arbitrariness and violence involved in any comparative strategy, Jameson seeks to emphasize the baleful nature of the comparative process itself.

Traditionally, scholars of Comparative Literature have assumed that we are justified in creating a semic complex that links together two entirely unrelated cultural texts across whatever reaches of time and space, an assumption that has become increasingly difficult to defend since the advent of poststructuralist difference and grammatology. However, if we proceed metacritically and remain sensitive to the violent nature of concepts themselves— to the way in which a concept by definition will imperiously and balefully impose order—then we may also creatively and productively harness this inevitable tension between two obviously different historical situations, especially in the service of effective praxis in the classroom. Respecting the differences between various situations, and at the same time conceptually juxtaposing them and thereby "making strange" (*ostranenie* in the Russian Formalist sense), or shocking us into a sense of historical awareness, is, as Jameson reminds us, one of the chief benefits of dialectical thinking: or, as Jameson also states in *The Prison House of Language,* "The application of

the techniques of ostranenie to the phenomena of social life is contemporary
with the dawn of historical consciousness in general" (57).

Hence, the pedagogical aim of situational comparison is the creation of a
"pseudo-totality," or a Benjaminian constellation or representation (*darstel-
lung*), which may contribute towards facilitating historical consciousness:

> Pseudo-totality: the illusion of the total system is aroused and encouraged by the
> systematic links and cross-references established between a range of concepts,
> while the baleful spell of system itself is then abruptly exorcised by the realiza-
> tion that the order of presentation is non-binding, that it might have been
> arranged in an utterly different fashion, so that, as in a divinatory cast, all the ele-
> ments are present but the form of their juxtapositions, the shape of their falling
> out, is merely occasional. This kind of *Darstellung,* which seeks specifically to
> undermine its own provisional architectonic, Benjamin called configuration or
> constellation. (*Late Marxism* 50)

While comparative situational studies for Jameson involve a neo-allegorical
(or perhaps Benjaminian) method of interpretation, the "pseudo-totality" created in this case fundamentally differs from the allegorical operation recommended in *The Political Unconscious* (in Jameson's tripartite hermeneutic
system, the transcendence of the purely historical or political level towards
the horizon of the social) in that the latter involves a comparison of cultural
documents, especially as "symbolic utterances" within a syntactic or even
"linguistic" order, whereas the former involves a dialectical comparison of
fundamentally different situations, especially in an effort to establish kinship
(or identity) and for the sake of pedagogical expediency (see Ross 672–74).

The dialectic itself then serves as an attempt to resolve the tension between
facts and theory, between history and the forms that we forever (and hopelessly) employ to meaningfully describe history. Nevertheless, to juxtapose
two significantly different situations within the same semic complex does not
necessarily mean that we have now resolved all existing tensions, or that our
creative pseudo-totality may somehow will away contradiction and difference altogether. As Jameson makes clear, one could just as easily assert that
the dialectic is ripped asunder by such contradictions, that it is necessarily
torn in two different directions at the same time, and that it will be ever-fail-
ing in its attempts to mediate between the baleful nature of abstraction and
history itself, which ultimately will refuse *any* conceptual scheme, however
well-wrought or self-negating.

For this reason, Jameson points out that it is precisely when the comparative investigation *succeeds* in identifying an authentic connection between
two radically different situations that the laboratory experiment inevitably
begins to lose its validity. The absolute and unavoidable disjunction between
two situations will occasionally reveal to us a link that could only have
resulted from the transmission of cultural traditions across different social

environments, an historical irony that Jameson compares to a "contamination in the laboratory" ("State" 22). This is the sense in which history now extracts its "vengeance" for our attempts to impose upon it any supra-historical or eternally reified form (22). It is, then, as Jameson argues, "(T)he coming into being of a global culture, with capitalism and imperialism (that) suddenly deprives us of those laboratory conditions. History returns in a new and dialectical way, as the history of all these various local histories, and the dialectical unification of a great variety of semi-autonomous local processes" (22).

Hence, situational comparison must now involve a new discipline in its own right, serving to conceptualize for us the larger phenomenon of cultural imperialism (22). Here again, the third and final interpretive phase of the hermeneutic system in *The Political Unconscious, "the ultimate horizon of human history as a whole,"* may help clarify what is at stake in Jameson's suggestion that we inaugurate a new academic discipline centered on cultural imperialism. In the final interpretive horizon of "human history as a whole," the various ideologemes, after having been identified, are situated within the larger system of ideologemes itself, or "the whole complex sequence of modes of production" (*The Political Unconscious* 76). This final interpretive horizon, Jameson contends, "becomes an index of an entity of study which greatly transcends those earlier ones of the narrowly political and the social" (89). The goal of this final interpretive phase is to reveal "cultural revolution" in action, which is to be understood as a "permanent process" in human society. History in this sense is defined as the "experience of Necessity," or as that force that "refuses desire" (102).

Here, it will be remembered that in classical Marxism, as well as Jameson's theory, there are either seven or eight modes of production, depending on whether or not the category of socialism may be considered as a mode of production separate from communism proper. In critical terms, Jameson therefore creates a system of mediation between the various modes of production and their corresponding ideological codes, or related theoretical formations. These correlations Jameson conceives of in the following terms: (1) The *primitive* mode of production, which we see manifested in terms of the magical or mythical; (2) The *gens* mode of production within hierarchically organized societies, which we see manifested in terms of kinship; (3) The *Asiatic* mode of production, which we see manifested in sacred or religious terms; (4) The *polis* mode of production, found in oligarchic, slave-holding societies, which we see manifested in "political" terms, according to the conception of politics in the ancient city-state; (5) The *feudal* mode of production, which we see manifested in relations of personal domination; (6) The *capital* mode of production, which we see manifested in terms of commodity reification; (7) The *social* and/or *communal* mode of production, which at present is "nowhere fully developed" (89).

In case we are tempted to interpret these various modes of production as giant typological bins, in which we can deposit cultural artifacts according to their corresponding modes of production, Jameson reminds us that no single text is a pure product of any one mode of production. Rather each text must be understood as a symbolic space "crisscrossed and intersected by a variety of impulses from contradictory modes of cultural production all at once" (95). Like Bakhtin, who argues for narrative polyphony, Jameson believes that within any single text there coexist any number of political voices and narrative overlays, revealing a kind of ideological or "Homeric" battlefield. In other words, rather than approaching a cultural document with an easy and "preordained resolution of system and reality," Jameson would have us instead carefully search for the discrepancies and contradictions that necessarily dominate any given historical situation, often demonstrating the way in which history itself will normally *refuse* any easy solution to most social dilemmas ("State" 24).

Similarly, Jameson suggests that the traditional hermeneutic task of establishing continuities between past cultural traditions and the historical present should give way to the establishment of genealogies in the Nietzschean sense, which would serve the "essential function of renewing our perception of the synchronic system as in an X-ray" (134).[13] Such a genealogy would in no way function as a historical narrative or teleology, but would instead enable us to perceive the various generic discontinuities within any given text under critical scrutiny (144). Recently, Jameson has even stated that "the conception of 'genealogy' largely lays to rest traditional theoretical worries about so-called linear history, theories of 'stages' and teleological historiography" ("Postmodernism" 55).

Hence, during his third and final phase of the interpretive process, Jameson is most interested in cultural revolution or imperialism: "the moment in which the coexistence of the various modes of production becomes visibly antagonistic" (*The Political Unconscious* 95). If the various modes of production may be said to be criss-crossed and intersected within any social text, the concept of genealogy is then especially helpful to Jameson insofar as he is also enabled to examine the overlay and coexistence of these various modes all at once. Hence, genealogy may be understood as a means of examining cultural imperialism itself as a "*permanent* process in human societies . . . a *permanent* struggle between the various coexisting modes of production" (97, italics mine). History then, or the process of cultural revolution, must be understood as the "ultimate ground" or "untranscendable limit" beyond which we are not allowed to pass. In this sense, Jameson does not consider Marxist theory as merely one more critical alternative within the postmodern academic marketplace. Rather, he sees it as the "completion" and "fulfillment" of every imaginable theoretical position.

CONCLUSION: TOWARDS A PEDAGOGY
OF THIRD WORLD LITERATURE

In "The State of the Subject" Jameson voices what many scholars have felt for quite some time, though have hesitated to articulate: namely, that as a theoretical methodology, Comparative Literature has become increasingly difficult to defend, if not wholly untenable, in the aftermath of any number of developments within the academy over the last twenty-five years. In the past, Comparative Literature has often been defended insofar as its practitioners have rightly attempted to organize their discipline in terms of a coherent set of theoretical strategies that improve upon the mostly arbitrary nationalistic conceptual schemes that determine the agendas of English, French, Spanish, and similar programs. As Jameson demonstrates, however, Comparative Literature as an academic discipline cannot really press any claim to a superior methodological status too far, once we also consider that, from its earliest beginnings, Comparative Literature's concept historically comes into being precisely at the moment of the great bourgeois revolutions of Western Europe, which also brought into being the discursive formation of the nation-state, as well as a whole new era of global imperialism (24).

Jameson demonstrates that Comparative Literature never really sought to rise above the logic of national literature programs—its existence has always depended upon comparison between already existing national traditions and the well-established canonical lists drawn up by national literary departments (20). In this sense, Comparative Literature has *always* been an ancillary development of the national literary program, especially within the United States, and only extricates itself from national literary programs at the risk of jeopardizing its very existence: its theoretical structure thus depends for its very life upon canonical and nationalistic thinking, which also means that it cannot help but serve the same ideological functions and goals as departments of English, French, Spanish, and so on.

Far then from being able to boast a sense of methodological superiority over the more obviously ideological agendas of national literary programs, Comparative Literature has complicitously sanctioned and supported the bourgeois nation-state, especially as a component of a larger governmental superstructure, from its earliest days to the present. However, at a moment when the bourgeois nation-state has become increasingly suspect as an adequate foundation for any approach to literary study, or at least any approach which hopes to remain culturally relevant, we might do well to consider what the future may hold in store for traditional Comparative Literature programs, or whether such programs will continue to serve a justifiable function in the immediate future. In other words, we must ask ourselves if the cultural problems of the twenty-first century can in any way be adequately addressed by an increasingly obsolete "Romantic" model of literary study, or any model founded upon the cultural logic of the bourgeois nation-state. In opposition then to traditional or Wellekian models, what is needed at present is a concept of Comparative Literature fully adequate to the task of cultural studies at a moment when the old nation-state as an independent entity can no longer be defined outside of its relative and interdependent position within the ever-expanding grid of multinational capitalist culture.

Within such a context, Jameson's approach to cultural and literary studies offers a flexible, working alternative to the so-called crisis of Comparative Literature, not least because Jameson does not simply dismiss or glibly negate national and traditional comparative approaches.[14] Rather, Jameson calls for *"an internationalism of national situations,"* or a method of literary study in which we recognize a new internationalism, though not as a monolithic totality that attempts to impose a single pattern upon all peoples and cultures (22). Obviously, such an approach to comparative literary and cultural study implies a new *global* perspective rather than a strictly Eurocentric or Western point-of-view. However, in opposition to theorists like Ahmad and R. Radhakrishnan, it is important to emphasize that Jameson has repeatedly insisted that his aim is not to offer a general theory of Third World literature but rather to imagine a *"relational* way of thinking about global culture, so that we cannot henceforth think 'first-world' literature in isolation from that of other global spaces" ("A Brief Response" 27, Jameson's emphasis). Jameson's approach to cultural documents thus attempts to offer a truly global (or "decentered") means of conceptualizing both the radical difference and identity of contemporary human situations. Far from "orientalizing" Third World literature then, as Ahmad charges, Jameson creates a practical and useful methodology in which "we ourselves (in the First World) are 'compared' and relativized along with everyone else" ("State" 25).[15]

Thus, rather than merely revitalizing an exhausted university system (though this surely plays a role in the contemporary explosion of postcolonial studies in Western academies), the cultural documents of the Third World are of crucial significance to the First World insofar as they may reveal "the dynamics of dependency and resistance, exploitation and internal development" (23). Another way of saying this might be to accept Gayatri Chakravorty Spivak's (and Pierre Machery's) suggestion that the primary task for us today is *not* to recover a lost consciousness, but rather to examine the "itinerary of the silencing" (31). Among other reasons, cultural artifacts from places as widely divergent as Africa, the West Indies, and the Middle East are not only intrinsically valuable for their own communities and social orders, but also for other geographical regions (including the United States as well as those countries that are systematically underdeveloped by the United States), as "so many structural variants of the developments of national capitalism" ("State" 23).

NOTES

1. For further examples in this regard, see Radhakrishnan. Also see Montag, Davis, and Kaplan. Ironically, even Best and Kellner's *Postmodern Theory: Critical Interrogations* tends to oversimplify Jameson's theoretical writings, whereas in other published essays Best and Kellner have proven to be among Jameson's most sensitive readers (see Best's "Jameson, Totality, and the Poststructuralist Critique" and Kellner's "Jameson/Marxism/Postmodernism."

2. In a recent article on the testimonial in Latin America, Jameson has described the cultural form of the novel as a kind of "neutral technology," not unlike the automobile, the television, and the computer. I am extending Jameson's analogy to include literary criticism and theory as a "neutral technology" of sorts.

3. Jameson defines the fundamental concepts of Marxism as follows: (1) the "nature, dynamics, and polarizing logic of social class"; (2) the "labor theory of value"; (3) the "commodity form and the four types of exchange value"; (4) "alienation and commodity reification"; (5) the "hidden logic of historical dynamics"; (6) "a commitment to the problem of ideology"; and (7) the "organizing concept of Marxism of the mode of production" (31). This list, however, should not be understood as definitive or restrictive in any sense. For example, Jameson has also stated that, though "it would be possible to devise a list of those basic positions which characterize Marxism . . . such an approach would seem to encourage a premature hardening of our various personal views, at a time when most of us feel that it is important to avoid the factionalism and the polemic divisiveness of which we would otherwise be only too capable" ("Notes" 35).

4. In *Postmodernism,* Jameson states that "in terms of political positions and ideologies, all the radical positions of the past are flawed, precisely because they failed . . . History progresses by failure rather than by success, as Benjamin never tired of insisting; and it would be better to think of Lenin or Brecht as failures—that is, as actors and agents constrained by their own ideological limits and those of their moment of history—than as triumphant examples and models in some hagiographic or celebratory sense" (209).

5. As a case in point, Jameson's book-length study of Wyndham Lewis, *Fables of Aggression: Wyndham Lewis, the Modernist As Fascist* (1979), demonstrates that even the most asocial or even fascist cultural artifacts contain significant utopian elements that enable the critic to rewrite such texts in terms of Lévi-Strauss's concept of the *pensée sauvage,* or as an imaginary resolution of a real social contradiction (*The Political Unconscious* 79).

6. For Jameson's reading of Benjamin in this regard, see "Conclusion: The Dialectic of Utopia and Ideology," in *The Political Unconscious* 281-99.

7. See Jameson's "Part I: Baleful Enchantments of the Concept," especially chapter three, "Sociology and the Philosophical Concept," in *Late Marxism* 35-42.

8. In "A Brief Response," written as a postscript to Aijaz Ahmad's "Jameson's Rhetoric of Otherness and the 'National Allegory,' " Jameson states that the "codeword" for cultural situations is the Marxian category of the mode of production (27).

9. Jameson has promised a forthcoming manuscript on Gadamer's *Truth and Method* ("Afterword" 384). Also see Gadamer's "The Logic of Question and Answer" in *Truth and Method* 369-79.

10. The full quote from Marx, which Jameson employs, reads as follows:

The realm of freedom actually begins only where labor which is in fact determined by necessity and mundane considerations ceases; thus in the very nature
of things it lies beyond the sphere of actual material production. Just as the savage must wrestle with Nature to satisfy his wants, to maintain and reproduce life,
so must civilized man, and he must do so in all social formations and under all
possible modes of production. With his development this realm of physical
necessity expands as a result of his wants; but, at the same time, the forces of
production which satisfy these wants also increase. Freedom in this field can
only consist in socialized men, the associated producers, rationally regulating
their interchange with Nature, bringing it under their common control, instead
of being ruled by it as by the blind forces of Nature; and achieving this with the
least expenditure of energy and under conditions most favorable to, and worthy
of, their human nature. But it nonetheless still remains a realm of necessity.
Beyond it begins that development of human energy which is an end in itself,
the true realm of freedom, which, however, can blossom forth only with this
realm of necessity as its basis. (820)

11. For more on Jameson's employment of Emile Durkheim, see Dowling 42–45.

12. Jameson praises Mikhail Bakhtin for his landmark study of carnivalesque elements in Rabelais.

13. For a fuller definition of genealogy, see Foucault. A "genealogical" history (such
as Foucault's *History of Sexuality*) attempts to avoid a "linear" model of historiography that posits a knowable origin to a complex of historical problems. Rather, a genealogical historiographer will trace problems "backwards" in time, denying in advance the possibility of discovering a unifying "archeological" origin. The most
well-known genealogical study is Nietzsche's *The Genealogy of Morals*.

14. In discussing the importance of nationalism, especially in the Third World,
Jameson reminds us that "the vitality of a certain nationalism" must be respected
("State" 25), that we must be "attentive to the structural and historical difference of
the national situation of other cultures" (25).

15. In fact, in the article Ahmad considers so offensive, Jameson clarifies his (largely
pedagogical) reasons for intervening into Third World literary debates:

It would be presumptuous to offer some general theory of what is often called
third-world literature, given the enormous variety of both national cultures in the
third-world and of specific historical trajectories in each of these areas. All of this,
then, is provisional and intended both to suggest specific perspectives for
research and to convey a sense of the interest and value of these clearly neglected
literatures for people formed by the values and stereotypes of a first-world culture" ("Third World Literature" 68)

Clearly Jameson's chief concern is to alert first world intellectuals, academics,
and critics to their arrogance and blindness in neglecting Third World literature. In
this sense, much of Jameson's schematization is tentative, mere theoretical scaf-
folding that he constructs to promote the dissemination of Third World literature
and to emphasize the interrelatedness of contemporary world cultures. Similarly,
Jameson's situational pedagogy is intended to offer sorely needed classroom strate-

gies, or a pragmatic conceptual means for first world students to assess cultural artifacts from the Third World. Hence, Jameson argues that "one of the new tasks of the university system in the first world is to come to terms with the immense richness of Third World cultures and literatures . . . when, for better or worse, the unification of the globe is (becoming) a reality" ("State" 17).

WORKS CITED

Ahmad, Aijaz. "Jameson's Rhetoric of Otherness and the 'National Allegory.' " *Social Text* Vol. 17 (Fall 1987) 3-25.

Benjamin, Walter. *Illuminations.* New York: Schocken Books, 1969.

Best, Stephen. "Jameson, Totality, and the Poststructuralist Critique." *Postmodernism/ Jameson/Critique.* Ed. Douglas Kellner. Washington, D.C.: Maisonneuve, 1989.

————, and Kellner, Douglas. *Postmodern Theory: Critical Interrogations.* New York: Guilford, 1991.

Culler, Jonathan. "The Discipline of Deconstruction." *PMLA* 108.3 (May 1993): 533-34.

Davis, Mike. "Urban Renaissance and the Spirit of Postmodernism." *Postmodernism and Its Discontents.* Ed. E. Ann Kaplan. London: Verso, 1988.

Dowling, Brian. *Jameson/Althusser/Marx: An Introduction to* The Political Unconscious. Ithaca: Cornell UP, 1984.

Eagleton, Terry. "The Idealism of American Criticism." *New Left Review* (1981).

Foucault, Michel. *Language, Counter-Memory, Practice.* Ithaca: Cornell UP, 1971.

Gadamer, Hans-Georg. *Truth and Method,* Second Revised Edition. New York: Crossroad Publishing Corporation, 1989.

Jameson, Fredric. "Afterword." *Postmodernism/Jameson/Critique.* Ed. Douglas Kellner. Washington, D.C.: Maisonneuve, 1989.

————. "A Brief Response." *Social Text* 17 (Fall 1987): 27.

————. Interview with Leonard Green, Jonathan Culler, and Richard Klein. *Diacritics* 12.3 (Fall 1982): 72-91.

————. *Late Marxism: Adorno, or The Persistence of the Dialectic.* London: Verso, 1990.

————. *Marxism and Form.* Princeton: Princeton UP, 1971.

————. "Marxism and Teaching." *New Political Science* 1.2/3 (Fall/Winter 1979-80).

————. "Modernism and Imperialism." *Nationalism, Colonialism, and Literature.* Minneapolis: U of Minnesota P, 1990. 43-44.

————. "Notes Towards a Marxist Cultural Politics." *Minnesota Review* 5 (1975).

————. *The Political Unconscious.* Ithaca: Cornell UP, 1981.

————. *Postmodernism: or, The Cultural Logic of Late Capitalism.* Durham: Duke UP, 1991.

————."Postmodernism and Consumer Society." *Postmodernism and Its Discontents.* Ed. E. Ann Kaplan. London: Verso, 1988.

————. *The Prison House of Language.* Princeton: Princeton UP, 1972.

————. "The State of the Subject." *Critical Quarterly* 29.4 (Winter 1987).

————. "Third World Literature in the Era of Multinational Capitalism." *Social Text* 15 (Fall 1986): 65-88.

————, and James H. Kavanagh. "The Weakest Link: Marxism in Literary Studies." *The Left Academy: Marxist Scholarship in American Campuses.* Ed. Bertell Ollman and Edward Vernoff. New York: Praeger, 1984.

Kellner, Douglas. "Jameson/Marxism/Postmodernism." *Postmodernism/Jameson/Critique.* Ed. Douglas Kellner. Washington: Maisonneuve, 1989.

Lyotard, Jean-François. "The Unconscious, History, and Phrases: Notes on *The Political Unconscious.*" *The New Orleans Review* 11:1 (Spring 1984).

Marx, Karl. *Capital III.* New York: International, 1977.

Montag, Warren. "What Is at Stake in the Debate on Postmodernism?" *Postmodernism and Its Discontents.* Ed. E. Ann Kaplan. London: Verso, 1988.

Radhakrishnan, R. "Poststructuralist Politics—Towards a Theory of Coalition." Ed. Douglas Kellner. Washington, D.C.: Maisonneuve, 1989.

Ross, Kristen. "World Literature and Cultural Studies." *Critical Inquiry* 19 (Summer 1993): 666–76.

Spivak, Gayatri Chakravorty. *The Post-Colonial Critic.* Ed. Sarah Harasym. New York: Routledge, 1990.

Weber, Samuel. "Capitalizing History: Notes on *The Political Unconscious.*" *Diacritics* 13.2 (Summer 1983): 14–28.

11

Subversion and Oppositionality in the Academy

Barbara Foley

My topic in this essay is the rhetoric of subversion—or rupture, or disruption—that is so frequently encountered in critical discourse these days; my purpose is to raise some questions about the implications this rhetoric carries for a politically oppositional practice in the academy. I shall address some important features of poststructuralism and deconstruction, as well as certain components of feminist theory, but I shall try to minimize my focus on theory as such and instead stress a related concern that has increasing influence on our everyday critical practice and pedagogy—namely, the matter of challenging (whether opening up, jettisoning, or, as my former colleague Michael Warner calls it, busting) the literary canon. When I use the term "new scholarship" in this essay, I refer primarily to this canon-busting activity, in conjunction with its roots in poststructuralist, deconstructive, and feminist theory.

Before tackling these critical and literary-historical questions, however, I shall briefly summarize the historical context within which our current discourse about theory and pedagogy is taking place, since any recommendations about political oppositionality necessarily address themselves to a specific situation. This context is profoundly anomalous and contradictory. On the one hand, we seem to be inhabiting a wasteland that makes T. S. Eliot's spiritual desert a comparative oasis. The super session of Cold War rivalries by a race for newly opened markets that will align emergent and declining superpowers in highly competitive—and increasingly warlike—alliances; the desperation of a declining American empire that is doggedly supporting fascist regimes around the world while creating a massive new poverty class within its own proletariat; the reestablishment of gross inequalities of race and gender, even after decades of popular resistance; the reconversion of the campuses into centers for CIA recruitment and war research: these and other phenomena signal the deepening of a capitalist crisis that can only result in increasing repression and impoverishment for a vast number of the globe's inhabitants.

On the other hand, while CIA recruitment is on the increase, in the academy we seem to be experiencing exciting and progressive developments that signal a very different sort of trend: the number of canon-busting scholars and poststructuralist theorists is also on the increase. A generation of 40ish scholars, whose social and political consciousness was shaped in the crucible of the 1960s and has now reached full maturity, is writing many of the books and articles we now read, and is attaining (or seeking to attain) tenured positions in English and literature departments. Academic Marxism is experiencing a popularity and prestige unprecedented since the 1930s. While fifteen years ago it was heresy to treat literary works as anything other than apolitical, ahistorical, and transcendental, and privileged, now, in the wake of poststructuralism, deconstruction, and feminism, it is almost a new orthodoxy to proclaim that everything is ideological, everything is textual and political. And in the wake of the canon-busting movement, the literary tradition emerges as variegated and full of pockets of resistance, rather than monolithic and hegemonic. Ethnic-minority, female, and working-class writers now draw the attention of many of the best younger scholars, and even the stodgy oldsters of the canon are discovered to have been secretly in rebellion against the dominant ideologies of their time.

As a result, the humanist's role as the gatekeeper of tradition seems to have undergone a profound alteration. Where once we were charged with pointing up the uniqueness of works of undisputed genius and the darkness and ambiguity of the human condition, we are now empowered—indeed, encouraged—to relativize, historicize, contextualize. Subversion is the new order of the day, and we appear to inhabit a decidedly oppositional stance in relation to dominant ideology. Allan Bloom and William Bennett may be building up a dangerous case for cultural traditionalism among the populace at large, but we in the academy know that pluralism and decentering constitute a truer and better (kinder and gentler?) approach to cultural matters.

Does this anomalous disjunction between the situation in literature departments and that in the body politic at large indicate that the academy is exempt from the rightward drift I described before? Do we in fact look to semiotics and post-structuralism for political guidance in the moral limbo exemplified by Tammy Faye Bakker and Geraldo Rivera, Donald Trump and George Bush? Is the Chapel Perilous located in departments of comparative literature? Is the canon-busting scholar the Fisher King? Or does the apparent progressiveness of contemporary literary scholarship make for only thunder over distant mountains, but no rain?

No doubt my own skepticism is signaled by my irony. Before explaining the reasons for this irony, however, I should acknowledge the most significant achievement of the canon-busting movement. First, and most obviously, the movement has profoundly democratized literary study, for students are now asked not only to read but also to understand and respect significant numbers of previously marginalized writers and traditions. No major shake-up occurs, of course, when a few women writers or writers of color are given grudging admission to course syllabi, or when old analytical paradigms remain intact. (I think here of a professor who incorporated Charlotte Perkins Gilman's "The Yellow Wallpaper" into his survey of American literature but taught it as an instance of Nabokovian unreliable narration!) But when the critic pays careful attention to those very features of neglected literary texts that have provided the basis for their exclusion from the canon in the first place, then there can occur a profound rupture in literary study—not only with inherited models of literary history but also with the elitist politics undergirding traditional notions of aesthetic value. For example, Cleanth Brooks's valorization of literary texts as setting forth not ideas, but what it would feel like to hold certain ideas (731), can take shape not merely as an expression of an aesthete's disdain for political commitments in general, but as a conservative's reaction against the leftist politics that many texts of the 1930s had worn on their sleeves.[1]

Second, the canon-busting movement invites us to rehistoricize canonical writers as well, and thus rescues them from the toils of the New Critical and archetypal interpretations in which they have been enmeshed for so many years. It becomes difficult indeed to stress Herman Melville's metaphysics to the exclusion of his materialism when "Benito Cereno" is taught not with "The Turn of the Screw" but with Frederick Douglass's *Narrative of the Life of an American Slave* (1845) or Harriet Wilson's *Our Nig* (1859). *The Adventures of Huckleberry Finn* (1884), when viewed in conjunction with Charles Chestnutt's *The Marrow of Tradition* (1901) or W. E. B Du Bois's *The Souls of Black Folk* (1903), requires the critic to address questions quite different from those invited through a comparison of Mark Twain's novel with *Walden* (1854). As Carolyn Porter has pointed out, Ralph Waldo Emerson's early essays gain a crucial social dimension when seen in the context of the author's anguished reactions to the commodification and alienation of labor in New England mill towns of the 1830s (*Seeing*). After decades of a critical hegemony exercised by the intentional and affective fallacies, by paradox and ambiguity, by epistemological skepticism, and by archetypal patterns of Adamic innocence in a fallen world, history reenters the domain of literary study—not simply as background or source, but as a constitutive component of discourse and textuality. (See also the recent excellent revisionary readings in Karcher, Sundquist, Arac, and Wilding, as well as Russell Reising's theoretical study of the politics of traditional American literary scholarship).

Despite the significant achievements of the canon-busting movement, however, I believe that in many ways it falls short of its emancipatory rhetoric and frequently ends up reconfirming those very structures of authority to which it purports to be opposed. There are a number of axes along which this process of cooptation and reincorporation occurs. It is to a scrutiny of these that I now turn, first focusing on more exclusively critical issues and then exploring their implication for our political practice in the academy.

II

First, the maneuver of opening up the literary tradition—and the curriculum—to previously silenced or marginalized voices is often conflated with the notion that these voices, *because* excluded, must somehow constitute a significant threat to the hegemony of dominant social groups. Now, I do not want to be misunderstood as saying that works such as Jessie Redmon Fauset's *Plum Bun* (1829) or Rebecca Harding Davis's *Life in the Iron Mills* (1861) fail to query important facets of class, race, and gender inequality in American culture and in the discourses by which that culture represents and validates itself. But I am bothered by the argument that these writers, simply by virtue of their race and/or gender positioning, necessarily articulate a counter-discourse that is intrinsically subversive of dominant power relations.

For an instance of this phenomenon—of which there appear more and more examples every day—I refer to Sandra Gilbert's introduction to the recently issued Penguin edition of *The Awakening* (1899). This essay is in some ways politically astute, but also, in my view, injuriously one-sided. Gilbert argues—with considerable force—against the antifeminist reading that would invoke standards of "realistic" plausibility and would accordingly treat the novel's conclusion as " 'a defeat and a regression, rooted in a self-annihilating instinct, in a romantic incapacity to accommodate . . . the limitations of reality.' " Accordingly, Gilbert claims that Edna's final act of suicide represents instead "a resurrection, a pagan female Good Friday that promises a Venusian Easter." The protagonist's final gesture thus "expresses not a refusal to accommodate to reality but a subversive questioning of both reality and 'realism' " (31).

I am in considerable sympathy with Gilbert's desire to point out the oppositional, even triumphant, aspects of Edna's rejection of a patriarchal society that would restrict her possibilities for growth. I also agree with Gilbert's corollary assumption that feminist criticism should address itself not simply to textual patterns of victimization but also to representations of defiance. I would moreover second the view that the presumably "realistic" invocation of probability and common sense as criteria for evaluating Edna's character carries with it a freight of conservative patriarchal judgments. But I also think that, in treating Edna Pontellier as a kind of transcendent pagan goddess, Gilbert profoundly distorts the contradictory nature of Kate Chopin's portrayal of her protagonist—a woman marked by considerable weakness of intellect as much as by greatness of spirit, by a narrow selfishness as much as by a generous identification with cosmic regenerative forces.

In arguing that Edna engages in a "subversive questioning of both reality and 'realism,': in short, Gilbert mistakes the part for the whole, substituting a univocal—and somewhat anachronistic—celebration of female sexual identity for what is, in my view, in fact a highly tension-filled and ambivalent representation of the cost of woman's emancipation. In particular, I would point out, it is precisely at the text's moment of closure that this conflict emerges most sharply. For in its attempt to synthesize the divergent claims of individual and social identity, Chopin's valorization of her protagonist's courage is substantially qualified by profoundly ambiguous patterns of symbolism and imagery that suggest infantile regression at least as much as Venusian transcendence.[2]

The problem I have pointed out in Gilbert's introduction to *The Awakening* is repeated, I believe, in a substantial number of works of the new scholarship. Recent critics are often eager to demonstrate that a noncanonical—or, in this case, recently canonized—writer occupied (and occupies) an oppositional stance in relation to dominant institutions of power. But in arguing their case, these critics too frequently select various subversive moments in the text while overlooking the ways in which these moments are frequently subordinated to larger narrative patterns, most particularly patterns of closure, that negate or at least blunt the text's sporadic querying of hegemonic conceptions of character and social relations. The critic's own brand of oppositional politics, in other words, becomes conflated with authorial intention.[3]

Second, practitioners of the new scholarship too often conclude not only that noncanonical writers possessed subversive politics but also that long-canonized writers experienced significant sympathy with oppressed social groups—or at least ironized or otherwise problematized the more reactionary ideas that their texts would appear to assert. As I mentioned before, Porter's discovery of Emerson's awareness of the alienation of labor in 1830s New England mill towns, and her postulation that this awareness is centrally involved in his formulation of a transcendentalist epistemology, puts Emerson's philosophical enterprise in a badly needed historical context. But this discovery does not in itself demonstrate that Emerson has any particularly strong sympathy for the oppressed masses, who figure in his essays as a somewhat rowdy and undesirable presence—"the unintelligent brute force that lies at the bottom of society [and] is made to growl and mow" (Emerson 960). In Emerson's complex political epistemology, the great unwashed contribute to the anguish suffered by the all-seeing "eye" at least as much as they themselves suffer from a comparable alienation. Nor does demonstrating Emerson's awareness of alienation in itself prove that, in his own philosophical practice, Emerson managed to contest or overcome the commodification that he perceived and decried.

Moreover, Porter extends her analysis of Emerson as a radical—which, given his association with Margaret Fuller and other progressive transcendentalists, is at least plausible—to Henry James, Henry Adams, and William Faulkner as well:

> Each of them [the four cited above] responds critically to his society, and the related terms in which these several radical critiques take shape reveal at once the deepening structure of reification in American society as it moves from the nineteenth century into the twentieth, and the exemplary efforts of four of America's most formidable critical minds to overcome and resist that reification. ("Reification" 188–217)

Emerson, James, Adams, and Faulkner do indeed offer compelling analyses of the costs of living in modern industrial society, but their criticisms are largely articulated from a conservative viewpoint. It does little to clarify these writers' political stands to treat them as sympathetic participants in an essentially Marxist critique of capitalist commodification. (For an interesting discussion of the distinctly nonradical aspects of Emerson's thought, see Grusin).

I invoke the example of Porter's *Seeing and Being* not to negate the value of her discoveries about the centrality of the problem of alienation in the works of Emerson and other American writers, but simply to point out a certain lack of dialectical thinking that is prevalent in a number of even the most valuable works of the new scholarship. In the attempt to pull canonical writers down from the clouds of idealist critical discourse and to reground them in history, writers who have for decades been seen as bearing the standard of traditional moral values are suddenly seen as querying these values. By a curious turn of the wheel, then, the effort to historicize produces a new kind of dehistoricization, albeit on a different plane. To be sure, writers are no longer seen as espousing human truths divorced from time and space. But in their insertion into time and space they frequently take on an aura of anachronistic political correctness. Their firm commitment to elitist, sexist, or racist social values is waved aside so long as their works contain the germ of a concern with decentered subjectivity or the problematics of reference.[4]

Indeed, such a privileging of postmodernist concerns can result in a very troubling bypassing—verging on whitewashing—of reactionary politics in canonical texts. Andrew Parker, for example, argues that Ezra Pound's virulent hatred of Jews stemmed from his perception that "Judaism, writing, money and rhetoric . . . all belong to the same tropological series, each term functioning analogously as a figure of 'excess,' as an inscription that deflects any immediate connection between the sign and its intended referent." Although Parker claims that his argument "will enable us to reject the widely-held critical position that considers Pound's anti-Semitism as a merely 'contingent' phenomenon, ancillary to his poetic achievement," I remain skeptical of a rehistoricizing that virtually collapses politics into poetics (81, 71). Parker is certainly not arguing that there is anything progressive about Pound's anti-

Semitism. But his contention that Pound worked out his poetic anxieties through his social attitudes has the effect of dignifying those attitudes. Pound's obsessive concern with the relation of signifier to signified makes him "one of us"; even his repellent politics takes shape as a protest, however, distorted, against the epistemological dilemma of modern humanity.

I can anticipate various objections to these arguments. It might be stated, for example, that in invoking critical categories such as "larger narrative patterns," "closure," and "intention," it is I who am reproducing dominant ideology, especially when I apply these notions to noncanonical texts. Concepts of totality, coherence, and authorial subjectivity can be seen as Aristotelian or Jamesian mediations of phallogocentric hegemony. Counterinvoking Jacques Derrida or Paul de Man, the canon-busting critic might argue that oppositional ideology necessarily asserts itself in gaps, fissures, and discontinuities in the text—that opposition itself is by definition a marginalized phenomenon. It is enough for the text to have flaunted the logocentric conventions that support patriarchy and racial domination; subversion consists not in the negation of this hegemony, but simply in its interrogation.[5]

I am bothered by this argument, even though we hear it often enough these days, uttered in a tone of radical panache. For what it amounts to is an admission that subversion and oppositionality are essentially formalistic operations—maneuvers of which the target and goal remain unspecified. The *act* of rupture is valorized. But what this act is subversive of, and oppositional to, is too often left unclear—as is the extent of the text's commitment to its disruptive stance. The enemy would seem to be an epistemological nexus defined by stability, fixity, realism—but beyond this we know little else. The result of this insistently structural definition of the antagonist is that we are left with only a hazy notion of the actual political praxis involved in textual subversion. Power, in this critical paradigm, lurks everywhere; but it is not always clear where power comes from or whose interests it serves. There is no cause for despair, however, since polysemous subversion waits everywhere in ambush, forcing dominant ideology continually to cover its flanks against guerrilla harassment from what Derrida calls the "marginalized others" of the West (134-35). There are romantic echoes here of the discourse and practice of Regis Debray, so popular among certain elements of the New Left in the 1960s. We may wonder, however, whether such a formulation of subversion and oppositionality is as sure a safeguard against reincorporation as it would claim to be.[6]

It is not necessary, I believe, to throw out the subversive baby with the traditional bath: to recognize that texts do not always succeed in negating dominant ideology is not to deny that they may try to do so. For such notions as intention, totality, and closure do not rule out the importance of considering *contradiction* in literary texts. Indeed, they enable us to view the text as an ideological battleground where contradictions in representation fight out the broader struggles of the society at large. But within the dialectic of the text's unity, there are nonetheless primary and secondary aspects of contradiction. If the "pockets of resistance" in a text constitute a secondary aspect—as is, in my view, most often the case with works written in the bourgeois tradition, even with noncanonical texts—so be it. Let us appreciate these pockets for all they are worth, and point out their significance to our students. But this does not mean that others aspects of authorial consciousness may not—however, unfortunately—end up winning the battle. Indeed, to posit that an insurgent, secondary aspect of a contradiction is, simply by virtue of its existence, a primary, essence-determining phenomenon is to trivialize the very urgency of the political issues that the canon-busting movement invites us to consider. For such a contention makes it appear that battles that have been bitterly waged in the historical world—and often continue to be waged—have achieved a comparatively easy victory in the realm of literary discourse.

It might also be objected, as a kind of fallback position, that even if I am right about the limited subversiveness of the majority of texts produced in the bourgeois tradition—or even at its margins—I am misconstruing literature's relation to ideology when I hold writers accountable for the formulable social views that their texts project. Some, invoking a more traditional distinction between the languages of science and poetry, might maintain that literary discourse is pseudostatement. Others, calling upon the post-Althusserian description of literary discourse as positioned midway between ideology and ordinary propositional discourse, might declare that literary texts are distanced from the politics they appear to articulate. To hold Emerson as a "subject" accountable for the views he expresses is to miss the point, since what the new scholarship is doing is precisely to demonstrate how subjectivity is constructed by discourse. Rather than affix praise or blame to the formulable politics explicit or implicit in a text, the critic's task is to reveal how the multiplicity of language continually disrupts ideology as such; indeed, the real subversiveness of literature (and of the criticism that treats it) resides in precisely this antipathy to the confinements of univocal meaning and reference.[7]

In response to this argument, I would note that it is quite illogical to assert on the one hand that "literary" texts must be understood within the fuller context of contemporaneous discourse, and on the other that there is something distinctive about "literary" language that overturns the text's apparent commitment to the ideological content it appears to set forth. Indeed, what this argument does is again not to foreground but to bracket—or at least to marginalize once again—the issues of politics and history. For if poets and novelists necessarily become rebellious when they start tangling with literary language, then there must be something intrinsically subversive about literary discourse as such. Politics thus becomes an abiding feature of discourse rather than a historically specific matter of social analysis and intervention. Writers might in their personal lives (which are after all historical lives) adhere to politically retrograde beliefs—for example, Faulkner on the subject of black equality. Nonetheless, when such writers take pen in hand, they become deft interrogators of dominant ideology. Ideological contradiction is thus displaced from within authorial ideology—where I for one think it belongs—and inserted into the epistemological space between literature and ideology (see Eagleton, Macherey, Bennett). Despite its insistence that everything is political, everything textual, then, much of the new scholarship—even in some of its neo-Marxist variants—ends up hypostasizing the realm of the aesthetic as a terrain somehow exempt from the political constraints that ordinarily shape the operations of consciousness. Perhaps Brooks has not, after all, been completely left behind.

III

We may now address the implications that this critique of the politics of the new scholarship has for our practice as citizens of the world—and, in particular, as teachers in the universities and colleges of the empire whose troubled situation I touched upon in the opening part of this essay.

There is, I believe, a distinct oppositional potential in the critical movements I have been describing here. In challenging both the makeup of the canon and the values that sustain the canon, we are in a position to subvert key tenets of dominant ideology. We therefore do potentially occupy an adversarial position in relation to the centers of power in American society—centers that are represented, among other places, on the boards of trustees of the colleges and universities that pay our salaries. And while it is our colleagues in the sciences and social sciences who are called upon to do weapons and counterinsurgency research for military escapades in Central America, we should not minimize our importance to ruling-class hegemony. After all, it is our job to furnish—and make compelling, beautiful, and inevitable—views of the human condition that, if they do not glorify, generally justify and permit social inequality and the separation of personal morality from public policy. The humanities, Herbert Marcuse once observed, serve to inure people to their own and others' want of bread by demonstrating that man does not live by bread alone (109). If we successfully and undermine such assumptions, pointing up their specious universalism and ahistoricity, and brining to our students' attention entire submerged subcultures that have queried such values, then we pose a threat to ruling-class hegemony.

But if this is the case, why do our boards of trustees generally tolerate—indeed, actively cultivate—our presence? Why, indeed, has the move for integrating race, gender, and class into the curriculum been promoted—over the objection of harshly hostile elements—at major universities such as Duke and Stanford, where the sons and daughters of the wealthy receive their training? This happens, I believe, not because financiers and industrialists shed their

crude commercialism when they enter the groves of academe, but because
we oppositional scholars by and large make ourselves safe—and because, to
some extent at least, the captains of industry actually need us to do much of
what we do. I shall now translate my earlier criticisms of the canon-busting
movement and the new scholarship into a critique of the political practices,
both liberal and neo-Marxist, that they imply.

To begin with, the movement to open up the canon to new voices and traditions is readily enough assimilable to the myth of American democratic pluralism: the melting pot has simply finally made it to the academy. What a celebration it is of "representative" American institutions if female and minority
writers now receive "representation" in anthologies and course syllabi! Even
if the largest poverty class in the U.S. consists of families headed by single
women, and even if millions of unemployed and working-class people of
color confront continually worsening prospects for housing and jobs—what
a testament the new cultural pluralism is to the "sensitivity" of the leading
institutions in our society! My sardonic tone here should not be taken to signify, of course, that I think it negative that such an opening up has occurred.
(On the contrary: we should always recall that the decisions about inclusion
and exclusion that take place nowadays in the quiet halls of W. W. Norton are
the fruits of the very unquiet decisions—and demonstrations—about inclusion and exclusion that took place in other halls some twenty years ago).

My point is simply that, if we really want to "politicize" the study of literature, we should juxtapose Richard Wright's *Uncle Tom's Children* (1938)
with William Faulkner's *Absalom, Absalom!* (1936) in a way that fully recognizes the fundamental antipathy between the two. For unless we incorporate a re-creation of social struggle into our presentation of these writers to
our students, we are simply perpetuating—and doing nothing at all to subvert—quintessentially logocentric conceptions of the American body politic.
Wright and Faulkner are not simply two sides to the democratic coin. The
social views articulated in their texts are as irreconcilable now as they were
in the 1930s. Any pedagogical strategy that simply juxtaposes them in a pluralistic exploration of literary representations of race and racism violates the
motives that prompted both writers to take pen in hand.

By no means, however, are all scholars involved in opening up the canon
so conventionally liberal as I have just suggested. Rather than validating the
myth of the melting pot, some of the new scholars would claim, they are blast-
ing it open and demonstrating that social life—and discourse—are constituted not by unity and consensus, but by difference, alterity, heterogeneity.
Indeed, they would argue, the politics implied by their critical practice is
emancipatory, even revolutionary. For they are seeking out pockets of resistance and envisioning social change coming from autonomous groupings of
dispersed elements—women, blacks, Hispanics, Native Americans, gays—
who fashion what Stanley Aronowitz calls a "micropolitics of oppositional

movements," or what Felix Guattari calls the "proliferation of marginal groups" that all bring about "molecular revolution" (Aronowitz 123–26; Guattari 268–72).[8]

Traditional Marxism, according to this analysis, is logocentric and authoritarian, since it posits the primacy of production in determining social relations, situates change in the class struggle rather than in the activities of "interest groups" such as those cited above, and makes the fatal mistake of supposing that a "third term"—revolution—will synthesize and resolve the destructive binary oppositions upon which bourgeois society founds itself, and by means of which it justifies itself. True resistance, in short, can come only from "pockets" that take the "refusal of mastery" as a guiding political principle. If these pockets should turn into phalanxes, much less armies, then the margins would become the center, and logocentric structures of authority would reassert themselves, albeit in a different guise. According to this argument, which is endorsed by a number of feminists and neo-Marxists involved in the new scholarship, to overturn the canon is neither to reaffirm liberal democracy nor to contribute to a class-based movement for social revolution, but rather to carry on rear-guard guerrilla actions that will interrogate hegemonic discourses without superseding or replacing them.[9]

Such a politics, in my view, amounts to little more than a rewarming of the liberal pluralism I mentioned before, although I know its adherents would strenuously disagree with me. To be sure, many feminists and neo-Marxists are quite correct to point out the "old left"'s fatal failure to understand the centrality of questions of race and gender within the overall class contradiction. And a class-based Marxism need not—indeed should not—seek the eradication of plurality, which is not the same thing at all as pluralism. But to concede that race and gender cannot simply be collapsed into class does not mean that the class struggle is no longer the main contradiction shaping historical processes. Nor does it mean that provisional coalitions of dispersed and molecular interest groups can successfully confront the powers that be, which have proven themselves remarkably efficient in accommodating—at least rhetorically—demands for cultural self-determination. Indeed, our political experience of the last decade or so reveals that this presumably radical politics of heterogeneity and difference is readily enough absorbed into the conservative pluralism of "*E pluribus unum*," which celebrates the openness and flexibility of American capitalist democracy while guaranteeing the continuing segregation and subjugation of the great number of its citizens. Interrogation from the margins is kept safely at the margins.

Indeed, in its extreme form this politics of decentering and marginality becomes a politics that actually enshrines impotence as a positive good. For the "refusal of mastery," apparently an act of heroic disengagement from the epistemology that fosters oppression, can lead to a kind of defiant passivity. This passivity may console the conscience of the individual, but it forecloses in advance the possibility of engagement in a praxis that will encounter hegemony on its own turf. The adherents of this refusal of mastery become avatars of Eliot's Fisher King—incapable of determinate action, but by their very presence continually emanating the promise of a redemptive rain that will magically fall from the sky. One might note, indeed, that some practitioners of the new canon-busting scholarship seem actually to relish the continuing existence of ruling-class hegemony, insofar as they take their own marginality as a condition of their scholarly being and conceive of themselves as a kind of loyal opposition. Fearing that should the margins become the center, they would be transformed into sites of a new Power that would be, *quâ* power, as oppressive as the old, these scholars prefer to engage in skirmishes that never take as their goal the actual reconstruction of textual value and literary tradition—let alone the seizure of power in the society at large—according to a new plan.[10] Better, they counsel, to drop in our lines from the dock behind the gashouse, turn our backs on the devastation of the global wasteland, and restrict ourselves to setting our own lands—demarcated by the new pluralistic geography—in order. What starts out as a radical refusal to engage in the coopting discourse of power can easily enough end up as a resort to the solaces of the wordprocessor and the conventional prestige rewards of the profession.[11]

I'd like to point out, however, that such questions of *how* most effectively to oppose the machinations of power are frequently rendered moot—for liberals and neo-Marxists alike—by what I have argued to be the greatest drawback of much of the new scholarship: namely, the tendency to find subversion under every textual bush. For if it is true not only that marginalized texts subvert the established canon, but also that canonical texts subvert the traditional and conservative ideologies that they seem to endorse, then bourgeois ideology—at least when embodied in literary texts—really poses no sort of threat at all. It self-destructs when touched—or, at least, when touched by the posstructuralist critic or pedagogue.

However, inadvertently, the scholar who holds such a view of literature actually ends up bolstering bourgeois hegemony. For if literature *quâ* literature offers, when deconstructed, such a trenchant critique of dominant values, and if it takes the oppositional scholar to point out the full extent of this critique, then what are universities and colleges if not privileged zones where the mysteries of textual subversion can be plumbed? The logic of the new scholarship *ought* to extend to a critique of those institutions that help to maintain hegemony. But it can actually end up legitimating the hegemonic view that campuses are apolitical centers where disinterested research and pedagogy take place, and, moreover, where the future leaders of society can receive the humanistic enlightenment that will equip them to respond effectively to the discursive plurality—if not the material needs—of the citizenry.

Poststructuralist scholarship thrives on the perception of ironic incongruities. I can think of no more ironic incongruity, however, than the situation of poststructuralist scholars who affirm the latently self-critical capacities of bourgeois culture while their campus administrations are recruiting students for the CIA or training officers to lead working-class G.I.'s into battle in Central America—or, on the more mundane level, preparing the new generation of business leaders to meet the challenge posed by an increasingly multicultural work force. For the view that both literature and criticism subvert and disrupt dominant ideology implies that the discourse carried on in departments that teach these subjects is somehow not complicit with the discourses and operations in which the university as a whole is engaged. Despite its up-to-date post-Saussurean dress, then, an its insistence that literature purveys not sweetness and light but counterhegemonic subversion, much of the new scholarship ends up valorizing literary study on grounds that are hardly unfamiliar. As I noted before, the numbers of both canon-busting scholars and CIA recruiters are increasing on our campuses these days; let us not be context with a conception of either literature or literary study that facilitates a peaceful coexistence between the two.

NOTES

1. For a discussion of the problems minority and female writers have encountered with the ideological premises encoded in inherited genres, see, respectively, Reilly and Abel. The definitive treatment of the relation of questions of aesthetic value to the activity of canon revision remains the final chapter of Jane Tompkin's *Sensational Designs.*

2. Similar dynamics and difficulties underlie Deborah McDowell's recent introduction to the reissued edition of *Plum Bun:*

> *Plum Bun* has the hull but not the core of literary conservatism and convention.
> . . . It passes for conservative, employing "outworn" and "safe" literary materials
> while, simultaneously, remaining suspicious of them. . . . *Plum Bun* dares to
> explore questions about unconventional female roles and possibilities for devel-
> opment using the very structures that have traditionally offered fundamentally
> conservative answers to those questions. Fauset's answers were risky, in the lit-
> erary marketplace, but powerful, liberating alternatives nevertheless, both for
> herself as a writer and for the image of blacks and women in literature. (xxii)

(For this example I am indebted to conversations with Carla Kaplan during our joint explorations of Harlem Renaissance literature in a graduate independent-study course at Northwestern University.) There are abundant examples of these sorts of radical claims in recent feminist scholarship. See also, for example, Lee Edwards, who encounters a dilemma frequently found in works of scholarship that aspire to demonstrate the oppositionality of a submerged tradition in women's writing. On the one hand, Edwards asserts that her study, unlike Sandra Gilbert and Susan Gubar's *The Madwoman in the Attic* (1979), finds not "covert reappraisals" of patriarchal domination but "overt and radical attacks" (15). On the other hand, she is forced to conclude that in work after work of nineteenth-century fiction, the female hero ends up a "heroine," safely reincorporated into the dominant system of patri- archal marriage. I agree that many nineteenth-century novels featuring woman he- roes *do* exhibit this contradiction—and therefore wonder at Edward's claim to be discussing works that unequivocally contain "overt and radical attacks." For a con- siderably more dialectical assessment of the strengths and limitations of the "cult of domesticity" in nineteenth-century women's fiction, see Baym, especially 22–50.

3. See the final chapter of Foley (*Truth*), 233–64. For a discussion of ideological reincorporation in Afro-American literature, see Hogue. For a description of the ways in which an excluded cultural tradition develops its own oppositional poetics and countertraditions, see Gates. In stressing the issue of ideological reincorporation, I am not denying that it has been a salutary development in feminist criticism to move from analysis of women's distorted lives, anxious authorship, and conservative social roles (for instance, Heilbrun) to explorations of their strategies of cultural survival and re- sistance. I am simply arguing that it is crucial that we not heroize the achievements of victims of oppression in such a way as to end up minimizing the nature and extent of that oppression. What seems to me a very sensible analysis of the relationship be- tween oppositionality and reincorporation is presented in Radway.

4. For arguments along similar lines regarding the presumably self-reflexive (and hence antilogocentric and antiauthoritarian) quality of the American literary tradition in its entirety, see Dauber and Riddel. Porter avoids the solipsism of Dauber and Rid- del but mistakes the *foregrounding* of the problem of reification in classic American literature with a *radical opposition* to that reification.

5. For altering views on the extent to which the novel form itself is irrevocably pa- triarchal, see, on the one hand, Jehlen and Fetterley, and, on the other hand, Tomp- kins.

6. For a valuable critique of the pseudo-oppositionality of the leftist panache ac- companying much poststructuralist criticism, see Graff, Meyerson, and Larson. It is im- portant to note, however, that poststructuralism can produce the diametrically op- posed claim that literature—or at least narrative—is intrinsically so cooptative as to preclude opposition of any kind, deriving from either authors' explicit politics or their implicit subject positions. See Davis.

7. For an intelligent discussion of literary conventions as carriers of ideology—a dis- cussion that both acknowledges the force of dominant ideology and at the same time allows space for oppositional activity—see Rabinowitz.

8. Interestingly, Guattari notes that "it is impossible to make a clear cut distinction between the fringe ideas that can be recuperated and those that lead down the slip- pery slope to authentic 'molecular revolutions.' The borderline remains fluid, and fluc- tuates both in time and place" (269). This argument is similar to Michel Foucault's con- tention that Power and opposition are often indistinguishable from one another (141).

9. See Foley ("Politics") and, for the poststructuralist/Marxist critique of dialectics, Ryan. Among poststructuralists/Marxists who attempt to retain dialectics as an analyt- ical category, a common operation is to assert the importance of identity rather than struggle within contradiction, and thus to evade the necessity of determining which aspect of the tendencies locked in combat is essence-determining. See, for example, Jameson (281–99), who argues that in both literary texts and social experience,

Utopian gratification and ideological manipulation often become virtually indistinguishable from one another. It seems to me crucial for the Marxist critic—for any critic—to make distinctions in this arena.

10. For an instance of a critical stance that takes the refusal of mastery as both premise and goal, see Craig Owens's description of Martha Rosler's photographs of the Bowery, in which she purposefully undermines her own authority as photographer in order to impress upon her audience "the indignity of speaking for others" (her words, Owens 69). There is an urgent need for further inquiry into the extent to which such statements articulate not simply an antipathy to hegemonic discourses but also an unacknowledged anticommunism, one that conceives of Marxism as a reductionist discourse threatening to engulf all difference not immediately subsumable to class. Until such inquiry is undertaken, there is the continual possibility that current research into the intersections—textual and historical—of race, gender, and class will be inhibited by the assumption that these intersections are merely conjunctural, with the consequence that the last of these categories will, by a curious turn of the wheel, almost automatically be subsumed to either of the former two.

11. The extent to which careers are now built around this politics of marginality is exemplified in a 1987 *PMLA* advertisement that heralded the new collectively written *Columbia History of the United States,* which presumably embodies much of the new concern with canon-busting. We are told that the new survey is "thoroughly up-to-date in understanding and attitude . . . refreshingly contentious and crammed with bright and bold [scholarship]. . . . intellectually challenging and socially and politically provocative." Interestingly, the ad was headed by the following in boldface: **"Meet the new Authority."**

WORKS CITED

Abel, Elizabeth, et al. *The Voyage In: Fictions of Female Development.* Hanover: UP of New England, 1983.

Arac, Jonathan. "The Politics of *The Scarlet Letter.*" Bercovitch and Jehlen. 247–66.

Aronowitz, Stanley, *The Crisis of Historical Materialism: Class, Politics and Culture in Marxist Theory.* New York: Praeger, 1981.

Baym, Nina. *Woman's Fiction: A Guide to Novels by and about Women in America, 1820–1870.* Ithaca: Cornell UP, 1978.

Bennett, Tony. *Formalism and Marxism.* London: Methuen, 1979.

Bercovitch, Sacvan, and Myra Jehlen, eds. *Ideology and Classic American Literature.* Cambridge: Cambridge UP, 1986.

Brooks, Cleanth. "Irony as a Principle of Structure." *Literary Opinion in America.* Ed. Morton D. Zabel. New York: Harper, 1951. 729–41.

Dauber, Kenneth. "Criticism of American Literature." *diacritics* 7 (March 1977): 55–66.

Davis, Lennard J. *Resisting Novels: Ideology and Fiction.* London: Methuen, 1987.

Derrida, Jacques. *The Margins of Philosophy.* Trans. Alan Bass. Chicago: U of Chicago P, 1982.

Eagleton, Terry. *Criticism and Ideology.* London: Verso, 1976.

Edwards, Lee R. *Psyche as Hero: Female Heroism and Fictional Form.* Middletown: Wesleyan UP, 1984.

Emerson, Ralph Waldo. "Self-Reliance." *The Norton Anthology of American Literature* I, 3rd ed. 956-72.

Fetterly, Judith. *Provisions: A Reader from 19th-Century American Women.* Bloomington: Indiana UP, 1986.

Foley, Barbara. "The Politics of Deconstruction." *Genre* (Spring-Summer 1984): 113-34.

———. *Telling the Truth: The Theory and Practice of Documentary Fiction.* Ithaca: Cornell UP, 1986.

Foucault, Michel. *Power/Knowledge: Selected Interviews and Other Writings 1972-77.* Ed. Colin Gordon. Trans. Gordon et al. New York: Pantheon, 1980.

Gates, Henry Louis. "The Blackness of Blackness': A Critique of the Sign and the Signifying Monkey." *Black Literature and Literary Theory.* Ed. Henry Louis Gates. New York and London: Methuen, 1984. 285-321.

Gilbert, Sandra. Introduction. *The Awakening.* By Kate Chopin. Harmondsworth: Penguin, 1986. 7-33.

Graff, Gerald. "American Criticism Left and Right." Bercovitch and Jehlen. 91-121.

Grusin, Richard A. "Put God in Your Debt': Emerson's Economy of Literature." *PMLA* 103 (January 1988): 35-44.

Guattari, Felix. *Molecular Revolution: Psychiatry and Politics.* Trans. Rosemary Sheed. Harmondsworth: Penguin, 1984.

Heilbrun, Carolyn. *Reinventing Womanhood.* New York: Norton, 1979.

Hogue, W. Lawrence. "Literary Production: A Silence in Afro-American Critical Practice." Weixlmann and Fontenot. 31-45.

Jameson, Fredric. *The Political Unconscious: Narrative As a Socially Symbolic Act.* Ithaca: Cornell UP, 1981.

Jehlen, Myra. "Archimedes and the Paradox of Feminist Criticism." *The Signs Reader: Women, Gender, and Scholarship.* Ed. Elizabeth Abel and Emily K. Abel. Chicago: U of Chicago P, 1983. 69-95.

Karcher, Carolyn. *Shadow over the Promised Land: Slavery and Violence in Melville's America.* Baton Rouge: Louisiana State UP, 1980.

Larson, Neil. *Modernism and Hegemony: A Materialist Critique of Aesthetic Agencies.* Theory and History of Literature Series, Vol. 71. Minneapolis: U of Minnesota P, 1990.

Macherey, Pierre. *A Theory of Literary Production.* Trans. Geoffrey Wall. London: Routledge and Kegan Paul, 1978.

Marcuse, Herbert. *Negations: Essays in Critical Theory.* Trans. Jeremy J. Shapiro. Boston: Beacon, 1968.

McDowell, Deborah. Introduction. *Plum Bun.* By Jessie Redmon Fauset. New York: Pandora, 1985. ix-xiv.

Meyerson, Gregory. Review of *Universal Abandon: The Politics of Postmodernism.* Ed. Andrew J. Ross. *Ariel* 20 (October 1989): 192-96.

Owens, Craig. "The Discourse of Others: Feminists and Postmodernism." *The Aesthetic: Essays on Postmodern Culture.* Ed. Hal Foster. Port Townsend: Bay, 1983. 57-82.

Parker, Andrew. "Ezra Pound and the 'Economy' of Anti-Semitism." *Postmodernism and Politics.* Ed. Jonathan Arac. Minneapolis: U of Minnesota P, 1986. 70-90.

Porter, Carolyn. *Seeing and Being: The Plight of the Participant Observer in Emerson, James, Adams, Faulkner.* Middletown: Wesleyan UP, 1981.

————. "Reification and American Literature." Bercovitch and Jehlen. 188-217.

Rabinowitz, Peter J. *Before Reading: Narrative Conventions and the Politics of Interpretation.* Ithaca: Cornell UP, 1989.

Radway, Janice. *Reading the Romance: Women, Patriarchy, and Popular Literature.* Chapel Hill: U of North Carolina P, 1984.

Reilly, John. "History-Making Literature." Weixlmann and Fontenot. 85-120.

Reising, Russell. *The Unusable Past: Theory and the Study of American Literature.* London: Methuen, 1987.

Riddel, Joseph. "Decentering the Image: The 'Project' of 'American Poetics.'" *Textual Strategies.* Ed. Josué Harari, Ithaca: Cornell UP, 1979. 322-58.

Ryan, Michael. *Marxism and Deconstruction: A Critical Articulation.* Baltimore: Johns Hopkins UP, 1982.

Sundquist, Eric J. "Benito Cereno and New World Slavery." *Reconstructing American Literary History.* Ed. Sacvan Bercovitch. Cambridge: Harvard UP, 1986. 93-122.

Tompkins, Jane. *Sensational Designs: The Work of American Fiction 1790-1860.* New York: Oxford UP, 1985.

Warner, Michael. "Recanonization." Paper delivered at the Midwest Modern Language Association, Chicago, November 1986.

Weixlmann, Joel, and Chester Fontenot, eds. *Studies in Black American Literature, II: Belief vs. Theory in Black American Literature.* Greenwood: Penkevill, 1986.

Wilding, Michael. *Political Fictions.* London: Routledge and Kegan Paul, 1980.

12

World Bank Literature 101

Amitava Kumar

WORLD

> Doubtless there are many reasons why students, and people who work in fast-food restaurants, say, don't often produce intricate analyses of "Sunday Morning" suitable for publication in *PMLA*.
>
> —Evan Watkins (1989, 3)

Critical and insightful readings of John Milton or William Shakespeare in the *PMLA* and elsewhere now jostle for space with analyses of the job market for recent graduates in literature. Cary Nelson, to take an early example, has written a manifesto devoted entirely to this issue: "It is likely that no more than 25 percent of the English Ph.Ds produced in the 1990s will end up becoming tenured faculty members" (1997a, 5). The delegate assembly of the Modern Language Association has for the past few years found itself caught over debates about the correct stance to take vis-à-vis adjunct hirings, strikes, and university investments. The widespread activism of both graduate students and adjuncts has undoubtedly led to a greater sensitivity to issues of employment and exploitation in the ivory tower.

Even as I was preparing these remarks, there was a cover story in the *Chronicle of Higher Education* about "how one unsung professor played by the rules, worked hard at the same university for 27 years, and died worrying that he couldn't pay his bills" (Heller, 2000, A18). The report was a bleak, but also by now common, tale of a teacher, the late Harold Overton, who had taught at Charleston Southern University; Overton got crushed under a large course load, salary compression, and the plain momentum of a profession that leaves so many of us behind. And yet, that was not all. The report mentioned that when Overton had joined the academic profession, it had appeared "more expansive" but now, no longer:

> Today, the market calls the tune, and everybody dances to it. The distance between the haves and the have-nots is widening throughout higher education, not just at Charleston Southern University. Accounting professors at private institutions average $67,000 a year, their colleagues in communications about $20,000 less. Assistant professors of English start at $37,000, on average; in classical languages, $39,000. Meanwhile, a new assistant professor of management earns $61,000, his colleague in finance $77,000. (A22)

If the agitation of those most hurt by the inequities of the academic system has spurred debate and awareness, it has also led to the production of materials that help teachers inform their students and colleagues about these realities. In a moving documentary video-film, *Degrees of Shame, Part-time Faculty: Migrant Workers of the Information Economy* (1997) by Barbara Wolf, the viewer is made aware of the conditions under which part-time teachers labor. What is further provocative about the film is that it makes a connection between two spaces and two types of workers who have remained divided in the public imagination: academic workers and migrant workers.

The film begins with the camera pointed at a computer screen. A set of want-ads scroll up the screen. These ads advertise jobs for adjunct faculty. This set of shots is imposed over the footage from an earlier documentary that had portrayed the condition of migrant workers in North America—a hiring foreman shouts, demanding that farmhands gather near him. As this mixed footage unrolls, in the lower left corner of the screen, we witness the filmmaker's interviews with academic adjuncts who describe the process of their hiring. As we watch the footage from earlier in the century showing a truck driving away with its load of workers for the day, one of the interviewees takes up the full screen space. We hear him say: "The public as a whole, the students at the university, and even the administrators, have no idea how part-time faculty live—the conditions, the hardships, *and* the positive issues."

Even in its title, *Degrees of Shame* invokes Edward R. Murrow's 1960 documentary *Harvest of Shame.* There is also a reference in the film to another documentary, *New Harvest, Old Shame,* made thirty years later, in which its filmmaker discovered that, in spite of legislation and union efforts, the purchasing value of the farmworker's income had dropped 50 percent to 80 percent since Murrow's film. We hear this on the voice-over. As the camera follows an adjunct faculty member making her way through her office, the copier room, and her classroom—all super-imposed on the black-and-white footage from the earlier documentary—the voice-over continues to provide us the grim facts:

> The documentary you are about to see is not about agricultural workers. It is about a new migrant labor force. And while this group of laborers do not see

themselves as suffering to the same degree as the farm workers, the parallels are alarming. *Degrees of Shame* examines the working lives of adjunct faculty teaching in America's institutions of higher learning. These are the part-time faculty, the migrant workers of the information economy. (*Degrees of Shame* 1997)

One adjunct, Jill Munroe Frankhauser says: "It's fairly common knowledge that it is financially beneficial to the university. The part-time adjuncts don't cost as much as full-timers. They don't have to. They don't receive benefits, they don't get full pay, they are not a problem. They don't have to have tenure, they don't have to have pensions." Mark Lehman, another adjunct who tells us he has been a "a temporary worker for a third of a century," says: "An average student pays $600 to get my class. Multiply that with 26. And that's how much the university is taking in on my class . . . for which they are paying me 15 quid. It comes to what about 7 or 8 percent, I think, of the amount of money that is being taken from that class that is coming to me as a teacher. It is really unbelievable. That's what exploitation—it's carried basically as far as they could possibly go" (*Degrees of Shame* 1997).

The rest of the film is a grim testimony to the ways in which education, as a process that was supposed to enable upward mobility, has failed. And the toll it extracts from hardworking, highly educated, underpaid class of dedicated academic workers every day. "I figured out once that at 70 hours a week, I'm really not earning that much above the minimum wage," says another adjunct, and adds, "I might as well be working at a Macdonald's. Except that my long-term hope is to be a professor and being an adjunct professor looks better than working at a Macdonald's" (1997).

What emerges through this description of the working conditions of the "freeway faculty" are two principal concerns: one, how to better inform the students and public at large of these issues so that they can ask themselves whether they would like to be taught by people who feel marginalized and impoverished in such serious, despairing ways; and two, inspired by the success of the United Parcel Service strikers, how might adjuncts unionize and find allies among their colleagues and students who have been educated about the former's working conditions.[1] In *Harvest of Shame,* Murrow closed with an appeal for an "enlightened, aroused, and perhaps angered, public opinion." Wolf asks at the end of *Degrees of Shame* a simple question: "Have we as a culture rather than bring the migrant farm worker into the economic mainstream, have we instead begun to marginalize and impoverish new groups of American workers?"

For the purposes of this chapter, my own concern lies not so much in answering Wolf's question, which is only rhetorical anyway. Instead, my aim here is to present Wolf's film as an example of a "text" that, because of the connections it makes between the classroom and the world outside it, permits the development of a pedagogy that connects the "inside" with the "outside."

I have screened *Degrees of Shame* during union meetings as well as a professional meeting in Seattle; I have also used it in an introductory criticism
course designed for English majors. The other materials used in that course
included Andrew Ross's *No Sweat: Fashion, Free Trade, and the Rights of
Garment Workers* (1997), a book on sweatshop labor. We read several of the
essays in that book, documenting the labor as well as the organizing efforts
of sweatshop laborers. The book allowed us to bring home to the United
States the realities of capitalism. Take, for example, what Ross wrote in his
introduction: "During the bull market year of 1995, when many large corporations recorded capital growth of 35 percent, the bottom two-fifths of U.S.
workers received an all-time low 12.5 percent of the national income, and the
top one-fifth received a record 50 percent." My students read *No Sweat* in
conjunction with a novel, *Bone,* by Fae Myenne Ng (1993), an Asian American writer. Ng's narrator lives in San Francisco and her mother is a seamstress
in a sweatshop there. Ng's characters also deal with the question of narrating
their own lives, especially as they break into a difficult independence. In our
classroom, we went back to *No Sweat* to ask how were we to speak about
Nike sweatshops and on-campus organizing against sweatshop clothing for
the sports teams. The students in the class also heard the speeches during the
teach-in on academic labor organized by the graduate assistants on campus.

The issues of class, global economy, and academic labor linked by this particular chain of readings also allowed me to introduce a further twist. After
the Yale strike, which had witnessed an alliance among academic and nonaca-
demic workers, Robin D. G. Kelley had written: "We have to decide whose
side we're on and realize that our base of support has already been established by the very black and brown workers who clean our offices and to
whom most faculty don't even speak" (1996, 37–42). In saying that "instead
of looking to the classroom and their attendant culture wars, we should pay
more attention to the cafeteria" (37–42), Kelley was pointing toward the
future of academic organizing. In my undergraduate criticism course, a discussion of Kelley's article was a way of calling into question the liberal-diver-
sity model of education that any teaching outside the canon finds itself so
often trapped in; to take seriously the argument about the ways in which the
cafeteria rather than the classroom was the prime site for racial and political
cleavages meant linking culture and politics in a much more powerful, immediate, and challenging way.[2]

There is a further question, however. Let me return to the example with
which I started this section. In *Manifesto of a Tenured Radical,* Nelson, while
expressing his dismay at a senior colleague's particularly uninformed and retrograde fantasy of our political exigencies, asks: "Had he no sense of what life
is like in South Central Los Angeles, let alone in Bangladesh or Somalia?"
(1997a, 57) Well, what *is* life like in Bangladesh or Somalia? In our classes, and
perhaps even in our other places, we gesture at the world outside to bring

home the truth of conditions elsewhere. But, in the American academy in recent times, just like Vietnam had been in the 1970s, the outer world has been making a comeback. What is especially encouraging is that this world includes zones and regions both inside and outside the United States. A widely discussed report in *The Nation* points out that while on-campus activism has recently been focused on the $2.5 billion collegiate apparel industry and the university licensing policies in relation to those industries that rely on sweatshops, it should also be noted that anticorporate agitation on campus has paid attention to a wide variety of injustices, both at home and abroad: "This year, from UC–Davis to the University of Vermont, students have held globalization teach-ins, planned civil disobedience for the April IMF/World Bank meetings, protested labor policies at the Gap and launched vigorous campaigns to drive Starbucks out of university dining services" (Featherstone 2000, 12).

BANK

"Governor's Encounter with Prisoner"
Hyderabad. The Governor, Dr. C. Rangarajan, who visited the Central Jail today to distribute sweets to prisoners on the occasion of Ugadi, was told by a Naxalite prisoner, Mr. Sakamuri Appa Rao, to put a stop to fake encounters, and force the Government to order a judicial enquiry into the Koyyuru encounter in which three top Naxalite leaders died.

Mr. Appa Rao also told the Governor, "You are an eminent economist. You know the ills of the World Bank aid. The threat of the World Bank is real, and it means unbearable burden on the people. Do something about it." The Governor excused himself and walked away saying, "You are treading on a much wider context now."

The Hindu, India, April 6, 2000[3]

Is not the moment of pedagogy the moment also of the "wider context"? The recent student mobilizations on campus, and also, of course, the public protests against the World Trade Organization (WTO), the World Bank, and the International Monetary Fund (IMF) in Seattle and Washington, D.C., have had similar results: the protests and the debates they have provoked have helped supply broader, alternative frameworks for understanding the conditions of global existence under corporate control.

To teach literature or cultural studies in this scenario is to necessarily reflect on the relations between universities and corporations. Since November 1998, an event that has attracted controversy is the $25 million-agreement signed between University of California at Berkeley and Novartis, a Swiss pharmaceutical company that is a producer of genetically engineered crops. Its deal with Berkeley's Department of Plant and Microbial Biology gives

Novartis the first right to negotiate licenses on about one-third of the department's discoveries as well as the rights to determine how the money is spent. Many see this agreement as having detrimental effects not only on academic freedom, but also on the free exchange of ideas. According to one Berkeley researcher, "This deal institutionalizes the university's relationship with one company, whose interest is profit. Our role should be to serve the public good" (Press and Washburn 2000, 40).

When I read the report of the Novartis-Berkeley agreement, my first response was to make copies to distribute to my students. What did I hope to accomplish with this gesture? I had found the report chilling, and in its concreteness it offered evidence of what is otherwise experienced only as paranoia and fear among the academic community. Most disturbing for me was the report's following line: "What is ultimately most striking about today's academic-industrial complex is not that large amounts of private capital are flowing into universities. It is that universities themselves are beginning to look and behave like for-profit companies" (46). Many of my students, some of whom attended the protests in Seattle and Washington, D.C., do not even need to be told this. This is a truth they already know, and it is the basis of their activism. Whether it is an issue of tuition increases, links with sweatshop industries, solidarity with striking cafeteria workers, or, for that matter, solidarity with striking students in Mexico, student actions have been directed against the role of what Liza Featherstone calls "the reality of the university as corporate actor" (2000, 12).

According to one report, corporate contributions to the university have risen, unbelievably in less than a decade, from $850 million in 1985 to $4.25 billion. This is not an indication of corporate altruism but, instead, of corporate control. Thus, with the boom in industry-endowed chairs we have examples like the chair that K-mart has endowed at West Virginia University—and whose holder needs to spend up to thirty days a year training assistant store managers (Press and Washburn, 2000, 41).

Despite these changes in the university's character—and also despite the students' focused campaigns against the increasing corporatization of the university—the pundits in mainstream media have painted portraits of misguided, and indeed infantile, protesters. On the eve of the April mobilization in Washington, D.C., media-critic Norman Solomon pointed out how a range of publications from *Newsweek* to *Foreign Affairs* had refused to shed light on underlying issues; instead, wrote Solomon, *Time* magazine repeatedly described the protesters as a "kooky crowd" and the *Wall Street Journal* began its lead editorial with the declaration that protesters that week would be "bringing their bibs and bottles to the nation's capital" (2000).[4]

Charles Krauthammer, writing in the pages of *Time,* described those protesting corporate control of our lives as "luddites" (quoted in Solomon 2000), but are the critics of the World Bank–IMF hegemony in any real sense backward-looking citizens? One important tool for addressing this issue with one's students is to be found in a book that is part-memoir and part-criticism, Manthia Diawara's *In Search of Africa* (1998). The passage of Africans into the twenty-first century, Diawara writes, will be marked by an articulation of a modern, democratic African identity, or, in other words, an unsentimental and passionate embrace of modernity. What is visible to Diawara, even while he opposes corporations, is a dynamic view of markets; this vision is neither rooted in backward-looking nativism nor the postmodern logic of rootlessness. Contesting right-wing celebration of the market as a free space, and left-wing shibboleths about the market as the repressive site of capital's deployment, Diawara sees markets as vital, contested, cultural zones. He writes that the markets of West Africa are traditional "centers of international consumption and cross-cultural fertilization [that] pose a serious challenge to globalization and to the structural adjustments advocated by the World Bank and other multinational corporations vying to recolonize Africa" (142). Even as slave markets, these places were where the mixing of cultures, customs, and languages took place; today, too, they continue to be sites where a "regional imaginary" is created and developed. The West African merchants, in the pages of *In Search of Africa,* emerge as genuine cosmopolitans. They are the ones who, struggling against the homogenization enforced by the dominant world culture, revitalize traditional cultures by introducing new commodities into the market.

In other words, it is *Time*'s Krauthammer who is a Luddite, not the protesters or those on whose behalf they agitate. In Diawara's view, it is the West African markets—and the right they grant to the peoples who come there, the right to consume—that are being brought to a "slow death" by the World Bank–IMF-driven structural adjustments, including the devaluation of the CFA (African Financial Community) franc. It is possible to fault Diawara on the ways in which he romantically considers the markets utterly inclusive, but it is incontestable that his opposition to devaluation as well as the recommendation of "a regional identity in motion" promise a way to political and cultural redress.

In his 1946 study of the Accra market (1998, 151), Diawara tells us, C.L.R. James had discovered a basis for revolutionary action; by paying attention to a myriad generative forces in the market, Diawara articulates a logic of the marketplace that is neither nativist nor hegemonic. I have found his analysis useful in addressing a confusion among some commentators on the World Bank–IMF protests: these social movements are not against globalization, they are against imperialist and capitalist exploitation.[5] Of course, my purpose here is not to stop at a reunderstanding simply of markets. The "wider context" of postcolonial studies can become one of helping our students understand, in a fundamental way, the global complexity of the relations between the economic, social, and physical aspects of the world we inhabit. Even in a class on postcolonial literature, in fact, *particularly* in a class on postcolonial literature, we can try to denaturalize culture. In this context, the protests against the WTO and the World Bank–IMF have given me added impetus to address the commonest ways in which my students access postcolonial real-ities. For example, when speaking of the most conventional ways in which they encounter India and Bangladesh in the dominant U.S. media—as natural disaster areas, appearing under headlines like "Thousands Feared Killed"—it becomes helpful to present the views of Vandana Shiva who has been promi-nent in the recent protests. Shiva wrote in late 1999 after a "supercyclone" tore through the eastern coastal state of Orissa in India: "The cyclone is not an ordinary natural disaster. It is a result of destroying coastal mangroves and shelter belts for industrial shrimp farms which today continue to operate ille-gally because in 1996 the Supreme Court ordered their closure. It is a disas-ter resulting from the profligate ways of a fossil fuel–based industrial society and the globalization of trade" (1999).

This manner of seeing does not come "naturally" in literature classes. Not even in those devoted to postcolonial literatures, where this absence has troubled radical scholars. Ania Loomba has engaged the criticism advanced by Terry Eagleton and Arif Dirlik that postcolonial writing does not deal with economic issues. Making a useful distinction between "postcolonial thought" and "postcolonial studies," Loomba asks:

> But is it postcolonial "thought" or postcolonial "theory" that displays such lack? Many writers on postcolonial and neo-colonial issues such as Amartya Sen, Van-dana Shiva or Bina Aggarwal . . . do have plenty to say on questions of global as well as local economies, and their impact on gender, culture, and class configu-rations. . . . *Postcolonial studies* have certainly not raised the economic question rigorously, and *postcolonial studies* have not taken on board the work of so many writers who *do* talk about it. (Loomba 1998–1999, 40)

In order to make the kind of link that Loomba is arguing elsewhere in post-colonial studies, we need to teach postcolonial literature under the sign of World Bank literature. After witnessing the kind of political action we have seen in the streets of Seattle and Washington, D.C., this analytic shift cannot but admit the importance of the Bretton Woods institutions. Their power and the struggles against it can and must be a part of this pedagogical paradigm. Can we, in our teaching, also follow the principle of organizing that the recent protests have displayed? This is a question surely worth examining.

In the pages of *The Nation*, Naomi Klein has written that "what emerged on the streets of Seattle and Washington was an activist model that mirrors the organic, decentralized, interlinked pathways of the Internet—the Internet come to life" (2000, 19). What Klein finds politically attractive about this pop-ular organizing is that its principles are pitted against those of the corporations it opposes. Against centralization, we see fragmentation; against globalization, flexible localization; against power consolidation, radical power dispersal. If we accept this analysis, the only curricular direction in which I feel motivated to move is one of radical public pedagogy. This would be one where the control of academic-industrial complex is opposed by public bodies; the four walls of the classroom are opened and challenged by the streets outside; and the discussions in class are critically supplemented by dialogue with a broader public that does not otherwise have access to the educational experience.

LITERATURE

> I worked as a waitress, a copy-shop clerk, a messenger—all those jobs that you get when you have nothing but a couple of community-college credits in highly useless things like World Literature.
>
> —Marisa Silver (2000, 115)

Let us read the previous epigraph. The narrator outlines a journey for us. If you make your start taking classes in world literature, you end up with useless jobs. My own travel has been in the opposite direction. I worked on poetry and protest in an Indian province—and, when I applied for a teaching job in the American academy, I was handed a course teaching world literature.

Both of these accounts, despite their differences, are haunted by the question of employment. To talk of jobs is to consider, even at its most basic, the question of the economy. If I were to meet the narrator of Silver's story, I would like to ask her if what she read in her course on world literature taught her anything about employment and the world. My attempt in this chapter has been to show that the teaching of world literature or even postcolonial literature should indeed take up the hitherto ignored task of making links with issues of jobs, structural adjustment, and social change.

Although the Western press in the recent past has been celebrating literature written in the postcolonial world, especially works by Indian writers, I have been hard-pressed to find among these writings much about the new global realities. Searing critiques of the semifeudal, semicapitalist existence in rural India, yes; shallow, glitzy portrayals of city life in modern India, well, lots of that. But, to date, I have read only one Hindi short story that could be described as a self-conscious critique of life under the World Bank–IMF dictates of the past decade.[6] Where is the literature of the new economic policy?[7]

In my courses, I have had to rely on an older body of literature that recalls a past, residual order of global exchange; I try to provoke students to think about what is absent in those writings, for example, the global exchanges under the WTO or the North Atlantic Free Trade Agreement (NAFTA). R. K. Narayan's short story "A Horse and Two Goats" (1970), slyly narrates the tale of a transaction between the East and the West. The story takes place in the village of Kritam, which we are told is probably the tiniest of "the seven hundred thousand villages dotting the map of India." At the tale's center is an old man Muni who lives in Kritam with his wife and two goats. They are a poor couple with hardly any means of survival, except for what Muni's wife, who remains unnamed, is able to glean from any chores she is able to perform. Most of the story takes place beside the statue of a horse at the edge of the village beside the highway. While his two goats graze on cactus and lantana bushes, Muni, the narrator tells us, sits on that pedestal beside the highway because "it gave him a sense of belonging to the larger world."

On this particular day, a van runs out of gas and stops by Muni. From it emerges, a "red-faced foreigner," an American. Muni does not speak English, the American does not speak Tamil. The reader gets to be the privileged anthropologist in this story, able to understand the man's speech, which is presented in the story in English. In other words, the reader is the only one who is able to travel in both worlds. The naive narratives of both the American traveller and the Indian peasant are available only to the reader. The drama and the jest of the story lie in the twists and turns of the mistaken transaction that takes place. Muni comes to believe that the red-faced foreigner is interested in buying his goats, the American assumes that Muni is the owner of the horse statue beside the highway. Muni accepts the hundred rupees the foreigner offers him and walks home quickly so that the goats do not follow him. The foreigner puts the horse in his van and drives away. It is not till the goats bleat outside their hut that Muni's wife accuses him of thievery. That is where the story ends.

Now, Narayan's charming story does not seem contemporaneous with the world in which the NAFTA and the WTO are familiar words, a world in which there are frequent exposes of sweatshops in the Third World that earn profits for Americans, or a world in which a lot of frequent flier miles are earned by people who make fun of Americans earning a lot of frequent flier miles while travelling to remote parts of the world. In my classroom, it seems all I can do is register the story's delight. And, filled with something I recognize as piety, I stress that its delight might lie in the erasure of unpleasant details: when you finish reading the story, you might be pleased that no one is worse off than before. For you to register a loss, and to protest against it, means that you have to refer to words and concepts that seem to lie so much outside the universe of the story. A part of the pleasure of the story lies in its portrayal of Muni. Old and lazy, Muni can still eke out a living. You are likely to applaud his comfortable transaction because he comes out a survivor. He certainly seems more than a match for the American. We do not need to appeal to the history of the legendary, organized peasant protests of Telengana and Naxalbari in India. If you were so inclined you might even argue that the Indian peasant is a figure of resistance even in the most ordinary of ways. But, of what use are such extravagant consolations? Even if we accept that the figure of the revolutionary peasant of Telengana and Naxalbari might have been the product of a generalization, it is certainly also true that Narayan romanticizes in the figure of Muni. A more adequate complexity will begin to emerge if we discard, among other things, the idea of the American as the sole traveller. In an altered landscape, which, to be fair to Narayan, is also more a landscape of the present, Muni might be a migrant laborer, a traveller himself. The van that stops in front of him could be a Maruti, its driver a wealthy Indian industrialist who is interested in introducing a bit of an ethnic touch in the verandah of his farmhouse. He might pay Muni only for the labor of helping him put the horse in the van. Or he could be an Indian living in the United States, a consumer of postcolonial fiction and artifacts. Or, indeed, even as Muni sits at his remote post beside the horse, his life might be getting changed irredeemably by the invisible forces of the World Bank–IMF guided structural adjustments in the world around him.

It is this last possibility that emerges in the writings of the Booker Prize-winning author Arundhati Roy. In Roy's *The God of Small Things* (1997), the untouchable Velutha, unlike Narayan's Muni, carries a red flag. He is a Naxalite. At the same time, however, it also needs to be acknowledged that when you put down the novel, you hardly know any more about what Velutha's politics can still mean. Velutha was dead. He barely spoke in the narrative, and it is likely that when the story was over, all you could remember of him was his glittering smile. The subaltern with perfect teeth.

But, in the hollow left by the death and emotional devastation chronicled in the novel, the reader is offered the bare outlines of the changes that have overcome the India of the new economic policy. Comrade Pillai's son, Lenin, ends up working as a technician in the Dutch and German embassies in Delhi. "Levin he called himself now. P. Levin." The house of history, the home of the Communist Party chief, has been turned in the novel into a five-star tourist hotel for affluent visitors from the West. The old feudal order has sunk to the ground and there are weeds growing around it.

However, it is in the essay that Roy wrote protesting the building of the dam on the Narmada River that we get a more direct and developed portrait of India under the economic policies of globalization (1999). In "The Greater Common Good," Roy notes: "India is in a situation today where it pays back more money to the Bank in interest and repayment installments that it receives from it. We are forced to incur new debts in order to be able to repay our old ones. According to the *World Bank Annual Report,* last year (1998), after the arithmetic, India paid the Bank $478 million more than it borrowed. Over the last five years (1993 to 1998) India paid the Bank $1.475 billion more than it received" (1999, 29).

It needs to be conceded that this might not be the most complicated or even sufficient analysis. However, what this inspired polemic allows me to do is make a connection where none existed between literature and the World Bank. In *Culture and Imperialism* (1993), Edward Said reads the dynamism of postcolonial responses in the rewritings of Western classics like Joseph Conrad's *Heart of Darkness* by writers like Tyeb Salih in *The Season of Migra-*

tion to the North. What I am arguing here is that a part of the postcolonial literature of resistance—what we can call World Bank literature—must include a countercanonical formation that mixes together novels with pamphlets, short stories with journalism, memoirs with economic reports. Novels are not consumed in a world separate from the world of commodities; to return insistently to this rather familiar fact is also to help our students examine aspects of their own lives in relation to the political world around them.

The reality is that our students, juggling jobs and working on their careers, when they offer observations on their own lives, also work as producers of World Bank literature. When I watched on my television the lines of protestors in Seattle and then again in Washington, D.C., I saw among them youth who I could easily imagine were my students. One of them had written in a paper during the same semester that riots in Seattle took place:

> When I'm at work, the machine that washes the dishes borrows my spirit and my soul for about six hours. The job is simple and mindless. The machine runs on a minute and forty second cycle. Everything I do revolves around this time-cycle. The second I shut the door, the machine starts. No matter where I go in the restaurant or what I do, I have been conditioned to return to it seconds before the cycle is complete so that I can move more dishes through. If I died of exhaustion, or merely burned out, I could be replaced immediately and for this reason, they can keep the pay as low as the law permits.

This student and many others like him find in Roy (whose *The Cost of Living* I used in my class) an inspiration to speak and act against—against what? The Narmada River, with its source in the Shahdol district of Madhya Pradesh in central India, will perhaps never flow through the lives of most of my students again. But, in finding in Roy's lyrical diatribe the occasion to grapple with capitalist exploitation in its contemporary forms, the American youth in my classes are also protesting against the condition of their own lives. They gather confidence from the fact that Roy was protesting the way in which half a million inhabitants in the Narmada Valley, mostly Adivasis or aboriginal Indians, were arrogantly written out of the social contract by the World Bank and its collaborators in India. And if we pay attention to our students and to their responses, we find, mixed up in their idealism and frustrations, in their ambitions and their anxieties, an active rewriting of the culture that has produced them as scriptless subjects in the Wal-Mart called America.

NOTES

This chapter was published in its earlier form under the title "World Bank Literature: A New Name for Post-colonial Studies in the Next Century" in *College Literature* 26.3 (Fall 1999): 195–204. My thanks to Henry Giroux for his helpful comments on that paper. A longer version of this chapter will be in Amitava Kumar, ed., *World Bank Literature* (Minneapolis: University of Minnesota Press, 2000).

1. For some responses on both issues, see Nelson (1997b) and Martin (1998). How might these questions be connected to the public sphere? For some answers, see Kumar (1997). I agree with a reviewer's comment that we need to ask "the next set of questions"; for example, "what would a pedagogy of the job crisis look like?" See Alessandrini (1998).

2. For another useful elaboration of critical multiculturalism, see Giroux (2000), especially the chapter "The Limits of Academic Multiculturalism." An earlier, valuable critique can be found in Mohanty (1989-1990, 179-208).

3. "Naxalite" is a term that has been used since the late 1960s to describe Maoist and Marxist-Leninist activists in India.

4. The web journal TomPaine.com also ran a series of features to contest media bias. See "The *New York Times*'s Slanted Op-Ed Coverage of the World Bank and IMF," <www.tompaine.com/features/2000/05/01/1.html>. Last accessed: January 15, 2001. Also see Seth Ackerman (2000).

5. For a succinct analysis of these distinctions, see Henwood (2000).

6. See Prakash (1997). For a longer discussion of this narrative, see Kumar (1999).

7. My question—rather the claim buried in it—cannot be sustained when it comes against the recent writing and activism of Arundhati Roy. I take up Roy's work a little later in this chapter.

WORKS CITED

Ackerman, Seth. 2000. "Prattle in Seattle." *Extra!* (January-February).

Alessandrini, Anthony. 1998. "Teaching (and) the Crisis." *Mediations* 21 (Spring): 126-129.

Degrees of Shame, Part-time Faculty: Migrant Workers of the Information Economy. 1998. Produced and directed by Barbara Wolf. Cincinnati: Barbara Wolf Video Work. Videocassette.

Diawara, Manthia. 1998. *In Search of Africa.* Cambridge, Mass.: Harvard University Press.

Featherstone, Liza. 2000. "The New Student Movement." *The Nation,* 15 May, 11-18.

Giroux, Henry. 2000. *Impure Acts.* New York: Routledge. See especially the chapter, "The Limits of Academic Multiculturalism."

"Governor's Encounter with Prisoner." 2000. *The Hindu,* 6 April.

Heller, Scott. 2000. "The Lessons of a Lost Career." *Chronicle of Higher Education,* 16 May, A18-A22.

Henwood, Doug. 2000. "What Is Globalization Anyway?" In *World Bank Literature,* ed. Amitava Kumar. Minneapolis: University of Minnesota Press.

Kelley, Robin D. G. 1996. "The Proletariat Goes to College." *Social Text* 49 (Winter): 37-42

Klein, Naomi. 2000. "The Vision Thing." *The Nation,* 10 July, 18-21.

Kumar, Amitava. 1999. "Louder Than Bombs: What's Hot about Indian Writing?" *Transition* 79:80-101.

———, ed. 1997. *Class Issues: Pedagogy, Cultural Studies, and the Public Sphere.* New York: New York University Press.

Loomba, Ania. 1998-1999. "Postcolonialism—or Postcolonial Studies." *Interventions* 1.1: 39-42.

Martin, Randy, ed. 1998. *Chalk Lines.* Durham, N.C.: Duke University Press.

Mohanty, Chandra Talpade. 1989-1990. "On Race and Voice: Challenges for Liberal Education in the 1990s." *Cultural Critique* 14 (Winter): 179-208.

Narayan, R. K. 1970. "A Horse and Two Goats." In *A Horse and Two Goats,* by R. K. Narayan. New York: Viking.

Nelson, Cary. 1997a. *Manifesto of a Tenured Radical.* New York: New York University Press.

———, ed. 1997b. *Will Teach for Food.* Minneapolis: University of Minnesota Press.

Ng, Fae Myenne. 1993. *Bone.* New York: Hyperion.

Prakash, Uday. 1997. "Paul Gomra Ka Scooter." In *Paul Gomra Ka Scooter,* ed. Uday Prakash. New Delhi: Radhakrishnan.

Press, Eyal, and Jennifer Washburn. 2000. "The Kept University." *Atlantic Monthly* (March): 39-54.

Ross, Andrew, ed. 1997. *No Sweat: Fashion, Free Trade, and the Rights of Garment Workers.* New York: Verso.

Roy, Arundhati. 1999. *The Cost of Living.* New York: Random House.

———. 1997. *The God of Small Things.* New York: Random House.

Said, Edward. 1993. *Culture and Imperialism.* New York: Vintage.

Shiva, Vandana. 1999. "A Lesson in Humility." *The Hindu,* 3 November.

Silver, Marisa. 2000. "The Passenger." *The New Yorker,* 19 and 26 June, 114-128.

Solomon, Norman. 2000. "Protests in Washington Clash with Media Spin." Creators Syndicate. Circulated on "Fifty Years Is Enough" electronic list-serve, 13 April.

Watkins, Evan. 1989. *Work Time.* Stanford: Stanford University Press, 1989.

IV

MAKING THE PEDAGOGICAL MORE POLITICAL

13

Going Postal: Pedagogic Violence and the Schooling of Emotion

Lynn Worsham

The point of critique is not justification but a different way of feeling, another sensibility.

—Gilles Deleuze

[D]ecolonization is always a violent phenomenon.

—Franz Fanon

GOING POSTAL IN PRACTICE AND THEORY

A phrase with a rather short history, "going postal" has proven to be quite portable during its brief life. I came across it most recently in *Premiere Magazine* where it serves as the clever title of the letters-to-the-editor section. To get to the glossy pages of a magazine devoted entirely to the promotion of the entertainment industry and the manufacture of celebrity, the phrase had to travel quite a distance from its place of origin: the inner workings of U.S. postal facilities where incidents of violence, usually deadly, have occurred with alarming frequency in the last decade. Since the mid-1980s, post office employees are said to be going postal when they murder and injure coworkers, often their supervisors, as a way of settling workplace grievances perceived to be beyond resolution or appeal. Coined in this context and in an effort to wrest from senselessness a sense of something unprecedented in labor history, the phrase then moved with surprising speed into the vernacular of postmodern America, where it now may be used to refer to any violent outburst, however mundane and inconsequential. Its appearance in the pages of *Premiere Magazine* seems to suggest that once "going postal" goes to Hollywood to entitle a popular court of opinion and appeal, the meaning of the phrase has forever changed. Perhaps "going postal" has now become merely a catchy phrase whose attenuated power exists only in its ability to incite the anonymous letter-writer to a verbal display that is worthy of fifteen seconds of notice. If so, then perhaps here the full deadly force of "nobodi-ness" can be contained and will not collide head on with the full force of the desire for "somebodiness," and thus in this venue the circuit may be rewired—the short circuit that transforms, for example, a "nobody" like Mark David Chapman into the "somebody" who killed John Lennon. Or perhaps "going postal" has become just another empty catchword that preserves no memory of what was originally carried in its terms, no memory of the outrage that begets rage and further outrage. If so, then the lines of articulation must be wide open, and "going postal" may soon turn up as the name for an updated version of that adolescent kissing game once called "post office." In any event, the strange career of this phrase—its increasing distance and abstraction, alienation and estrangement, from the objective conditions that gave rise to it—has followed a wild logic that we can neither bear to remem-ber nor afford to forget.

In this chapter, "going postal" will therefore remain a canny phrase for remembering, for example, the execution of fourteen women by a man who, on December 6, 1989, walked into an engineering classroom at the Univer-sity of Montreal and reportedly shouted, "I want the women!"[1] There was laughter—everyone thought it was a joke, a game—as he ordered the women to one side of the room and the men to the other. Before he opened fire, he called the women a "bunch of feminists." In a desperate effort to quickly reeducate the gunman and reverse the inevitable course of events, one woman screamed, "You have the wrong women; we are not feminists!" But this disavowal alone could never have reversed the momentum of a paranoid logic which, in abject misrecognition, crossed the personal and the political to justify the annihilation of difference.

"Going postal" will also remember the senseless mayhem created in Stock-ton, California, by Patrick Purdy, who armed himself with an assault rifle, walked onto a schoolyard at midday recess, and began shooting. Five children were killed and twenty-nine were injured before Purdy turned the gun on himself. Although news reports indicated that the slaughter might have been motivated by racial bitterness—an influx of Southeast Asian immigrants into the area in the 1980s had taken jobs that Purdy felt should have been his—public memory has since erased the gunman's smiling face and its recitation of euphoria and rage. In the aftermath, what remained for most of us was only an abstract sense of the event as another moment in the ongoing stalemate over constitutional rights and gun control. What remained for a time in the daily lives of the surviving children of Stockton was a game they called "Purdy." This child's play took two forms: the players either reenacted the slaughter with a toy assault rifle placed in the hands of an appointed villain, or they revised the original event by taking up toy guns and, in righteous and justifiable vengeance, staging the villain's ritual execution.[2] In 1989, Stockton was the fifth in a series of school assaults that year that began when a woman walked into a Winnetka, Illinois, schoolroom, saying, "I'm going to teach you a lesson about guns," and then shot and killed an eight-year-old boy and critically wounded five others.

Then, too, there is the national teaching that took place, also in 1989, in the wake of the Central Park rape. The principal lesson here would reinforce a familiar teaching—the catechism of fear and shame that schools women to accept responsibility for their own brutalization—but it focused attention primarily on the terrible relation that may link boredom and urban violence. "Wilding" entered the national vocabulary and the postmodern imaginary through this case to describe the seemingly random acts of unmotivated savagery committed by bored and restless groups of youths looking for something to do. Nothing, at least initially, explained the wilding in Central Park, none of the usual social or psychological topoi for locating, naturalizing, and, in a sense, organizing urban crime for its profit of meaning.[3] Wilding, by definition, seems to refuse to wear the face of poverty, race, gender, sex, or even madness. The term itself suggests a form of play, except that here the disappearance of the players (i.e., their anonymity) in this brutal game may not signal a suspension of the rules as much as render them more deceptive and more desperate.

If it is to be defined by a poverty of reason, then perhaps wilding should not be associated with the incidents of violence that occurred in Montreal, Stockton, or Winnetka, or with any of the incidents of school, workplace, and family violence that, in the last decade, have increasingly punctuated the everyday—most recently, in Jonesboro (Arkansas), Newington (Connecticut), Milwaukee (Wisconsin), Orange (California), West Paducah (Kentucky), and Pearl (Mississippi). From Pearl to Paducah, the incidence of certain forms of violence in the United States is on the rise—for example, workplace homicide is the fastest growing category of murder, where the number has tripled in the last decade; murder is the leading cause of workplace death for women. The phenomenon of wilding, because it appears to be in a category of its own, may not shed any light on these forms or on more symbolic forms of violence or their effects—for example, the repeated broadcast of the videotaped beating of Rodney King by Los Angeles police officers; or the ritual humiliation of Anita Hill by the all-male, all-white Senate Judiciary Committee and before the American people, whose need for an education on the issue of sexual harassment has been suggested as justification for her public shaming.

However, in my view, wilding is an exemplary instance of going postal. It will therefore prove instructive for what it will offer a rhetoric of "pedagogic violence," a study that would seek to describe both the forms and effects through which violence is lived and experienced and its objective or structural role in the constitution of subjectivities and in the justification of subjection. The increase in violence, especially incidents of going postal, suggests to me that it is time to reconsider the real and symbolic function of violence. In the liberal view, violence occurs at the very limit of the social order where it points to the fragility of meaning, identity, and value; and the "progress" of modern society can be measured in the successful substitution of persuasion and consent for violence and force. However, this view draws attention away from the fact that violence also (and increasingly) arises from within the authority of existing social, political, and economic arrangements and serves quite effectively to reinforce their legitimacy. Given that violence seems to be a permanent and pervasive feature of capitalist societies, circulating its effects widely through the reiterative teaching of media, a study of pedagogic violence may add an additional chapter to Michel Foucault's (1979) history of disciplinary society by returning again to the bodily rhetoric of violence, to its visible and invisible scarification of the individual and social psyche.

More specifically, the concept of pedagogic violence seeks to make visible the relationship between discipline and violence, between what is most legitimate and what is most illegitimate, to open for examination the symbolic violence implied in teaching and learning, the real violence prepared in schooling, wherever schooling happens to occur. The concept of pedagogic violence brings together phenomena set apart from one another by the partitioning and individuating techniques of discipline; therefore, I see it as a horizontal or border concept that locates the point at which one kind of thing becomes visible as something entirely different. In its origin and effects, wilding is, as I will suggest later, far less pathological than it is normal (and normalizing), for it demonstrates and confirms the efficacy of dominant pedagogy.

A rhetoric of pedagogic violence will focus specifically on the way violence addresses and educates emotion and inculcates an affective relation to the world. In the view I develop here, "emotion" will refer to the tight braid of affect and judgment, socially and historically constructed and bodily lived, through which the symbolic takes hold of and binds the individual, in complex and contradictory ways, to the social order and its structure of meanings. School, workplace, and family violence are pedagogies of emotion, and as such they are particularly effective ways of locating and anchoring us in a way of life. They are an integral part of the political machinery of what I will call, following Ann Ferguson, the sex/affective production system of advanced capitalism, and they arise from within and extend (rather than radically destabilize) its logic. The paradigmatic instance here is the institution of domestic violence (including incest) that has been criminalized in First World societies, though only recently and unevenly.[4]

In what can only be a limited treatment of the subject here, I am moved by the exorbitant instances of pedagogic violence, suggested by the examples opening this chapter, to consider more subtle forms while nevertheless insisting on their relation. In this chapter, I want to return to what I think we already know but have learned to forget—namely, that the discourse of emotion is our primary education (primary in the sense of both earliest and foundational). And I argue that if our commitment is to real individual and social change—change that would finally dissolve the relationship between pedagogy and violence—then the work of decolonization must occur at the affective level, not only to reconstitute the emotional life of the individual, but also, and more importantly, to restructure the feeling or mood that characterizes an age. To be sure, our most urgent political and pedagogical task remains the fundamental reeducation of emotion. This project cannot succeed by mapping a new regime of meaning onto an old way of feeling, one that has only intensified with the so-called waning of affect in the era of the postmodern (see Jameson 1984). Face-to-face with the indomitable and archaic spirit of sex-hatred and race-hatred, for example, critical social theories have helped to shape an intellectual understanding of the practices and the costs of othering. However, a tear is not simply an intellectual thing, and a change of heart does not follow, naturally or simply, from a change of mind (see Neu 1987). Grief, hatred, bitterness, anger, rage, terror, and apathy as well as emotions of self-assessment such as pride, guilt, and shame—these form the core of the hidden curriculum for the vast majority of people living and learning in a highly stratified capitalist society. This curriculum holds most of us so deeply and intimately and yet differently within its logic that our affective lives are largely immune to the legislative efforts of social critique and to the legislative gains of progressive social movements.

I am compelled therefore to make the ultimate destination of this chapter a consideration of the turn to pedagogy in American literary and cultural studies. This pedagogical turn arguably represents an effort to change, through the language of critique and empowerment, the emotional constitution of the postmodern subject. In literary and cultural studies, the pedagogical turn is relatively recent, beginning only in the late 1980s. By the early 1990s, education and pedagogy had become, in Gerald Graff's words, the "boom subject" of the academic humanities (1994). In a brief account of the growing interest in pedagogy in literary and cultural studies, Graff finds in the very nature of theory what I have called, in the context of composition studies, a pedagogical imperative to spell out theory's implications for teaching (see Worsham 1992). But, in my view, the pedagogical turn in literary and cultural studies is driven by a recognition of the failures of theory—on the one hand, its failure to effectively counter the successes of the conservative educational agendas of the 1980s; and, on the other, its failure to meaningfully confront the political consequences of postmodernism understood as the cultural logic of late capitalism. Interestingly, the decade of the 1980s also closed with the incidents of going postal suggested earlier and with the so-called global triumph of capitalism represented by the fall of the Berlin Wall in 1989. In the 1990s, "Capitalists of the World Unite!" has replaced the failed slogan for worker solidarity, and the triumph expressed in this phrase threatens to foreclose the possibility of any oppositional theory that could effectively organize collective political action (see *New York Times* 1997, C28; Eagleton 1996, 5). In this context of failure and triumph, of despair and euphoria, pedagogy finds the political imperative to reconceive itself as a form of radical politics with goals that are formulated with a sense of utmost urgency: to reclaim education as a terrain of struggle crucial to the reconstruction of a public political culture and to constitute a revolutionary subject capable of transforming the world.

Ambitious, to say the least, this project and these goals have been important in the recent history and development of composition studies, a field that has been devalued ("feminized" and "proletarianized," it claims) precisely because its labors have been deemed "unscholarly"—that is, practical, pedagogical, and applied. Apparently undisturbed by rumors of the failure of theory, composition studies has rapidly adopted the *lingua franca* of theory during the last fifteen years as a way of enfranchising itself as a fully vested member of English studies, while more recently it has appropriated the political language of radical pedagogy as a way of claiming a key role for itself (and writing instruction) as a revolutionary agent of change. The irony for those of us in composition studies is that the pedagogical turn in literary and cultural studies has accomplished what composition has not had the power to achieve on its own: pedagogy has become not only a legitimate object of intellectual inquiry in English studies, a boom subject in the humanities, but also a matter of urgent social and political interest. More sobering is the fact that composition studies, in an anxious effort to travel the circuit from "nobodiness" to "somebodiness" (if only in the culture of English studies), has continued to pursue a relatively uncritical relation to the boom subject that has been such a boon to the field. Understandably, content to capitalize on the terms of political vision and to translate them into the more lucrative tokens of professional self-interest, composition studies generally has asked too few questions.

One pivotal question that should be asked—and a question that gives sharp focus to the nature of the failure of theory—concerns the fact that the spectacle of excessive violence returns as an all too familiar form of the everyday, while the category of violence all but disappears in recent theoretical and pedagogical discourse, where the focus is on detailing forms of desire, pleasure, and consent. Teresa L. Ebert, among others, also has focused attention on this preoccupation in critical theory and in a way that helps to situate the present inquiry. Ebert suggests the concept of the "post-al" as a name for various new knowledges including poststructuralism, Lacanian and post-Lacanian psychoanalysis, postmodernism, post-Marxism, postlesbian and postgay queer theory, and almost every brand of feminist theory. These new post-al (a.k.a. ludic) knowledges, and the pedagogies they inspire, are thus differentiated from classical Marxism and are identified as the specific forms that failure takes.

In general, the concept of the post-al designates discourses and practices that concentrate critical attention on the body, that substitute desire for labor as the basic process of late capitalism, that erase the relations of production and class struggle from contemporary analyses, and that in effect reduce the scope of politics to cultural and discursive (or ideological) analysis (Ebert 1996a, 1996b). Reclaiming the priority of the categories of labor and class, Ebert seeks to end theory's long digression into discursive and cultural materialism by setting it on the proper path of historical materialism. A central part of this project is to expose post-al theory as merely a form of bourgeois ideology outfitted in the latest jargon to appear to be "knowledge" and thereby to expose its role in the elision of issues of exploitation and emancipation. To this end, Ebert excoriates cultural materialists for combating phrases with phrases, for thinking they are combating the real problems of the existing world and waging real political struggle with discourse about discourse. Her point is not that ideology, cultural practices, and significations are peripheral to political struggle. Rather, her point is that they are not autonomous and must be linked, through materialist critique, to the nondiscursive, to the " 'real existing world'—whose objectivity is the fact of the 'working day' " (Ebert 1996a, 45). Post-al knowledges and pedagogies have failed to perform such a critique and have successfully shifted critical attention from the "working day" to the "everyday," to popular culture and consumption (see also Kelsh 1998). For Ebert and her cohorts, going post-al is a particularly heinous form of violence because it has effectively paralyzed political will and action. It may not be going too far to suggest that, in this view, going post-al in theory is tantamount to a form of going postal—that is, post-al theory is merely a route for a very few enterprising "nobodies" to become "somebodies" in the academic star system by trading on the misery of the most exploited and oppressed; going post-al in theory is nothing more than a verbal display, even a mode of play or entertainment, that serves the professional and political interests of bourgeois intellectuals (see also Shumway 1997).

In specific cases, I might agree. I too seek a form of critique that links the discursive and the nondiscursive, the working day and the everyday, beyond the mystifying focus on pleasure and desire. However, I cannot endorse the rather sharp line drawn between (classical) Marxism and all other theories gathered under the rubric of post-al or ludic knowledges. Such strict categorization, coupled with a rather dogmatic return to classical Marxism, ignores the historicality of Marxism as well as the historicality of capitalism. It also suggests a rather undialectical relation to so-called post-al theories that refuses to recognize that history also happens in these theories, that they too may have their moment of "truth" as well as their moment of "falsehood." At the very least, such strict categorization is arguably another instance of the kind of dividing practice that is the genius of disciplinary thinking, an "up against the wall" rhetoric that historically has been used so effectively against those who are identified as others and enemies. Granted, there is a critical edge given to thought when it can clearly and decisively name the problem and identify the enemy. Perhaps this is the only certain way to achieve the necessary critical distance that leads to oppositional struggle and change. Still, it may be useful here to suggest a distinction between "enemy" and "adversary," as post-Marxist theorist Chantal Mouffe urges (1993). An enemy is one to be annihilated; an adversary is respected as one to struggle *with* and *against* in the formation of a new hegemony (2–4, 84–85). Capitalism—complicated and abetted by interacting regimes of white supremacy, racism, neocolonialism, patriarchy, and heterosexism—is the enemy. On this, Ebert and I agree. But Ebert also sees enemies in all of the various post-al knowledges, whereas I see some worthy adversaries and even a few friends. Ebert seeks a correction in the course of theory through the substitution of labor for desire, through the substitution of one way of knowing and its phrasings (historical materialism) for another way of knowing (post-al knowledge); I seek in theory's various phrasings a "critical articulation" that may claim a role in producing, in the real and existing world, a different way of feeling, a different sensibility.

The crucial insight here is that what the working day produces and reproduces as its primary and most valuable product is an affective relation to the world, to oneself, and to others. This is in large part what is meant by the social relations of labor. "Going postal" will serve as a representative anecdote and a guide for the kind of critique that I have in mind, one that links the working day and the everyday. Although we may prefer to be comforted by the view that violence is the unfortunate result of individual pathology, we must remember that the phrase "going postal" originates in the objective conditions of the working day in U.S. postal facilities and should tell us something about those conditions: conditions of exploitation and domination; humiliating and alienating conditions that produce rage, bitterness, frustration, and indignation. The violence that must be remembered through this phrase is of two orders: the outrage of exploitation and domination and the rage such outrage produces. In the phenomenon of going postal, we have evidence that violence begets further violence; violence legitimized and justified as the existing economic and social arrangements begets further violence that, within these arrangements, must be set apart and termed "illegal," "unjustified," and "unjustifiable." Furthermore, the strange career of "going postal" offers a record of the kind of symbolic violence through which a phrase or sign loses its ideological edge, its contact with the objective conditions that gave rise to it, and its potential to call those conditions into question and make them an object of struggle. An oppositional reading of "going postal" and its career would return power to this phrase by retracing the path of disarticulation, alienation, and estrangement and by reconnecting the domains of working day and everyday, of "productive" labor and "nonproductive" emotional labor.

I should say from the outset that I am not overly sanguine about our prospects for reeducating emotion given the prevailing "pathos of theory" (a phrase that includes a theoretical discourse on teaching)—in other words, given the role theory and pedagogy play in reproducing an affective relation to the world. Here, my specific concern is that the new commitment to pedagogy may effectively redeploy key distinctions that mystify the work of decolonization—in particular, the distinctions between public and private and between reason and emotion as well as the gendered and racialized authority of these distinctions. A more general worry is that the turn *toward* pedagogy may constitute a turn *away* from the family as a locus of critique and a site for reconstructing social and emotional life. Although the family has compelled some of the most important social criticism of the post–World War II period, it is rarely discussed in recent pedagogical discourse, except in the feminist pedagogy of nurturance, where it is often treated ahistorically. The argument that advanced capitalism reduces the role of the family to a minimum (and that the primary determinants of social and psychic life therefore are to be found in forms outside the family, especially in popular culture and consumption) certainly compels us to look elsewhere if we are going to make fundamental social changes. "The domestic sphere," as Gayatri C. Spivak observes, "is not the emotion's only legitimate workplace" (1987, 103). Still, the claims of any form of radical politics must be qualified by the fact that women of most social locations are still enlisted to take primary responsibility for caretaking and nurturing—in isolated nuclear families, in single-mother homes, in daycare centers, in elementary and secondary schools, and, some would argue, in college writing classrooms. Their working day is also an everyday that takes shape in the objective conditions of emotional labor—largely unpaid, unrecognized, yet socially necessary labor. The education provided by women in an otherwise male-dominated society remains the primary pedagogy on which all subsequent learning is mapped; and, as many feminists before me have argued, it continues to affix the struggle for identity and agency to the emotional repudiation of that which is coded feminine and maternal. My question is whether radical pedagogy is committed in theory and practice to altering what Jon R. Schiller calls "the social conditions of psychic matriarchy" set up by a gendered (and racialized) division of emotional labor (1981, 84).

To develop the notion of pedagogic violence further, I return to this primary pedagogy and its role in the education of emotion in the next section of this chapter. Then, in the third section, I consider the way in which some versions of radical pedagogy may actually work to remystify violence and mask their own ambivalence about the work of decolonization. In general, my effort here might be read as a reworking of Louis Althusser's notion of the family-education couple as our dominant pedagogy and therefore as a crucial place to struggle for the political reconstruction of our emotional lives.

SCHOOLING EMOTION

Psychoanalysis has taught that the individual's emotional attitudes to other
people are established at an unexpectedly early age. . . . The people to
whom [the child] is in this way fixed are his parents. . . . His later acquain-
tances are . . . obliged to take over a kind of emotional heritage.

—Sigmund Freud

The idea of pedagogic violence assumes a distinction between two senses of
pedagogy: the familiar and specialized sense of pedagogy as a philosophy (or
ideology) of teaching, including classroom practices and instructional methods; and the broad sense of pedagogy as education in general, or what the
Greeks once called *paideia*. The view of pedagogy as the general education
appropriate to members of a culture receives its contemporary formulation,
for example, in Althusser's conception of ideological state apparatuses and in
Michel Foucault's notion of discipline. Inasmuch as both of these formulations
emphasize that modern society makes state-sanctioned violence increasingly
unnecessary as a mode of social control, I want to begin to rework the family-
education couple along the lines suggested by Pierre Bourdieu and Jean-
Claude Passeron's *Reproduction in Education, Society, and Culture* (1977),
where the relationship between pedagogy and violence receives explicit treatment. In the following discussion, I identify two kinds of pedagogic violence
or two related domains where it operates and organizes its effects: first, the
pedagogic violence authorized by and implied in education in general; and,
second, the pedagogic violence that initially organizes the emotional life of the
individual, approached here through Julia Kristeva's notion of abjection
(1982). Finally, I question whether postmodernism constitutes, in Fredric
Jameson's words, "a whole new emotional ground tone" and as such represents a break with the dominant pedagogy of emotion (1984).

For Bourdieu and Passeron, "pedagogy" (in the general sense, above) refers
to the power held by dominant discourses to impose the legitimate mode of
conception and perception. "Pedagogy" refers to the power to impose meanings that maintain and reinforce the reigning social, economic, and political
arrangements as legitimate when in fact they are entirely arbitrary. The dominant pedagogy in a disciplinary society consists of the ruling ideas of the ruling class or group—or, the framework of meanings that most thoroughly,
though most indirectly and inconspicuously, expresses and safeguards the
material and symbolic interests of the dominant group or groups (1977, 7-9).
Dominant pedagogy is a structure that produces individuals and groups who
are recognized as such because they have internalized the legitimate point of
view. Pedagogy retains its authority precisely through violence, through its
power to impose the legitimate mode of conception and perception, and
through its power to conceal and mystify relations of domination and exploita-

tion. The specific goal of pedagogic work is the transmission of knowledges appropriate to the position of an individual in a hierarchy of social relations that reproduces the authority of the dominant group and sustains its continued legitimacy. Pedagogy is an apparatus for creating, maintaining, and perpetuating the legitimacy of the interests of the dominant group across many different kinds of discourse that cultivate "the educated individual" as an ideal type of pedagogical subject who possesses the propensity to consume the legitimate products of dominant culture and is predisposed to be used and consumed according to its interests. Dominant pedagogy depends on the social misrecognition of the objective truth of pedagogic work.

To ensure its success, dominant pedagogy develops a system of subordinate educational ideologies that serves to mask its truth: philosophies and practices that claim to be nonviolent and nonrepressive are particularly useful in promoting misrecognition, such as pedagogies (Socratic or psychoanalytic or ludic) that focus on the erotics of teaching and learning; or pedagogies (deconstructive or collaborative) that are premised on decentered authority in the classroom; or even pedagogies that emphasize affective understanding (feminist pedagogies of maternal nurturance) that exert power through a subtle instrument of coercion, the implied threat of the withdrawal of affection.

Bourdieu and Passeron argue that these pedagogies do not (and cannot) recognize the extent to which their authority is based in dominant pedagogy and contributes to its legitimacy. They also argue that blindness to the structure of domination among classes or groups makes possible and persuasive the "liberating" and "humanizing" project of "culture for the masses" that gives subordinated groups the means of appropriating legitimate culture. It also produces and authorizes the "democratizing" and "declassing" project that gives legitimacy to the cultures of others, a project that begins, as they point out, with the erasure of the distinction between high culture and popular or mass culture and may extend, it seems to me, to include at least some versions of multiculturalism (1977, 12). That is, these projects serve to bind individuals and groups ever more closely to the authority of dominant pedagogy. In this context, Bourdieu and Passeron's reminder is especially relevant: it is one thing to teach the arbitrary nature of all culture to individuals who have already been educated according to the ideas of the ruling class; it would be quite another to claim to give the kind of education that makes an individual a native, as it were, of all cultures (23–24). Radical pedagogy, as I will suggest later, does not claim to offer the latter, but the key to its emancipatory project and its promise of empowerment is the claim to teach the arbitrariness of all culture.

This view of pedagogy clarifies the kind of work that decolonization requires and suggests that the intervention needed to change a hierarchical social order can be nothing less than a radical conversion or complete substitution of one kind of social formation for another. Bourdieu and Passeron argue that pedagogic work is not reversible. In other words, we cannot simply unlearn what dominant pedagogy teaches by mapping a new regime of meaning onto an old one (1977, 31–43). Such a strategy, as I have already indicated, offers an education in the arbitrariness of all culture to individuals who have already appropriated (and who have been appropriated by) the prevailing ideas of the ruling class. This means that the work of decolonization cannot consist simply in a struggle for the recognition and legitimacy of an alternative pedagogy in terms set by the dominant pedagogy, for such a struggle would inevitably neutralize the radical change promised by the alternative. Dominant pedagogy is always able to accommodate (and subordinate) alternatives in a way that does not seriously disrupt its own authority. The work of decolonization requires that we change the terms of recognition. Bourdieu writes, "To change the world, one has to change the ways of making the world, that is, the vision of the world and the practical operations by which groups are produced and reproduced" (1991, 137). The crucial stakes of political struggle are the categories of perception and the systems of classification and conceptualization—in other words, the words, names, and phrases—that construct the social world, the real and existing world. In this view, we must fight phrases with phrases.

The success of decolonization depends, it seems to me, on a recognition that the primary work of pedagogy is more fundamental than the imposition of a dominant framework of meanings. Its primary work is to organize an emotional world, to inculcate patterns of feeling that support the legitimacy of dominant interests, patterns that are especially appropriate to gender, race, and class locations. Pedagogy locates individuals objectively in a hierarchy of power relations; more importantly, it also organizes their affective relations to that location, to their own condition of subordination, and to others in that hierarchical structure. Pedagogy binds each individual to the social world through a complex and often contradictory affective life that remains, for the most part, just beyond the horizon of semantic availability, and its success depends on a mystification or misrecognition of this primary work. In particular, pedagogy provides and limits a vocabulary of emotion and, especially to those in subordinate positions, it teaches an inability to adequately apprehend, name, and interpret their affective lives. This is its primary violence. Primary pedagogic work mystifies emotion as a personal and private matter and conceals the fact that emotions are prevailing forms of social life, that personal life always takes shape in social and cultural terms (Ferguson 1989; Rosaldo 1984; Lyman 1981; Bartky 1990, 83–98; Foucault 1979, 194). Decolonization and the struggle for social change must therefore take place at the primary level of emotion.

The way in which dominant pedagogy organizes emotion may be understood in terms of Ferguson's notion of systems of sex/affective production. Ferguson argues that historically there are diverse ways to organize, structure, and reproduce what she calls sex/affective energy (or emotion) as a social energy that is bodily lived (1989, 77-99). The main task of any society is to create the social desire to cooperate and unite with others and to organize this social energy by identifying the appropriate objects, aims, and persons for emotional attachments and by prohibiting others as legitimate loci of interest. The overall task of the dominant pedagogy of a given society, then, is to coordinate and maintain a system of sex/affective production with a regime of meaning and with an economic system of production. Dominant pedagogy provides a complex system for the production of "goods"—that is, forms of recognized and legitimate affect, meaning, and value. Furthermore, what Alison M. Jaggar (1989) calls outlaw emotions—women's anger or worker rage, for example—are produced by dominant pedagogy, which views them as forms of insubordination, subject to retraining, because they are clues to suppressed social relations and may become resources for political resistance and social change (145-149). Legitimate and illegitimate (or appropriate and inappropriate) objects of affective attachment, in other words, are structurally or systemically related and, in prohibiting particular objects or persons as legitimate attachments, a society automatically invests them with great value and interest—if only for their disciplinary value in reproducing or policing authorized distinctions.

I want to focus for a moment on the dominant pedagogy of emotion for American middle-class society, a pedagogy that includes an explicit teaching about emotion—in other words, what it makes available at the semantic level in the way it theorizes the category of emotion—and the more implicit education of emotion itself. Through its explicit teaching, dominant pedagogy historically has held emotion in a relation of opposition to reason and has masked the fact that emotion is, in Catherine Lutz's words, "a master cultural category" in the West, fundamental to the way we organize understanding and experience (1988, 54). This pedagogy mystifies emotion as a natural category and masks its role in a system of power relations that associates emotion with the irrational, the physical, the particular, the private, the feminine, and nonwhite others.[5] In linking emotion to such negatively valued categories, pedagogy deploys emotion to secure the ideological subordination of women and minorities. Lutz also shows that the pedagogy of emotion is more complicated than this: it teaches us to define and value the concept of emotion in a contradictory way—negatively, in terms of its opposition to reason and rationality (as the core of the true self); and positively, in terms of its opposition to estrangement and disengagement from the world (55-59). Here, dominant pedagogy invests emotion with the authority to ensure the authentic engagement of the true self over and against estrangement and to provide motivation for taking moral positions and making ethical investments (76-80).[6]

Pedagogy develops more specific ideologies of emotion that conceal the ways in which it makes emotion an object of cultivation. The positivist approach to emotion, for example—or what Elizabeth V. Spelman (1989) calls the "dumb" view because it silences emotion—restricts emotion to the realm of the body (to sensation, physical feelings, and involuntary bodily movements) where it remains a purely private and internal event. Positivism makes emotion independent of any object or meaning or intention, and it directs attention to the way in which emotion disrupts rational judgment, thoughts, and perceptions. In recent years, the cognitivist theory of emotion has provided an alternative to positivism and has made emotion the explicit and legitimate object of pedagogic work. Emotion, in this view, can be educated, reeducated, or miseducated according to what pedagogy expressly establishes as appropriate, reasonable, and justifiable (Spelman 1989; Jaggar 1989). If emotion is to be a legitimate object of pedagogic work, it must be provided with cognitive content—in other words, its reasons, objects, and intentions that can be known and judged. In this way, cognitivism permits something of a rapprochement to occur between reason and emotion, though it also maintains their essential distinction and resubmits emotion to the authority of reason and the body to the direction of mind. The point here is that cognitivism works indirectly on emotion, which remains "dumb," through reason (or through the meaning or content to which it is attached).

Neither cognitivism nor positivism, however, unworks that odd bit of reasoning that historically has made members of subordinate groups allegedly more emotional (and "dumb"—irrational and therefore "stupid") than members of groups that are dominant politically, socially, and economically (Spelman 1989, 264). Their increased emotionality does not need reasons; it is simply given and justified by the structure of subordination. Cognitivism nevertheless capitalizes on the fact that those in subordinate positions can and must be taught, especially in school and workplace, that emotional responses (such as anger, rage, or bitterness) are always inappropriate and unjustified personal responses—forms of emotional stupidity, so to speak, if not psychopathology—rather than suppressed social responses to the objective conditions of humiliation wrought by structures of subordination and exploitation. In general, the dominant pedagogy of emotion refuses the expression of anger by subordinates. More importantly, it schools anger to turn inward so as to become silent rage or passive bitterness, where the energy for political action can be derailed in the pathos of the personal (see Spelman 1989, 266; McFall 1991, 153; Lyman 1981, 68–72). It makes it almost impossible to see that sometimes and in some contexts active bitterness might be a move away from self-deception and hence not only a moral achievement, but also a form of political insight because it more accurately apprehends the true source of injury and disappointment.

For much of the twentieth century, anger (or its prohibition) has been the target of workplace training and the effort to inculcate a proper emotional style for work (Stearns and Stearns 1986; Stearns 1988). Forms of pedagogic violence, developed through and authorized by industrial psychology, have so successfully disqualified the legitimacy of worker anger that by the 1960s it was said that anger had been eliminated from the workplace and no longer posed a problem to productivity. Attention then shifted to the cultivation of empathy, friendliness, and consideration[7] (through T-groups or sensitivity training) as an appropriate emotional style for the workplace. However, the increasing incidence of workplace violence in the last decade suggests that anger was not eliminated by the 1960s, as Peter N. Stearns and Carol Zisowitz Stearns contend, but that it has been driven deeper into silence where it festers into rage. The result: the number of workplace homicides has tripled in the last ten years.

Positivism and cognitivism are two specific pedagogies, then, that support the general way that dominant pedagogy understands emotion and organizes emotion-work by channeling it into appropriate and legitimate objects, aims, modes of expression, and stages—all of which are socially and historically produced and organized. While the workplace remains an important site for the education of emotion, the bourgeois model of the family has been the preferred instrument for the production and organization of emotion and the production of the kind of individuals whose affective organization best supports the social order needed by capitalism. The principal work of the family, in other words, is to transmit an affective orientation to authority, an orientation that changes with changes in the economic realm. Although the family has undergone dramatic changes, especially under the pressures of advanced capitalism, the role assigned to women in most social positions has not changed: they remain the primary nurturers and caretakers of men, children, and elders. Ferguson, among other theorists, argues that what I am calling the dominant pedagogy of capitalist patriarchy is a structure of exploitation that organizes the unequal exchange of emotion-work between men and women. The gendered imbalance in the provision of emotional support (which is a form of pedagogic violence) is a significant part of the gendered division of labor. This arrangement gives men a privileged position in the sphere of sex/affective production, where women are required to produce more nurturance than they receive. And they are required to engage in more nurturing labor not only in the home, but also in the workplace (see Schell 1998). Sandra Bartky extends Ferguson's analysis to argue that this structure of unequal exchange disempowers women at the same time that it binds women to a conviction that their moral worth and epistemic power consists in their greater capacity for love and nurturance (1990, 99–119). The ideology of nurturance, in short, is a key example of the mystificatory violence of dominant pedagogy.

More to the point here, the nurturing labor assigned to women arguably sets them up to be the first objects of pedagogic violence on which all subsequent education is mapped. Primary pedagogic violence occurs in what Kristeva (1982) calls the crisis of abjection that founds meaning, identity, and value—not only for the individual but also at the social level. Kristeva regards abjection as a universal psychological mechanism that operates to create the distinctions through which self-consciousness and culture (or the social) develop, but I see it as a way of understanding how social order is organized for the patriarchal domination of women by men. In Kristeva's view, each individual undergoes the violence of abjection at the time of his or her earliest attempt to break away from the mother and to establish boundaries as an autonomous ego. Abjection, she writes, is "a violent, clumsy breaking away, with the constant risk of falling back under the sway of a power as securing as it is stifling" (13). That power is the mother, and abjection serves to situate a first, fragile sense of place, before full subjectivity and objectivity emerge, upon which the psyche is built. The psyche is built on this primordial act of violence, and it is rocked by the ambivalence of attraction and repulsion, of fascination and terror, in its struggle for separation from the mother. The first fragile position the future subject takes, then, is defensive. The crisis of abjection is not, precisely speaking, a crisis of identity but of position and location: the decisive question is not "who am I?" but "where am I?" Before the subject is, it is abject and atopic (7–8).

Through interaction with the mother, which is its first contact with authority, the future subject learns about its body in a process Kristeva calls the "primal mapping of the body" (1982, 72). This is essentially an affective mapping, or education, in which the future subject learns rudimentary emotional orientations that distinguish between "inside" and "outside," "clean" and "unclean," "good" and "bad," "proper" and "improper." Abjection is, then, a kind of emotional boundary-work. It is a mechanism that works affectively to create a sense of place, orientation, and, ultimately, a sense of self. Abjection knots affect and judgment together and does its boundary-work especially through what we would call emotions of self-assessment such as pride, shame, and guilt. Abjection is a precondition of oedipalization, or the process of repudiating the maternal and of internalizing and identifying with paternal authority. Kristeva argues that abjection and the repudiation of women and maternal authority are the precondition for social order, the precondition of the subject's entry into the symbolic and the acquisition of language. Abjection sets in motion a process that oedipalization completes: the primordial estrangement that haunts the future subject. The experience of emotion will offer the thread leading back to the maternal, or to the constellation of contradictory emotions the maternal signifies in a patriarchal symbolic economy: bliss and terror, euphoria and rage, desire and disgust (1986, 316–317). Abjection and oedipalization provide a particular organization and education of emotion; they describe a violent movement from a world without shame to a world of shame and more violence. Shame, according to Thomas J. Scheff and Suzanne M. Retzinger (1991), is the consequence of estrangement, or the loss of social bonds, and this loss is, in their view, the major cause of destructive violence of all kinds. They argue that shame leads to violence when it goes unacknowledged, silenced, and repressed. Silenced shame produces anger and rage that are then turned inward to destroy the self or turned outward to destroy others (also see Bartky 1996).

Abjection is continually restaged in a kind of psychic drama that maintains identity; as a consequence, the subject remains in process and on trial, so to speak, and is always in danger of falling back into indifferentiation. Dominant pedagogy works reiteratively from the foundation of this initial affective mapping to continually educate emotion. It employs a regime of meaning that affectively identifies the abject with the experience of whatever disturbs identity, system, order—with whatever does not respect borders, positions, and rules (Kristeva 1982, 4). Dominant pedagogy sets up an equation, at the level of meaning or signification, among the abject, emotion, the maternal (or the feminine), and the profane—all of which are made to signify a threat to established authority and thus are made the legitimate objects of repression, control, and consumption; or denial, rationalization, and rage. Historically, this equation is then extended to include racialized others.

There is nothing necessary, of course, in the organization of emotion through a process that begins with and sustains itself on the pedagogic violence of abjection and the repudiation of women and the maternal. Nancy Chodorow (1978) makes an important point about the emotional heritage of women's mothering as it is organized in isolated nuclear families and single-mother families and in the context of women's social and economic inequality. Her point pertains to the organization of emotion and the education of gender personalities through a distinction between "positional" and "personal" identification processes (173–190). Women's mothering sets up an affective organization in boys that requires that they not only give up their primary identification with the maternal, but that they also deny this primary attachment. Their emotional education stresses differentiation from others and the repudiation of relationship and nurturance—and all things feminine. Boys learn proper gender identification negatively through a repudiation of the feminine and a movement from the personal (identification with the mother) to the impersonal and positional (identification with aspects of the masculine role, especially economic power, rather than specific attributes of the absent or remote father). Gender education through positional identification breaks the tie between affective processes and gender role learning (175).

Women's mothering and nurturing labor sets up an affective organization in girls based on personal identification with the mother, with her general personality, behavior, and values. In the process of personal identification, the affective processes and gender role learning are not severed. In girls, hostility toward the mother (the affective memory of abjection) tends to be more personally tied to an individual rather than generalized to all women as it is in masculine development. I want to extend Chodorow's argument here and say that women's mothering and nurturing labor organizes in men an identification (and preoccupation) with position, with "where" as an authoritative answer to the question of "who." It tends to establish in women an identification (and preoccupation) with the authority of the personal, with the affective relation of "who" and "where." These preoccupations are reiterated throughout recent discourse—for example, in Jameson's pedagogy of "cognitive mapping," which foregrounds the role of theory in producing a sense of position (1984); and in Adrienne Rich's "politics of location," which emphasizes the sense of personal locatedness provided in feelings and the body (1986). I will return to these two kinds of education later on.

Oedipalization—or the internalization and identification with an authority figure to which one is attached emotionally—is the specific way the patriarchal and bourgeois family produces individuals whose affective orientation to authority best supports the early period of capitalist development. With the development of capitalism and the corresponding changes in the social and cultural realm that are identified with postmodernism, the process of oedipalization is disrupted and it is argued that our affective lives are organized differently. In Jameson's view, postmodernism constitutes "a whole new emotional ground tone" (1984); in Fred Pfeil's view, it is a new "structure of feeling." More specifically, postmodernism produces a subject who is variously described as deoedipalized, narcissistic, feminized, lost, fragmented, and schizophrenic. The deoedipalized subject is deeply ambivalent because it is locked in a perpetual crisis of abjection in which it oscillates between self-exaltation and dejection, between euphoria and hostility or rage. With the loss of paternal authority in home and workplace and the consequent loss of oedipal struggle to fortify ego boundaries, the postmodern subject is also narcissistic, bored, and apathetic, isolated by its possessive individualism, incapable of feeling solidarity with any social or cultural group, unable to feel truly connected in love or work or to make lasting emotional commitments (Lasch 1979). Both deoedipalization and narcissism are said to represent the feminization of the postmodern subject, a change that is described both positively and negatively. On the positive side, deoedipalization produces a change in the social organization of emotion allowing for what Mike Featherstone calls "controlled de-control," or the greater range of emotional expression for both men and women (1991, 81). It also loosens the bonds of male domination and allows for the expression of the epistemic and ethical vision of women, especially figured in terms of nurturance and reciprocity (Pfeil 1988). Deoedipalization coincides with, and indeed authorizes, some of the progressive social movements of the last thirty years—in addition to feminism, the environmental movement, civil rights, and gay rights. On the negative side, feminization is the sentimental education of the postmodern subject who, on the other side of boredom and apathy (as the total defeat of all desire), feels its power only in feeling too much or in feeling for the sake of feeling, in the absence of the possibility of anything more significant. "It is not that nothing matters," Lawrence Grossberg says of the postmodern condition, "but that it doesn't matter what matters" (1989, 108).

To the extent that postmodernism constitutes a whole new emotional ground tone or a new structure of feeling, we would expect it to constitute a new pedagogy, one that breaks with the one I have discussed thus far. However, postmodernism as historical reality and cultural dominant is arguably not a pedagogy at all, for it produces a mutation in the disposition of the subject and in the external world that makes impossible the kind of pedagogic work I have outlined earlier. In other words, this pedagogy, if we can call it that, does not bind the subject to its place in the social order through the organization of emotion. If it can be said to be a pedagogy, then postmodernism is a wild pedagogy; the subject it educates, a wild subject. As such, it inculcates a kind of ultimate estrangement or dissolution from the structures that traditionally have supported both self and world. More specifically, the "waning of affect" is one of the defining features of this new epoch, a feature that Jameson correlates with the condition of alienation that coincides with the extension of commodity fetishism to the human subject. The waning of affect is the liberation from the structures of recognition that bind meaning to feeling. Jameson explains, "This is not to say that the cultural products of the postmodern era are utterly devoid of feeling, but rather that such feelings . . . are now free-floating and impersonal, and tend to be dominated by a peculiar kind of euphoria " (1984, 64). Jameson's view suggests that the pedagogy of postmodernism offers an extreme version of the dumb view of emotion, where emotion no longer can have any appropriate objects, aims, or interests. Indeed, postmodernism would seem to provide for the decolonization of all feeling. For Jameson, even the term "emotion" has lost all relevance and has become obsolete with the deconstruction of the bourgeois ego and the modernist ideology of expression. Furthermore, a whole range of cultural experiences corresponding to such concepts as anxiety and estrangement are no longer appropriate to the postmodern world since there is no longer any self to feel anxious, estranged, or even neurotic.

This mutation in the subject corresponds to changes in the external world as a consequence of the penetration of capital into hitherto uncommodified areas—specifically, nature and the unconscious. This latest development of capitalism creates an utterly alien and alienated object world in which the subject cannot recognize the results of its own activity in the world and, as a consequence, is unable to recognize the subjectivity of the other. The inability to recognize the subjectivity of the other, as Jessica Benjamin explains, is another aspect of the inability to recognize one's own subjectivity (1978, 41). Subjectivity and agency are denied to the other at the same time they are denied to the self. Hence, the collapse of the demarcation between human and nonhuman in diverse forms of explicit violence is the final lesson in the pedagogy of postmodernism, whose symbolic violence leaves nothing and no one exempt from commodification.[8] The logic that sorts people into two legitimate forms, consumer and consumed, is as crude as it appears: "eat or be eaten," "commodify or die" (also see Bourdieu and Passeron 1977, 34-39).

This wild postmodern space transcends the capacities of the individual human body to locate itself, to organize its immediate surroundings perceptually, and to map its position cognitively. Jameson identifies this wild postmodern space with the great global multinational and decentered communicational network. This is the *other* in the postmodern era, or the postmodern experience of the sublime. Confronting "the impossible totality of the contemporary world system"—confronting an object world that renders the subject wholly inadequate psychically, cognitively, perceptually, and physically—the postmodern subject experiences the intensities of euphoria, exhilaration, apathy, and terror. For Jameson, these changes in the subject and object world are both the moment of truth of postmodernism and the "demoralizing and depressing" situation of this new global space. Driven by a need to both affirm and intervene in this situation, he calls for a radical cultural politics, a pedagogy of cognitive mapping that would return authority and agency to the subject. Through the pedagogy of cognitive mapping, Jameson claims, "we may again begin to grasp our positioning as individual and collective subjects and regain a capacity to act and struggle which is at present neutralized by our spatial as well as our social confusion" (1984, 92). Cognitive mapping provides specifically for "the practical *reconquest of a sense of place,* and the construction or reconstruction of an articulated ensemble which can be retained in memory" (89; emphasis added). In other words, it provides an internalized authority that allows the individual subject to locate him- or herself in relation to what is radically other, in relation to what disturbs identity, position, and rule. As a process of internalizing a critical orientation, it works to transform the subject into a revolutionary agent who will once again be able to act and to struggle to transform the world.

Although postmodernism may constitute a whole new emotional ground tone, much of Jameson's mapping of the postmodern condition seems all too familiar. His postmodern subject is a universal subject, apparently unmarked by class, gender, and race (1984, 91). Those who have been othered are less likely to recognize themselves in this postmodern subject, for they are less likely to be lost in postmodern space but continually located and oriented affectively by the organization of gender, race, and class. In my view, Jameson's postmodern subject is most likely a deoedipalized but nonetheless patriarchal subject, a marginalized white man who has lost his economic position and cultural authority and is relatively dissatisfied with (or can be made to feel dissatisfied with) a more feminized identity as consumer and consumed. For this subject, emotion does not offer a resource for critical positioning or coalition-building because, given the power of dominant pedagogy, emotion remains reason's other. The pedagogy of cognitive mapping represses and diminishes emotion as an effect of alienation and a source of postmodern estrangement. From this perspective, the reeducation of emotion will be achieved only indirectly through the return of substantive reason and critical consciousness that alone offer the capacity to hold a position in relation to the only ultimate object that remains—the maternal, figured here as the postmodern sublime, a figure more terrifying than ever in its ability to disturb, confuse, and neutralize a sense of self and agency. Jameson's revolutionary project provides for a reoedipalization (and a remasculinization) of the subject's relation to the symbolic (see Pfeil 1988, 395). Through the pedagogy of cognitive mapping, the postmodern subject is meant to internalize the authority it needs to recapture a position from which to act and struggle in a world it once again recognizes and reconquers as its own. In this context, multiculturalist reforms to pedagogy appear to intervene in the postmodern situation to recognize the other's subjectivity and agency but may serve more effectively to reclaim agency for the historically privileged subject (white, male) who has most recently undergone an erosion of authority and lost a sense of place and position. Again, the danger is that these reforms will commodify difference in a way that safeguards the privilege of those historically constituted as subjects (and as legitimate consumers).

If ours is an age besotted with a sense of loss (of authority and position), then wilding should be remembered as a uniquely postmodern expression of pedagogic violence, one that may be structurally linked to the cult of emotional restraint that Stearns calls "American cool" (1984). Conceived in boredom and apathy, which is the utter defeat of all desire, wilding may be the ultimate expression of "cool" and the consequence of the kind of postmodern alienation that marks the absolute limit of meaning and feeling, the limit of the human. If it is defined by its lack of motive, then wilding would seem to possess no content to its message—no reason to it, no justice for it. From a kind of post-positivist but nonetheless dumb view, wilding is perhaps the predictable form violence takes when meaning is cut loose from affect: free-floating violence, so to speak, and its apparent randomness makes it seem purely anonymous and impersonal, even unintentional in the sense of having no proper object or aim. In the way the phenomenon is represented and defined, a second, more symbolic violence is committed. In other words, much of the lesson of wilding can be read in the gesture of abstraction committed in the way it is taken up into discourse and circulated. As symbol or figure, wilding posits a disjuncture between the real and the symbolic, suggesting that violence gone wild achieves a pure or sublime form that is made especially horrific by its refusal to be understood or explained. The definition of wilding masks the origin of the phenomenon in the othering practices that we call gender, race, class, and sexuality that still map the postmodern topography. Gender, race, class, and sexuality are the authorized tropes that name and mask the disfigured faces of hatred, bitterness, and rage that the definition of wilding further mystifies. The symbolic transformation of wilding into a random and unmotivated act of violence mystifies the fact that the phenomenon itself confirms the dominant pedagogy of emotion in which violence always finds

its "appropriate" object in any audacious and insubordinate refusal of pedagogic work, such as a woman jogging alone at night in a public park or a Vietnamese child in carefree play at last. Kristeva reminds us that those besotted
with archaic conflicts are always vulnerable to the paranoid rage to dominate,
to transform, and to annihilate what threatens position and rule (1982, 4). The
question that haunts the wild subject is not "who am I?" but "where am I?"

RETHINKING PEDAGOGY

> [D]ecolonization is always a violent phenomenon. At whatever level we
> study it . . . decolonization is quite simply the replacing of a certain
> "species" of men by another "species" of men.
>
> —Franz Fanon

In the United States, teaching has been women's work since at least the late
nineteenth century when a gendered division of labor was established to
secure higher status administrative positions for men and to place women in
low-paying, labor-intensive teaching jobs (Gorelick 1982). This gendered division of labor is reiterated in the distinction between scholarship and teaching, a distinction that associates scholarship and theory with productive labor
and assigns it a masculine position and that associates teaching with reproductive labor and assigns it a feminine position (see Scholes 1985; Watkins
1989). This division of labor also correlates with the distinction between the
two senses of pedagogy that invests one form of pedagogy with the productive power to organize a way of life and gives the other (in the form of educational ideologies or instructional methods) only a reproductive role. This
series of distinctions locates some of the kinds of questions that need to be
asked of the recent pedagogical turn which, not incidentally, has been driven
in large part by male intellectuals. Will radical pedagogy unwittingly sustain
the gendering of these categories by symbolically remasculinizing pedagogy
and materially remarginalizing women in traditional roles? Will it work to produce a new affective life for the contemporary period or extend the dominance of an old one and thereby remystify pedagogic violence? Is the euphoria of some of radical pedagogy's central claims—to enlighten, empower, and
emancipate—structurally related to the rage expressed in pedagogic violence? In other words, are euphoria in the classroom and rage in the streets
products of the same pedagogy and, if so, is radical pedagogy (or at least some
instances of it) a symptom rather than the cure for our cultural pathology?
These questions, though they cannot be fully answered here, are motivated
by a concern that radical pedagogy will take a position in the reconstruction
of political life that will work against its explicit claims and goals.[9] To consider some of these questions, I first need to map the territory to which I refer.

"Radical pedagogy" refers to any number of different kinds of oppositional pedagogies—poststructuralist, psychoanalytic, Marxist, critical, feminist, postmodernist, and even subcategories within each of these—that are offered as alternatives to the dominant pedagogy. Given this variety, I want to quickly organize the field with a distinction, borrowed from Donald Morton and Mas'ud Zavarzadeh (1991b), between two approaches: pedagogies aligned with critical cultural studies and pedagogies aligned with experiential cultural studies.[10] In reconceiving pedagogy in the broadest terms available, these two approaches have much in common, but the distinction between them turns on what each identifies as its principal object of critique: critical cultural studies seeks to unwork the power/knowledge relation that produces the objective conditions of domination and exploitation; experiential cultural studies focuses on experience as the medium through which the conditions of domination and subordination are articulated and resisted. Both seek to empower the pedagogical subject by creating in students a critical position in relation to the authority of those objective conditions and to the authority of experience. In other words, they both emphasize and authorize the political importance of positional identification and thus may be said to be remasculinizing the pedagogical subject. For the sake of clarity, and to use the term each employs to identify itself, I will refer to the former as "postmodern" pedagogy and to the latter as "critical pedagogy" in the following very general, and all too cursory, observations.[11]

Through the language of critique and the rhetoric of empowerment, both critical pedagogy and postmodern pedagogy arguably seek to change the emotional constitution of the postmodern subject so as to produce either a democratic citizen who participates fully in public life or, more radically, a revolutionary subject who is capable of the kind of political struggle that will transform the world. However, in both discourses, emotion is a vague figure, present but also absent in some substantial sense. Emotion appears as a phantom limb, so to speak, more nearly felt than precisely seen, and thus it remains undertheorized and mystified in many important respects. More to the point, its mode of existence in pedagogical discourse (as a phantom limb) is itself an effect of the phenomenon I seek to describe in this chapter. That the vocabulary of emotion in pedagogical discourse might be rather limited should not be particularly surprising, but it should be read as a sign that critical and postmodern pedagogies still operate within the closure set by dominant pedagogy.

Critical pedagogy, unlike postmodern pedagogy, develops an explicit discourse on emotion where it refashions but does not break significantly with the dominant pedagogy of emotion.[12] Critical pedagogy approaches emotion along the lines suggested by both the cognitivist and the positivist view, though necessarily politicized (sort of) for the contemporary context. Critical educators place emotion within an economy of meaning that contrasts emotion and meaning (or reason) and emotion and disempowerment, which arguably is the postmodern figure for alienation and estrangement. They separate emotion from meaning, empty it of content, and relate it specifically to the body. In other words, they smuggle in a rather traditional pedagogy of emotion, though one that is more closely tuned to the postmodern situation. Their discomfort with the category of emotion and its potential reception in theoretical discourse is evident in this statement from Henry A. Giroux and Roger I. Simon: "[W]e are not trying to privilege the body or a politics of affective investments over discourse so much as we are trying to emphasize their absence in previous theorizing for a critical pedagogy" (1989, 16). Following Grossberg, critical educators distinguish between the affective and semantic planes of experience and discourse, where emotion pertains to the intensity or desire with which we invest the world and our relations to it with meaning (1988). The distinction between affect and meaning (or ideology) simply reformulates the distinction between emotion and reason, and while emotion is not negatively valued in an explicit way, it retains its subordinate status. From this perspective, the pedagogical problem in the era of the postmodern is to place emotion, which has been severed from meaning, at the disposal of meaning once again and thereby produce affective investments in forms of knowledge that will lead to empowerment and emancipation. If, as Grossberg says, it is not that nothing matters but that it does not matter what matters, then the pedagogical problem is to link emotion and meaning in a way that provides orientation and a sense of commitment to social change.

In developing a discourse on emotion, critical pedagogy has focused almost exclusive attention on pleasure and desire. This focus is a function of the attention given to popular culture and its manufacture of pleasure. It is also part of the affirmative stance that critical pedagogy takes in relation to students who "not only unwittingly consent to domination but sometimes find pleasurable the form and content through which such domination is manifested" (Giroux and McLaren 1991, 169). With attention focused on knowledge and its relation to "the politics of pleasure, the typography of the body, and the production of desire," the discourse of critical pedagogy moves constantly from making a general claim about emotion to a specific reference to pleasure or desire, as if the emotional constitution of the student were described entirely by these two figures (see Ebert 1996b). This interest may be explained by the focus on popular culture and the everyday, but the overall effect is to seriously limit the discourse of emotion.

A similar limitation occurs in the way that critical pedagogy understands the nature of what Giroux and Grossberg call affective struggle. For example, critical pedagogy sees affective struggle in terms of empowerment rather than resistance. Giroux and Peter L. McLaren quote Grossberg to make the point: "Affective struggles cannot be conceptualized within the terms of theories of resistance, for their oppositional quality is constituted, not in a negative dialectics, but by a project of or struggle over empowerment, an empowerment which energizes and connects specific social moments, practices and subject positions" (1991, 170). Giroux and McLaren go on to say that resistance must be understood as a way of gaining power. Resistance, as a sign of affective investment, is read positively as a sign of engagement with other forms of knowledge outside school culture as well as a sign of political and social disempowerment. This view of the affective struggle for empowerment expresses the affirmative stance of critical pedagogy, a stance that recognizes in students' resistance their affective investments in popular cultural experience and knowledges. The job of the educator is to understand this investment, even better than students understand it, and to harness its potential for engaging students in and empowering them through self-criticism and cultural critique. However, this view of the nature of affective struggle is not sufficiently nuanced, it seems to me, and it may be reductive in two ways. First, it does not recognize, or perhaps it misrecognizes, the fact that the work of the dominant pedagogy of emotion has given affective struggle a negative moment, its moment of pure resistance and repudiation. Our earliest affective struggle requires that we pass through a negative moment (actually, a series of such moments) of resistance and repudiation in which resistance clears the ground, so to speak, for an initial defensive position from which to begin to constitute identity and existence. In ignoring this moment, critical educators misrecognize the dynamics of struggle imposed by dominant pedagogy and are likely to misread their students' affective lives. Without wanting to sound glib, I would suggest that in the pedagogical relationship what sounds like "no" may in fact constitute a "no." It might also sound like anger, hostility, or apathy—not pleasure and investment in popular cultural forms. Also noteworthy here is the fact that the affective struggle for empowerment places the teacher in the rather traditional patriarchal role as the sign of power and the agent of empowerment, as the one who has the power to know students better than they know themselves and to transform their relation to the world (see also Gore 1992; Weiler 1988).

Second, in its development of an affirmative pedagogy of empowerment, critical pedagogy does not seem to require a particularly nuanced understanding of disempowerment beyond its origin and perpetuation in the ideological mystifications of race, class, and gender. (This is true of postmodern pedagogy as well.) Specifically, it does not read the many different faces of disempowerment—in particular, disempowerment as boredom, apathy, bitterness, hatred, anger, rage, generosity, nostalgia, euphoria, sorrow, humiliation, guilt, and shame, or the ways these emotions are organized and practiced differently across differences of race, class, gender, age, and sexuality. Beyond a consideration of a few of the familiar tropes (particularly pleasure and desire), critical discourse does not apprehend its own limitation of the discourse of emotion—that is, what it places beyond the horizon of semantic availability. In this respect, critical pedagogy fails to be sufficiently critical; it does not carefully consider, through a subtly articulated discourse of emotion, how students have been taught to name their affective lives, how they might begin the process of renaming and rephrasing. Critical pedagogy does not make emotion and affective life the crucial stakes in political struggle. With its rhetoric focused on pleasure and empowerment, critical pedagogy works against itself to remystify not only the objective conditions of human suffering, but also the varied experience of suffering.

From the perspective of postmodern pedagogy, critical pedagogy reduces exploitation to the experience of exploitation and represses the objective logic of domination by privileging the local site of the experience of the dominated. Morton and Zavarzadeh suggest that a focus on experience depoliticizes cultural work precisely at a time when we need to depersonalize experience in order to analyze domination as a global strategy. In contrast to critical pedagogy, postmodern pedagogy pursues what it considers to be a rigorous critique and demystification of the structures of authority, including the authority of experience. In particular, this pedagogy examines dominant discourse and the way it situates people at "posts of intelligibility from which the reigning economic, political, and ideological social arrangements are deemed to be uncontestably true" (Morton and Zavarzadeh 1991a, vii). Dominant discourse here means liberal humanism, and postmodern pedagogy, at least as Morton and Zavarzadeh develop it, focuses its effort on the displacement of the traditional humanistic subject and its posture of unthinking obedience to authority—whether that authority is the text, the tradition, or the teacher (see Strickland 1990).

The specific way this displacement occurs is through the figure of the teacher who takes an adversarial role in relation to the student. The confrontational teacher seeks to depersonalize the student's understanding of him- or herself and the world by showing how the student's "ideas and positions are the effects of larger discourses (of class, race, and gender, for example), rather than simple, natural manifestations of this consciousness or mind" (Morton and Zavarzadeh 1991b, 11–12). The goal of such an adversarial relation is to develop in the student a critical position that never defers obligingly to any authority and, most immediately, the authority of the teacher and other students. Practically, this may take the form of the polarization of classroom dynamics where students and teacher alike write position papers that argue against (even "attack") other positions presented in the course (Strickland 1990). Morton and Zavarzadeh continue: "Having denaturalized himself, such a partisan subject will see the arbitrariness of all the seemingly natural meanings and cultural organizations based on them" (1991b, 12). The idea here is to create an alternative pedagogy that does not consolidate into a new norm because it is a relentless critique of authority and invites students into the game of power/knowledge. What this approach does not fully acknowledge is that students have already learned the dominant pedagogy, which radical pedagogy then suggests is purely arbitrary. It also does not consider the distinction between the demystification of authority and the dispossession (or decolonization) of its effects. Demystification operates at the level of meaning; dispossession or decolonization, at the level of both meaning and affect. Through demystification, the postmodern pedagogical subject may intellectually understand the arbitrariness of dominant culture— for example, the arbitrariness of the teacher's authority or of the patriarchal or racist psyche. But intellectually grasping the arbitrariness of a way of life does not then lead naturally or simply to the power to change it (see Bartky 1996, 45–62).

In demanding a confrontational and adversarial relation between teacher and student, especially as "the only way to achieve an *intellectually* responsible pedagogy," postmodern pedagogy may successfully demystify authority and give students a way to achieve a practical reconquest of a sense of place and position (Strickland 1990, 294; emphasis added). But it also triangulates the pedagogical situation and gives the teacher the authority to stage the kind of oedipal conflict that the deoedipalized family and postmodern society no longer provide. The authority that has become disembodied and abstract as a consequence of the bureaucratization of postmodern space is reembodied in the (impersonal) figure of the teacher. The teacher actively confronts the student who is required to take a position and defend it. In what critical theorists have called a world without fathers, postmodern pedagogy offers the conflict and critique needed for internalizing authority that, according to classical psychoanalytic theory and critical theory, is the only basis for the subsequent rejection of authority and for political action (Benjamin 1978). This agonistic pedagogy offers a reoedipalization of emotion that requires a conscious denial of the experience of fear in the presence of the teacher who is, all posturing aside, still an authority figure. It requires a reassertion of the dominance of emotions of self-assessment (such as pride, guilt, and shame), and it requires submission to the constant examination and assessment of individual adequacy. Shame is a key instrument of this pedagogy, as it is in what I have called dominant pedagogy, for as the student struggles to articulate a critical oppositional position and defend it, the student will meet his or her "betters" in the figure of the teacher, if not in other students (see Bartky 1996). The demoralized postmodern subject is, in effect, remoralized and capable of differentiating the good from the bad. In general, the turn to pedagogy might be read, at least in part, as a form of crisis intervention and management in the postmodern age; it suggests that what is needed is a kind of psychodrama in which the radical educator stages an affective relation to the wildness of postmodernism. In my view, the recent fascination with the pedagogical, at least in some quarters, may have as much to do with meeting the needs of (white, male) intellectuals for a sense of position and authority as with addressing the needs of students.

Stated plainly, I read the recent interest in pedagogy in literary and cultural studies at least in part as an expression of a crisis of (white) masculinity that coincides with postmodernity and late capitalism. In *The Hearts of Men: The American Dream and the Flight from Commitment* (1983), Barbara Ehrenreich offers a history of this crisis, which begins in the 1960s and 1970s with a male revolt against what has been called the breadwinner ethic. She reads this revolt ambivalently (as do I) as a childish flight from responsibility, as an effort to legitimate a consumerist personality for men, and as a libertarian movement that parallels the women's movement and other progressive social movements associated with the New Left (171). The pedagogical turn in the academic humanities may be part of this history. It may be an expression of a (white) masculinist subject's recommitment to the social order, of his effort to *reconquer* the social order and replace the breadwinner ethic and consumerist personality with a revolutionary ethos. And if this pedagogical subject reconquers a sense of place and position, the question remains whether or not the reinvestment in pedagogy will significantly alter prevailing patterns of feeling organized by gender, race, and class.

In this context of crisis and management, feminist pedagogies of maternal nurturance offer no escape from the recolonization of the postmodern imaginary and little hope for real resistance to the process of reoedipalization. Feminist pedagogies of nurturance, we must remember, receive their pedagogic authority from a dominant discourse that sets up the ideology of nurturance and its gender duality. Pedagogies of nurturance work alongside (often cheerfully) radical pedagogies of critique and confrontation to reproduce and reauthorize the affective relations typical of the middle-class nuclear family and thus constitute the latest version of the family-education couple. Here the feminist mother-teacher provides a personal education, and the postmodern teacher triangulates the pedagogical relation to produce a positional education. This new situation, still charged with archaic conflicts, resubmits women to the disempowering effects of nurturing and to the hostility of pedagogical subjects who are schooled to recognize the prevailing authority of position in a highly stratified society.

This view runs contrary, of course, to the claims made by feminists engaged in developing the political significance of nurturance. In "The Politics of Nurturance," for example, Margo Culley and her coauthors (1985) join with many other feminists working in the areas of epistemology and ethics to make broad claims for the importance of the maternal (idealized as metaphor and experience) not only in reconstructing the pedagogical relation in the classroom, but also in replacing the fundamental structures of patriarchy with a new pedagogy that protects and promotes the welfare of all.

Specifically, the authors of "The Politics of Nurturance" argue that nurturance is the topos that will alter the fundamental construction of gender in our culture, that it will "heal" the cultural split between mother and father (or, more accurately, maternal authority and paternal authority), and that it will "heal" the existential, ethical, and epistemic fragmentation caused by capitalism and patriarchy. Women intellectuals in the academy do this important work, they argue, by virtue of their contradictory position in a culture that separates the role of nurturer from the role of intellectual and makes these roles gender-specific. They argue that the fusion of these roles in the woman intellectual produces the power to create changes in what I have called dominant pedagogy. However, this is more nearly a dualism than a fusion, for the pedagogic authority of women intellectuals devolves from their role as the "fathers," who are the "word-givers" and "truth-sayers," at the same time that they bring to the classroom their inscription in the symbolic as "mothers," as nurturers and caretakers. This contradictory position elicits a "highly charged" affective response from students, and while these authors focus on women students for whom this pedagogical relation is a return to the preoedipal mother/daughter configuration, psychoanalytic theory suggests (and my own experience confirms) that this pedagogy can elicit an equally volatile affective response from male students. "Powerlessness, rage, and guilt conflate with longing, love, and dependency," these authors write, "just when our students are confronted by a woman professor, purveying at the same time the maternal breast and the authoritative word" (16). The classroom becomes a transferential space for reliving preoedipal and oedipal emotions but, as these authors see it, in a way that allows new patterns to emerge (17; see also Grumet 1988). Furthermore, this "intrusion/infusion of emotionality" into the classroom provides the occasion for the reconstruction of knowledge and ethics through the fusion of affect and intellect.

From this perspective, the feminist classroom is the *locus desperatus* for reenacting and transforming, through the emotional labor of the feminist teacher, "threatening and joyous psychic events" and thus offers the best chance to reformulate our relationship to others, to knowledge, and to the world (Culley et al. 1985, 17). Feminism, accordingly, must "assert that its project is not to abandon the *feminine standpoint,* but to insert its best qualities into history" (18; emphasis added). Again, maternal nurturance and care are considered the best qualities of this standpoint, and a key place to insert them into history is the feminist classroom. From my perspective, however, nurturance is, at this time, an *impossible topos* for the feminist teacher, one that simply resubmits women intellectuals to the pedagogic authority of dominant discourses that sets up the ideology of nurturance for the benefit of men and at the expense of women. This kind of feminist classroom makes women responsible in their professional lives for the emotional labor of "tending wounds and feeding egos," to use Bartky's apt phrase for describing women's traditional role, and we must remember that this is unpaid labor that is expropriated from women.[13] For nurturance to operate politically toward the ends previously outlined, it must be entirely reconstructed and, along with it, so must the sex/affective system that sustains and justifies pedagogic violence of all kinds.

The symbolic reconstruction of nurturance will require, at minimum, an understanding that the development of individual identity need not require (or posit) an originary oneness with the mother (or caretaker) and abjection as the mechanism for creating and sustaining boundaries—for defending against the overwhelming desire for and fear of reabsorption into a state of indifferentiation associated with the maternal. Neither will it focus so exclusively on the intrapsychic world of the subject and the way in which the subject incorporates and expels, identifies with and repudiates the caretaker-as-other, not as a real being, but as a mental object. Nor will it privilege autonomy, separateness, and position as the principal goals of the psychic struggle for identity and authority. In *The Bonds of Love: Psychoanalysis, Feminism, and the Problem of Domination* (1988), Jessica Benjamin suggests a different conceptualization of the formation of individual identity based on the idea of intersubjectivity and the process of mutual recognition. She argues that subjectivity emerges in an interaction with significant others and through a paradoxical process of balancing the need for self-assertion and autonomy with the need for connection and recognition. In her view, theories (such as Kristeva's) that posit an original state of oneness and symbiosis that must be resisted and repudiated distort our understanding of individuation. Early infancy studies show that from the beginning the child's interest in the external world alternates with absorption in internal rhythms. Before consciousness of difference, and because of prevailing woman-centered parenting/caretaking styles, the child *affectively* associates the excitement and difference of the external world with the father and the safe but dangerous inner world with the mother who regulates the emotional life of the child by satisfying or thwarting basic needs. The father is idealized and his authority internalized because he represents the external world and the way into that world. What the child wants above all is recognition that he or she is an agent who can make things happen in the external world. The recognition necessary for individuation can only come from one whom the child recognizes as subject and agent. Benjamin stresses that mutual recognition as a form of emotional attunement (and the basic form of social bonding on which all other bonding is built) is a goal that is as important to the formation of self as separation and autonomy. Ideally, the world "recognizes" the child as subject and agent; the child becomes subject and agent in a world that is responsive to his or her needs and actions. While individuation may ideally require two subjects in interaction with one another, the real and existing world does not offer an economy based on recognition and mutuality. Women are enlisted and exploited as nurturers in a society that does not recognize this labor as labor, as the most necessary labor if the social is to exist. Moreover, it does not confer on women and racialized others the status of full psychic, economic, social, or political subjects and agents. Dominant pedagogy requires that women seek recognition of themselves as subjects and agents through emotion-work and nurturing labor but in a system that withholds recognition of the necessity and value of this work. Maria Mies calls this situation "super-exploitation" (1986, 48). It is a system that is calculated to ensure that women are the "appropriate" targets of further violence, real and symbolic.

The failure of mutual recognition—the loss of social bonds that leads to shame (understood as a sense of personal inadequacy)—promotes a premature formation of a defensive boundary between inside and outside. It fosters an intensification of the desire for omnipotence and of the expression of narcissistic rage. At the social level, the failure of mutual recognition takes the form of relations of exploitation and domination. A hierarchical social order is nothing more than an efficient arrangement for doling out what Richard Sennett and Jonathan Cobb (1972) call badges of recognition and unequally distributing tokens of human dignity. When Patrick Purdy walked onto that Stockton schoolyard at midday recess, a schoolyard he himself played on as a child, he was arguably acting out the kind of omnipotence and rage that results from the failure of mutual recognition and a thwarted sense of agency (see Benjamin 1988, 70; Miller 1981, 30–48). Likewise, the surviving children also sought to reclaim a sense of agency by revising the event through a make-believe game that restored their power. That Purdy misrecognized the children as the enemy, as the source of injury to his dignity, is significant. News reports compared Purdy to Rambo and remarked that because many of the children were Vietnamese, his actions should be read as an effort to settle America's political score with Vietnam (see also Schneiderman 1995, 59–99). Perhaps his was another demented expression of rugged (white) masculinity attempting to reclaim a sense of position and agency and thereby to remasculinize the postmodern wild(er)ness and reassert dominance over women, children, and racialized others (see Jeffords 1989). If so, then surely it must be time, as Pfeil suggests, to end a collective silence and "to get up the strength and wisdom to call [our] foremost enemy by its right name, corporate capitalism, the enclave of those (largely) white men who really own the field and call the shots" (1995, 124). However, the odds are against any success here, if for no other reason than that too many anonymous (white) men want to maintain a belief in a system that gives them the advantage. The sex/affective production system of corporate capitalism (or the dominant pedagogy of emotion) ensures the continued misrecognition of the enemy, the source of injury and cause of violence. It ensures the continued misrecognition of incidents of going postal as the pathological or purely criminal behavior of isolated and disaffected individuals. And yet the dramatic increase in the number of incidents of workplace and school violence in the last decade demands another explanation.

The challenge for radical educators (feminist, critical, postmodern) is to offer that explanation. The intersubjective model gives recent pedagogical discourse a way to begin to rethink its goals of returning agency to the subject and of recognizing the other as subject and agent—that is, an alternative to the postmodern pedagogy for the reconquest of the external world, or what is radically other. Without a fundamental revision in our conception of subjectivity and of our affective relationship to the world, the radical potential of recent pedagogy to reconstitute our emotional lives may be recontained, in spite of its best intentions and the euphoria of its claims, as a strategy of condescension. Bourdieu points out that condescension occurs in situations in which agents occupying a higher symbolic position (by virtue of race, class, gender, or education, for example) deny the social (and, I would say, emotional) distance between them and those to whom and for whom they speak (1990, 127-128). This distance does not cease to exist simply because it is symbolically denied through claims of identification and recognition. Rather, the purely symbolic negation of distance ensures that the profits of recognition and distinction will confer the status of somebodiness on self-styled radical agents but without necessarily producing significant structural change in the social conditions of those who are subordinated. If radical pedagogy operates in this manner, its condescension might be the unfortunate result of a misrecognition of the kind of work required for decolonization, or it might be symptomatic of a predictable (and perhaps historically inescapable) ambivalence toward decolonization. In any event, strategies of condescension always appear otherwise than as instances of pedagogic violence concealing the power relations that are the condition of possibility for so-called radical alternatives and for their alleged success.[14]

NOTES

1. See *Time* (December 1989) and *New York Times* (9 December 1989) for typical reports of this incident. See also Cameron and Frazer (1987) on gender issues in mass murder.

2. See *Newsweek* (30 January 1989) for a typical report of the Stockton assault. Daniel Goleman discusses Purdy, the rage that led to such violence, and the game the children created in its aftermath (1995, 200-201, 208-209).

3. After the initial news report on the Central Park rape, which tended to downplay the issue of gender and race, a number of editorials called into question the mystification around the phenomenon of wilding. See, for example, Pogrebin (1989), Krauthammer (1989), and Zuckerman (1980).

4. For a more global perspective on domestic violence and an illuminating discussion of the political economy of dowry murder in India, see Mies (1986).

5. Richard Dyer (1988) is particularly helpful in clarifying the ways in which emotion and emotional expression have been racialized.

6. Feminist work on morality and ethics often focuses on the role of emotion. Nel

Noddings, for example, bases an ethic of caring on the priority of what she calls sentiment or feeling, and distinguishes natural sentiment (which is experienced in the caring relationship established between mother-child) and ethical sentiment (which is the memory of natural feeling and the basis for ethical action) (see 1984, 79–103). The ethical ideal driving this view is not an abstract principle or rule of right action but maintenance of the caring relation, both care for the other and care for the self. Ethics, in her view, does not focus on the problem of justification and justified action but on the issue of our obligation to maintain caring relations.

7. Interestingly, this shift to a more personal style coincides with the entrance of many more women into the labor force. Perhaps sexual harassment, which surfaced finally, as an issue, in the 1980s, should be understood in the context of this history of workplace emotion. Specifically, I am suggesting that dominant pedagogy authorizes a style of work emotion that cultivates the conditions for sexual harassment to occur with greater frequency and for harassment to be misrecognized and tolerated by training women workers to accept a more personal and friendly style. To the extent that anger has been eliminated from the workplace, the victim of sexual harassment is subject to a secondary violence that may short circuit or censor her anger as a legitimate response to violation.

8. The pervasiveness of commodification does not nullify the hierarchy that renders women, children, and people of color the preferred objects of consumption. Here, the film *The Silence of the Lambs* is especially instructive as a parable of the patriarchal psyche of postmodern America and illustrates many of the issues I deal with in this chapter. Of particular interest is the pedagogical relation established, on the one hand, between Federal Bureau of Investigation trainee Clarice Starling and her mentor, Jack Crawford, and on the other, between Clarice and the serial killer, Hannibal "the Cannibal" Lecter. Starling is positioned between two fathers, the good father and the bad, both of whom feed off the emotion she is made to confess. This film is also relevant in the way it treats skin as a signifier of difference and a commodity in postmodern America. A reading of the film appears in my article "Reading Wild, Seriously" (1992).

9. Jennifer Gore (1992) also focuses on the "overly optimistic" claims of recent pedagogical discourse, especially its claim to empower students. On the subject of violence and pedagogy, see Lewis (1992).

10. Morton and Zavarzadeh identify Jameson with critical cultural studies, and Raymond Williams and E. P. Thompson with experiential cultural studies (1991, 23–29). They also associate Janice Radway and Teresa de Lauretis with the experientialists. They want to suggest, through this distinction, that a focus on personal experience depoliticizes cultural work precisely at a time when we need to depersonalize experience to analyze the objective conditions of existence. Morton and Zavarzadeh say these two approaches to cultural studies and to pedagogy are necessarily in competition. My own treatment of pedagogic violence in the second section of this chapter recognizes that we need both a critique of the objective conditions of domination and a phenomenology of the forms in which we live and experience domination and oppression. Merged in this manner, these two approaches to cultural analysis and pedagogy constitute what I call a political phenomenology. See Bartky (1990) and Lyman (1981) who also recommend a political phenomenology of emotion.

11. This nomenclature is bound to be confusing in light of the fact that critical ped-

agogy has begun to engage the discourse on postmodernism and to move away from its commitment to a modernist agenda and consequently has begun to call itself a post-modern pedagogy. See Giroux and Simon (1989); Aronowitz and Giroux (1991); and Giroux (1991).

12. Morton and Zavarzadeh recognize that emotion constitutes a "frame of intelligibility" on a par with ideas and texts, but they make no specific effort to develop a discourse on emotion. I see their relative inattention to emotion as a participation in the dominant tradition that continues to marginalize this category of existence and instead privileges reason.

13. This highly charged classroom sets up women to be the targets of violence and harassment. For example, several years ago a student offered this crude assessment of my teaching: "A good teacher but she has invisible tits." The hostility expressed in this statement, the way in which it retaliates against (perhaps even repudiates) authority through objectification, suggests that women teachers always labor under the obligation to provide the (maternal) breast. Nurturance, in other words, is an obligation for women who live and labor in an economy that recognizes them only as providers of an all too often sexualized nurturance.

14. This chapter is a revised and expanded version of "Emotion and Pedagogic Violence." Research for the earlier article was supported by a fellowship at the Center for Twentieth Century Studies, University of Wisconsin at Milwaukee. I thank Shelley Circle and Gary Olson for their careful reading of this revision.

WORKS CITED

Aronowitz, Stanley, and Henry A. Giroux. 1991. *Postmodern Education: Politics, Culture, and Social Criticism.* Minneapolis: Minnesota University Press.

Bartky, Sandra. 1996. "The Pedagogy of Shame." In *Feminisms and Pedagogies of Everyday Life,* ed. Carmen Luke. Albany: SUNY Press.

———. 1990. *Femininity and Domination: Studies in the Phenomenology of Oppression.* London: Routledge.

Benjamin, Jessica. 1988. *The Bonds of Love: Psychoanalysis, Feminism, and the Problem of Domination.* New York: Pantheon.

———. 1978. "Authority and the Family Revisited; or, A World without Fathers?" *New German Critique* 13:35–78.

Bourdieu, Pierre. 1991. *Language and Symbolic Power,* trans. Gino Raymond and Matthew Adamson. Cambridge, Mass.: Harvard University Press.

———. 1990. *In Other Words: Essays towards a Reflexive Sociology,* trans. Matthew Adamson. Stanford: Stanford University Press.

Bourdieu, Pierre, and Jean-Claude Passeron. 1977. *Reproduction in Education, Society, and Culture,* trans. Richard Nice. London: Sage.

Cameron, Deborah, and Elizabeth Frazer. 1987. *The Lust to Kill: A Feminist Investigation of Sexual Murder.* Oxford: Polity.

Chodorow, Nancy. 1978. *The Reproduction of Mothering: Psychoanalysis and the Sociology of Gender.* Berkeley: University of California Press.

Culley, Margo, et al. 1985. "The Politics of Nurturance." In *Gendered Subjects: The*

Dynamics of Feminist Teaching, ed. Margo Culley and Catherine Portuges. New York: Routledge.

Dyer, Richard. 1988. "White." *Screen* 29.4: 44–64.

Eagleton, Terry. 1996. "Introduction." In *Marxist Literary Theory,* ed. Terry Eagleton and Drew Milne. London: Blackwell.

Ebert, Teresa L. 1996a. *Ludic Feminism and after: Postmodernism, Desire, and Labor in Late Capitalism.* Ann Arbor: University of Michigan Press.

———. 1996b. "For a Red Pedagogy: Feminism, Desire, and Need." *College English* 58:795–819.

Ehrenreich, Barbara. 1983. *The Hearts of Men: The American Dream and the Flight from Commitment.* New York: Anchor.

Featherstone, Mike. 1991. *Consumer Culture and Postmodernism.* London: Sage.

Ferguson, Ann. 1989. *Blood at the Root: Motherhood, Sexuality, and Male Dominance.* London: Pandora.

Foucault, Michel. 1979. *Discipline and Punish: The Birth of the Prison,* trans. Alan Sheridan. New York: Vintage.

Giroux, Henry A. 1991. *Postmodernism, Feminism, and Cultural Politics: Redrawing Educational Boundaries.* Albany: SUNY Press.

Giroux, Henry A., and Peter L. McLaren. 1991. "Radical Pedagogy As Cultural Politics: Beyond the Discourse of Critique and Anti-Utopianism." In *Theory/Pedagogy/Politics: Texts for Change,* ed. Donald Morton and Mas'ud Zavarzadeh. Chicago: University of Illinois Press.

Giroux, Henry A., and Roger I. Simon. 1989. "Popular Culture As Pedagogy of Pleasure and Meaning." In *Popular Culture, Schooling, and Everyday Life,* ed. Henry A. Giroux and Roger I. Simon. Granby, Mass.: Bergin.

Goleman, Daniel. 1995. *Emotional Intelligence.* New York: Bantam.

Gore, Jennifer. 1992. "What We Can Do for You! What Can 'We' Do for 'You'?: Struggling over Empowerment in Critical and Feminist Pedagogy." In *Feminisms and Critical Pedagogy,* ed. Carmen Luke and Jennifer Gore. New York: Routledge.

Gorelick, Sherry. 1982. "Class Relations and the Development of the Teaching Profession." In *Class and Social Development: A New Theory of the Middle Class,* ed. Dale L. Johnson. Beverly Hills: Sage.

Graff, Gerald. 1994. "The Pedagogical Turn." *Midwest Modern Language Association Bulletin* 27:65–69.

Grossberg, Lawrence. 1989. "Pedagogy in the Present: Politics, Postmodernity, and the Popular." In *Popular Culture, Schooling, and Everyday Life,* ed. Henry A. Giroux and Roger I. Simon. Granby, Mass.: Bergin.

———. 1988. "Postmodernity and Affect: All Dressed up with No Place to Go." *Communication* 10:271–293.

Grumet, Madeleine R. 1988. *Bitter Milk: Women and Teaching.* Amherst: University of Massachusetts Press.

Jaggar, Alison M. 1989. "Love and Knowledge: Emotion in Feminist Epistemology." In *Women, Knowledge, and Reality: Explorations in Feminist Philosophy,* ed. Ann Garry and Marilyn Pearsall. Boston: Unwin Hyman.

Jameson, Fredric. 1984. "Postmodernism, or the Cultural Logic of Late Capitalism." *New Left Review* 146:53–92.

Jeffords, Susan. 1989. *The Remasculinization of America: Gender and the Vietnam War.* Bloomington: Indiana University Press.

Kelsh, Deborah. 1998. "Critiquing the 'Culture' of Feminism and Composition: Toward a Red Feminism." In *Feminism and Composition Studies: In Other Words,* ed. Susan C. Jarratt and Lynn Worsham. New York: Modern Language Association.

Krauthammer, Charles. 1989. "Crime and Responsibility." *Time,* 8 May, 104.

Kristeva, Julia. 1986. "Psychoanalysis and the Polis." In *The Kristeva Reader,* ed. Toril Moi. New York: Columbia University Press.

———. 1982. *Powers of Horror: An Essay on Abjection,* trans. Leon S. Roudiez. New York: Columbia University Press.

Lasch, Christopher. 1979. *The Culture of Narcissism: American Life in an Age of Diminishing Expectations.* New York: Warner.

Lewis, Magda. 1992. "Interrupting Patriarchy: Politics, Resistance, and Transformation in the Feminist Classroom." In *Feminisms and Critical Pedagogy,* ed. Carmen Luke and Jennifer Gore. New York: Routledge.

Lutz, Catherine. 1988. *Unnatural Emotions: Everyday Sentiments on a Micronesian Atoll and Their Challenge to Western Theory.* Chicago: University of Chicago Press.

Lyman, Peter. 1981. "The Politics of Anger: On Silence, Ressentiment, and Political Speech." *Socialist Review* (May–June): 55–74.

McFall, Lynne. 1991. "What's Wrong with Bitterness?" In *Feminist Ethics,* ed. Claudia Card. Lawrence: University Press of Kansas.

Mies, Maria. 1986. *Patriarchy and Accumulation on a World Scale: Women in the International Division of Labour.* London: Zed.

Miller, Alice. 1981. *The Drama of the Gifted Child,* trans. Ruth Ward. New York: Basic.

Morton, Donald, and Mas'ud Zavarzadeh. 1991a. "Preface." In *Theory/Pedagogy/Politics: Texts for Change,* ed. Donald Morton and Mas'ud Zavarzadeh. Urbana: University of Illinois Press.

———. 1991b. "Theory Pedagogy Politics: The Crisis of 'The Subject' in the Humanities." In *Theory/Pedagogy/Politics: Texts for Change,* ed. Donald Morton and Mas'ud Zavarzadeh. Urbana: University of Illinois Press.

Mouffe, Chantal. 1993. *The Return of the Political.* London: Verso.

Neu, Jerome. 1987. " 'A Tear Is an Intellectual Thing.' " *Representations* 19:35–61.

Newsweek. 30 January 1989, 35.

New York Times. 25 September 1997, C28.

———. 9 December 1989, A6.

Noddings, Nel. 1984. *Caring: A Feminine Approach to Ethics and Moral Education.* Berkeley: University of California Press.

Pfeil, Fred. 1995. "Sympathy for the Devils: Notes on Some White Guys and the Ridiculous Class War." *New Left Review* 213:115–124.

———. 1988. "Postmodernism As a 'Structure of Feeling.' " In *Marxism and the Interpretation of Culture,* ed. Cary Nelson and Lawrence Grossberg. Urbana: University of Illinois Press.

Pogrebin, Letty Cottin. 1989. "Boys Will Be Boys?" *Ms.* (September): 24.

Rich, Adrienne. 1986. "Notes toward a Politics of Location." In *Blood, Bread, and Poetry.* New York: Norton.

Rosaldo, Michelle. 1984. "Toward an Anthropology of Self and Feeling." In *Culture*

Theory: Essays on Mind, Self, and Emotion, ed. Richard A. Shweder and Robert A. LeVine. Cambridge: Cambridge University Press.

Scheff, Thomas J., and Suzanne M. Retzinger. 1991. *Emotions and Violence: Shame and Rage in Destructive Conflicts.* Lexington, Mass.: Lexington.

Schell, Eileen E. 1998. "The Costs of Caring: 'Feminism' and Contingent Women Workers in Composition Studies." In *Feminism and Composition Studies: In Other Words,* ed. Susan C. Jarratt and Lynn Worsham. New York: Modern Language Association.

Schiller, Jon R. 1981. "The New 'Family Romance.' " *Triquarterly* 52:64–84.

Schneiderman, Stuart. 1995. *Saving Face: America and the Politics of Shame.* New York: Knopf.

Scholes, Robert. 1985. *Textual Power: Literary Theory and the Teaching of English.* New Haven: Yale University Press.

Sennett, Richard, and Jonathan Cobb. 1972. *The Hidden Injuries of Class.* New York: Vintage.

Shumway, David R. 1997. "The Star System in Literary Studies." *PMLA* 112:85–100.

Spelman, Elizabeth V. 1989. "Anger and Insubordination." In *Women, Knowledge, and Reality: Explorations in Feminist Philosophy,* ed. Ann Garry and Marilyn Pearsall. Boston: Unwin.

Spivak, Gayatri C. 1987. *In Other Worlds: Essays in Cultural Politics.* New York: Methuen.

Stearns, Carol Zisowitz, and Peter N. Stearns. 1986. *Anger: The Struggle for Emotional Control in American History.* Chicago: University of Chicago Press.

Stearns, Peter N. 1994. *American Cool: Constructing a Twentieth-Century Emotional Style.* New York: New York University Press.

———. 1988. "Anger and American Work: A Twentieth-Century Turning Point." In *Emotion and Social Change: Toward a New Psychohistory.* New York: Holmes.

Strickland, Ronald. 1990. "Confrontational Pedagogy and Traditional Literary Studies." *College English* 52:291–299.

Time. 8 December 1989, A9.

Watkins, Evan. 1989. *Work Time: English Departments and the Circulation of Cultural Value.* Stanford: Stanford University Press.

Weiler, Kathleen. 1988. *Women Teaching for Change: Gender, Class, and Power.* New York: Bergin.

Worsham, Lynn. 1993. "Emotion and Pedagogic Violence." *Discourse* 15:119–148.

———. 1992. "Reading Wild, Seriously: Confessions of an Epistemophiliac." *Rhetoric Society Quarterly* 22.1: 39–62.

———. 1991. "Writing against Writing: The Predicament of *Écriture Féminine* in Composition Studies." In *Contending with Words: Composition in a Postmodern Age,* ed. Patricia Harkin and John Schilb. New York: Modern Language Association.

Zuckerman, Mortimer B. 1980. "Meltdown in Our Cities." *U.S. News and World Report,* 29 May, 74.

14

The Politics of Teaching ~~Literature:~~ The "Paedagogical Effect"

Robert Miklitsch

This problem ["the general question of language"] can and must be related to the modern way of considering educational doctrine and practice, according to which the relationship between teacher and pupil is active and reciprocal so that every teacher is always a pupil and every pupil a teacher.

—Gramsci 349-50

As for the technique that needs to be developed for all such operations [for transforming the radio into an apparatus of communication], it must follow the prime objective of turning the audience not only into pupils but into teachers.

—Brecht 52

What is the difference between the politics of teaching and the teaching of politics? Assuming there is a difference (a genuine question, for some), does it reduce to the difference between teaching and politics? In other words, is teaching irreducible to politics (and vice versa), or is teaching always already—as some argue—an instance of politics?

There is a certain vertiginous self-reflexivity to such questions. Which is not to say they are merely rhetorical; indeed, I will return to these questions below. Given the topic, however, it will be obvious by now that the above interrogative structure elides one of the terms of the topic: "Literature."[1]

A Brechtian maxim: do not build on the good old days, but the bad new ones (Benjamin 219.)
[Molly Case's] room might have been the one in Chiba where he'd first seen Armitage. He went to the window, in the morning, almost expecting to see

Tokyo Bay. There was another hotel across the street. It was still raining. A few letter-writers had taken refuge in doorways, their old voiceprinters wrapped in sheets of clear plastic, evidence that the written word still enjoyed a certain prestige here. (Gibson 88.)

The above "erasure" would seem to suggest that Literature today is marginal or peripheral, and in the conclusion to *The Noise of Culture* (1988), William Paulson argues as much:

What I am trying to propose . . . is a way of understanding the reading and teaching of literature, *not* in a society in which such reading and teaching appear [*sic*] to be an essential aspect of society's continual self-reproduction, but rather in a civilization where such teaching and reading are not essential or no longer appear to be. . . . At this juncture our strongest move may be to suppose that literary studies *are* something marginal, to argue from the assumption that they are indeed no more than a source of perturbations on the edge of a cultural system that gives the appearance of being able to get along without them. (155)

Though I am sympathetic, it should be obvious, to Paulson's point of view, his stress on appearances—subordinate as it is—blunts, if it does not altogether sabotage his argument. It may also betray a residual nostalgia for the "good old days," for Literature with a capital L. Indeed, Paulson's rhetoric intimates, *à la* Nietzsche, that we might perish if we knew the Truth about Literature: that its sociocultural centrality is (was?) mostly illusory. Hence the, for me, uncanny appearance in the above passage of the presumably consoling logic of Truth-and-Appearances. Hence also the not-quite-subliminal pathos.

Yet one does not have to get apocalyptic about the future of Literature (LITERATURE IS DEAD!) to wonder about the individual and institutional anxiety about the question of its marginality. In order to understand this anxiety, however, it seems to me that it is necessary to investigate the historicity of the concept of Literature. In *Marxism and Literature* (1977), for instance, Raymond Williams explains that the concept of "literature" did not emerge in its modern form until the eighteenth century and "was not fully developed until the nineteenth" (46). Moreover, "literature"—as "a category of use and conditions rather than of production" (that is to say, of reading rather than writing)—"specified a particular social distinction" (47).

But if it "is relatively difficult to see 'literature' as a concept," it is even more difficult to see "literature" as a class concept, a concept *for* a class—that is, a concept used by a particular class to construct its ideological hegemony: "[The] forms of the concepts of *literature* and *criticism* are, in the perspective of historical social development, forms of a class specialization and control of a general social practice, and of a class limitation of the questions which it might raise" (Williams, "Literature" 49).[2] Literature, of course, is not simply a class concept, nor for that matter one of race or gender, sexuality or ethnicity. Inasmuch as it is associated with "the relatively uniform and specializing technology of print" (53), it is a historical category as well. Which does not, as William notes, "diminish its importance" (53). In fact, the concept of "literature" is important precisely because of its historicity, because it tells us so much about history, and not only literary history, but history "as such," our history.

And yet with the emergence of the new technologies and the consequent "information revolution"—to return to the subject of Paulson's book—it would appear we are entering a new postprint phase where Literature will no longer constitute the central medium for the cultural reproduction of society. In other words, if, in William's terms, the new technologies are now emergent, not to say dominant, Literature and *its* "means of production" ("the particular technology of print" [54]) are, or will soon be, residual. The institutional consequences of this "event" should be equally apparent: English departments should not restrict themselves to Literature, even when/where Literature has been redefined—according to a liberal-pluralist logic—to include popular, multicultural, and/or postcolonial literatures.

It may well be that Literature has served its usefulness as a concept and even, perhaps, as a discipline. Cultural Studies may not be the answer (either as a discipline or, in particular, as a concept), but one thing is clear: history is ultimately about change, and the dominant hegemonic moment of (English) Literature—real or otherwise—is over. Such a claim has, it seems to me, profound implications for "The Politics of Teaching Literature," implications that teachers of literature are going to have to address if we are going to resist the present powerful current of nostalgia ("the good old days") in the name of the future and the forces of change.

THE POLITICS OF TEACHING

And your education? Is not that also social, and determined by the social conditions under which you educate, by the intervention of society, direct or indirect, by means of schools, etc.? (Marx and Engels 100.)

The work of teaching and organising the others fell naturally upon the pigs, who were generally recognised as the cleverest of the animals. (Orwell 25.)

We should begin, then, with political questions. . . . (Kampf and Lauter 7.)

My emphasis in this part will be on "the politics of teaching" or, as I want for strategic reasons to rephrase it, "the politics of pedagogy."[3]

Today, according to a disciplinary logic that Michel Foucault has reconstructed in all its micrological discursivity, the teacher-student relation frequently displays a "master"/"slave" structure where the student is positioned as a child, a child *to be educated* (that is, "socialized"). Education in this sense is an apparatus of or a vehicle for social reproduction, and the aim of a "normal education" (as in "normal science") is to school students in the interests and ideology of the "ruling class." Though scholastic reproduction—even and perhaps especially in the most totalitarian circumstances—is never and can never be complete (there are always pockets of resistance, of struggle and contestation), there is, I think, more than a grain of truth to the educative-reproductive thesis. In other words, the above pedagogical paradigm remains the dominant one.

I rehearse these familiar arguments about education-as-social-reproduction and the master/slave model of pedagogy in order to frame the following openly autobiographical remarks about the politics of teaching and what I want to call, recollecting Noam Chomsky via James Merod, the responsibility of the teacher. Part of this responsibility devolves, I want to argue, to the proposition that teachers must begin from the pedagogic subject-position to which they have been assigned.[4] If the latter position is not necessarily one of mastery (in either sense of the word), it nonetheless remains one of authority. In other words, to attempt absolutely to renounce the pedagogic subject-position—from whatever motivation, liberal or otherwise—is not only to accede to a "bad" egalitarian logic, it is to evade our responsibility as teachers. And that responsibility—which, needless to say, is an implicitly political one—involves recognizing those structures (social, cultural, economic, and so forth) that both enable *and* constrain our activities.

Let me relate an anecdote. A couple of years ago I was scheduled to teach a course at Tufts, primarily for freshmen, entitled "Politics and Writing."[5] Now, with such "seminar" courses, I typically arrange the seats in a circle so as to encourage intimacy and facilitate discussion. However, in this case, the room to which we had been assigned—I found out the first day of class—was not amenable to such an arrangement as the desks were nailed to the floor. Moreover, to my horror (I exaggerate only slightly!), there was at the front of the room a raised platform and, upon the platform, a lectern from which I was supposed to preach—I mean, teach. Faced with this explicitly disciplinary *mise-en-scène,* I elected—in what I thought was a radical gesture—to teach from the back of the class.

It will come as no surprise that although my antihegemonic gesture did have a certain effectivity (mostly short-lived), the class was not ultimately a successful one, at least according to my "subjective" standards, and I'm starting to think it had something to do with my decision to teach from the back of the class—or, as some might say, ass backwards. And yet, causal and other possible explanations aside (perhaps I performed poorly; perhaps it was just a bad class or a bad time), this specific class—precisely because of its unique *architexture*—afforded me an opportunity to think about certain things that I might not otherwise have thought about, in particular what I have called the pedagogic subject-position as it relates to the physical space of the classroom.

In retrospect, I now realize that although I did effect a palpable change in the spatial relations of the room, I did not sufficiently articulate my reasons for doing so. In Brechtian terminology, I failed to *demonstrate* the point of my gesture, with the net result that the gist of my gesture, the *gestus,* was almost immediately neutralized. I'm not suggesting that given the quasi-fixed configuration of the room, I should have resigned myself to its potentially negative pedagogic implications. What I am suggesting—and I don't make any claims for novelty here—is that it is not enough simply to reverse a dominant-inflected structure. Indeed, a reversal of sorts having been effected, it might have been more useful to switch back to the original arrangement, all the while remarking—perhaps with some help from Foucault—the disciplinary nature of the classroom as it is conventionally arranged.

My response to and reading of the above scenario are not, needless to say, the only ones. I could, for example, have found another classroom or, better yet, another, different space. When possible, I have in fact done so. My point, though, is that it is not always possible to do so, that sometimes there are structural limits to situations, and that this is precisely when/where the question of strategy comes into play.

Admittedly, all of this architextural analysis may seem much ado about nothing, but it seems to me that too many teachers and theorists of teaching neglect this aspect of the educative process. As I have tried to illustrate, the materiality of the classroom is ineluctably a practical *and* theoretical affair. In other words, the classroom is one of the contexts—a *material,* not negligible one—within which both the discourse of knowledge and the student/teacher relation are constructed.

Having focused in the above on context (generally speaking), I would now like to address the subject of text(s). However, before I broach the question of the general political economy of the American student as it intersects with *Animal Farm* (1945), I want to describe in some detail my pedagogic approach to the text with which I chose to begin the aforementioned "Politics and Writing" course. Though the course in fact began with a discussion of what exactly we all meant by the word "politics" (also asked students to narrate on paper what they thought was their most political act), the first book I assigned was a quasi-canonical one: *The Communist Manifesto* (1848). Given this choice, a difficult pedagogical problem posed itself: How does one go about teaching this particular text, a text that for many students is not only intellectually demanding (all that Hegelian jargon!) but ideologically suspect.

True to Hegel and Marx, the best approach to the *Manifesto* was, I felt, a dialectical one. In other words, I felt it was necessary to bring out—if possible, Socratically—its "positive" and "negative" moments. To accomplish this, to make Marx and Engels's treatise materialize as the prescient *and* historically determined text it is, I endeavored to situate it in its historical-intellectual context (for example, the "revolutionary" 1840s and post-Hegelianism). But if it was crucial to see the *Manifesto* as a work that simultaneously reflects and transcends its historical preconditions, it was also crucial, I felt, to situate it within a larger, explicitly critical context.

To this end, I assigned A. J. P. Taylor's Introduction to the Penguin edition of the *Manifesto,* an eminently readable and witty preface to what is at times a rather ponderous and tendentious text. Taylor's donnish *esprit,* though, tends to negate whatever force, rhetorical or otherwise, the *Manifesto* possesses. Hence, as a "positive," dialectical foil to Taylor and because it is committed to democracy but critical of both American capitalism and Soviet-style "socialism" (so-called "actually existing socialism"), I also assigned "The Democratic Essence," the second chapter of Michael Harrington's neglected American "classic," *Socialism* (1972).[6] Together, Taylor and Harrington would, I hoped, effectively legitimate the *Manifesto* as a text to be read and reread like any other "classic."

I might add that as an audio-visual coda of sorts, I also screened *Red Nightmare* (1952), a Defense "docudrama" directed by one George Waggner and narrated by none other than Jack Webb of *Dragnet* fame. Let it suffice to say that I hoped this film would cast a retrospectively comic light on the anticommunist rhetoric of the fifties even as it pointed up the decidedly unfunny causes and consequences of such Cold War propaganda (that is, Soviet expansionism and McCarthyism).

After *Red Nightmare,* we went on to Bertolt Brecht's *Galileo* (1947), V. S. Naipaul's *A Bend in the River* (1979), Nadine Gordimer's *The Late Bourgeois World* (1966), Graham Greene's *The Quiet American* (1955), and *Bloods* (1984). The *Manifesto,* however, set the tone for the course, a tone that I would characterize, not unfavorably, as an explicitly *ideological* one (in other words, left, but not "communist"). But despite my efforts to present Marx and Engels's work in as dialectical a light as possible, the students were extremely skeptical about its critique of capitalism, not to mention its proletarian-inspired vision of a future state of classlessness. Today, with recent events in the Soviet Union and Eastern Europe as well as China still reverberating across the world stage in all their revolutionary and counterrevolutionary repercussions, not to be skeptical about the claims of classical Marxism is to be hopelessly naive. Indeed, one might argue that one of our tasks as teachers is to encourage a "healthy" skepticism on the part of our students. The irony, of course, is that the kind of skepticism I encountered was more reactive than radical.

As Nietzsche says, do not misunderstand me. I am not saying that my students' response was merely reactive (which would be to represent it as a form of "false consciousness"). Nor that their skepticism was not radical simply because they did not share my point of view, a point of view which—as I have said—was explicitly ideological. In fact, one might argue that in *their* extreme skepticism, *their* openly ideological posture (what I would characterize as, at best, Right-centrist and at worse, "anticommunist" *à la* Ronald Reagan), these students were vigorously contesting my authorial subject-position—as in some sense, to some degree, they were. And that inasmuch as my posture was also openly polemical, they were "right" to do so.

None of these explanations, however, speaks satisfactorily to my experience of teaching the *Manifesto*. Which is only to say that they do not sufficiently explain the force and complexity of my students' response. But at this point I need to recontextualize what has become a rather speculative reading in order to problematize that response.

The *Manifesto,* Taylor, and Harrington read, I decided—according to that dialectical imperative of which I sketched an instance earlier—to assign *Animal Farm.* Though I will not attempt to reconstruct any approach to this text, I do want to try to convey, albeit briefly and impressionistically, my sense of teaching Orwell after Marx and Engels. What struck me most about student response to *Animal Farm* was its relatively uncritical character: after having been forced to read the "bible" of communism, they were more than willing, it seemed, to engage in some real suspension of disbelief. Overnight, extreme skepticism turned to anxiety-free enthusiasm. (*Now, this is a classic!*) Orwell's fable spoke deeply and directly to their beliefs—about Power, about Intelligence, about Totalitarianism, about Human Nature.

Again, I must bracket a number of absolutely crucial issues here (the formal qualities of *Animal Farm,* the difference between reading fiction and reading nonfiction, and so forth) in order to isolate one: the subject-position, or general political economy, of the American student. Bluntly, I was unable to interest students in a reading of *Animal Farm* that was as critical as their reading of the *Manifesto.* It didn't matter, finally, that Orwell was something of a "chauvinist pig" (pun intended)[7] or that his dogmatically binary characterization of, say, pigs and horses—that is, of intelligence and stupidity and, still more, power and powerlessness, dominance and subalternity—was less than persuasive from any considered, critical point of view. Unlike Marx and Engels (who were pathologically interested in what I call Other-interest), Orwell understood "man" and his "nature," a "nature" which is determined, *essentially,* by self-interest. Human Nature is Human Nature, and damn the critics.

The conclusions that follow from such a premise go something like this: Communism doesn't work because of its fundamental miscomprehension of Human Nature; Communism inevitably reduces to Totalitarianism (*Look at Stalin! Look at Napoleon!*); Capitalism is not only the American Way, it's the best way (and/or vice versa). Though this may be to generalize to the point of caricature my students' political-economic subject-position (even Socrates turns into a straw man in my hands, says Nietzsche), one problem with the above argument is that it misconceives capitalism, which, at least in its contemporary, welfare-state form, no longer corresponds to the object of Marx's critique and cannot therefore be diametrically opposed to communism. More to the point, if Marx was all wrong about communism, in particular its dialectical-historical inevitability, his insight about "human nature"—that it is, like communism and capitalism, historical, not natural—remains.

All of which brings me to the following questions: How can we empower students to interrogate not only their teacher's but their own beliefs? In other words, what can we do—as teachers—to encourage them to think, and to think long and hard, about those things they hold dearest to their hearts? *Is* it possible somehow to teach students to read themselves as carefully as they read the text that is their teacher's politics?

THE TEACHING OF POLITICS

We want education that teaches us our true history and our role in the present-day society. ("What We Want, What We Believe," Black Panther Party Platform and Program [1966])

I don't see how teachers and departments and university faculties can make intelligent professional choices without consciously making them political choices. (Ohmann 304)

The traditionalism inherent in our project may make the list seem to some an obstacle to desired change. But wise change comes from competence, and that is what our list really addresses. (Hirsch 137)

In this final part I want to take up not only the question of "the teaching of politics"—as the subtitle indicates—but what I want to call "political literacy."

By the latter I mean what used to be called "civic education," the process of being schooled in the discourse of democracy as well as in the active exercise of citizenship with its duties and prices, institutions and responsibilities. if on the subject of the political-as- "paedagogical" Brecht has been an important influence8 (in addition to the recent work of, in particular, Henry Giroux), my sense of "political literacy" is a function of the recent dramatic— and, occasionally, melodramatic—debate about the concept of "cultural literacy," especially as that concept derives from the work of E. D. Hirsch, Jr.

Though it is dangerous to let the opposition define the terms and terrain of a problematic, what I intend by the term "political literacy" is not unlike what the author of *Cultural Literacy* calls "cultural politics," the aims of which, according to Hirsch, "are fundamentally different from those of teaching literacy"—"cultural literacy":

A chief goal of cultural politics is to change the content and values of culture. But the principal aim of schooling is to promote literacy as an enabling competence. Although our public schools have a duty to teach widely accepted cultural values, they have a duty *not* to take political stands on matters that are subjects of continuing debate. Only a descriptive list accords with these fundamental goals of universal education. (137)

Hirsch is right about one thing: the principal aim of "political literacy" or "cultural politics" is not merely "competence" but transformation, *social transformation*. Hirsch is right as well, in a negative-theological way, about another thing: "political literacy" implies that both educators and institutions have a duty not only "to teach widely accepted cultural values" but different, less widely accepted—even dissenting—ones.

Moreover (more importantly, that is), educators and institutions have a duty "to take political stands on matters that are subjects of continuing debate" (137). *Pace* Hirsch, teachers cannot and should not reify the undecidability of "continuing debate" (which can all too easily become, in Hegel's terms, a bad infinity). Every debate must be repeatedly punctuated, whether individually or collectively, although—and this can't be emphasized enough—the potentially infinite "textuality" of the dialectical imperative necessitates that each and every *decision* must be negotiated anew.

Of course, a transformative as opposed to what Giroux calls a "transmission pedagogy" also has a duty *not* to be dogmatic (or, for Hirsch, "prescriptive"). The "paedagogical" imperative is, as I have insisted throughout this essay, a dialectical one. If it recognizes, explicitly, the primacy of the political in any and every act of pedagogy, such a recognition does not rest on an assumption of their equivalence. (The "unequal sign," like Jacques Derrida's concept of *sous rature,* can be put to good use here: the political $\neq$ the pedagogical.) Thus, if—compared to a fundamentalist pedagogics such as Hirsch's—Graff's notion of a conflictual vis-à-vis a consensual pedagogy is a step in the "right" direction, from another, "paedagogical" perspective, his valorization of "cultural conversation" ("the cultural text"-as-"the context of teaching" [258]) is necessary but not sufficient. It is necessary because it situates Hirsch's ostensibly "neutral" but—as we shall see—extremely interested notion of competence within a wider, more material field of forces and interests. It is not sufficient because it is not sufficiently political. That is to say, it is neither decisive nor transformative.

In order to sharpen the distinction I have been drawing between "cultural literacy" (or "cultural politics") and "political literacy," I want to return to Hirsch's text. In "The Decline of Teaching Cultural Literacy" (a title that recollects, tiredly, the rise-and-fall-of-the-Roman-Empire trope), Hirsch argues that his notion of "universal education," or what he elsewhere calls his "traditionalism" ("a descriptive list . . . necessarily emphasize[s] traditional materials, because widely shared information is not likely to be new" [137]), is neither an overt nor a covert affirmation of the "status quo." The claim that "universal cultural literacy" reinforces the dominant hegemony is paradoxical, according to Hirsch, "because in fact the traditional forms of literate culture are precisely the most effective instruments for political and social change" (22). Read this way (with the grain, as it were), "competence" is *the* medium of and for transformation.

To illustrate this argument—that "all political discourse at the national level must use the stable forms of the national language and its associated culture"—Hirsch cites a number of passages from *The Black Panther*, "a radical and revolutionary newspaper if ever this country had one" (22). This is an extremely clever rhetorical device on Hirsch's part, and true to the device, the passages are representative, not to say paradigmatic. However, the ideological frisson aside (you can almost hear the grumbling of neoconservatives everywhere: "What's with this Panther stuff?!?"), Hirsch's reading of these rhetorically *and* politically rich passages illustrates the poverty of his theory—a conservative and counterrevolutionary theory if ever there was one.

Take, for example, this claim: "The *Panther* was highly conservative in its language and cultural assumptions, as it had to be in order to communicate effectively" (Hirsch 22). Yet if the following language is "highly conservative" (in the narrowest, formalist sense), its "cultural assumptions" are anything but: "The present period reveals the criminal growth of bourgeois democracy since the betrayal of those who died that this nation might live 'free and indivisible.' It exposes though the trial of the Chicago Seven, and its law and order edicts, its desperate turn toward the establishment of a police state" (17 January 1970, 22). What is interesting about this passage for me is the conflict between what one might call the language of nationalism (" 'free and indivisible' ") and the international language of Marxism ("bourgeois democracy").[9] In other words, a counterdiscourse—a discourse counter, that is, to the official discourse of late "state" capitalism—is deposited in and can be constructed around the word "bourgeois" and its "*associated* culture" (Hirsch 22; italics mine), a culture whose history and language—whose language of history—*The Black Panther* is specifically drawing on.[10]

The construction of such a counterdiscourse—significant as it is—is not, however, sufficient, politically speaking, inasmuch as it is predicated on Hirsch's own premises about "cultural competence." Politics is never simply a matter of reading or discourse, just as empowerment is never simply a matter of competence. Just because you have mastered your ABC's—not to mention the appendix to *Cultural Literacy*—does not mean that racists will stop being racists, sexists sexists, and so on. Prejudice and its disabling effects cannot be countered wholly by communication, especially when communication is understood reductively—as it is in Hirsch—in terms of "effectivity." Indeed, in Hirsch's hands communication comes to seem yet another, belated version of instrumental rationality: cultural Taylorism, post-Fordist literacy for the underprivileged.

From a different, not unrelated perspective, Hirsch's "traditionalist" reading of the above passage from the *Panther* elides absolutely the historical specificity of the BPP's indictment of "this nation" and its "criminal campaign," especially as that campaign and its "law and order edicts" crystallized around "the trial of the Chicago Seven."[11] This "idealization" or de-materialization—the fact that Hirsch does not provide any context for the *Panther* passage (except to remark, repeatedly, the radicality of its "sentiment")—exposes the ahistoricism of his method. On the other hand, for Hirsch to have invoked, even cursorily, the history of the Black Panthers and that larger history within which their discourse must be situated if it is to be at all politically intelligible would have been to educate readers in the kind of "literate knowledge" that his model is expressly designed to suppress.[12]

Finally, the *Panther's* "radical sentiment," its "cultural *politics*," cannot—however incoherent—be separated from its supposedly "conservative language." As Marx would say, it is cutout of whole cloth. In this sense, Hirsch's analytical distinction between "sentiment" and "language"—a distinction that is no longer, I would argue, a critical one—is not "neutral" but political. That is to say, Hirsch's nonreading is not so much a misreading as a pointedly political act.

After suggesting that "the writers for *The Black Panther* had clearly received a rigorous traditional education in American history, in the Deceleration of Independence, the Pledge of Allegiance to the Flag, the Gettysburg Address, and the Bible" (and here the warm-cockle-hearted cheers of neo-conservatives can, I think, be heard), Hirsch adds that the *Panther* writers "also received rigorous traditional instruction in reading, writing, and spelling" (23). His conclusion:

> I have not found a single misspelled word in the many pages of radical sentiment I have examined in that newspaper. Radicalism in politics, but conservatism in literate knowledge and spelling: to be a conservative in the *means* of communication is the road to effectiveness in modern life, in whatever direction one wishes to be effective. (23)

In the last part of this passage, he sounds less like a critic than like a Rotarian Polonius. The peroration and its "wise," palpably condescending tone aside, it is hard to imagine a more perfect illustration of how *not* to read: after having read (?) "many pages" of the *Panther,* Hirsch is struck not by its politics but by its grammar ("I have not found a single misspelled word"). And this from the "content" critic!

One can only conclude that if Hirsch's reading of the *Panther* is an instance—as it well should be—of the kind of rigorousness and traditionalism that American public schools are desperately in need of, then it is clear that rigor and tradition—not to say grammar—are not, by themselves, enough. (I have not found a single misspelled word in the many pages of conservative sentiment. . . .) From what I have said, it should be equally clear that the kind of "conservative" education in "literate knowledge" and, in particular, "American history" that Hirsch's pedagogic model privileges is not only narrowly conceived, dangerously so, but as ideologically interested as the "cultural politics" that is the manifest object of his polemic. Which is to say that "cultural literacy"—at least as Hirsch formulates it—is, in the final analysis, a form of political illiteracy.

In the space that remains I want to return to some of the claims and concerns of this essay in order to advance—against the above language of critique—what Giroux calls a "language of possibility." Bluntly, I want to present a positive instance of what I mean by "politically literacy." To do so, however, I need to reengage the rhetoric of critique in order to examine the problem of print versus visual culture as it is played out in Giroux's *Teachers As Intellectuals* (1988).

In "Mass Culture and the Rise of the New Illiteracy: Implications for Reading," a chapter that both begins and ends with an epigraph from Brecht,[13] Giroux argues that not "visual" but "print technology" is "emanicipatory at the present time" (81). Unlike "reading," which, historically speaking, "created a class-specific audience because of the technical and critical skills needed to use it" ("reading," for Giroux, is synonymous with "print culture"), "visual culture" "has all but eliminated any reliance upon a class-specific audience to use its technology or to understand its messages" (80). One would think that this democratic effect would be a good thing, especially for a class-sensitive critic like Giroux, but according to him, the very concept of "mass culture"—tied as it is to the emergence of the electronic media as "the most dominant form of communication"—"suggests not only the importance of quantity but also the reduction of thought and experience to the level of mere spectatorship" (80).

However, because "the written word is governed by the logic of conciseness, clarity, and cogency" (rather than the "logic" of emotion, diffusion, and fragmentation associated, for Giroux, with the image or the spectacle), print culture or, more precisely, the "technology of print media" "necessitates a form of rationality that *contains* room for critical thinking and analysis" (80; italics mine). Moreover, it is "inexpensive to produce and consume," at least compared to the mass media, which "are centrally controlled by the ruling interests" (81). The left, in any event, "simply does not have access to the visual culture," as the latter's "modes of communication are much too important to the corporate interests to be democratized" (81). The "sociopolitical" bottom line: the visual media—in particular television—present "much greater possibilities for manipulation and social control" than the print media. Put another, epigrammatic way: "The visual media are presently demagogue of one-way communication" (81).

Right off, I feel like saying that Giroux has been reading too much Theodor Adorno and Hans Magnus Enzensberger (the Adornian Enzensberger). If, as Williams says, concepts are problems, then concepts like the "culture industry" and the "industrialization of consciousness" are especially problematic because they lend themselves all too easily to monolithic characterizations of the "mass media." Giroux is not unaware of this Orwellian perspective, which can lead in turn to what he calls "technological fatalism." As he himself says: "the electronic media, as well as print culture, are not a causal agent as much as a mediating force in the reproduction of consciousness" (79). Despite such caveats, however (phrases like "reproduction of consciousness," with their functionalist inflection, are of course equally problematic), Giroux's rationalist rhetoric of containment falls prey to precisely the kind of "technological determinism" and "cultural pessimism"—in Williams's words—that he warns against at the beginning of his essay (Williams, "Culture" 129).

For instance, to argue—as Giroux does—that "the left simply does not have access to the visual culture" is to leave that culture, uncontested, to the right. To this kind of argument—which represents, for Giroux, "a noble but misguided position"—he submits instead the solace of a unilateral cultural politics:

> The electronic media are in the hands of the corporate trust, and it would take a redistribution of power and wealth to place them at the public's disposal. This is an important task, but it must be preceded by a change in the collective consciousness and accompanied by the development of an ongoing political struggle. (83)

But in a society where literacy is increasingly more an audiovisual rather than a "verbal" matter, what is the future of a cultural politics that renounces outright—in the name of a revolutionary historical strategy—the emancipatory potential of the mass media?

If the recent presidential election, not to mention the rise of the Moral Majority, does not offer sufficiently convincing proof that the visual media are indispensable to any hegemony, counter or otherwise, than the work of Williams— from *Preface to Film* (1954) to, say, *Television: Technology and Cultural Form* (1974)—can and should be read as an extended cautionary tale to the effect that the electronic modes of communication are too important not to be democratized. For critics like Williams, the task of the left is not to abandon but to find ways to gain access to visual counterpart, the argument that it is more "logical" than the "tactile" technology of the image ("print culture . . . is not as obtrusive as the visual culture; it lacks the 'tactile' qualities of the latter" [80]) is specious. Print is neither more "rational" nor more "intentional" than visual culture. In the final analysis, the dominative or liberatory force of print or visual technology depends, in Giroux's own terms, on "use," not "potential."

It is not surprising, given Giroux's conjunctural thesis about the liberatory potential of print culture, that his analysis of "the construction of citizenship" in Hollywood films and television programming in *Schooling and the Struggle for Public Life* (1988) is located squarely within the parameters of the *critique* of "the ideology of the new nationalism and chauvinism" (23). If his theoretical understanding of ideology is not, as he himself argues, the "orthodox, classical Marxist" one (ideology as economic last instance or "false consciousness"), his critical practice is decidedly Western-Marxist or, more pejoratively, Frankfurtian. Thus while his general discussion of, for example, "the new anti-communism" in *Rambo* (1982), *Rocky IV* (1985), *White Nights* (1985), *Red Dawn* (1984), *Invasion U.S.A.* (1985), and *Moscow on the Hudson* (1984) is instructive on "the progressive ideological contradictions" at work in such films, his reading is not really persuasive because it privileges uncritically—that is to say, reflexively—the language of critique. And despite his own insistence on "the latent possibilities, needs and hopes" that often constitute the subtext of "reactionary" films, his reading is compelled to privilege the language of critique because it privileges certain films rather than others: *Rambo* rather than *Missing* (1982), *Red Dawn* rather than *Under Fire* (1983), *Rockey IV* rather than *Salvador* (1986).[14]

If films such as *Missing, Under Fire,* and *Salvador* are more evocative of the "history of Hollywood itself" than of their professed historical subject or "political provenance" (Smith 46 *n*12), they nonetheless mobilize considerably different subject-positions than the above manifestly "conservative" films. To be indifferent to this difference is to be dumb to the politicality of art in general and film in particular. To be fair to Giroux, in his most recent work—for example, "Popular Culture As a Pedagogy of Pleasure and Meaning" (written with Roger Simon)—he offers a "positive" but not uncritical reading of *Dirty Dancing* (1987). Unlike his analyses of *Rambo, Rocky IV,* and others, which are marked by a certain "critical" (modernist) self-distance, Giroux's reading of *Dirty Dancing* re-marks his "white working-class" investment in the film even as it lays bare those "semantic" elements that conflict with and contradict it.[15] In fact, partly because of the element of transference (the critical impulse is, as we have seen, a given), Giroux's reading of *Dirty Dancing* as a "popular cultural" text is more dialectical, and therefore more persuasive, than his remarks on "Hollywood films and television programming." More importantly, perhaps, it suggests a real reconsideration on his part not only of the role of the visual media in contemporary culture but *its* potential for "critical thinking and social action" ("Mass Culture" 84).

Given my critique of—among other things—English Studies, Hirsch's notion of "cultural literacy," and Giroux's valorization of "print culture," I want to conclude by briefly describing the first, very successful part of a course I recently taught entitled "Differences" as a "positive" instance of what I mean by "political literacy." The texts for this, the first section of the course—which was subtitled "Reading Race-as-Difference"—were *The Autobiography of Malcolm X* (1963), Martin Luther King, Jr.'s "Black Power" (1967), Cornel West's "The Paradox of the Afro-American Rebellion" (1984), and Spike Lee's *Do the Right Thing* (1989). As will no doubt be obvious by now, I chose these texts in this particular order because I felt they enacted that dialectical imperative which, I have been arguing, is crucial to the "paedagogical effect." In crudely Hegelian terms (crude Hegel, that is): if Malcolm X's autobiography is the thesis to which King's essay is the antithesis, West's article represents one (historical-theoretical) synthesis. More simply, if "Black Power" is a response of sorts to Malcolm X and his successors, "The Paradox of the Afro-American Rebellion" constitutes on organic-intellectual attempt historically to situate and theoretically to mediate between the two.

And yet, insofar as West's article privileges King at the expense of Malcolm X (and rather reflexively at that, at least as I read it), the above discursive set also tends toward a certain closure. Given this constrained dialectic, the advantage of *Do the Right Thing* is that it not only *cinematically* puts into play both King's and Malcolm X's positions but, insofar as it privileges the latter (again, as I read it),[16] contests West's reading of the "logic" of the Civil Rights movement. Lee's film is not, of course, without its totalizations: for instance, nothing seems to have changed at the end of the film, despite the fact that certain members of the neighborhood have acted collectively to avenge Radio Raheem's death, an act that can be read as a symbolic confirmation of Malcolm X's politics of violence-as-"intelligence." However, if the latter act is read as a catharsis devoid of any larger political meaning, the film's conclusion—in particular, the final ludic-musical shot (a parody, arguably, of the classic Hollywood ending)—appears as a spiked, ironic reflection on the present impasse of "the Afro-American rebellion," an historical "aporia" to which neither Malcolm X nor King is the answer. From this perspective, *Do the Right Think*—which is clearly both a product of and meditation on the racially regressive Reagan '80s—poses the politically fraught question: Where, exactly, do we go from here?

Though my construction of the "race question" is obviously only one among many, such a construction illustrates—to take up the points with which I began this conclusion—that "TV and film should be taught within English courses" (a potentially "positive" effect of Cultural Studies [McCabe 32 *n*5]); that literacy is as much a political as a "cultural" issue (Is it possible to divorce Lee's film from that history and politics of which it is so manifestly a product?); and that "print" and "visual culture" *can* "complement each other" "at the present time" (indeed, they may even productively, dialectically interrupt each other). The reconstructive principle at the heart of the above construction—a principle that can and should be extended to include other discourses of rights, such as the gay and woman questions[17]—also illustrates the power of the language of possibility, what Giroux and Simon call "the affirmation of difference" and "the difference of affirmation": both "the possibility of a social imaginary for which a politics of democratic difference offers up forms of resistance in which it becomes possible to rewrite, rework, recreate, and re-establish new discourses and cultural spaces that revitalize rather than degrade public life" *and* the possibility of "claiming one's experience as a legitimate ground for developing one's own voice, place, and sense of history" (13).

If that teaching of politics which is both different from yet implicated in the politics of teaching is going to mean anything today and in the future, it is going to have to come to terms with these different needs and discourses: the possibility of criticism and the irreducible, equally critical demand for affirmation.

NOTES

1. Literature—in the upper case—refers in this essay to that general, dominant-hegemonic conception of "the literary" that still circulates in most departments of English. Literature, in this sense, is something like "work" as opposed to "text"; for this distinction, see Barthes. This is *not,* however, to endorse the Barthesian concept of the Text.

I have put Literature "under erasure" in order to mark the historical contingency of this particular concept-metaphor.

2. I bracket here the question of the historicity of the concept of "criticism." I would only add that "theory," though a historical category and activity as well, is tied to the deconstruction of both "literature" and "criticism."

3. I emphasize the word "pedagogy" because its etymological history is particularly instructive in this context. "Pedagogy" derives from *paidagōgos,* which derives in turn from *paidos* ("child") and *agein* ("to lead"). For the Greeks and Romans of antiquity, it referred to "a slave who attended the children of his master and conducted them to school, often also acting as a tutor." The irony, at least loosely speaking, is that the "original" master/slave relation has now been reversed.

4. Paul Smith is instructive on this point: "In order to learn to resist a text or texts students need to come up against resistance from it and, by extension, from teachers. Teachers . . . not only cannot abrogate their responsibility to their own voices and their own cultural experience and knowledge; they are obliged to present those elements as needing to be taken into account by students" (42).

5. "Politics and Writing" is the title of one among a number of different sections ("Differences," "Love and Sexuality," "Conformity and Rebellion," and so on) that structure the second half of the two-semester writing requirement at Tufts. Tufts is a small, expensive "liberal arts" college located in Medford, a working-class suburb northwest of Boston.

6. For Harrington, the years between 1848 and 1850 mark "the period of Marx's antidemocratic temptation" (49), a period that is "a classic source for the Bolshevik, and then the Stalinist, version of Marxism" (56). Need I add that according to the dialectical imperative I have outlined here, Harrington's quasi-continuist democratic reading of Marx must also be put into critical circulation? For a countercritique of Harrington, see Cohen.

7. See, for example, Orwell's characterization of Mollie, "the foolish, pretty white mare" with her sugar and ribbons: "The stupidest questions of all were asked by Mollie. . . . The very fist question she asked Snowball was: 'Will there be sugar after the Rebellion?'" (26). See also the scene in Jones's house when she is found primping in the mirror (31), the scene after the counterrevolution when she is found hiding in the stall (49), and her final ignominious defection to Foxwood (51–52).

8. For my understanding of what Brecht calls "the paedagogical effect," see for instance "An Example of Paedagogics (Notes to *Der Flug der Lindberghs*)," in *Brecht on Theatre* 31–32.

9. Though the phrase "free and indivisible" appears to be a citation (Hirsch alludes later to the Pledge of Allegiance), this is in fact a conflation.

10. The Panthers' Marxist-Leninist (and Maoist) orientation is both well known and well documented. I cite an article that appeared in *The Black Panther* on the same

date as Hirsch's citation (17 January 1970): "The Black Panther documents step by step the actions taken by, and programs instituted by the Black Panther Party in its unstoppable drive to serve the people; and documents before the whole world the repression and murders committed by Amerikka's corrupt monopoly capital in its dastardly attempts to stop this move to institute people's power" (Foner 8). See also the "Introduction" to *The Black Panthers Speak* (Foner xvii–xix).

11. It is important to note—inasmuch as it is irrelevant, apparently, to Hirsch's argument—that J. Edgar Hoover repeatedly issued directives to his Counterintelligence Program personnel (COINTELPRO) to move against not only the BPP in general but also "the distributors of the [Black Panther] Party newspaper, *The Black Panther*" (Churchill and Vander Will 68).

12. For an account of that larger history within which the history of the BPP must be situated—I am of course referring to the '60s—see Gitlin, in particular "The Bogey of Race" 348-351. For an account of *The Black Panther,* see Peck, esp. 65-66, 76-77, 130-31, and 223-25.

13. "Secure yourselves Knowledge, you who are frozen! Your are starving, grab hold of a book: It's a weapon. You must take over leadership" (74 and 85). Though Brecht did not approve of, for example, G. W. Pabst's production of *The Threepenny Opera* (1931), he was not adverse—at least early on—to "visual culture"; on the contrary, he recognized its revolutionary potential. See for instance "The Film, the Novel and Epic Theatre (From *The Threepenny Lawsuit*)" (47-51).

14. Though I cannot recommend its understanding of *cinematic* language (which is, alas, almost nonexistent), *Camera Politica* provides a more dialectical reading of the "discourse of anti-Communism" than Giroux. See Ryan and Kellner. I might add that if, for Giroux, the "discourse and anti-Communism" reflects a "reactionary" educational reform movement on the state and federal level that is a function in turn of the neoconservative hegemony of the '80s, the year 1986-87 may well be—as Michael Ryan and Douglas Kellner note—"a pivotal one in Hollywood film and in American culture" (297). For one particularly revealing instance of this popular-cultural "turn leftward"—an aftereffect of the Iran-Contra Affair—see the pulp *policier Above the Law* (1988) where the typically "right," self-reliant hero of the conventional action picture (Clint Eastwood, Sylvester Stallone, Chuck Norris) is rewritten as a counter-hegemonic figure. In fact, though the tension between the film's genre and its politics complicates the issue (a critical question, to say the least), the Nicaraguan subtext suggests that Nico Toscani (Stephan Seagal), the ex-CIA protagonist, represents an ironic, if not politically motivated recoding of Oliver North himself.

15. Giroux notes that although the dichotomous construction of "reason and passion" in *Dirty Dancing* lines up along class lines (bourgeoisie-as-head, proletariat-as-body), "Baby"'s introduction to the proletarian pleasures of "dirty dancing" (embodied in the person of Johnny Castle, the dance instructor at Kellerman's Resort) evokes Giroux's own adolescent initiation into the differently inscribed "body politic" of black working-class dances.

16. I hope to develop this reading of *Do the Right Thing*—in conjunction with the West—on another occasion. I would only note that Mookie's garbage-can throwing not only ignites the arguably self-defensive violence of the crowd but that this act of violence is consonant with the politics of Malcolm X, who was—as it were—the last word (cf. the epigraph).

17. Accordingly, the other sections of "Differences" addressed these "new social movements" as well as the "class question": "Coming Out: The Gay Question" (James Baldwin's *Giovanni's Room* [1956]), "Feminism, Fantasy, and Science Fiction" (Joanna Russ's *The Female Man* [1975]), and "Class Dance: Pictures of the American Proletariat" (Mike Nichol's *Working Girl* [1988].

WORKS CITED

Barthes, Roland. "From Work to Text." *Image/Music/Text*. Trans. Stephen Heath. New York: Hill & Wang, 1977. 155–64.

Benjamin, Walter. "Conversations with Brecht." *Reflections*. 1978. Trans. Edmund Jephcott. New York: Schocken, 1986.

Brecht, Bertolt. *Brecht on Theatre*. 1964. Trans. John Willet. London: Methuen, 1987.

Churchhill, Ward, and Jim Vander Will. *Agents of Repression: The FBI's Secret Wars against the Black Panther Party and the American Indian Movement*. Boston: South End, 1988.

Foner, Philip S., ed. *The Black Panthers Speak*. Philadelphia: Lippincott, 1970.

Foucault, Michel. *Discipline and Punish: The Birth of the Prison*. 1978. Trans. Alan Sheridan. New York: Vintage, 1979.

Gibson, William. *Neuromancer*. New York: Ace, 1984.

Giroux, Henry. "Celluloid Patriotism in Hollywood Films and Television Programming." *Schooling and the Struggle for Public Life: Critical Pedagogy in the Modern Age*. Minneapolis: U of Minnesota P, 1988. 23–28.

———. "Mass Culture and the Rise of the New Illiteracy: Implications for Reading." *Teachers As Intellectuals: Toward a Critical Pedagogy of Learning*. South Hadley: Bergin and Garvey, 1988. 74–85.

———, and Roger Simon. "Popular Culture As a Pedagogy of Pleasure and Meaning." *Popular Culture, Schooling, and Everyday Life*. Eds. Giroux and Simon. South Hadley: Bergin and Garvey, 1989. 1–29.

Gitlin, Todd. *The Sixties: Days of Hope, Days of Rage*. New York: Bantam, 1987.

Graff, Gerald. *Professing Literature: An Institutional History*. 1987. Chicago: U of Chicago P, 1989.

Gramsci, Antonio. "The Study of Philosophy." *The Prison Notebooks*. Ed. and trans. Quintin Hoare and Geoffrey Nowell Smith. New York: International, 1971. 323–77.

Harrington, Michael. "The Democratic Essence." *Socialism*. 1972. New York: Bantam, 1973. 41–64.

Hirsch, E. D., Jr. *Cultural Literacy: What Every American Needs to Know*. Boston: Houghton Mifflin, 1987.

Kampf, Louis, and Paul Lauter, eds. Introduction. *The Politics of Literature: Dissenting Essays on the Teaching of English*. New York: Vintage, 1972.

Marx, Karl, and Friedrich Engels. *The Communist Manifesto*. Trans. Samuel Moore. Harmondsworth: Penguin, 1987.

McCabe, Colin. "Class of '68: Elements of an Intellectual Autobiography 1967-81." *Tracking the Signifier: Theoretical Essays*. Minneapolis: U of Minnesota P, 1984, 1–32.

Merod, James. *The Political Responsibility of the Critic.* 1987. Ithaca: Cornell UP, 1989.

Ohmann, Richard. *English in America: A Radical View of the Profession.* New York: Oxford UP, 1976.

Orwell, George. *Animal Farm.* New York: New American Library, 1946.

Paulson, William. *The Noise of Culture: Literary Texts in a World of Information.* Ithaca: Cornell UP, 1988.

Peck, Abe. *Uncovering the Sixties: The Life and Times of the Underground Press.* New York: Pantheon, 1985.

Ryan, Michael, and Douglas Kellner. "Vietnam and the New Militarism." *Camera Politica: The Politics and Ideology of Contemporary Hollywood Film.* Bloomington: Indiana UP, 1988. 194–216.

Smith, Paul. "Pedagogy and the Popular-Cultural-Commodity-Text." Giroux and Simon. 31–46.

Taylor, A. J. P. Introduction. *The Communist Manifesto.* 7–47.

Williams, Raymond. "Literature." *Marxism and Literature.* 1977. Oxford: Oxford UP, 1985. 45–54.

———. "Culture and Technology." *The Year 2000.* New York: Pantheon, 1983. 128–52.

15

Guerrilla Pedagogy: Conflicting Authority and Interpretation in the Classroom

Jody Norton

> The truth of art lies in its power to break the monopoly of established reality (i.e., of those who establish it) to define what is real.
>
> —Marcuse

I teach in the English Department at Albion, a small Midwestern liberal arts college that has recently adopted a two-semester gender and ethnicity course requirement. In attempting to develop a survey course in American literature that would reflect both the exhaustion of canonicity and an awareness of the multiple problematics of race, ethnicity, gender, and sexual orientation, I found myself confronted with three interrelated questions:

1. Will traditional literary issues—form, theme, figuration—be a sufficient agenda in dealing with works that reflect a set of values and assumptions that differ from those of the dominant culture, or whose importance may be as much historical or political as "literary"?
2. If analysis of the course materials moves beyond the staple questions of practical criticism into political and historical concerns, what happens to evaluation? If, in this post-postmodern era, evaluation cannot be thought of as turning solely on internal criteria, but must be recognized to involve the dynamics of the individual reader's relation to the text within a specific historical and cultural context, how is one to establish a viable theory and practice of evaluation?[1] Or is the practice of evaluation itself anachronistic? Are all texts potentially of equal value? If so, what does *value* mean?

3. If meaning and value are both thrown open to new and unpredictable determinants will I, as teacher, be an effective and sufficient locus of interpretive authority?

Having decided that a non-canonical range of materials would indeed necessitate a broadened set of critical issues, that evaluation seemed, if anything, *more* important (if far more difficult) under the conditions of an exploded canon, and that to hope to be a sufficient authority on meaning and value would do nothing more than betray my own blindness as well as incapacity, I engaged my colleague Judy Lockyer to team-teach a course with me entitled *The Subject of American Literature: A Dialogic Approach.*

We began by scrutinizing various individual texts to determine whether, in what ways, and from what perspectives they might be said to involve themselves with questions of gender and ethnicity. Could *Uncle Tom's Cabin,* for example, be studied as an example of the African-American presence in literature? African-American history and culture are usually, we feel, best studied in texts by authors who have written about blackness from within (see Baldwin). Would teaching *Uncle Tom's Cabin* renew Whiteness (White anxieties, White gods, White values) as the dominant color/culture, by its very selection (as opposed, for example, to *Narrative of the Life of Frederick Douglass, An American Slave)*?

Or should *Uncle Tom's Cabin* be thought of as more crucially having to do with gender—as a work that, according to Jane Tompkins, was "in almost any terms one can think of, the most important book of the century" (83), a principal exemplar of the popular domestic novel, the generic project of which was no less than "to reorganize culture from the woman's point of view" (83)?

This process of attempting to classify literary works as importantly "feminist," "African-American," "gay/lesbian," and then "African-American feminist," "lesbian separatist," "AIDS literature," etc., inexorably led to a maze of difficult questions about the relation of texts to socio-ideological formations, and about the construction of those formations. For example, as is clearly demonstrated by scholarship pertinent to gays, lesbians, bisexuals, and an emerging men's studies, gender studies cannot be regarded as synonymous with women's studies. A further question: if men's studies, for instance, chooses to define itself by reference to negative as well as politically exemplary literary materials, are we not back where we started, that is, at a position in which Hemingway and Woolf are equally conceivable authors for a literature course now defined as gender-conscious?

Yes, we *are* back where we started. The difference, of course, is not that the texts have changed, or need to change—except insofar as voiding canonicity and placing all texts, initially, on an equal footing changes them. What has changed is the point(s) of view from which they are approached.

Mikhail Bakhtin writes that "The novel begins by presuming a verbal and semantic decentering of the ideological world, a certain linguistic homeless-ness of literary consciousness" ("Discourse" 367). It began to be clear to us that in our efforts to decenter the ideological world of "class" (in both the social and academic senses of that word), to go beyond traditional literary/ aesthetic evaluative criteria, and to make the teaching and study of literature a field for socio-political critique we had, in effect, to make ourselves *home-less* in Bakhtin's sense. We decided then to see whether ideological vagrancy—a wandering in and out of canonical bounds, a conscious divest-ment of prior interpretive and evaluative positions (accompanied, crucially, by the acknowledgment both of our continuing institutional and professional authority, and of our personal characteristics and experiences as possible sources of value inflection)—might not be a productive "foundational" con-dition from which to undertake a survey of American literature, and in par-ticular of representations of subjectivity and its historical, cultural, and mate-rial determinants.

Our assumption—which is carefully explained to the class—is that literature has political potentiality, and that through the experience of the class we expect this potentiality to take shape in the form of possibilities for more "real" (less constructed) engagements with self and other. We aim to enable the class experience to be, in Bakhtin's words, "the process of coming to know one's own language as it is perceived in someone else's language, coming to know one's own belief system in someone else's system" ("Discourse" 365).

After an opening session in which the design of the course is explained to the class, and a second day devoted to explicating basic Bakhtinian terms (*het-eroglossia, social language, dialogism, voice, ideology, authoritative* versus *internally persuasive* discourse), illustrated with passages from *Pride and Prejudice, The Red Badge of Courage,* Flannery O'Connor's *Wise Blood,* and Matthew Lewis's *The Monk,* I conclude the conceptual preparations for the course with a lecture on literature and literary value (see Norton).

In my lecture I pose two complex questions: what constitutes literary expe-rience, and what are the consequences of such experience? Working out of reception theory developed by Wolfgang Iser, Hans Robert Jauss, and Bakhtin, each of whom, in different ways, describes the reading process as a dialogic relation between text and reader, I argue that *to use a text as liter-ature is to read it responsively:* to read oneself into the world of the text through provisional identifications with a character or characters (or by imag-ining oneself beside them, in their world), while at the same time reading *one-self,* and one's difference—in personality, materiality, values, experience— from the people, places, and things of the text.

There is a difference in meaning, according to Bakhtin, between my expe-rience of a character's (or another human being's) suffering, say; and the experience of the character or individual him- or herself:

> The other's co-experienced suffering is a completely new *ontic* formation that I alone actualize *inwardly* . . . . Sympathetic understanding is not a mirroring, but a fundamentally and essentially new valuation, a utilization of my own architectonic position in being outside another's inner life. ("Author" 103)

"Meaning," as Michèle Barrett writes, "is not immanent; it is constructed in the consumption of the work" (702).

One of the explanatory limits of the reader-response theory of Iser and Jauss, and of Bakhtin's "Author and Hero in Aesthetic Activity," is that the reader is treated as a role or position rather than a personality replete with cultural and historical specificity. The introduction of psychoanalytic and object-relations theory to my account of reader/text dynamics allows me to propose that *in order to function as literature for a reader, a tenet must recall and anticipate a psycho-structurally significant event in the reader's life.* The engaged text initiates a process of *rememoration,* which Jacques Lacan defines as "a retroactive effect . . . specific to the structure of symbolic memory" (185).

Freud hypothesizes that identity is formed "by a process of stratification: the material present in the form of memory-traces being subjected from time to time to a *re-arrangement* in accordance with fresh circumstances—to a *retranscription*" (qtd. in Laplanche and Pontalis 112). Literary experience activates rememoration in the reader by engaging her in an aesthetic event that duplicates/recreates/metonymizes psychic experience of her own involving loss, exclusion, affection, connection, and so on.[2] Rememoration allows us to reflect on our own construction, and to intervene in patterns of fear and denial that may be limiting our potential to actualize ourselves as subjects with choices.

The summary ideas that I propose to the class, then, are that literary experience requires engagement, which in turn requires an active willingness; that engagement (with a particular text) makes possible rememoration (for a given reader);[3] and that rememoration is transformative, involving the reader in a continually revisioning relation to herself and to the individuals and communities that make up her social, political, cultural, and spiritual worlds. As the critical legal studies theorist Roberto Mangabeira Unger envisions it, literature should present "a window upon possibilities of other social relations" (Gagnier 720).

I assure the class that no text can be expected to work equally well, or in the same way, for every reader. No matter how critically esteemed (or vilified) a text may be, and no matter now iconized (or ignored) by cultural institutions, its usefulness as literature must always be determined in the *present,* by and for a particular reader. At the same time, formal, thematic, we-respond ideological analysis of a work can not only tell us more precisely why we respond to it as we do, but in doing so, suggest contingent evaluative grounds that other readers may verify (or discard), extrapolate, and apply to other works on an experimental basis.

Art is almost always harmless and beneficent; it does not seek to be anything else but an illusion. Save in the case of a few people who are, one might say, obsessed by art, it never dares to make any attacks on the realm of reality.

—Freud

Art, if you want a definition of it, is criminal action. It conforms to no rules.

—John Cage

I call the method of our course *guerrilla pedagogy.* The term derives from the guerrilla theater of the Vietnam War period, which borrowed the name and some of the tactics ("simplicity of tactics, mobility, small bands, pressure at the points of greatest weakness, surprise") of guerrilla warfare (Schechner, "Guerrilla" 163). As practiced then, guerrilla theater was a radically politicized street theater, loosely plotted and improvisational, dedicated to bold, brief, and easily accessible critical representations of institutions and ideologies. Its point was to suspend political, cultural, and social "business as usual" (the title of a 1970 guerrilla action protesting racism and the Kent State killings), and to challenge a complacent (or complicitous) citizenry by raising political issues abruptly and dramatically in public spaces (see Schechner, "Guerrilla" 16; other practical and theoretical texts on guerrilla theater include Schechner's *The Future Ritual,* Davis, Estrin, Klein, Munk, and Weisman).

The initial point of guerrilla pedagogy is to split the traditionally univocal interpretive authority of the instructor in two. The authority of each pole of this dyad is further decentered by the open practice of illusion: Judy's and my interpretive positions do not represent the "truth" for either of us, but comprise a critical method-acting. As an opening to the discussion of each work, Judy and I assume critical/theoretical/social positions we do not necessarily "really," or fully, hold, and role-play their consequences in a critical dialogue. For example, I identify myself with Baldwin's objections to *Uncle Tom's Cabin* ("a very bad novel . . . activated by what might be called a theological terror, the terror of damnation" [14–17]), and with the imputations of authoritarianism and sentimentality that that novel is open to. Judy identifies with feminist and historical approaches to the novel, producing a different thematics and inevitably suggesting a different set of values and evaluations.

In discussing *Thelma and Louise,* I take the position that Thelma and Louise self-destructively act out internalized masculine scripts (driving too fast, drinking too much, using guns to commit violent crimes—murder, armed robbery), and that the film's ending demonstrates the non-feminist dead end to which their retrogressive behaviors inevitably lead. Judy argues that, on the contrary, the women's new-found ability to make positive choices for themselves ("I can't go back"), and their determination to respond in active, empowering ways to male aggression—whether by force or evasion—rather than passively submitting to the domination of institutions and individuals, are indeed both feminist and effective.

Thelma and Louise generated powerful responses from the class—responses that very markedly broke down along gender lines. Many of the men saw Thelma and Louise's blowing up of the tanker as an outrageous, violent, and morally unjustified act. Many of the women recalled personal incidents of sexual harassment, including affronts by truck drivers on 1–94. The intensity, and the voices, rose. Scatological expressions entered the discourse. Finally, one young man, unconsciously producing the perfect justification for both Scott's film and a guerrilla pedagogy approach observed, "I don't see why the girls are getting so upset."

Several characteristics of guerrilla pedagogy link it to its theatrical antecedent:

1. It belongs to (the practice of) the people. Guerrilla teachers are provocateurs and interrogators—instigators, not didacts. The theatrical portion of guerrilla pedagogy—the initial teacher/teacher exchange—quickly gives way to interactions with and among the "audience."
2. It is activist, in its commitment to an egalitarian, community-wide critical process, and in its skepticism concerning positions of authority, authoritative voices and discourses, truth statements, and pronouncements of all kinds. Its fundamental point of faith is that individual and collective action (within and outside the classroom) can produce change.
3. It is dislocative, decentering, confounding—and clarifying.
4. It is mobile, improvisational, contingent, and unpredictable—ideologically venturesome at the conscious level, while simultaneously acknowledging the limiting force of social construction in the unconscious. It is alternately covert and open, evasive and forthright, disingenuous and honest.[4]
5. It is liberatory. Guerrilla teachers should be aggressive toward practices of domination and oppression, supportive and compassionate toward human beings, regardless of their views.

There are two crucial ways in which guerrilla pedagogy is unlike guerrilla theater. First, whereas guerrilla theater presented explicitly radical messages, guerrilla pedagogy does not have an agenda, other than textual analysis, ideological critique, and self-examination. Conservatives can interrogate and affirm (or modify) their own ideas and values as easily as liberals or radicals. The guerrilla teachers are open about their politics, but work hard to keep authority separate from belief systems, so that the latter must convince or not on their own merits. The presentations often role-play conservative or anti-feminist, as well as radical, positions.

Secondly, whereas guerrilla theater, operating rapidly in noisy public areas, had a practical need for "simplicity of tactics" and was self-consciously "not subtle" (Klein 121), guerrilla pedagogy, carried on over eighty minutes in the quiet, private space of the classroom, can afford as much complexity and difficulty as the discussants can generate and absorb.[5]

Although we use feminist strategies of consensus-building, team-work, and dialogue (particularly in small groups) as well as conflictual approaches, there is a certain rhetorical violence involved in the practice of guerrilla pedagogy. This methodological violence metaphorizes the violence, both of language and representational content, in the texts we choose for the course, and in particular, those I discuss in this chapter. We feel that a fascination with violence *per se* is symptomatic of pervasive American (especially American male) anxieties about domination and control, and the tendency to reduce complex moral questions to a dialectics of power. At the same time, discursive conflict can be intellectually and emotionally challenging, and can produce more complex understandings, not just of texts, but of worlds and selves. With sensitive facilitation, it can be made relatively safe. We feel strongly that the appropriate ethical response to free-floating or institutionalized aggressivity is not passivity, or evasion, or false consensus.

Furthermore, the adoption of conflict as praxis both acknowledges and appropriates the postmodern axiological condition. As John Guillory notes:

> no concept of value circulates within the intercultural conditions of modernity which is not the product of the interrelation of all of the apparently subcultural forces constituting the social totality.
> The concept of value, then, must be referred to that totality, even though the latter is, strictly speaking, unimaginable *as a totality*; it is a totality of conflict and not of consensus. (282)

Hence, while the value of any given cultural object will be differential according to its assessment within any particular valuing community, the judgments of the individual members of that community will never be unaffected by the conflicting (and congruent) values of all other individuals and communities in the society. Pedagogical practice too often avoids inter- and intra-cultural controversy (it is instructive to notice whose pictures are displayed in your child's elementary school during Black History Month: there will certainly be many pictures of Dr. Martin Luther King, Jr.—often drawn by the children themselves. But is Malcolm X there as well? Or Anita Hill? Huey Newton? Or Angela Davis?).

I would like, at this point, to work through two exemplary texts, of very different genres, as a means of illustrating our approach and the issues and conflicts we address. These are *A Narrative of the Captivity and Restoration of Mrs. Mary Rowlandson,* written by the wife of a Puritan minister, and published in 1682, and "Straight Outta Compton," a rap by N.W.A. (Niggas With Attitudes), released in 1988.

Each of these works involves the self-representation of a social community, as well as an individual. That is to say, they are not simply "auto biographies," to borrow Eazy E's neologism, they are ideologies. As such, they can be analyzed in terms of the social consciousness they display. It is possible, in each case, to suggest that the work should indeed be taught in an appropriately designed literature course—not because (or only because) it can be rehabilitated in traditional literary terms, but because, critiqued as an ideological production, it will perform precisely the function that I have quoted Bakhtin as claiming for the genre of the novel—that is, of enabling one to come "to know one's own language as it is perceived in someone else's language, coming to know one's own belief system in someone else's system."

It would be possible to have this kind of exploration carried out along a pre-arranged path, to have it led by a single teacher, and to have it arrive at a nicely balanced (and thoroughly finalized/authorized) conclusion. To some extent, that is what happens in this essay. In explaining the project with a Single voice and with no doubt about where I'm going next, I have had to pull its pedagogical teeth. In accepting the irony of trying to write in an orderly fashion about radical pedagogy, I will trust that despite my best masculinist attempts to be utterly clear and convincing, occasional shadows of doubt will pass from time to time across the reader's face—the adumbrations, perhaps, of a guerrilla dialogue that might take place between her and me in some shabby bar near the next MLA Convention.

In any case, things are different in the classroom, where two—and ultimately twenty-two or more—critical agencies are simultaneously in operation. As the class becomes active, we become engaged in a polylogue with an indefinite number of more or less independent and distinct student and student-team voices. The responsibility for the direction of inquiry, for the questions that get raised, and for the views that get expressed belongs to the interpretive community as a whole. The critical process goes on with Judy's and my support, but without our control.

Mary Rowlandson's memoir is a well-known example of a very popular, and "uniquely American" (Slotkin 301) colonial literary genre. The captivity narrative detailed the putatively non-fictional adventures of a White Euro-American (usually female) from the time of her capture by hostile Indians to her eventual "repatriation." Part of the interest in these documents was historical, but because narrative and novelistic detail are foregrounded, their effect is literary. And because fiction (romances, tales, etc.) was frowned on by the Puritan fathers as morally dubious, captivity narratives took their place as literary entertainment.

They also formed the basis of an ideological myth of colonial experience. In Richard Slotkin and James Folsom's synopsis, "a white woman, symbolizing the values of Christianity and American civilization, is captured and threatened by a racial enemy and must be rescued by the grace of God (or, after the Puritan times, by an American hero)" (302).

The following passage, which describes the Indian attack on the settlement at Lancaster (outside Boston) in 1675, illustrates quite clearly the terms in which Mary Rowlandson conceives herself and her captors:

> Oh the doleful sight that now was to behold at this house! *Come, behold the works of the Lord, what desolations he has made in the earth.* Of thirty-seven persons who were in this one house, none escaped either present death, or a bitter captivity, save only one, who might say as he, Job 1.15, *And I only am escaped alone to tell the news.* There were twelve killed, some shot, some stabbed with their spears, some knocked down with their hatchets. When we are in prosperity, oh the little that we think of such dreadful sights, and to see our dear friends, and relations lie bleeding out their heart's blood upon the ground. There was one who was chopped into the head with a hatchet, and stripped naked, and yet was crawling up and down. It is a solemn sight to see so many Christians lying in their blood, some here, and some there, like a company of sheep torn by wolves. All of them stripped naked by a company of hell-hounds, roaring, singing, ranting and insulting, as if they would have torn our very hearts out; yet the Lord by his almighty power preserved a number of us from death, for there were twenty-four of us taken alive and carried captive. (325)

In this passage, we understand that historical events are "the works of the Lord," and that God's "almighty power" determines salvation in this world and, implicitly, in the next. The "Christians" here are not only topical but categorical victims. They are "like a company of sheep torn by wolves"—wolves who on closer inspection turn out to be "hell-hounds," the minions of the devil.

The theological frame of the narrative implies that the Puritans are in need of chastisement for their thoughtlessness in times of prosperity. This punishment contains a lesson for the surviving members of the Christian community, whom God has elected to protect from the (only barely metaphorical) cannibalism of these "ravenous beasts." As Rowlandson says elsewhere, "The Lord hereby would make us the more to acknowledge his hand, and to see that our help is always in him" (324).

Rowlandson understands the events of her life as part of the history of God's chosen people (for whom the Jews of the Old Testament were merely the types), whose calling was to bring the word of God into the wilderness. Political and economic factors could have no reality for her, independent of God's will. Yet the passage above contains real horror that does not escape representation. This "touch of the real," as Mitch Breitwieser calls it (39), reveals an incongruous gap between rote ideology and historical experience.

Is Richardson's *Narrative* literature? One could argue—and I do in presenting the work to the class—that its mix of dogmatic theology, sensational violence, crude moralism, rigid social definition, and lack of sensitivity to a cultural other, combined with its author's severely underdeveloped capacity for self-criticism, allows the work as a whole to amount to little more than purblind xenophobia, that it is racist, elitist, self-exculpatory, and unworthy of serious readerly attention.

The capstone of my negative reading of the *Narrative* is the argument that Rowlandson's incoherence in this particular passage—the most wrenching naturalistic description of violence, combined with a highly artificial and purely cerebral transliteration of the events described into the parabolic language of the Bible—derives from her intention in the *Narrative* to produce the events of her life as an example of the power of God; and that, in Mitch Breitwieser's words, "Exemplification, rather than a sufficient resume of its material, is on the contrary a violent social epistemology that seeks a forgetting of the existential-historical actuality of what it claims to represent" (33).

In the words of Per Amicum, the pseudonymous author of the Preface (probably Increase Mather), the *Narrative* documents "the wonderfully awful, wise, holy, powerful and gracious providence of God" in delivering Rowlandson and two of her children from the Indians (319). Per Amicum concludes that it would be

> altogether unmeet that such works of God should be hid from present and future generations: and therefore though this gentlewoman's modesty would not thrust it into the press, yet her gratitude unto God made her not hardly persuadable to let it pass, that God might have his due glory, and others benefit by it as well as herself. (320)

We are to linger, not with the particularity and horror of the events and emotions of the *Narrative,* but with a typology that merges the individual into the generality of Christendom. To do otherwise would risk leaving Rowlandson's raw suffering dangerously unaccounted for. Thus, Breitwieser argues that the *Narrative* involves an unwieldy and massive repression of an experiential knowledge that would conflict with Puritan orthodoxy:

> there is another way of reflecting on what happened to her that might have dominated her had she not scrupulously eradicated it. This *other-than-pious scope* would have been a forgetting not of the experience itself, but of the ways in which the experience was an episode of "God's dealing with her." The writing therefore opposes a way of remembering that would be a forgetting of the right way of remembering. (103)

I conclude that Rowlandson's *Narrative* is comparatively difficult to use as literature because it blocks the reader's engagement by its failure to honor the phenomenological truth of the experience it represents, losing the identificatory magnetism of the grief and pain it expresses in an ideological justification of God's will that appeals to few contemporary readers.

But when one reads Rowlandson's account of the death of her child, wounded in the Indians' raid, the text takes on a different character:

One of the Indians carried my poor wounded babe upon a horse, it went moaning all along, I shall die, I shall die. I went on foot after it, with sorrow that cannot be expressed. At length I took it off the horse, and carried it in my arms till my strength failed, and I fell down with it: Then they set me upon a horse with my wounded child in my lap, and there being no furniture upon the horse's back, as we were going down a steep hill, we both fell over the horse's head, at which they like inhuman creatures laughed, and rejoiced to see it, though I thought we should there have ended our days, as overcome with so many difficulties. . . . After this it quickly began to snow, and when night came on, they stopped: and now down I must sit in the snow, by a little fire, and a few boughs behind me, with my sick child in my lap; and calling much for water, being now (through the wound) fallen into a violent fever. My own wound also growing so stiff, that I could scarce sit down or rise up; yet so it must be, that I must sit all this cold winter night upon the cold snowy ground, with my sick child in my arms, looking that every hour would be the last of its life; and having no Christian friend near me, either to comfort or help me. . . . Thus nine days I sat upon my knees, with my babe in my lap, till my flesh was raw again; my child being even ready to depart this sorrowful world, they bade me carry it out to another wigwam (I suppose because they would not be troubled with such spectacles) whither I went with a very heavy heart, and down I sat with the picture of death in my lap. About two hours in the night, my sweet babe like a lamb departed this life, on Feb. 18, 1675, it being about six years, and five months old. It was nine days from the first wounding, in this miserable condition, without any refreshing of one nature or other, except a little cold water. I cannot, but take notice, how at another time I could not bear to be in the room where any dead person was, but now the case is changed; I must and could lie down by my dead babe, side by side all the night after. I have thought since of the wonderful goodness of God to me, in preserving me in the use of my reason and senses, in that distressed time, that I did not use wicked and violent means to end my own miserable life. . . . When I had been at my master's wigwam, I took the first opportunity I could get, to go look after my dead child: when I came I asked them what they had done with it? Then they told me it was upon the hill: then they went and showed me where it was, where I saw the ground was newly digged, and there they told me they had buried it: there I left that child in the wilderness, and must commit it, and myself also in this wilderness condition, to Him who is above all. (326-29)

In these passages, Judy argues, Rowlandson provides a stark record of events, and of her own and her child's suffering. The loss she expresses is real and palpable, despite what strikes us as the odd rhetorical distance she maintains from her unnamed, ungendered daughter.

Rowlandson's comparatively ideologically unconstructed language allows us to hear her more effectively than we may be able to in the first passage. With the exception of "inhuman creatures"—itself a response to lack of compassion on the Indians' part—Rowlandson is more concerned to write her own life than to judge the lives of the Indians. And where her Christian beliefs surface, they do so in conjunction with feelings with which we can identify, such as the longing for a friend and gratitude for survival, expressed with a degree of acceptance and humility that we can admire regardless of our own ideological persuasions. This second passage, then, works to deconstruct Per Amicum's apologia, in that in it, the certainty of suffering sounds far more clearly than the possibility of redemption.

When we compare Rowlandson's spare, intensely focused narrative voice in this passage with her propagandistic reification of the Indians and her equally ideologized rationalization of destruction in the earlier section, we feel the literary potential of her *Narrative,* but also its limitations. Rowlandson can feel for her child to the core of her being. And the language of her loss—the more charged by its very simplicity—facilitates our engagement with the experience it represents. But in relation to the Indians, she can feel only a violent difference. And in relation to God she dares not feel.

Our interpretation and evaluation of Rowlandson's *Narrative,* then, needs to be flexible and open-ended (we try, of course, to enable the class to work through to their own versions of this ambivalent closure). To read it only as Judy presents it, as a powerfully affecting tale of a mother's devotion and faith ("history as 'what hurts'" [Breitwieser 156]) is to blink its doctrinaire antipathy to the Indians. Yet to dismiss it—as I pretend to do—as a piece of racist myth-mongering is to ignore Rowlandson's capacity to present intense feeling and concrete detail vividly, economically, and powerfully.

Students have had some difficulty engaging Rowlandson's text. The ideology, the language, and the historical context all seem far removed from their own cultural reality, and the pathos of the mother/child relation is less accessible to them than it is to me, who am myself a parent. In our modeling of this conflict, through adopted critical stances, Judy and I attempt to enable the students to engage the text and its tensions dialogically, and to consider analogously conflicting tendencies toward candid self-expression and ideological mystification in their own lives.

The second representative work that I wish to discuss is N.W.A.'s "Straight Outta Compton."

In bringing N.W.A. and other rap groups into the literature classroom, we anticipate some hard questions. I would like to address the three that seem to me the most challenging.

First, there is the question we want asked of each of the course materials: can we use this text as literature? In terms of the theory of literature outlined above, the answer will depend on whether we can engage and respond to it in a way that precipitates rememoration and transformation in us. In order to break down any preexisting assumptions that low cultural practices cannot possibly function as literature, however, I examine "Straight Outta Compton" in the light of John Ellis's definition of literature as comprising texts that are lifted "out of the context of their origin" (44), are "used in a way that is characteristically different from other uses of language" (50), and finally, are "worth treating in the way that literary texts are treated" (51). My assumption is that if

I can justify the literary use of "Straight Outta Compton" in the terms set by Ellis—a widely respected but also fairly intellectually conservative theorist—resistance to a putative "lowering of standards" (or in Guillory's terms, disdain for the low cultural capital of "Straight Outta Compton") will be overcome.[6]

By being produced as a tape, "Straight Outta Compton" has already been taken out of a particular context: it is no longer purely oral, a transient utterance on a California ghetto street. It is open to being played and read in a classroom 2,000 miles and sociocultural light years away. When this takes place, N.W.A.'s work is automatically being treated as literature, according to Ellis's second criterion.

"Straight Outta Compton"'s worthiness for this treatment will, as I have suggested, be part of the intentional problematics of the course. But one can begin by pointing out that the title piece is indisputably artistically controlled: it has a triadic structure, each strophe ending with an identical refrain, and a loose accentual tetrameter line, grouped in irregularly rhymed couplets. It presents three identifiable dramatic voices engaged in complex dialogue with each other, with unvoiced characters ("you too boy," "I'ma call you a bitch"), and with the audience ("This is the auto biography of the E / and if you ever fuck with me / you'll get taken"). That it may strike us as peculiar to explicate the form of "Straight Outta Compton" in this high-critical language reveals more about our assumptions concerning art and propriety than it does about the literariness of rap.

In addition to its elaborate stylistics, "Straight Outta Compton" is structured by an identificatory thematics. Each speaker combines his own fantasmatic name (Ice Cube) with the name of the group/gang (N.W.A.), in the larger context of a mythic community (Compton). The boasts, insults, confrontations, and fantasies of violence, domination, and evasion of authority are all directed toward constructing identity and creating power.

Merely in terms of aesthetic form, it is easier to justify treating "Straight Outta Compton" as literature than, say, the Rolling Stones' or Bob Dylan's songs, which depend far more than rap on melody for their full effect. Rap is much closer to *a cappella* singing, with the addition of a rhythm apparatus and special effects. It is quite literally an oral poetry, and its roots lie in signifying, "the dozens," and jailhouse ballads.

Stylistically, rap has its own originality. Its refusal to be "merely" art is implicit in its total linguistic openness. No word is taboo. But more important than its refusal to limit itself to polite discourse is its insistence on speaking its own scatological, violent language. Conceptually, while truth on a certain level is required—the realness and integrity of the character and his language are necessary illusions—verbal scamming of all kinds, intimidation, hyperbole, evasion, duplicity, etc. are all legitimate generic tools. N.W.A.'s rage at oppression, their misogyny, even their braggadocio are both veracious psychosocial expressions and studied rhetorical effects, providing tone to a rapidly shifting, kaleidoscopic series of street fantasies.

Unlike most heavy metal, rap is hard to write off as mere pop trash or adolescent hormonal relief. Its anger, while it is not rhetorically innocent, carries significant social and political consciousness and intentions. As a genre, rap dialogizes contemporary art and social reality relentlessly. One is not allowed to read "Straight Outta Compton" simply as a universally human *cri de coeur:* it insists on its temporal, cultural, political, and economic particularity. "Straight Outta Compton" cannot be trivialized or dismissed as boring, unless one is ready to dismiss the conditions it expresses as boring and trivial as well. Wittgenstein writes that "the truth can be spoken only by someone who is already *at home* in it" (35e), and the voices of "Straight Outta Compton" are nothing if not at home.

One could go into great detail about post-deconstructive senses of language, intertextuality (raps often "sample" passages from earlier songs, speeches, radio and t.v. broadcasts or simulations, real-world urban noise, etc.), fragmented, abrasive sound effects (scratching, abrupt cuts) as postmodern mimesis of social chaos, and so on. But in class there is neither the time nor the necessity for such arcane investigations. "Straight Outta Compton" clearly displays the high degree of aesthetic self-consciousness, the formal, stylistic, and thematic complexity, and the creative use of language that are traditional measures for inclusion within the category of literature. Therefore, I argue (somewhat disingenuously, since my own theory of literature does not depend on stylistic criteria for their own sake, but on language, voice, and value as they enable or fail to enable a specific kind of text/reader relation) that "Straight Outta Compton" is an appropriate object of study in the literature classroom.

The other initial questions concerning the appropriateness of including "Straight Outta Compton" in our course on *The Subject of American Literature* have to do not with the work itself, but with who's talking about it. To begin with, what gives me, a gay White male college professor from Michigan, the right to talk about Compton, California, N.W.A., Black culture, Black people, or anything else Black (except, perhaps, the poetry of Langston Hughes or Essex Hemphill)? Certainly not the presumption that I am intimately acquainted with those subjects. If, indeed, I *have* any business taking up a piece like "Straight Outta Compton," my legitimacy depends on my being a trained reader of language and cultural semiotics. I call this the Gates defense.

When Henry Louis Gates visited Albion to lecture on Afro-American Studies, a Black student stated that she felt it was wrong to have a White professor teaching African-American literature (as we have at Albion), since this individual could not possibly be familiar with, as she put it, "the Black experience." Professor Gates' reply was, "Does that mean I can't teach Shakespeare?" One may clearly be more or less qualified in terms of cultural background, life experience, and professional training to teach Dostoyevsky, Han Shan, Camus, or Eldridge Cleaver; but a literature teacher will know a lot about how to approach a text by any of these authors. As teachers in any discipline are aware, it is often less important to have a vast supply of answers than to be able to pose a handful of significant questions.

My other response to the question of what business I (or Judy, who is also White) have talking about N.W.A. is political. I simply reject the extreme of political separation that holds, for example, that only "out" gays and lesbians should teach gay/lesbian studies, only women should teach feminist theory, and only Hispanics should teach Chicano/a literature. Such positions seem to me to parochialize intellectual inquiry, and to reduce rather than foster intercultural dialogue and social consciousness.

The final of the three credibility questions I broach is a social rather than an individual one. One might ask, isn't the introduction of "Straight Outta Compton" into a predominantly White learning community made up of students from upper-middle-class backgrounds, by White instructors, yet another rip-off of Black culture, another consumption of Black identity by a devouring mainstream?

Answering this question is not easy. My own feeling is that much depends on the extent to which the politics of race, culture, production, and consumption are made active agendas in conjunction with the use and study of art. To fail to engage such issues is to risk being a voyeur and an exploiter. To make and keep them present is to treat both the art and the people and culture from which it springs with respect.

In another sense, the problem of appropriation, dilution, etc.—the Vanilla Ice effect—is a recurrent phenomenon in the dynamic relation between the *avant garde,* the modes of cultural production, the critic, and the consumer. As a critic, I feel that my social use is to bring to light work of an aesthetic, imaginative and intellectual caliber that suggests its usefulness as politieizable art within the historical and multicultural context I speak from, even if a negative consequence of broader use of a particular work, or genre, is the proliferation of third-rate imitations.

I have already discussed the ways in which it seems to me "Straight Outta Compton" more than holds its own in the "Is it art?" kind of argument. I want to look, for a moment, at the ways in which one might read it as a socially productive (Jody) or counter-productive (Judy) text.

N.W.A. does gangster rap. They specialize in attitude and exploits rather than more evolved political consciousness (though attitude, to be sure, is already political). Hence, they are harder to legitimate than KRS-One, the Jungle Brothers, or even Public Enemy. There is anger, however, and without anger there can be no liberation from oppression. Paulo Freire writes that "Functionally, oppression is domesticating. To no longer be prey to its force, one must emerge from it and turn upon it" (36). The anger in "Straight Outta Compton" is envisioned immediately as action, and its destructiveness is simply predictable. Turning again to Freire, we are told that

Violence is initiated by those who oppress, who exploit, who fail to recognize others as persons—not by those who are oppressed, exploited, and unrecognized. It is not the unloved who initiate disaffection, but those who cannot love because they love only themselves. It is not the helpless, subject to terror, who initiate terror, but the violent, who with their power create the concrete situation which begets the "rejects of life." (41)

The act of defiance—of negation—inherent in "See, I don't give a fuck / that's the problem" is a valuable first step in the transformation of a condition of oppression. We can also point to an honesty of address (the language is absolutely as spoken), pride in oneself and one's cultural location (however ironic)—"I'm comin' straight outta Compton"—and determination ("The police are gonna have to come and git me").

On the other hand, as Judy notes, the violence here is all Black-on-Black. The reputations are made at the expense of brothers (and sisters). And the ethic of aggressivity is so dominant that absolutely anything goes: the only wrong is to be a punk.

The reinscription of oppression is most noticeable in the terms with which women are designated: "a good piece of pussy," "bitch," "'ho." The value of a woman for a man is programmatic and explicit: "You think I give a damn about a bitch? / I ain't a sucker." Even to care about a woman is to be a fool, in this language. And one derogates another male by transgendering him through modifiers like "pussy-ass." This aspect of attitude is a vivid example of the adoption by the oppressed of the most extreme negative models offered by the dominant culture. White misogyny, as well as racism, is reflected in the heavy sprinkling of "muthafuckas," "niggas" and the general virulence and aggressivity of the language not about White people, but about Black.

The question of whether "Straight Outta Compton" is successful or not on purely aesthetic terms finally seems far less important than its pedagogical value as a tool for the examination of social consciousness, through the kind of reading process I have described as responsive. As such it sparkles, in the force and clarity with which it exemplifies a highly defined and active ideological community, and the deep flaws that threaten to destroy the real and moving vitality of that community. Tony Bennett writes that for Louis Althusser and Pierre Macherey,

> literature's specificity . . . consists in its capacity to help us "see," "feel," or "perceive" the ideologies to which it alludes and which provide the ground upon which it works—and works precisely to transform by rendering the occlusions and contradictions of those ideologies perceptible. (129)

"Straight Outta Compton" generates considerable force as literary discourse through its overwhelmingly evident wish to represent exactly its own occlusions and contradictions: the self-loathing of the glorified self, the self projected as the other-who-cannot-be-loved, and so on.

Yet if rap remains at an emotional distance from its audience it cannot function as literature, however powerful its language—perhaps not as art in any sense. The point of access for the dominant culture reader/listener is the cycle of destitution central to rap. Raps typically arise out of self-esteem issues and emotional, economic, and political needs that move the protagonist to "talk the talk, and walk the walk"—to speak up and act up. The speaker's frustration concerning social inequities and the failure of his personal attempts to change his situation for the better lead to rage, destructive consequences for self and other, and a downward spiral of self-esteem. The speaker can only renew his quest for strategies of amelioration, this time from a still more disadvantageous position.

What functions as testimonial and praxis for the rapper can operate among White middle-class audiences as an extended metaphor for their own anxieties about self-value, frustration concerning options, anger at unequal distributions of social power (family, school, work, court), and tendencies toward self-destruction. Rap can also provide a connective education in the social reality of the Black subclass that can spur political engagement—no mean feat amongst the axiologically impoverished members of generation X. As Paul Lauter writes, "Is not merit determined by the capacity of a work to engage genuine feelings and thus to open us to others' lives, and worlds, and needs? Even to prod us to action in the world?" (68).

The class predictably enjoyed all the rap music we studied. Discussion of lyrics was always preceded by listening to the original recording at full volume, since volume, rhythm, and tone are all crucial elements of the rappers' styles. In discussion of "Straight Outta Compton," students seemed to be accustomed to, and unfazed by, the rough language, and to accept the threats of violence as metaphors for resistance to oppression. The gender politics of the piece seemed most problematic, in that if "Straight Outta Compton" is read as a resistance statement, its divisiveness in regard to gender (the gang life is a male thing) and its unreconstructed (and transparently anxious) misogyny are difficult to accommodate without judgment.

For literature to work its transformative effects, examination of the consciousness of others, as it is represented in their language, must ultimately become the individual student's critique of his or her own ideological system, and the extent to which illegitimate practices of dominance, devaluation, and exclusion are part of it. As Steven Knapp writes, "The moral benefit of literary interest lies not in any capacity to tell us which values are the right ones, but far more modestly, in the way it helps us find out what our evaluative dispositions *are*" (100). If the student—and here I include the socially disempowered as well as the privileged minority who inhabit the liberal arts college classroom—is to transform what he or she may come to experience as negative patterns of thought and action, pedagogical practices—whether in the classroom or on the street—must be designed to avoid top-down ideological transmission, and to maximize individual critical growth.

In *Theory and Resistance in Education,* Henry Giroux stresses the following points as fundamental to the establishment of a process of self- and social criticism:

> The active nature of students' participation in the learning process must be stressed. This means that transmission modes of pedagogy must be replaced by classroom social relationships in which students are able to challenge, engage, and question the form and substance of the learning process. Hence, classroom relations must be structured to give students the opportunity to both produce as well as criticize classroom meanings. . . .
>
> Students must be taught to think critically. They must learn how to move beyond literal interpretations and fragmented modes of reasoning. . . .
>
> The development of a critical mode of reasoning must be used to enable students to appropriate their own histories, i.e., to delve into their own biographies and systems of meaning. That is, a critical pedagogy must provide the conditions that give students the opportunity to speak with their own voices. (202-03)

In our class on *The Subject of American Literature,* dialogue between Judy's ("female") and Jody's ("male") pedagogical, critical, and theoretical voices, ventriloquized through a series of characterologically and critically subjective positions is, as soon as possible, broadened to include the engaged and engaging voices of our students (a process facilitated by small groups, class panels and presentations, directed exercises, essay topics, post-essay postmortems, sessions exploring feelings generated by the class process, and so on). Our aims are three-fold:

1. to dialogize the personal, political, and critical voices/languages of our students, in ways that will carry far beyond the limits of our class;
2. to dialogize the imaginative texts, essays, and theoretical discourses that form the materiality of the course (but not simply centrifugally—we try to work through to some provisional readings, which involve closures as well as openings); and
3. to dialogize the relations of pedagogical authority in relation to the study of literary texts: we aim to dramatize the power of dialogue—involving the mutual and voluntary questioning of our own authority/credibility— to enable levels and complexities of critical consciousness that are largely unavailable in the univocal, authoritarian classroom.

Finally, our wish is that the challenge, humor, inspiration, intensity, and pleasure that Judy and I—I hope visibly—feel in our interactive pedagogical process (and the anxieties as well) may provoke an analogous but richer and broader range of intellectual and emotional experience in our students.

NOTES

1. Barbara Hernstein Smith writes: "literary value is not the property of an object *or* of a subject but, rather, *the product of the dynamics of a system*" (15). The relation between text and reader occurs within the context of a larger economic system, according to Smith: "our experience of 'the value of the work' is equivalent to *our experience of the work in relation to the total economy of our existence*" (16). Along similar lines, Richard Shusterman writes, "For all its power to speak, art is dumb without a dialogical intelligence for it so speak to. It cannot therefore be judged on its own, apart from its manner of appropriation" (142).

2. Ronald de Sousa describes a related pattern of emotional repetition through literature, via what he calls "paradigm scenarios":

> We are made familiar with the vocabulary of emotion by association with *paradigm scenarios*. These are drawn first from our daily life as small children and later reinforced by the stories, art, and culture to which we are exposed. Later still, in literate cultures, they are supplemented and refined by literature. Paradigm scenarios involve two aspects: first, a situation type providing the characteristic *objects* of the specific emotion-type . . . and second, a set of characteristic or "normal" *responses* to the situation, where normality is first a biological matter and then very quickly becomes a cultural one. (182)

The key differences between the process de Sousa describes and the Lacanian concept of rememoration, as I am applying it here, are first, that paradigm scenarios are bio-cultural norms to which the child is educated. They do not account for particularities of individual psychosomatic experience. Secondly, paradigm scenarios, as normative structures, do not change in their essentials, whereas rememoration is always a reformation of the content of experience.

3. Bakhtin writes, "A given human being is the condition of aesthetic vision" ("Author" 230).

4. In response to a letter questioning the ethics of presenting guerrilla actions as though they were "real," Marc Estrin writes:

> The critical measure is option, degree of freedom. The critical question: does the "audience" emerge from the experience with more options or less? Have the degrees of freedom been increased or decreased? The guideline I have formulated for myself is: *if people emerge with more options, more freedom, go ahead and do it. If people emerge with fewer, watch out—it's fascism.* (Letter)

In guerrilla pedagogy, the class is aware that the teachers' interpretive *contretemps* are staged (though this fact tends to disappear from the consciousnesses of both teachers and students in the midst of discussion). Time for debriefing and disavowals is budgeted for the close of a session.

5. We try, however, to keep the importation of highly specialized terminologies to a minimum, excepting the Bakhtinian tools with which the class is initially familiarized.

6. As Trevor Ross points out, one can choose from a variety of genres of definitions of literature, including fictive, verbal, generic, aesthetic, institutional, and historicist. Ellis' definition involves elements of the generic, which Ross defines as follows:

literature . . . is but a conventional grouping, a separate genre in effect, that includes within loose boundaries a range of forms and modes . . . related not by a defining essence but by contingency, including changing notions of literary value. (582–83)

Ellis' definition is also, at least potentially, institutional, according to which, as Ross describes it, "The definition and value of literature . . . are primarily determined in accordance with the changing disciplinary interests of academic and cultural institutions" (583).

WORKS CITED

Bakhtin, Mikhail M. "Author and Hero in Aesthetic Activity." *Art and Answerability: Early Philosophical Essays by M. M. Bakhtin.* Trans. Vadim Liapunov. Ed. Michael Holquist and Vadim Liapunov. Austin: U of Texas P, 1990. 4–256.

———. "Discourse in the Novel." *The Dialogic Imagination.* Trans. Caryl Emerson and Michael Holquist. Ed. Michael Holquist. Austin: U of Texas P, 1981. 259–422

Baldwin, James. "Everybody's Protest Novel." *Notes of a Native Son.* Boston: Beacon, 1955. 13–23.

Barrett, Michèle. "The Place of Aesthetics in Marxist Criticism." *Marxism and the Interpretation of Culture.* Ed. Cary Nelson and Lawrence Grossberg. Urbana: U of Illinois P, 1988. 697–713.

Bennett, Tony. *Outside Literature.* New York: Routledge, 1990.

Breitwieser, Mitchell. *American Puritanism and the Defense of Mourning: Religion, Grief, and Ethnology in Mary White Rowlandson's Captivity Narrative.* Madison: U of Wisconsin P, 1990.

Davis, R. G. "Guerrilla Theatre." *Tulane Drama Review* 10.4 (1966): 130–36.

De Sousa, Ronald. *The Rationality of Emotion.* Cambridge: MIT P, 1987.

Ellis, John. *The Theory of Literary Criticism: A Logical Analysis.* Berkeley: U of California P, 1974.

Estrin, Marc. "Four Guerrilla Theatre Pieces from The American Playground." *The Drama Review* 13.4 (1969): 72–79.

———. Letter to *The Drama Review* 14.1 (1969): 189.

Freire, Paulo. *Pedagogy of the Oppressed.* Trans. Myra Bergman Ramos. New York: Continuum, 1990.

Freud, Sigmund. *New Introductory Lectures on Psychoanalysis.* New York: Norton, 1933.

Gagnier, Regenia. "Value Theory." *The Johns Hopkins Guide to Literary Theory and Criticism.* Ed. Michael Groden and Martin Kreiswirth. Baltimore: Johns Hopkins UP, 1994. 719–23.

Gates, Henry Louis. Lecture on Afro-American Studies. Albion College. Albion, Michigan, 1991.

Giroux, Henry A. *Theory and Resistance in Education: A Pedagogy for the Opposition.* New York: Bergin and Garvey, 1983.

Guillory, John. *Cultural Capital: The Problem of Literary Canon Formation.* Chicago: U of Chicago P, 1993.

Klein, Maxine. *Theatre for the 98%*. Boston: South End, 1978.

Knapp, Steven. *Literary Interest: The Limits of Anti-formalism*. Cambridge: Harvard UP, 1993.

Lacan, Jacques. *The Ego in Freud's Theory and in the Technique of Psychoanalysis 1954–1955*. Trans. Sylvana Tomaselli. Ed. Jacques-Alain Miller. New York: Norton, 1988. Book 2 of *The Seminar of Jacques Lacan*. 4 vols.

Laplanche, Jean, and J.-B. Pontalis. *The Language of Psycho-Analysis*. Trans. Donald Nicholson-Smith. New York: Norton, 1973.

Lauter, Paul. *Canons and Contexts*. New York: Oxford UP, 1991.

Lesnick, Henry, ed. *Guerilla* [sic] *Street Theater*. New York: Avon, 1973.

Lewis, Matthew. *The Monk*. New York: Oxford UP, 1973.

Marcuse, Herbert. "On Science and Phenomenology." *The Essential Frankfurt School Reader*. Ed. Andrew Arato and Eike Gebhardt. 1978. New York: Continuum, 1982. 466–76.

Munk, Erika. "Booking the Revolution: An Interview with Saul Gottlieb and Oda Jurges of the Radical Theatre Repertory." *The Drama Review* 13.4 (1969): 80–88.

Norton, Jody. "History, Rememory, Transformation: Actualizing Literary Value." *The Centennial Review*. Spring, 1994.

N. W. A. *Straight Outta Compton*. Cassette. Produced by Dr. Dre and Yella. Priority, 4XL57102, 1988.

Ross, Trevor. "Literature." *Encyclopedia of Contemporary Literary Theory: Approaches, Scholars, Terms*. Ed. Irena R. Makaryk. Toronto: U of Toronto P, 1993. 581–83

Rowlandson, Mary. *A Narrative of the Captivity and Restoration of Mrs. Mary Rowlandson*. Slotkin and Folsom 315–69.

Schechner, Richard. *The Future of Ritual: Writings on Culture and Performance*. New York: Routledge, 1993.

———. "Guerrilla Theatre: May 1970." *The Drama Review* 14.3 (1970): 163–68.

Shusterman, Richard. *Pragmatist Aesthetics: Living Beauty, Rethinking Art*. Cambridge: Blackwell, 1992.

Slotkin, Richard, and James K. Folsom, eds. So *Dreadfull a Judgement: Puritan Responses to King Philip's War, 1676–1677*. Middletown: Wesleyan UP, 1978.

Smith, Barbara Herrnstein. *Contingencies of Value: Alternative Perspectives for Critical Theory*. Cambridge: Harvard UP, 1988.

Stowe, Harriet Beecher. *Uncle Tom's Cabin or Life Among the Lowly*. Ed. Ann Douglas. New York: Penguin, 1986.

Thelma and Louise. Dir. Ridley Scott. MGM-Pathe, 1991.

Tompkins, Jane. "Sentimental Power: *Uncle Tom's Cabin* and the Politics of Literary History." *The New Feminist Criticism: Essays on Woman, Literature, and Theory*. Ed. Elaine Showalter. New York: Pantheon, 1985. 81–104.

Weisman, John. *Guerrilla Theater*. Garden City: Anchor, 1973.

Wittgenstein, Ludwig. *Culture and Value*. 1980. Trans. Peter Winch. Ed. G. H. von Wright. Chicago: U of Chicago P, 1984.

with the opposition movement to the War in Vietnam. Because such issues have surfaced repeatedly in Republican diatribes against the President, it was predictable that, when DeLay defended the slash-and-burn, scorched-earth campaign to overthrow Clinton, the Republican whip framed it within the larger "debate about relativism vs. Absolute Truth" (Impeachment Coverage).

DeLay's invocation of Absolute Truth refers to a larger historical frame that has contextualized this debate for neoconservatives over the last 30 years. Spurred on by preachers like Pat Robinson and Jerry Falwell, politicians such as DeLay and Newt Gingrich have depicted the positions of their adversaries as Evil incarnate. Although many contemporary critics see the dyad of Absolute Truth vs. moral relativism as a reductionistic indicator of experience, it does provide a perceptual window onto the type of thinking that has influenced academic politics in recent years. As many people know, right-wing caricaturists have depicted progressive academics according to the binary logic of the culture wars, which flamed white hot after Starr investigated Lewinsky. Such caricatures have not always been countered, however, for several reasons: because many academic critics have so little respect for the intellectual acumen of their accusers and, as a practical matter, because professors have been preoccupied with departmental and curricular issues. Anyone who has attended a department meeting knows how much work is involved in updating the curriculum and democratizing teacher-student relations in the multicultural classroom. Although these projects take time and effort, we should not be diverted from looking beyond the confines of the campus to see how progressive pedagogical practices are being challenged at state houses across the country. If we have learned anything from the Clinton impeachment, it is that we can no longer blink away the "holy" war currently ravaging Washington, nor pretend it won't take a pedagogical turn toward conservatism in the foreseeable future. For at the end of the twentieth century the site of contestation over the cultural production of meaning is within the confines of the university and beyond— in the managerial halls of state governments where neoconservative politicians are attempting to affect an academic rollback that fits their reactionary agenda.

Believing that left-wing intellectuals pose a threat to the neoconservative revolution, far-right policymakers have decided to leapfrog the educational institution to appeal directly to state and local legislators. Through such tactics, they hope to make wholesale changes in the way state colleges and universities are run. Reactionary conservatives have deployed this strategy because they feel threatened by critics who use poststructuralist, postmodern, and postcolonial theories to critique gender, race, and class biases in contemporary society. Such approaches, suspicious of oversimplified binary categories deployed by reactionary traditionalists, have used contemporary theory to deconstruct the magical abracadabra of a marketplace discourse utilized to reproduce existing power relations. Combining enormous reserves of money with ready access to the media, neoconservative spokespersons have rhetorically smeared "academic radicals" with the same broad brush they used to characterize Bill Clinton. Spurred on by an uncompromising religious fundamentalism, conservative hardliners have depicted academic intellectuals as cultural pariahs intent upon subverting "traditional values" and the cultural practices based on them. The university is under siege by right-wing critics wary of academic professors capable of contextualizing a broad intertext of cultural representations, which challenge the ideological "ground" of conservative cultural representations, customs, and practices. While neoconservatives strive to reproduce existing power relations based on a set of previously agreed-upon evaluators (truth vs. falsity, good vs. evil, absolute objectivity vs. relative subjectivity), contemporary critical theorists have crafted a "double articulation" of culture, conceptualizing it as both the "ground of analysis" and "the object of study" (Nelson, Treichler, Grossberg 1992, 5). For sophisticated linguistic analysis is not solely content-based; it acts as a gatekeeper onto the very structure of discourse itself. And this is intolerable to neoconservative ideologues who believe they have unfettered access to Absolute Truth consecrated by time-honored traditions.

Influenced by groups like the Christian Coalition, zealous right-wing conservatives have refused to examine the limitations of their ideological positions. They have sought instead to naturalize mythic concepts presented for public consumption as objective, depoliticized Truths. Their semiotic myths assume the existence of a prepolitical social order and the material conditions guaranteed by it. In the past year they have ceaselessly trumpeted the rule of law, which, they claim, is capable of reading across class, gender, ethnic, and ideological boundaries in an "evenhanded" manner. They insist values are inherited, not produced, and that "bottom line" objective knowledge somehow escapes dialectical contestation. They insist it is possible to forge transcendental signified-concepts by converting cultural representations into the particulars of "natural" signification and, taking it a step further, into universal Truth itself. Roland Barthes contends that universal Truths function mythically by freezing meaning in a state of arrest. According to this paradigm, static transcendental signification holds all competing meanings at a distance while mythic signification postures as an unlimited and unbounded generating process unified across time and space. As part of a project of demystification, multicultural critics show that the rule of law is constructed by empowered groups who control the dissemination of politicized signs across the culture. They link the rule of law to its internalized correlate, the superego, the critical agent that codes desires according to their acceptability. Multicultural theorists prove threatening to neoconservative traditionalists precisely because they challenge the constructed aspect of those rules, which guarantee laws. Instead of taking for granted the rules that underpin legal and cultural practices, cultural critics emphasize the context-specific nature of institutional structures. Instead of blindly accepting propagated discursive truth as fact, cultural critics subject such claims of veracity to dialectical accountability. In this way, they demonstrate how discourse cuts across boundaries of race, class, and gender to delineate the limitations of knowledge as well as the ideological functions that prop up existing regimes of power.

By encasing themselves within a uni-signifying, legal language to camouflage their unabashed political desires, right-wing critics have gained semiotic cover to claim the transcendental high ground. Calling on a depository of "neutral" claims, they have sought to dissociate their mythological project from their discursive practices, particularly from their chosen strategies of representation. As ideological purists, they wield the law to reinforce respect for their privileged positions in society, all the while fending off the threat of auto-critique and self-judgment. To accomplish this objective, they link "legal truths" to a larger frame of reference: the conflict between religious fundamentalists and secular critics who posit with their materialist calculus terrestrial answers to "universal" questions. This conflict has intensified recently for several reasons: Republicans have gained increased political power since the Reagan revolution, and society is rapidly approaching the millennial moment that has revived fundamentalist fears about apocalyptic collapse and the impossibility of human survival.

SUNDAY MORNING MILLENNIAL FEVER

Anyone who has watched television recently knows about the media's preoccupation with marking the millennium and the symbolic sweep of time it signifies. Millennial hype has been graphed onto a definable moment symbolizing everything from anxiety over the eschatological Last Judgment to concern about the Y2K computer bug. Millennial sensationalism is predictable considering how the media handled the Simpson trial and the Clinton impeachment crisis. Once again the media are giving heightened importance to an exploited event, this time to the fabled temporal transposition signaling the third thousand-year cycle. Ironically, the media approach the advent of the third millennium as a project in need of constant revision if it is to command consumer attention to sell products. Because doomsday predictions of the world's end are too pedestrian to capture most people's attention, look for the appearance of the staged event—millennial madness—to square exponentially in the foreseeable future to draw large-scale consumer interest.

There are already addresses on the web like "everything2000.com," which sensationalize such subjects as "UFOs, Aliens, and the Antichrist" and "multicultural prophecies"—a site concerned with cyberspace homing devices and cosmic teleportation spells. The mainstream media are also complicit in constructing the palpable outlines of a pseudo-millennium which doesn't quite have the same cachet as its religious affiliate, since the former is a hyperreal construction calculated to capture high ratings and a significant market share. For instance, members of the Israel Tourist Board are launching a "worldwide campaign to promote the country as a destination for millennium tourists" ("Israel" 1998). But this microevent pales next to Hal Uplinger's plans for a New Year's mega-event to produce a 24-hour broadcast that would forgo the usual "pop-the-cork celebrations" in favor of a historical format looking "at our world over the last 100 years" (Markovich 1998). But even Uplinger's high-tech millennial celebration, which begins "with dawn's first light at the equator," will pale in comparison to Zvi Dor-Ner's millennium broadcast of a 24-hour show circling "the globe with each country passing off the hosting baton to a neighboring country in the next time zone" (Markovich 1998). As if this weren't grandiose enough, Dor-Ner wants NASA to "open the show from space where the astronauts in MIR will see the sun first at the moment of the new millennium" (Markovich 1998).

It is not just the mainstream media that have linked millennial activities to transhistorical fantasies related to these communal signifying systems. Even distinguished publishing outlets have joined their voices to the syncopated mantra calculated to exploit the millennial moment for crass commercial reasons. For instance, Indiana University Press recently sent a "Pre-END of the MILLENNIUM" catalogue encouraging its readers to "get a jump on all the festivities at the end of 1999" by "celebrating NOW" this extended moment of commercial bliss. When groups like I.U.P. participate in the dissemination of end-of-the-year fantasies, it becomes apparent millennial fever is part of a larger fixation linking individual media events to a wider chain of equivalency. In the computer industry, for instance, words like "catastrophe," "crisis," and "time bomb" are routinely employed in "trade journalism to describe the potential trouble" awaiting computer industry laggards who don't convert systems in time (Schanzer 1997, 263). In the graphic arts community, the obsession with apocalyptic art has become a signifier of survival on a "post-nuclear planet" (von Ziegesar 1997, 284). In philosophy, the acceleration of time imperils the referential orbit of history itself—an important component in a postmodern project obsessed with the hysterical flow of media images which, caught in structural overdrive, broadcast a 7/24 schedule. Even environmentalists have joined the millennial chorus by decrying the ecological apocalypse they believe will occur if we don't use technology to reverse quantifiable trends like global warming. Although we need to take steps to reverse course, when environmentalists color the apocalypse green, they inadvertently bolster the forces of production seeking to superimpose regulated corporate desires upon transhistorical apocalyptic fantasies.

The third millennium has always had special meaning for religious devotees whose spiritual narratives have privileged it as an indicator of historical seed change. Since the musical *Hair* was produced in the '60s, New Age astrologers have been obsessed with determining precisely when the Age of Aquarius begins. The argument turns on distinguishing when Neptune will phase in sync with Aquarius. Some believe Neptune is currently passing in and out of

Aquarius, while others claim the New Age is upon us. Still others predict that in 2012 or even 2160 the Age of Pisces will conclude. Because such divergent beliefs make it more difficult to determine the precise moment of "cosmic transition," it becomes absurd to use the millennial marker as a signifier of the Aquarian Age. Yet it remains a distinguishing moment for New Agers as well as for Christian fundamentalists, who use it to demarcate the final sweep of time which symbolizes more than century's end. For fundamentalists, *the event* foregrounds in top-of-the-chart letters the easy-to-read signposts of the apocalypse. Fundamentalists believe a supreme judgment will rise above the fog of postmodern confusion to trumpet in the judicial timetable of the Holy Spirit's third age. Signaling this milestone is part of a larger apocalyptic project bound up with fundamentalists' broadcasting to the public their belief in Armageddon, the reign of Christ in the new millennial kingdom, and the rapture for "you-got-it-right" true believers.

Part of the obsessional project of forecasting this fatal eschatological endgame is to reread cosmic narratives in order to convert ontological calamity into epistemological certitude. Armed with the Bible's predictions yet lacking evidentiary assurance, conservative Christians spin experience to fit within the frame of their tortured expectations. If we consider narrative's performative aspect (its ability to do things with words), it becomes apparent that fundamentalist fantasies convey apocalyptic desires projected onto the body politic to produce the very circumstances that will help realize those fantasies. Through such event-labeling, right-wing fundamentalists construct a set of microdescriptive evidentiary details which, combined into a macrosequence of historical events, indicate the big story of apocalypticism customarily referred to in the Bible. While they claim such detective work merely reads signs for wonders of God-promised events, they have embarked on an expedition to structure causal plots into arranged time sequences that fit their pseudoscientific predictions. In this way, they combine the narrative bits and pieces of their self-conceived, self-sustaining, retheologized universe as premillennial circumstances allow. Since time is a major structuring principle of narrative flow, renascent fundamentalists need only revise their doomsday predictions once they are proven false to account for the delay in thermonuclear war, environmental collapse, and the annihilation of the known universe. Their argument remains credible, however, as long as they revise incorrect date-setting to accomplish several goals at once: (1) to slow the rapid acceleration toward the catastrophic end of history; (2) to chronicle God's plan in linear narratives that defend against a fear of death they have generalized into a universal system of symbol formation. In this way Christian narrators seek to reinterpellate true believers by constructing morality tales of good and evil around improvised sequences of historical causality.

Narrative causality often privileges one set of interpretations over another and, in so doing, elevates an identifiable protagonist over a scapegoated "miscreant" who is objectified in the process. In *The Scapegoat,* Renè Girard explains that people feel helpless when faced with the eclipse of culture—an event that takes on calamitous significance when we ponder the omnicidal catastrophe promised in these end-of-the-world scenarios (1986, 14). Typically, when true believers feel threatened by people who hold different values from theirs, they deny their subjectivity while casting them out of the cultural mainstream. Hitler, for instance, created this dangerous dynamic by setting up the camps, the gas chambers, the crematories, and the selection process that filled them with the living symbols of the Reich's disavowed Jewish population. Before Hitler was born, slave owners of the American South deprived displaced Africans of their civil rights by projecting upon them their own bestial Darwinian appetites, which dehumanized these captives as part of the enslavement process.

Today, another group of anti-Semitic racists has fabricated a selection process to rationalize persecutory narratives that sanction the grand design of their apocalyptic fantasies. Positioning themselves against dispensational fundamentalists whose biblical exegesis annexes narrative significance, anti-Semitic Christian Identitarians "avoid the potential embarrassments of date-setting by arguing that most biblical prophecies still remained unfulfilled, a condition that placed the end of history in the indeterminate future" (Barkun 1997, 193). In "Racist Apocalypse: Millennialism on the Far Right," Michael Barkun explains how Christian Identitarians characterize themselves as God's "chosen people" while they transpose their Jewish enemies into "Satan's agents" (1997, 194). In a bewildering display of epic racism, Christian Identity validates the group's imaginary fantasies of joining with Jesus as they do battle with Jewish identity-snatchers to achieve racial redemption at the end of time (1997, 195). For their blissful union will occur only after "the earthly battle between the forces of light" (Christian Identitarians) and darkness (the Jewish population) which, in this twisted scenario, pose as God's chosen people but are really the "Devil's spawn" (1997, 195).

Such narrative reversals should give us pause, not only because they help to justify the Holocaust itself, but because they base their beliefs upon a temporal narrative whose conclusion makes their project precarious. The apocalyptic narrative's temporary nature—the fact that it predicts its own imminent demise—makes narrative temporality so precarious that conservative Christian groups are furiously retelling their stories in the time they feel they have left. They believe that if they draw the outlines of God's plan with greater and greater frequency, they will compensate for each marked boundary that has passed into history without consequence. They are left, however, with a sequence of redrawn subplots that proliferate as the number of scapegoats grows because the disarticulation of the narrative project itself becomes more and more pronounced. Constructed by televisual realities providing us with hyperreal bytes of less and less duration, saturated with information flickering in hysterical rapidity that speeds up perceived notions of time and space, left observing structures that move quickly enough to become apparent in their movement—right-wing millennialists cringe in reaction to postmodern life, striking out at their enemies in a desperate attempt to slow the process down. They want to slow it down to make sense of it: to stop the world and get off *after* they get a handle on circumstances whose velocity threatens to pitch them from their conceptual orbits.

At this juncture academics find themselves cast as Evil incarnate along with rock and hip-hop musicians, graphic artists, Hollywood actors, and Democratic politicians, who have been scripted as scapegoats of the religious right. For neoconservative epistemologists realize that, in a postmodern world of media-disseminated images, the construction of meaning is bound up with the means of representation because representation is constitutive of the event itself (*Stuart Hall*). Although they hold there is one essential, fixed, true meaning against which distortion can be measured, they are savvy enough to utilize representational strategies to influence the process of meaning making. Thus their obsession with narrative ordering principles employed to conserve transcendental formulations from the Bible. We can measure their success in furnishing frameworks of intelligibility by their ability to erase the seam between language and experience so that, at the level of common sense, neoconservative frames of reference seem to unfold in a spontaneous, transparent, natural manner. By constructing prescient chronologies that claim to know how history will end, neoconservative mythologists divert attention from the premises upon which their stories are founded. In this way, they trace the closed circle of narrated events, which renders their own presuppositions invisible to true believers who refuse to interrogate formulations that attain, through their repetition, the taken-for-granted aspect of commonsense reality (Hebdige 1993, 362-63).

Cultural conservatives have reorganized the political horizon to emphasize the ability of narrative to depict the transcendental reality it claims to represent. To retain an illusion of universality, right-wing writers have set out to denigrate alternative storylines advocating a pluralist self-reflexivity which calls attention to its own epistemological limits. When attacking postmodern micronarratives that openly admit their inability to recuperate culturally assigned meanings, neoconservative writers posit an alternative: transcendental narratives, which function to underwrite cultural cohesion. Postmodern mininarratives rely upon signs that act differentially with other signs rather than the objects depicted by them. In a world where signs become so self-referential they displace the objects of reference themselves, it is understandable why neoconservative theorists would trade the provisional, contingent aspects of signification for a series of macronarratives of duration whose purpose is to reinstate the grand narrative vision of human perfectibility. That is why ultraconservative technocrats use the information superhighway and other communication networks to build bridges to a forbidding future they hope will empty time of alternative possibilities.

In the struggle for cultural ownership, neoconservatives have been forced to work with media hybrids, which offer a dramatic proliferation of electronic outlets (radio, film, television, the Internet) that help to construct socio-cultural boundaries. In other words, the way information is conveyed to the public has itself become a subject of interest. If we consider the maxim previously examined in this essay—the construction of meaning is indissociable from the means of representation—the medium becomes as important as the message conveyed. It follows, then, that if representation helps to constitute the event, the same information staged in different mediums is capable of taking on different meanings. Because technocultural information is shaped by the medium of representation, people have become cognizant of the hyperreal gap between the event and its conveyance. Because there is a wide variety of media outlets at the turn of the century, we are able to watch media structures grow, mutate, and, in some cases, dissolve before our very eyes. Because of this dynamic, the fixed, unitary nature of structure has been undermined in a way that it has never been before. In a time of rapid technological innovation, where people can fly from one end of the planet to the other to witness firsthand experience previously unavailable to them, cultural rituals become framed by historicized geographical references. Even those who live in close proximity to where they were born have access to television, which provides them with innumerable experiences undreamed of a century ago. The saturation of electronic technologies in our image-driven society has enabled people to see cultural structures change in their lifetimes, and this has had a detrimental effect for right-wing propagandists intent upon conserving past traditions for future generations.

Such rapid epistemic transformations have produced a cultural urgency on behalf of neoconservative critics who have taken to the airways with a vengeance in the last 10 years. One issue hotly debated since the Simpson case emerged as a national obsession is the place of the rule of law in our culture. This topic has become a political football in a litigious contact sport carried out by televisual intermediaries who insinuate themselves into the ideological debates of the times. Besides Court TV (a 24-hour network which covers courtroom trials), cable and satellite television stations like MSNBC, CNBC, and the Fox News Channel have top loaded their programming with an influx of prosecutorial shows that judge people along partisan lines. Shows like *Hardball* with Chris Matthews, *News Chat* with John Gibson, *Rivera Live, The O'Reilly Factor, Hannity and Colmes,* and *Drudge* have rocketed into prominence by sensationalizing legal issues whose shelf life has been extended to garner higher ratings. These shows are littered with former prosecutors, defense attorneys, and judges whose prosecutorial leaps of judgment are more often based on critical hunches than well-reasoned arguments. If this spate of TV court shows were not enough, talk radio shock jocks like Don Imus and Rush Limbaugh have gained so much influence over the past decade they are now helping to shape public policy. We have not witnessed such a prosecutorial feeding frenzy since Senator Joseph McCarthy left the Senate. This time, however, the players include overzealous independent counsels like Ken Starr and investigative journalists who excoriate their enemies in the press. Unfortunately, radio and television talk show hosts have even more latitude than McCarthy did in the fractious '50s to level unsubstantiated claims against perceived enemies.

Neoconservative media critics have manipulated technological signs to prop up one of the structural backbones of our culture: the rule of law we have heard so much about in the last year. Attempting to shrink the ensemble of postmodern subject positions into a limiting conservative context that situates us in their hegemonic narratives, right-wing traditionalists have appealed to the rule of law in order to underpin conventional structures that are disintegrating into empty, discombobulated rituals. Their overemphasis of legal issues underlines their obsession with converting institutional nodal points into permanent cultural fixations. This leaves us with a question: what responses can multicultural critics summon to undermine litigious right-wing McCarthyite tactics? Add to this a related question: what concrete political solutions can be employed to counter the Republican agenda of peopling the courts with an array of ultraconservative judges? To answer these questions, we must recognize that it is not the Supreme Court alone which has shifted sharply to the right; it is the entire judiciary branch of government that has tilted toward conservatism since Ronald Reagan took office. Don't be fooled into thinking that the ultimate aim of right-wing politicians is to capture the Senate, House, and presidency for an extended period of time. This is not the case, because they know that the majority of Americans hold contempt for the conservative branch of the Republican Party. Because of this circumstance, right-wing political operatives have rewritten an endgame calculated to stack the Supreme Court with their appointees and to flood the state and local court systems with unelected officials who hold allegiance to them. In this way they hope to produce the seismic cultural effects we witnessed in the Clinton impeachment. They know that disproportional power lies in the judiciary because it is the one branch of government filled with an inordinate number of political appointees, some of whom serve life terms.

Calling into question the undemocratic dimension of the American legal system, multicultural theorists have read the rule of law through the wide-cut lens of ideological theory, which contextualizes it as one aspect of a broader system of oppression. In "Ideology and Ideological State Apparatuses," Louis Althusser demonstrates how the legal system works hand in glove with "the Government, the Administration, the Army, the Police, the Courts, the Prisons" in comprising a "Repressive State Apparatus" (1971, 143). According to Althusser, the repressive State Apparatus maintains its clout by supporting a hierarchical structure of productive forces intent upon reproducing the conditions of production. In this way the State Apparatus manufactures goods and services as well as ideas and values so that those who have economic and ideological privilege can maintain it. This repressive apparatus, whose longevity does not depend upon any one regime in particular, reinforces its dominance by subjugating citizens who learn their "place" in a structural hierarchy of privilege. The SA accomplishes its goals primarily by the use of force (one goes to jail for breaking the law), but secondarily through subjugating us to a ruling ideology. In such cases the state maintains a veneer of objective neutrality to allow its legal system to dispense justice.

But with the massive exposure given the Simpson and Clinton cases, this veneer has become suspect of late. Because there is a growing perception that the rule of law cuts unfairly across race, class, and gender boundaries, those who wield power have endeavored to influence the ideological debate by mobilizing the Ideological State Apparatus—the press, educators, churches, family members, film industry, and political parties—to make their case (Althusser 1971, 143). In the past the ISAs were employed to persuade the public to accept traditional values, which enabled the State Apparatus to operate without resorting to force. Functioning "massively and predominantly by ideology," the ISAs have traditionally retained power by legislating ideological beliefs in the attempt to interpellate (or hail) its members into recognizing themselves in cultural narratives presented for mass consumption (Althusser 1971, 146). But today, when the media shape a range of conflicting ideological positions which reinforce and reject state biases, support for traditional perspectives must share airtime with positions that compete for media interest. The result is a proliferation of outlets and a less defined centralized and hierarchical control of news stories. Because the transmission of postmodern knowledge is dispersed through a lateral expanse of informational outlets, "the media play a central role in the creation and maintenance of the culture of heterogeneity" (Taylor 1994a, 9). Because the fragmentation of unitary perspectives has become a psycho-cultural indicator of postmodern America, universal codes of meaning that present unmediated representations and unbiased interpretations have become less and less convincing as the objective arbitrators of experience (Taylor 1994b, 4). One consequence of this new dynamic is interpretation-with-an-attitude, which has led right-wing ideologues to utilize conservative ISAs to bolster a legal system whose ethical credentials have become questionable of late. Because of this situation, neoconservative writers have insisted upon the universal validity of their narratives. But each retold narrative quantifies their desperation to parry the demonstrated amnesia postmodern America shows toward historical precedents that seem outdated, if not naïve.

What practical steps can be taken to problematize the myth of the democratic American judicial system? Before we answer this question, it is necessary to draw attention to several circumstances that bear on the matter. (1) Since judiciary officials are not often elected to their posts, idealized fantasies of democratic American relations have difficulty accounting for them. (2) The World War II generation is giving way to their baby boom, X, and Y successors who don't hold the same reverence for the rule of law as those that preceded them. (3) Brought up suspicious of the site of communicative engagement, younger generations are more likely to link the judiciary with the broader net of propagandizing ISA-outlets, which don't necessarily have their best interests in mind. One proof of this trend is Clinton's endurance in the face of the Lewinsky affair. Had their affair occurred 10 years ago, Bill Clinton would have likely followed Gary Hart into historical oblivion. But that's not the case today, because generational politics has affected the geopolitical mood of the country to such an extent that the structure of influence itself has become a target for reevaluation.

As prosaic as it may seem, it is vital for multicultural critics at the turn of the century to expose fantasies that enable hegemonic SA and ISA structures to continue as old. But that is not enough to stop coup attempts of the type we've witnessed this year in Washington. And it is certainly not going to stop right-wing conservatives from striving to overturn tenure statutes at state houses across the country. Nothing less than making all police chiefs, prosecutors, and judges (in traffic courts, state courts, and the Supreme Court) *elected, not appointed* officials can alter this untenable situation. By having them stand for election, we could slow the momentum achieved by neoconservative legal experts who have been engaged in silencing their enemies in the classroom. If we require elections every four years and impose term limits based upon a four-year cycle, members of the judiciary would become more responsive to public opinion than they are today. Then we could reinvest our energy in the counter-hegemonic struggle to influence public opinion. By retargeting the electronic media, we could take political and cultural responsibility for extricating ourselves from their magnetic allure long enough to denounce constructed consumer subjectivities which encourage a slavish subservience to media influences that often remain unconscious.

THE LOOK OF NARRATIVE

We have seen that to convince the public their narrative depictions of truth are authentic, neoconservative storytellers have produced semiotic myths, which preclude inspection of their basic premises. To erase from observation the conceptual limits of discourse, neoconservative narrators have tried to accomplish the following objectives: (1) produce subjects who unquestionably accept their narratives as nonnarrativized truth; (2) fashion a larger context of beliefs which augment a social order that right-wing writers hope to revive; (3) divert attention from the medium of communication itself so that its role in disseminating information is not called into question; (4) slow the historical becoming of structure so it appears static, unitary, and transcendental rather than historically contingent. These rhetorical maneuvers help to reconceptualize, recode, and recontain narratives that put at a distance aspects of their discourse which would otherwise call attention to their fictive, constructed nature. Earlier in this essay, I emphasized the difficulty of sanctioning master narratives that call for their own terminus in the near future; because of this difficulty, neoconservative mythologists are busy making revisions to their stories so they appear more believable. Such double-speak helps them to reproduce a supernumerary ambiguity about the precise date when the world will end even as they insist upon the accuracy of their narrative chronologies. Notwithstanding these efforts, they have had to take other steps to interpellate the viewing public to effect the changes they desire. As part of the process of producing consumable images, right-wing yarn-spinners have graphed the *look of narrative* onto their stories as a standardized part of their high-tech discourse.

The look, which is among Jean-Paul Sartre's "major philosophical innovation[s]," produces an intersubjective experience of being seen by others that reduces the person under observation to an object of visual politics (Jameson 1998, 103). In this process of becoming an object of scrutiny, the subject is turned into a thing whose own look is relegated to a secondary status evoked in reaction to the primary gaze of the other. In this dynamic the subject becomes an aspect of a visible field coming into focus from a "site" outside its purview. In "Transformations of the Image in Postmodernity," Fredric Jameson illustrates how the look becomes a "protopolitical phenomenon" bound up with dominating the object of examination (1998, 104). Here the observed subject is *othered* by a colonizing gaze, which is supplemented by power, money, and narrativized identity positions bearing the weight of ideological macrostructures behind them. When someone receives a determining look under these circumstances, the gaze of the other is validated by a system of pseudo-universal beliefs that wields truth like a weapon against the subject-turned-object. In this way, the objectified subject's convictions are relegated to the level of idiosyncratic particulars that are deemed to have little relevance for the larger population as a whole. Through such intimidating acts, the look "teaches" people their place in society.

In his essay on the transformation of the image, Jameson illustrates how the Sartrean look is reconstituted into the communal gaze of bureaucracy. In a bourgeois culture, the gaze melds into an attitudinal prototype obsessed with the tasks of measuring and marking, observing and examining the subject. Thus is born the epistemological look whose redirected focus generalizes itself into the mechanized *structures* that mediate the relationship between subject and object. In this paranoid age of teleprojected images, the look is always there as the prevalent presence of systemicity itself, subjugating the subject to the paranoid possibility of being seen in each frame of each event that unfolds. We are left, then, with the phenomenon of "being visible for a henceforth absent look . . . [that has been] generalized, to the point at which the individual act of looking itself is no longer required" since vision has been dispersed into the machinery of hierarchical power, specialized knowledge, and biased truth (Jameson 1998, 106).

In his final formulations on the look, Jameson transposes Foucault's epistemological gaze of dominance, discipline, and control onto the hyperreal sites of postmodern transmission—the screens, tubes, and LCDs that convey the surface array of imagistic and lexical signs which bombard us daily. Day after day, technocultural transmissions flicker across TV, film, and computer screens that present us with the possibility of seeing and, through self-conscious reversal, of being seen. As the twentieth century ends, we find ourselves caught between two antithetical looks: the depersonalizing gaze of bureaucratic determination that produces us as reified commodities and the euphoric gaze of technological innovation born of the spectacle. In our mixed-media society, we are left to negotiate the effects of these conflicting demands as well as their influence in circumscribing post-industrialist, designer identities sold to us as objects-of-value.

At this point we can add an old staple to Jameson's list, the conservative gaze of divine omniscience. It proffers the idealized look as a means of recuperating master narratives that guarantee the spiritual identities-from-above promised in their stories. But, as we have seen, to reaffirm their narrative claims and the criteria of Truth based upon them, neoconservative writers have reconstituted fictions which had previously provided less problematic access to the all-embracing mythos they had forged in their ideological texts. Recently, the sovereignty of their master narratives has been compromised by dynamically changing historical circumstances that have put into question the neoconservative project of reading the ahistorical signposts of the millennium. For it has become obvious in this age of semiotic fabrication that there is no one historical typology and no one omniscient look that accompanies it.

Because the mediums of exchange themselves have dramatically increased in the latter half of the twentieth century, information is circulating so rapidly that the older metanarratives have splintered into a temporal discontinuity related to the proliferation of alternative positions. Such stances carry with them a series of nonidentical, variable *looks* that have intensified ontological instability through the sheer enumeration of proffered positions. Jameson's sequence provides a useful, though not comprehensive, overview of the typological transformations of the gaze: from Sartre's look of domination (wherein a character like Prospero can intimidate Caliban by giving him the evil eye) through the look of bureaucracy (wherein members of the State Apparatus that Big Brother signifies endlessly spy upon its citizens) to the seemingly unbounded, generative look of the postmodern telecommunicational network (which busies itself with the production of images that reaffirm its simulacrum). The latter gaze has penetrated most aspects of American life at the end of the twentieth century, presenting us with the impossibility of omniscient overview because the narrative guaranteed by the gaze invariably lacks an end-frame.

Because ontological certitude confronts epistemological uncertainty at birth and death, human beings overwrite such transitional moments with symbolic stories to explain the incomprehensibility of these rites of passage. Because most people have some fear of death, they are particularly susceptible to such overwriting, which often leads one to accept forced narrative closure in compensation for an indeterminate, inapprehensible conclusion. Such unresolvable ambiguity leaves right-wing millennial narratives in the tenuous position of overcompensating for radical uncertainty as they rush past themselves to their final scene, writing people out of the script in the process. This situation is further compounded by the confused pluralism of the postmodern condition, which strips the narrative gaze of its omniscient pose, making it difficult to retain its primacy as a dominant cultural construct. This leaves conservative epistemologists having to contend with the augmented power of postmodern micronarratives which, forged in a technical era of maximized output, care more for the circulation of capital than the potential realization of truth. Such mininarratives stand firmly against the *grand religious récits* that have trumpeted the spirit as the principal driving force of life-experience. In the age of postmodern transmission, so many perspectives are generated that the construction of narrative subjectivity is sutured to a proliferation of societal looks organized around the means of reproduction as much as the ends of teleological transcendence. This confusion of means with ends further problematizes the status of the narrative end-frame, whose structure is in question as well as its ability to symbolize the puzzling experience it seeks to symbolize.

Conservative tacticians know that life in America today dictates that they continually revise conceptions of reality by converting hyperreal artifacts into art facts, which deny their own artificiality. To solidify an "authenticity of expression" yet weave fragmented, interrupted, and tenuous constructs into a seamless web of metaphysical facts, right-wing image crafters face the paradoxical task of piecing together postmodern microevents into a larger narrative whole which leads toward a discernible conclusion validating its overall design. In other words, they must be conversant with the language of postmodernism to use it against itself. Moreover, they must induce their base to accept historical changes without critical speculation *even as* mercantile technologies multiply to shape cultural identities as an extension of their organizational activities.

In times past, historical, scientific and religious narratives often prescribed "acceptable" behavior for acculturated subjects in the secular and religious domains of society. Before the twentieth century there were debates about elevated notions of truth conveyed in metanarratives elaborating the following themes: "the dialectic of Spirit, the emancipation of the worker, the accumulation of wealth, the classless society," the promise of truth, justice, and the American way, and the salvation of righteous true believers (Sarup 1989, 132). Although debates generated around these issues were heated, they often remained contextual rather than structural until one side gained enough influence to effect a definitive change in society. Except for the outbreak of war or revolution, structural changes in other eras occurred over much longer time cycles. For instance, the displacement of neoclassicism by romanticism took decades of conceptual and ideological struggle before the previous discourse was vanquished and the Age of Reason with it. The same can be said of the struggle between realism and modernism, which vied to construct a cultural paradigm capable of influencing the way people viewed their world during that period. Today, as contemporary theorists show how language structures experience while replacing the object of reference with semiotic signs in the field of representation, they scrutinize the pretence of narrative claims in light of this situation. Jean-François Lyotard goes so far as to contend that "the rules of language games do not carry within themselves their own legitimation," for every utterance has become a move in a rhetorical game that empowers one player over another, one group over others, one discourse over a competing ideological sequence of representations (Sarup 1989, 119). Popular stories, mythic legends, and tall tales attempt to bestow legitimacy upon an empowered group of privileged people who seek to establish rules and regulations that bind others to their social compact. But this project loses its capacity to certify its position once narrative is understood as a system of representations relying upon description to further its purpose. Because of this crisis in legitimation, televisual stories have used the camera's eye to validate point-of-view shots that sustain themselves through their equation with the omniscient narrator, author, director, and/or overall structuring principle which exerts influence upon the interpretative process. It is by sustaining the *look of narrative,* then, that right-wing storytellers hope to create continuity when faced with an open-ended, indeterminate future.

Once narratives lose their capacity to organize experience, the public's ability to interpret their lives in terms of them becomes less feasible. When signs generated by the grand narratives of legitimation become self-reflexive, the space for considering alternate stories becomes more contemplative. In today's media society, we see a proliferation of mininarratives that self-consciously undermine many of the deterministic claims associated with them. These micronarratives present a series of perpetual presents—interludes of short duration generated for technological consumption that elevate profit as a governing principle above the anchor of absolute and determinative Truth. Narrative sound bytes are screened for technical qualifications, then replaced like indissociable consumables giving way to other advertised products of planned obsolescence. In the society of the spectacle, narrative truth provides passage through shortened periods of duration, resulting in abridged attention spans focused on the moment rather than previous experiences which are all too quickly ferried into the past. As we have seen, what attempts to hold the narrative in place is a sequence of carefully constructed, ever-changing looks that interpellate subjects-turned-consumers—not in an epic instance of recognition as before, but through intermittent interludes of fixation giving way rapidly to other relatively brief moments of social organization.

If multiculturalists are to engage neoconservative narratives of human redemption, they must accept a simple fact: Sunday morning millennial fever no longer just occurs on Sunday mornings. It is a 24/7-televangelist enterprise broadcast on satellite stations promising eternal life in the celestial kingdom while they solicit donations in the day-to-day business exchanges of corporate religion. Their cosmological narratives would convince us that God's omniscient gaze will redeem "His" chosen elect at the end of history. The divine gaze is invoked to sanction the circularity of narrative progressions that assure us we were sundered from God only to be returned to "Him" after the Second Coming, which will confer universal visibility to Christ's transmundane project. This storied trajectory has been inscribed to convey the synoptic tale of universal history, the panoptic gaze of God, and the *raison d'être* for the neoconservative narrative enterprise. The question becomes, if neoconservatives have found a utilitarian technological means of reproducing the conditions of their narrative productions, how can multicultural critics counter the theocentric identity politics conveyed in these religio-political chronicles? This task is especially difficult because neoconservative narratives—conditioned by a sequence of revisionary looks—are bound to telecommunicational capital, simulated values, and hypervisual truths, three influential arbiters of turn-of-the-century experience.

MULTIMEDIA PEDAGOGY AT THE
TURN-OF-THE-CENTURY

If multicultural critics are to engage neoconservative strategists, they must avoid encasing their ideas in an aura of objectivity. If multiculturalists merely fold their all-embracing claims into the textual design of their work, they will replicate right-wing tactics used to produce their idealized metalanguages. A metalanguage creates a super-representation of a dominant perspective that supersedes all other viewpoints under its hegemonic control. An over-arching metalanguage accumulates under its aegis every aspect of textual content, every shred of divergent possibility under a single meaning. When validating pluralistic difference, progressive academics have the opportunity to draw attention to the performative aspect of their narratives. These critics would do well to acknowledge that their work will eventually be replaced by theories serving ideational desires born in another time and place. This has always been the case, so there is no reason to believe it will change in the future. Given enough time, even the greatest writer's historical reach finds its limit, but for most of us this process is much more accelerated. If we acknowledge discursive displacement, we will be less inclined to posit ourselves as subjects of certainty who take the historical stage to tie the knot between knowledge and self-promotion.

As we enter the twenty-first century, it becomes especially important to encourage our students to rent, not buy our explanations of interpreted information. It is helpful for students to maintain a healthy irreverence for right-wing, moderate, and left-wing formulations, which overreach themselves when framing non-parodic propositions in the political imaginary. In the multicultural classroom, it is not enough to condemn "value free" pedagogical strategies that reach past ephemeral principles to link universal codes to transhistorical Truths. Even the postmodern dismissal of devalued metanarratives, if conceived as an over-simplified reduction, can itself mutate into a repackaged mythic master-narrative based on this one-pointed insistence. We need to avoid parenting any system of signs that consolidates paternal power over other "delegitimized discourses." bell hooks is particularly helpful in this regard, when she asks cultural critics to encourage the articulation of divergent discourses in the classroom as a means of giving voice to noncanonical writers so long excluded from curricular syllabi. Hasn't the white male canon, she asks, sustained itself by rigidly wielding discursive power to the exclusion of alternative points of view (hooks 1994, 36)? Hasn't this been a central tactic in the struggle for cultural ownership? Don't ingroup conventions lay claim to foundational, definitional, and operational discourses that re-emphasize the established cultural consciousness of the day?

Progressive academics can convert the classroom into a viable space for constructive criticism by deconstructing outdated epistemological models while taking into account the limitations of their positions. By accepting the provisional nature of those positions, professors can encourage students to dismantle the pedagogical model produced for classroom consumption. If we authorize radical difference in the classroom—radical because we refuse to measure difference against a professorial position privileged as normative— then divergent viewpoints are recognized even when students define themselves in oppositional terms. If every theoretical discourse must repeatedly reproduce the conditions of its production to compel consensus, then geographical and historical factors join with gender, ethnicity, sexual preference, age, and class to contextualize one's discursive position. Such variability clears space for multiple interventions in the classroom, signaling the instability of any one perspective to sustain itself over an extended period of time. No doubt every governing principle will pass away just as surely as we will die. If we remain insensitive to geo-temporal disjunctions and the uncertainties produced by them, periodic visitations from future critics will regard our attempts to limit self-canceling endeavors in the harshest terms. Even if they go out of their way to be fair to us, their evaluations of our projects will distinguish useful contributions to their work from the well-worn propositions they dismiss as irreconcilable with their intellectual endeavors.

This observation leads me to ask the following question: how can we posit meaning while ridding ourselves of monological beliefs? One way to accomplish this goal is to convert universalizing concepts into local universals whose duration is based upon their difference from themselves and the unity they seek to consolidate. Local universals are terms that provide a provisional unity, which welcomes a deferral of its authenticity. They convert unanalyzed ideals into unstable signs, whose disjunction problematizes their claim as naturalized foundational concepts. Local universals are "universal truths" within quotation marks that allow for scrutiny of their contingent, utilitarian, functional aspects. In the end, their mythic quality is demystified as their theoretical efficacy is determined by their impact, duration, and functionality. In this way a local universal gives up the ghost, renouncing its claims as a singularly exhaustive resource that has no retro-ideological limitations. If we subject local universals to vigorous self-reflection and encourage others to rethink them in terms of larger cultural projects, they begin to circulate as part of a dialectical exchange of ideas which negates any pretence of their being distinctive, self-enclosed artifacts. For example, we can see this process at work in the construction of postmodern theory, which, at its worst, is in danger of converting all provisional, diverse, iconoclastic mininarratives into the macroscript of hegemonic postmodernism. This linguistic turn has the capability of checking all emancipatory shifts of thought which reconceptualize each historical premise at each stage of its development.

We need do more to combat discursive self-identifications. For identities, which persist through time by endlessly reinventing themselves have the capacity to remythologize local universals into constant designators of truth. Because postmodern suddenness functions at breakneck technological speeds that were incomprehensible a hundred years ago, critics of postmodern innovations need to examine how the look of discourse is produced by those who use multimedia outlets to construct the visible lineaments of their projects. Multicultural critics have a vested interest in examining a multiplicity of looks to prevent any one gaze from reinforcing a master narrative's hegemony over those competing with it. This is especially relevant when corporate money sponsors a set of reflexive looks that blend into the televisual apparatus itself. For while viewers are caught up in "inference programming" concerned with the dissemination of ideas based on logical inference from a set of facts, television shows further their own interests by fine-tuning conventional systems of representation while merchandizing consumptive knowledge. What drives this market strategy is the desire to transmit diegetic narratives whose aesthetic dimension is warranted by a sequence of stylized looks offering viewers interpellative choices of who to be and how to act.

One way to disrupt narratives guaranteed by the gaze is to point to the quiescent, docile, and obedient effects that can be created for those subjected to them. Even if we fracture a link in the chain of narrative transmission to interrupt its taken-for-granted progression of ideas, the look of narrative can embed itself in consciousness reflexively. It can transpose the subject within its field, subjugating the person to a projected look from a gestalt of visual data contextualized by a narrative flow, which problematizes any simplistic reading of subjectivity. Through such transpositions the gaze is capable of imprinting static representations upon cultural consciousness, a process that has consequences for the multicultural classroom endeavoring to enlist a multiplicity of viewpoints. The multicultural classroom best allows for disagreements when it jettisons the "melting pot" xideal of cultural difference, where students are "grouped together in our diversity" and everyone wears "the same have-a-nice-day smile" (hooks 1994, 30–31). This notion of harmonious difference pretends that economic, identitiarian, and political differences have no colonial interest, paternalistic bias, or material teeth. To expose this type of Ozzie-and-Harriet idealism for what it is, we need not only deconstruct happily-ever-after narrative fairytales, but also question the look appended to such narrative disclosures. To accomplish this goal, I suggest we place a heightened emphasis on Media Studies programs as we enter the next century—an emphasis that exceeds film and media courses to cut across the curriculum in every phase of academic education.

When deconstructing hyperreal image orders that nurture immaterial subjectivities, we can use tools provided by Media Studies programs that emphasize media theory, media culture, and media ethics. If "the buzzwords of the millennium are digital, interactive, multimedia/hypermedia, immaterial labor" and ideological image orders, we must become conversant with these issues to attain visual literacy when reading hyperreal phenomena ("Rhode Island College Proposal" 1999). This should not persuade us, however, to devalue the print culture because it enables us, among other things, to articulate subtle theoretical formulations as we read the nuanced narratives of print capitalism. On the other hand, a study of the mass-media culture with its emphasis on iconic telewriting refocuses attention onto imagological address. In our electronic technoculture, where communication-at-a-distance has become more and more prevalent, the digital gaze has been appended to a circular dynamic wherein technology produces knowledge and knowledge produces technology. In this telecommunicational interchange, identities are mapped by electronic narratives linking the subject to the community, which finds itself in screen-centered scenarios. On these screens of fostered visibility, we find ourselves mirrored by immaterial subjects whose experience is embedded in the overblown moment that provides a jumping off point to another saturated instant of televisual or filmic experience. This is one reason why the narrative is so important in creating a historical typology, for its progression can replicate or expose the encapsulating moment of media interpellation. Depending upon how it is used, electronic causality can reinforce or de-emphasize the regulatory practices contextualized in the sequence being depicted.

But narration is only one aspect of representation, and representation is only one constituent in the field of discourse. Although representation helps constitute the meaning of referential objects, interpretation is a vital aspect of the process. Utilizing skills from both the print and media cultures, academics can draw upon a range of interpretative models to provide alternative critiques in the classrooms of the twenty-first century. I believe that once professors introduce media theory to the print-oriented classroom, they can take the next step in deploying a system of multiplex discourses through the composite channels of distribution. By extension, once this process is initiated, interested academics can create a series of satellite TV stations to offer courses on a range of subjects as well as commentary on contemporary issues. This would provide a method of linking distance-learning instruction with televisual strategies that could reach a critical mass of people across the globe. Such a project would require a group of public intellectuals willing to speak to a broad audience ready to entertain alternate views about a variety of subjects. The public, it seems, is hungry to hear more credible spokespersons than Don Imus and Rush Limbaugh on the particulars of cultural experience. If multicultural critics are willing to provide an alternative to the barrage of right-wing propaganda currently broadcast on radio, TV, and the Internet, a democratic forum expressing divergent opinions could make a difference. Instead of waiting to appear on corporate stations that currently control the flow of information, cultural critics could sustain a discursive struggle over the construction of meaning by utilizing the academy's vast resources to create new channels of dissemination. They must be careful, however, not to reinstate an omniscient position which guarantees mythic truth, narrative finality, and the look of certainty. To protect against this atavistic tendency, multiculturalists can advance theories which accept their own provisional status and theoretical limitations. Considering that life ends shrouded in mystery, they can forgo any attempt to instate a narrative, which will endure the test of time because it too is missing a certifiable end-frame that could codify fixed meaning for the ages.

WORKS CITED

Althusser, Louis. 1971. "Ideology and Ideological State Apparatuses (Notes towards an Investigation)." Trans. Ben Brewster. In *Lenin and Philosophy and Other Essays,* by Louis Althusser. New York: Monthly Review Press.

Barkun, Michael. 1997. "Racist Apocalypse: Millennialism on the Far Right." In *The Year 2000,* ed. Charles B. Strozier and Michael Flynn. New York: New York University Press.

Girard, René. 1986. *The Scapegoat.* Trans. Yvonne Freccero. Baltimore: The Johns Hopkins University Press.

Hebdige, Dick. 1993. "From Culture to Hegemony." In *The Cultural Studies Reader,* ed. Simon During. London: Routledge.

hooks, bell. 1994. *Teaching to Transgress: Education As the Practice of Freedom.* New York: Routledge.

Impeachment Coverage. 1998. C-Span. 19 December, Providence, RI.

"Israel Tourist Board Seeks Ad Agency." 1998. *Daily Telegraph,* 8 March. Online Available: http://www.everything2000.com/new/events/isre.asp

Jameson, Fredric. 1998. *The Cultural Turn: Selected Writings on the Postmodern, 1983-1998.* London: Verso.

Markovich, Mark. 1998. "Worldwide Millennium Broadcasts in the Works." *Everything 2000* 1/31/98. Online Available: http://www.everything2000.com/index.html

Nelson, Cary, Paula A. Treichler, and Lawrence Grossberg. 1992. "Cultural Studies: An Introduction." In *Cultural Studies,* ed. Lawrence Grossberg, Cary Nelson, Paula A. Treichler. New York: Routledge.

"Pre-END of the MILLENNIUM." 1999. Catalogue (January). Bloomington: Indiana University Press.

"Rhode Island College Proposal for Media Studies Program." 1999 (January).

Sarup, Madan. 1989. *An Introductory Guide to Post-Structuralism and Postmodernism.* Athens: The University of Georgia Press.

Schanzer, Sandra. 1997. "The Impending Computer Crisis of the Year 2000." In *The Year 2000,* ed. Charles B. Strozier and Michael Flynn. New York: New York University Press.

Stuart Hall: Representation and the Media. 1997. 55 min. Directed and produced by Sut Jhally. The Media Education Foundation. Northampton. Videocassette.

Taylor, Mark C. 1994. "Syles." In *Imagologies: Media Philosophy,* ed. Mark C. Taylor and Esa Saarinen. New York: Routledge

Taylor, Mark C., and Esa Saarinen, eds. 1994. *Imagologies: Media Philosophy.* New York: Routledge.

Taylor, Mark C., and Esa Saarinen. 1994. "Simcult." In *Imagologies: Media Philosophy*, ed Mark C. Taylor and Esa Saarinen. New York: Routledge.

von Ziegesar, Peter. 1997. "After Armageddon: Apocalyptic Art since the Seventies: Tactics of Survival in a Postnuclear Planet." In *The Year 2000,* ed. Charles B. Strozier and Michael Flynn. New York: New York University Press.

Index

Arnold, Matthew (*continued*)
  liberalism, 109–14; and pluralism, 76
Aronowitz, Stanley, 21, 34, 39, 91
assessment, 154–56
audiovisual. *See* visual media
Austin, Texas, 95–99
authority, 6–7, 247–49, 254–55, 304
Autobiography of Malcolm X, The
  (Malcolm X), 280–81
Awakening, The (Chopin, Kate),
  198–99

Bahktin, Mikhail, 288–90
Bangladesh, 220
Bard College, 46, 50, 54
Barkun, Michael, 315
Barrett, Michele, 290
Barrio Student Resource Center (BSRC),
  96–98
Barrow, Clyde, 25
Barthes, Roland, 311
Benjamin, Jessica, 258
Benjamin, Walter, 181, 186
Bennett, Tony, 30
Bennett, William, 76–77
Ben-Peretz, Miriam, 154
Berkeley, University of California at, 4,
  217–18
Berlin Wall, 233
Bérubé, Michael, 5, 25
Bhabha, Homi, 103
Bible, 60, 314
Biden, Senator Joseph, 126
Blackmur, R. P., 66
Black Panther, The (newspaper),
  276–77, 282n10
Black Panthers, 276–77, 282n10,
  283nn11–12
"Black Power" (King, Martin Luther,
  Jr.), 280–81
Blacks, 78, 94, 167, 298–303
Bleich, David, 150
Bloom, Allan, 75
*Bonds of Love: Psychoanalysis,
  Feminism, and the Problem of
  Domination, The* (Benjamin,
  Jessica), 258

books. *See* specific book titles
Botstein, Leon, 50
Bourdieu, Pierre, 164–65, 169, 172n3,
  238–40, 260
bourgeois society, 205, 321–22
bourgeois state, 114–15, 118
Bové, Paul, 62–63, 66, 69n11
Brecht, Bertolt, 267, 272, 278,
  293n13
Bretton Woods institutions, 220
Bromme, Rainer, 154
Brown, Linda, 90
Brown University, 81, 158
*Brown v. Board of Education, Topeka,
  Kansas,* 89
BSRC (Barrio Student Resource Center),
  96–98
bureaucracy, 321–22
bureaucratic hero, 51
business-university partnerships, 34–37

California Civil Rights Initiative, 31
Call of Stories, The (Coles, Robert), 141
Calmecac, 99–101
Canada, 47, 49–50
canon, 61, 165–69, 178, 203–4, 288
canon-busting movement, 195–207
canonical method, 169, 171
capital. *See* capitalism
capitalism: and democracy, 33, 114–17,
  120–21, 127–28; and educational
  capital, 17–18, 49, 164–67; and
  educators, 216–17; and family
  sphere, 237; and liberalism, 112–13;
  and multimedia, 328; and
  postmodernism, 247; and student
  belief, 273–74; and violence,
  232–34, 236
Carlin, James, 37–38
Carlson, Scott, 90
Carnegie Mellon University, 81–82
Casa Education Office, 100
Castoriadis, Cornelius, 1, 2, 7
Castro, Sal, 93
CCCS (Center for Contemporary
  Cultural Studies), 92
censorship, 64–67

About the Editors and Contributors

Peter Baker is professor of English and cultural studies at Towson University. His books include *Deconstruction and the Ethical Turn* and *Onward: Contemporary Poetry and Poetics.*

Richard Feldstein is professor of English at Rhode Island College and the co-editor of *Literature and Psychology.* His most recent book is *Political Correctness: A Response from the Cultural Left.*

Barbara Foley is professor of English at Rutgers University, Newark, and the author of *Telling the Truth: The Theory of Practice of Documentary Fiction* and *Radical Representations: Politics and Form in U.S. Proletarian Fiction, 1929-1941.*

Henry A. Giroux is the Waterbury Professor of Education at Pennsylvania State University. He is the author of several books, including *The Mouse That Roared: Disney and the End of Innocence; Channel Surfing: Racism, the Media, and the Destruction of Today's Youth;* and the forthcoming *Public Spaces, Private Lives.*

Amitava Kumar teaches English at the University of Florida and is the author of *No Tears for the NRI* and *Passport Photos.*

John Lofty is associate professor of English education at the University of New Hampshire. He is the author of *Time to Write, The Influence of Time and Culture on Learning to Write.*

Robert Miklitsch teaches cultural theory and critical media studies in the English department at Ohio University. He is the author of *From Hegel to*

Madonna: Towards a General Economy of "Commodity Fetishism" and the forthcoming *Roll Over Adorno: Critical Theory and Popular Culture in the Post-Marxist Period.*

Kostas Myrsiades is a professor of comparative literature and editor of *College Literature* at West Chester University. He is the author, editor, and/or translator of sixteen books on modern and classical Greek culture and the teaching of literature.

Jody Norton is an instructor in the department of English and the women's studies program at Eastern Michigan University. S/he is the author of *Narcissus Sous Rature: Male Subjectivity in Contemporary American Poetry.*

Jerry Phillips is an assistant professor of English at the University of Connecticut. He has published articles on Herman Melville, Frances Hodgson Burnett, and Edmund White and has contributed chapters to *Recasting the World: Writing after Colonialism; Whiteness: A Critical Reader;* and *Cannibalism and the Colonial World.*

Ralph E. Rodriquez is an assistant professor of English and comparative literature at the Pennsylvania State University, where he is developing a Latina/o Studies program with his colleague Jane Juffer. He is currently completing a book project on contemporary Chicana/o literature and its political imperatives and cultural aesthetics.

Roger I. Simon is professor at the Ontario Institute for Studies in Education at the University of Toronto. He has written extensively in the area of critical pedagogy and cultural studies. He is the author of *Teaching Against the Grain: Texts for a Pedagogy of Possibility,* and, most recently, *Between Hope and Despair: Pedagogy and the Remembrance of Historical Trauma.*

Paul Smith is professor of media studies at the University of Sussex (England) and professor of cultural studies at George Mason University. His books include *Discerning the Subject; Clint Eastwood;* and *Millennial Dreams: Contemporary Culture and Capitalism in the North.*

Ronald Strickland is a professor of English at Illinois State University. He writes on Renaissance literature, pedagogy, and critical theory, and is coeditor with Christopher Newfield of *After Political Correctness: The Humanities and Society in the 1990s; Going Public: Academics and Public Culture after the PC Debate* (forthcoming), and *Mediations* (forthcoming).

Jeffrey J. Williams is an assistant professor of English at the University of Missouri, editor of *Minnesota Review,* and author of PC *Wars: Theory and Politics in the Academy; Theory and the Novel: Narrative Reflexivity in the British Tradition;* and *The Institution of Literature.* He has published widely on theory, the novel, the politics of professionalism, and the university. Most recently, he is coeditor of the new *Norton Anthology of Theory and Criticism.*

Christopher Wise is associate professor of English at Western Washington University. He is the editor of *The Desert Shore: Literatures of the Sahel* and *Yambo Ouologuem: Postcolonial Writer, Islamic Militant.*

Lynn Worsham is a professor of English at the University of South Florida and editor of *JAC.* She teaches graduate courses in rhetorical theory and undergraduate courses in cultural studies.

The following chapters were previously published.

Chapter 2 was originally published in *College Literature:* 26.3 (Fall 1999): 147-61, and is reprinted here with permission.

Chapter 4 was originally published in *College Literature* 22.2 (June 1995): 1-15, and is reprinted here with permission.

Chapter 5 was originally published in *College Literature:* 21.1 (February 1994): 1-14, and is reprinted here with permission.

Chapter 7 was originally published in *College Literature:* 25.3 (Fall 1998): 109-32, and is reprinted here with permission.

Chapter 8 was originally published in *College Literature:* 22.2 (June 1995): 16-41, and is reprinted here with permission.

Chapter 9 was originally published in *College Literature:* 17.2/3 (June/October 1990): 80-89, and is reprinted here with permission.

Chapter 10 was originally published in *College Literature:* 21.3 (October 1994): 173-89, and is reprinted here with permission.

Chapter 11 was originally published in *College Literature:* 17.2/3 (June/October 1990): 64-79, and is reprinted here with permission.

Chapter 13 was originally published in *JAC* 18.2 (1998): 214-45, and is reprinted here with permission.

Chapter 14 was originally published in *College Literature:* 17.2/3 (June/October 1990): 90-108, and is reprinted here with permission.

Chapter 15 was originally published in *College Literature:* 21.3 (October 1994): 136-56, and is reprinted here with permission.

Chapter 16 was originally published in *College Literature:* 26.3 (Fall 1999): 205-25, and is reprinted here with permission.